THE HOUSE DIVIDED: America in the Era of Civil War and Reconstruction

Second Edition

THE HOUSE DIVIDED: America in the Era of Civil War and Reconstruction

Second Edition

By

Louise A. Mayo
County College of Morris
Randolph, New Jersey

Abigail Press Wheaton, IL 60187

Design and Production: Abigail Press
Typesetting: Abigail Press
Typeface: AGaramond
Cover Art: Sam Tolia

The House Divided: America in the Era of Civil War and Reconstruction

Second Edition, 2003
Printed in the United States of America
Translation rights reserved by the authors
ISBN 1-890919-23-3

ABOUT THE AUTHOR

Louise Mayo is the Chairperson of the Department of History/Political Science at County College of Morris, Randolph, NJ, where she has been a professor for the past twenty-three years. She is the author of *The Ambivalent Image* (1988) and numerous articles and papers in the fields of women and minority history. She has an M.A. from Cornell University in Modern European and Russian History and a Ph.D. from City University of New York in American History, specializing in immigration and minority history. She teaches courses in Twentieth Century America, History of American Women, History of Minorities, History of American Cities and Suburbs, and Civil War and Reconstruction.

Contents in Brief

Contents

CHAPTER FIVE

PART III: THE CIVIL WAR

CHAPTER SIX

PREFACE

Like many Americans, my earliest knowledge about the Civil War came from *Gone With the Wind* and its romantic southern-oriented exaggerations. Even as an undergraduate in a northern college, I learned little in my history classes to challenge the myths about the Civil War and Reconstruction.

It was not until graduate school in the 1970s that I learned about newer interpretations of the events of that era. LaWanda Cox first made me reconsider the accepted images. Later, I was fortunate enough in my Ph.D. program to take classes with the late Herbert Gutman, a giant in the field of social history who exploded many of the preconceptions about slavery and black families. Eric Foner made it possible to gain a fuller understanding of the Reconstruction era.

After many years of teaching Civil War and Reconstruction to freshmen and sophomore students, I became more aware of the need for a relatively concise textbook that would incorporate the insights of social history with the political and military aspects of the era that are normally covered. I also wanted to include original documents that would give students a better understanding of the era, interesting anecdotal history, and references to the impact of Civil War and Reconstruction on modern America.

I would like to thank members of my department for reading and making helpful comments about my book before publication, particularly Rita Heller and Richard Phelps.

INTRODUCTION

More than any other conflict in American history, the Civil War has captured the imagination and interest of the American people. Terry Winschel, historian of the Vicksburg National Military Park, commented that, "Americans just can't get enough of the Civil War." He spoke from experience. Millions of Americans visit his and the other twelve national battlefield and military parks of the Civil War, particularly Gettysburg. More than a quarter million Americans characterize themselves as Civil War buffs or hobbyists. They subscribe to some or all of the half dozen magazines dealing with the Civil War, belong to one or more of the hundreds of Civil War societies or round tables, and, along with thousands more, buy and sell war souvenirs and memorabilia. Many thousands of them are Civil War reenactors who spend considerable sums of money to purchase replicas of weapons, equipment, and uniforms of the period. They travel to different parts of the country to reproduce Civil War battles with great enthusiasm.

Even more Americans read books on the war. More than fifty thousand books about the war have been issued since the final battle more than 135 years ago, many of them on national best seller lists. There have been numerous popular films based on the war and its aftermath, particularly one of the largest grossing films of all time: *Gone With the Wind.* Ken Burn's series, *The Civil War,* may well have been the highest rated documentary series on public television.

The reasons for this are complex. One involves the human tragedy involved. More than 620,000 soldiers on both sides lost their lives, as many as all other American wars combined up to Vietnam. The 25,000 casualties on the single bloodiest day at Antietam was four times as many as the number of American casualties on June 6, 1944, at the monumental D-day invasion. This enormous human catastrophe, however, was also suffused with the glow of romance, glory, and reverence. There were dashing officers leading doomed (or successful) charges. There were heroic and impressive leaders like Lincoln, Lee, Grant, and Jackson. There was the special pathos of a brothers' war in which families, particularly in the border states, were indeed divided. Mrs. Lincoln's brothers and brother-in-laws fought for the Confederacy, for one example. The famed Confederate cavalry general, Jeb Stuart, had a father-in-law who commanded Union cavalry. Unlike twentieth-century conflicts where soldiers were heavily censored, all these Civil War human interest stories, as well as detailed accounts of the terrors of the battles, have been preserved in letters and diaries. Many of these have been published as books.

The memories of the war have been particularly preserved in the South where, as William Faulkner once remarked, the past isn't dead; it isn't even past. Towns and cities throughout the South have monuments to Confederate soldiers in their squares. The symbolism of the Confederate flag continues to provoke passions from southern whites and blacks. The Confederate song, "Dixie," became an emblem of southern resistance to civil rights in the 1960s.

Most importantly, the issues that were at stake in this conflict were central to America's soul and future. One was the definition of "liberty," which both sides believed they were fighting to preserve. Obviously, each interpreted that concept in very different ways. The war resolved what was, in the words of historian James McPherson, "the great American paradox—a land of freedom based on slavery." The war also settled the issue of whether a democratic republic could survive and "whether the house divided would continue to endure half slave and half free."

As America grew dramatically in the nineteenth century, tensions arose from recurring crises, particularly over the issue of slavery. Almost from the beginning, the country was divided into free and slave states. The nation had endured for almost seventy-five years with two sections because the forces of nationalism and the common struggle for the survival of a new country were more powerful than the tug of sectionalism. Yet, from the beginning, there was conflict over slavery. In order to keep southern states from repudiating the Constitution, northern delegates were forced to agree to compromises protecting slavery. These included counting a slave as three-fifths of a white person for purposes of representation, forbidding interference with the importation of slaves for twenty years, and requiring the return of fugitive slaves who escaped to free states. Southern presidents and congresses pushed the expansion of American territory in hopes of gaining new slave states. The South dominated the national government for most of those seventy-five years. They had a majority on the Supreme Court, presidents for two-thirds of the time, and most of the leaders of Congress. But nothing could stop the growth of free state populations, so that, by 1860 there were nineteen million people in those states and only twelve million in the slave states of which four million were slaves. In the end, those northern states would assert their dominance and elect one of their own, an antislavery politician as president. The South would feel impelled to secede from the union. The Civil War would result. Although it would resolve the questions of slavery and union, other issues of race, caste, and human liberty would remain to plague the nation.

PART I

ANTEBELLUM AMERICA

ERIE CANAL

Chapter One

THE GROWING WEST AND NORTH

GROWTH AND EXPANSION

The antebellum era (1830-1860) was one of great dynamism. Eighteenth century travelers to America tended to criticize the supposed slothfulness of its citizens while nineteenth century travelers marveled at their incessant activity. At least, this was true of the North, as the North and South seemed to be developing into two distinct civilizations. Americans were fond of informing visitors that the United States was rapidly becoming a great power. In the first half of the nineteenth century, the United States grew at a rate unequaled in modern history. Land area quadrupled as a result of the 1803 Louisiana Purchase, the 1819 acquisition of Florida, the 1845 annexation of Texas, the 1848 Mexican Cession, and the Gadsden Purchase of the final strip of land in 1853. Population increased even more spectacularly as the six million Americans in 1803 grew to thirty-two million in 1860. Even more surprisingly, despite gloomy predictions that unchecked population growth would always outstrip its economy, rapid economic growth actually doubled average income. The American standard of living steadily improved until it was second only to Britain in the world. A modern market economy developed in combination with westward expansion and settlement. No other society imposed so few limitations on the marketplace and the ability to maximize profits.

This unprecedented growth came at great cost to many. Economic inequality increased. Territorial expansion rested on ruthless seizure of lands and forcible removal of Native Americans and Mexicans. The export of cotton, produced by slave labor, helped support economic development. The rapid growth caused social and political strains that led to continuous crises.

Population and Immigration

From 1820 to 1860 America's population increased at an average rate of 35 percent every decade. In the first part of this era a very high birth rate was accompanied by a relatively low rate of infant mortality (compared to the rest of the world, although ten times as great as it is today). By the 1820s the birthrate began to decline, bringing the median age in America **up** to 19 by 1850. In 1850 more than 70 percent of Americans were still under 30, compared to 50 to 60 percent in Europe. The youthful nature of the people may explain their extraordinary restlessness. They seemed to be constantly on the move. Alexis de Tocqueville, the remarkably perceptive French observer, noted, "In the United States a man builds a house in which to spend his old age, and he sells it before the roof is on...he settles in a place, which he soon afterwards leaves to carry his changeable longings elsewhere...." The population rushed westward seeking new possibilities so rapidly that, by 1860, almost half the people already lived in areas beyond the settlement lines of 1790. By 1850 one-quarter of New England's population had moved on to other states.

By the 1840s, an unprecedented increase in the numbers of immigrants accounted for one-quarter of the population growth. Agricultural disasters and displacements due to technological change made many European peasants expendable. Economic adversity in Europe, and political and religious persecutions, provided the push for many to leave their homelands. Job opportunities in growing American cities and the supposedly unlimited chance to own land pulled immigrants to the "land of opportunity." In the decade of the 1850s alone, some three million immigrants entered America, the majority of whom listed "no occupation." Philip Hone, a wealthy New Yorker, worried that, "All Europe is coming across the ocean; all that part at least who cannot make a living at home; and what shall we do with them? They increase our taxes, eat our bread and encumber our streets...."

Of the four million Irish who came to the United States in the nineteenth century, more than half arrived between 1840 and 1860. Irish peasants were already living in desperate poverty when the devastating Great Famine of 1845 struck. It was a fungus that destroyed the entire potato crop, the dietary staple of the Irish people. The resulting starvation and misery (more than a million died) pushed many of the survivors to America. They came with almost no money and

Irish are pictured here leaving Ireland for America, the land of opportunity. Irish immigrants flooded into ghettoes in northern cities.

few skills. They collected in city ghettos in old houses and warehouses, converted into overcrowded tenements. Sewage flowed in the streets attracting an army of rats. Cholera and tuberculosis took a fearful toll.

Many Americans believed these immigrants were the cause of disease, overcrowding, alcoholism, and breakdown in law and order found in many cities. Describing growing disturbances in New York, Hone concluded, "This state of things has been hastened in our case by the constant stream of European paupers arriving upon the shores of this land of promise." Irish workers often encountered signs warning, "No Irish Need Apply." Despite this, they found work in the dirtiest and lowest-paying fields, squeezing out the free blacks who had previously held those jobs. The new immigrant Americanized enough to express great animosity towards black competitors at the lowest end of the economic scale.

The Irish immigrants' deeply held loyalty to the Roman Catholic Church, which was the center of their community life, led to further hostility by Protestant Americans. Protestants feared the supposed Catholic devotion to the Pope. Anti-Catholic sentiment became the basis of a major political movement, as we will discover later. Catholics objected to enforced reading of Protestant prayers in public schools. In the 1840s, they began their own system of parochial schools at great cost to the community.

Their long political struggles against England had made the Irish a highly politicized people. That talent and their ability to speak English pushed them into the politics of the cities where they lived. This, in turn, enabled them to gradually move out of poverty through jobs such as policemen, firemen, and sanitation workers in the developing cities.

During the same period (1840-60), about as many Germans also came to America. Some were religious dissenters. Others fled the crushing of democracy after the Revolutions of 1848. Still more were peasants and artisans who had lost their livelihood as a result of modernization. In this era most German immigrants were Protestants. Some had enough funds to purchase farms in the West or to migrate to cities in the area, such as Milwaukee.

Thousands of Jews arrived among the immigrants from the German states and central Europe. Many settled in cities. Others took advantage of the opportunities created by the westward movement. They became peddlers who sold essential products to the scattered pioneers. Eventually, many were able to earn enough money to open their own general stores in towns throughout the West. They assimilated rapidly and found it difficult to maintain a Jewish community.

Other groups also became part of an increasingly diverse American mosaic. Some eighty thousand Spanish-speaking Catholics lived in areas acquired as a result of the Mexican War. The treaty ending the war guaranteed citizenship, religious liberty, and title to their property to those who decided to remain American. The federal government, however, did little to enforce these provisions. Anglo settlers took their lands. Some protested forcibly, leading to the emergence of bandit-heroes like Juan Cortina who raided towns and killed whites who had mistreated Mexican-Americans.

American merchants brought news of the California Gold Rush to China where stories of the "Golden Mountain" (America) spread among peasants. Thousands of young men came to seek gold. Most lost their claims and took jobs with mining companies or as laundry workers and servants. Traders and missionaries in China had described the Chinese as an immoral, dishonest, and backward people. Their religion was considered "heathen" and their culture very strange. Some communities in California expelled Chinese miners. The state legislature passed a tax of 50 dollars for each Chinese worker brought into California. In 1854 the California Supreme Court overturned a white man's murder conviction. They ruled that "Mongolians" could not testify against whites. Increasing anti-Chinese violence resulted, and it became almost impossible for Chinese immigrants to assert any rights.

Although the arrival of all these groups did not increase the portion of foreign born in the population to more than 15 percent, they were a vital factor in the expanding cities. In New York and Boston over half the residents were foreign born.

The Growth of Cities

One of the most remarkable changes in American life was the astonishing growth of cities. In 1790 only five cities could boast populations of 10,000 or more. By 1860 there were one hundred such cities. Only 5 percent of the population in 1790 lived in "urban" areas (defined by the Census Bureau as 2,500 or more). By 1860 the figure had risen to approximately one-fifth of the population. Eight American cities (three of them in the West), had populations of more than 150,000. A mania of city building swept the country. Boosters speculated on the quick development of their city, which meant quick profits to them.

Cities were "bursting at the seams." The populations of most doubled and tripled between 1840 and 1850. It was the greatest proportionate growth of city population in the nation's history, with the highest urban densities ever (136 persons per acre in New York). The need for services rapidly outstripped the ability of cities to provide them. Rural migrants were used to relieving themselves outside and throwing garbage any place they pleased. In the city this resulted in fearful odors, polluted water, and disease. Despite some improvement, by 1857 only one-quarter of the streets in New York had sewers.

Crowded urban terrain, tightly contested by antagonistic ethnic, religious, and racial groups, led to increasing disorder and crime. An 1844 conflict between Protestants and Irish Catholics in Philadelphia left thirteen dead. Another twenty died in an 1855 anti-German riot in Louisville. Nearly one thousand people died in various urban conflicts of the era. Cities began to establish professional uniformed police forces. There were far too few policemen, and they bogged down in political conflicts. They tended to concentrate protection in business and wealthy residential districts. Working class sections were ignored and abandoned to criminal control. Prostitution grew along with the cities. Authorities attempted to confine it to clearly marked red-light districts where madams ran established brothels and cooperated with police to clear out streetwalkers. Famous romanticized, red-light districts included New York's Bowery, San Francisco's Barbary Coast, and New Orleans' French Quarter.

Cities sought to respond to the most deadly danger, fire, by organizing professional fire departments. They operated out of fire stations and utilized steam engines, rather than the old hand pumps. These fire departments needed access to adequate water supplies to be effective. Cities also became aware that polluted water caused mass outbreaks of such diseases as yellow fever. A cholera epidemic hit New York City in 1849 and swept through St. Louis and Cincinnati. In New York City alone five thousand died. By 1860 the nations' 16 largest cities had built water works, most of them publicly owned. The wealthy were able to install indoor plumbing, but few systems provided running water to the homes of the poor.

The growth of mass transit was breaking up the old walking city. It had been a compact place where people could walk to their destinations, residences, and businesses; rich and poor were intermingled. By the middle of the century, the omnibus had become essential in most American cities. It was drawn by two horses and seated 12 but often carried 20 uncomfortable passengers on a "bumpy, noisy journey." One contemporary observer noted wryly, "Modern martyrdom may be succinctly defined as riding in a New York omnibus." The street or horse railway superseded the omnibus. Horse-drawn coaches ran over rails down the middle of streets. They could carry three times as many passengers in faster, smoother, and safer rides. By 1860 there were 155 miles of track in Philadelphia and 142 in New York. These advances enabled cities to expand physically and made it possible for wealthy people to live separately from the poor and the commercial areas.

An Austrian journalist wrote about "glorious and chaotic America." The mid-century northern city was a place of transition between a pre-industrial and industrial American society. It was filled with ethnic and class divisions, corruption, disease, crime, and violence. At the same time, it was the center of unparalleled change and growth.

Transportation Advances

The most important factor in creating a modernized, capitalist, industrialized economy was the dramatic improvement in transportation. Construction crews laid thousands of miles of modernized all-weather roads in the first third of the century, largely in the North. The real breakthrough, however, was the development of canals. The amazing success of the 1825 Erie Canal, built by New York State to link the Great Lakes to the Atlantic, launched the canal era. By the 1850s the per mile cost of shipping a ton of freight from Buffalo to New York City had fallen from 19.2 cents to .81 cents. The canal reinforced the primacy of New York City as the commercial hub of the nation. Other states went deeply into debt to build their own canals. Internal trade patterns began to shift away from traditional north-south routes down the Mississippi River to the new east-west links, connecting the Northeast with the Great Lakes area. By the 1840s tonnage on the Great Lakes-Erie Canal route was greater than that on the Mississippi.

The great railroad boom of the 1840s and 50s intensified this trend. The opening of the first railroad westward out of Baltimore in 1830 led to a frenzied competition by states and cities to construct railroads. Hundreds of independent lines were built, but they gradually consolidated into main lines, particularly in the North. Economic ties between the West and the Northeast increased. By the 1850s, east-west water and rail routes carried twice the tonnage of the north-south river artery. By 1860 America had as many miles of railroad as the rest of the world combined (31,000 miles). Railroads were the first billion-dollar industry, creating the first large corporations.

Foreign trade also continued to grow, although not as rapidly as domestic commerce. The 1850s was the great era of the glamorous clipper ships. These graceful vessels with their tall masts were the fastest ships at the time and were crucial in the trade with the Orient. At home, the river steamboat (first built in 1807 by Robert Fulton) developed rapidly. From a dozen in 1815, the number of steamboats had grown to three thousand by 1860. In the 1840s canals were widened and deepened to receive them. Others operated in the Great Lakes. The new steamboats combined design and technology, elegant, splendid staterooms, and gleaming, powerful machinery. The price in human life, however, was considerable. In one two-month period in 1841 alone, eight steamboats sank between St. Louis and the Ohio River. In an 1855 "race" between two steamers, down the Hudson River in New York, one of the boats caught fire, killing ninety passengers, including the famed landscape architect, Andrew Downing.

All of these transportation improvements aided economic growth. An interregional market economy developed. In 1817 it had taken fifty days to send freight from Cincinnati to New York. By 1852 the time was down to six days. All the resulting cost reductions lowered wholesale prices by approximately 40 percent in 40 years, causing equivalent reductions in the cost of living.

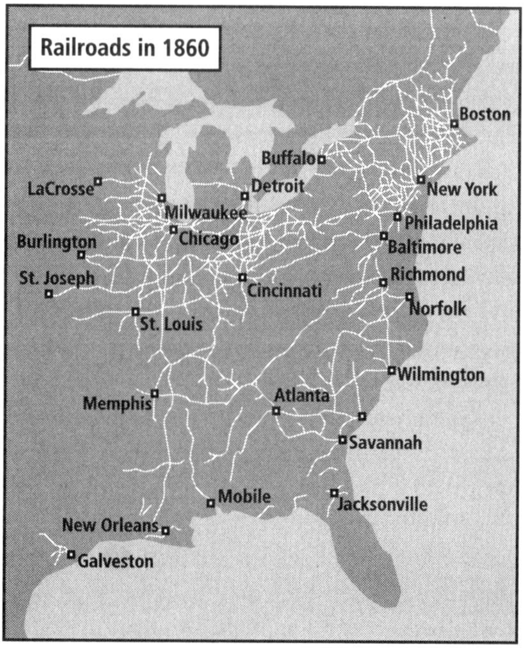

The network of railroad growth, established by 1860, reinforced economic ties between the Northeast and the West.

Agricultural Expansion

Transportation advances created a national market, leading to dramatic changes in agriculture. Although the majority of Americans continued to depend on farming for their livelihood, the proportion of farmers had fallen from 79 to 55 percent between 1820 and 1860. Nevertheless, the total output of food crops quadrupled, enabling farmers to feed the rapidly expanding cities. The nation exported an increasing percentage of the agricultural output, helping to pay for needed manufacturing imports and fueling industrial and urban growth.

One factor that made this possible was the extraordinarily rapid expansion of agriculture in the West and Old Southwest. The main business of the federal government at the time was the sale and management of a billion acres of public land. The government rapidly surveyed vast tracts of western land, offering them to the highest bidder. The remainder was sold for $1.25 per acre. Speculation ran wild, as investors bought huge blocks of the best land to resell to farmers. As land values boomed, farming became an increasingly speculative enterprise. Unlike the close-knit European farm villages, American farms in the boundless Western territory were isolated, often more than a day's travel apart. The first market crop produced in the West was the easily grown corn. But it was supplanted by wheat, which paid better and was easier to transport. Wheat production increased by 75 percent between 1849 and 1859. It vied with cotton as the major American export. The Crimean War of 1854-6, which closed off the Russian wheat source from Europe, added to the demand for American wheat.

Pioneer settlers migrated westward mostly by foot, pulling handcarts with their meager possessions. Many became squatters who borrowed money from speculators to buy necessary supplies. Squatters, striving for economic independence, pressed for laws that would lower the minimum purchase of federal land to 40 acres (rather than 160). What is more important, they succeeded in establishing the right of "preemption" in 1841. Under this law, settlers could cultivate as much as 160 acres of public land that they could then buy at minimum price before public sale. Without any national controls, pioneers ruthlessly stripped public lands of all resources, particularly trees. They rarely bothered to conserve the soil by fertilization or crop rotation. Americans tended to believe that western resources were inexhaustible.

Technological innovation played a significant role in the increase in food production. Farming had barely changed before 1800. One historian commented that "the colonists were not much advanced beyond Biblical times." The middle of the nineteenth century saw a revolution in the technology of agriculture. John Deere, who had produced the first steel plow, which could break up the tough prairie sod, was manufacturing 13,000 plows a year by 1858. Cyrus McCormack's horse-drawn reapers enabled two men and a horse to harvest as much wheat per day as twenty men using sickles. Northern farmers bought thousands of mass produced agricultural implements, transforming the nature of farming. Western farmers increasingly went into debt to pay for equipment. Growing specialization made them dependent upon the world market. The collapse of wheat prices in 1857 devastated the western farmer.

Farmers began attending protest meetings. There, reformers pushed for agricultural colleges to be financed by federal land grants. An even more popular demand was for free homesteads on the rest of the public lands. In the 1860 presidential election the slogan, "Vote Yourself a Farm," helped carry the West for Lincoln.

The Development of Northern Manufacturing

Changes in manufacturing paralleled advances in agriculture. Although the richest Northerners were still merchants, rather than industrialists, the 1850 census revealed that the value of industrial output now surpassed that of all agriculture, including cotton. As in Britain, the production of textiles launched the industrial revolution in New England. The factory system then spread to other industries after 1830. Much of the early technology was adapted from European advances. (Like Asian businessmen today, Americans of that era modified and tailored foreign technology to fit their own needs.)

American industry was far more oriented towards change than its British counterpart. British textile machines were made of metal to last for a long time. By contrast, American machinery was inexpensive and light, often made of wood. The accepted reasoning was that rapid technological changes would enable such machines to be easily and cheaply replaced by better ones when they wore out.

American inventiveness blossomed. The number of yearly patents issued increased sixfold from 1835 to 1850 (when over 4,300 were issued). The electric telegraph, patented by the artist Samuel F. B. Morse in 1840, revolutionized communication. In the public demonstration of his newly constructed telegraph line, the daughter of the Commissioner of Patents chose the first "official" transmission, "What hath God wrought!" The country, filled with awe, agreed. A Scottish visitor, reflecting the views of many, wrote, "The effect which this invention...has produced, and that which it is still likely to produce on many of the operations of society are almost beyond comprehension." Within four years of the erection of Morse's first experimental line, more than 5,000 miles of telegraph lines crisis-crossed the country and 3,000 more were under construction. The 1858 completion of the first Trans-Atlantic cable, a result of the unceasing efforts of two remarkable self-made men, Cyrus Field and Peter Cooper, was even more sensational. Charles Goodyear perfected the "vulcanization" of rubber. Before the automobile era, his product was used for shoes and boots (and a tougher new condom that gained widespread use in the 1850s).

Probably the most important American industrial advance was what the British called, "the American system of manufactures." This was mass production of machine-made interchangeable parts. It had first been used in the production of muskets. Later, the system expanded to such products as clocks, locks, plows, sewing machines, reapers, locomotives, boots, and, even to the astonishment of British observers, a machine that produced 180 hairpins a minute. At the 1851 London Crystal Palace exhibit of international products, American machinery and production techniques amazed European experts. Samuel Colt, inventor of the six-shooter, summed up the American attitude in testimony before the British Parliament in 1854: "There is nothing that cannot be produced by machinery."

The abundance of cheap and abundant resources, particularly water and wood, aided America's economic development. The general shortage of labor encouraged new methods to replace workers with machines. In addition, the world's highest literacy rate helped produce the "adaptive versatility" of Yankee workers who were renowned for their ingenuity. Elias Howe invented the sewing machine when he worked as a journeyman machinist in Boston.

A value system that glorified change over tradition promoted American modernization. One optimist in the 1840s announced: "WE ARE THE PEOPLE OF THE FUTURE. Custom hath lost its sway and Time and Change are Champions against the field." The American value system also rested on what has been called, "the Protestant work ethic." In this belief system success is a sign of God's favor and can be achieved by hard work, self-discipline, and thrift. Popular "how to succeed" books, often written by ministers, spread these views. According to one, "religion will teach you that industry is a SOLEMN DUTY you owe to God, whose command is, 'BE DILIGENT IN BUSINESS!'" It is not surprising that New England, where these views predominated, produced most of the inventors and entrepreneurs of the era.

American industry by 1860 was just beginning its dramatic transformation of American society. Most iron, for example, was still imported from Britain. Traditional small-scale forms of production, like artisan shops and the "putting out" system of home piecework, co-existed with the newer factories in many American cities. Nevertheless, the United States (its northern half) had already become the most rapidly modernizing nation in the world and was poised for the astonishing growth of American industry that would follow the Civil War.

Rough and Tumblers

One of the favorite side trips of proper English travelers in nineteenth century America was to the backcountry West to witness "rough-and-tumble" fighting. These brutal struggles by working class men often ended in the backwoods equivalent of the modern knockout punch: the gouging out of the loser's eye by the victor's thumb. One such tourist watched with mesmerized horror as one combatant kept his opponent down with his knees and "fixing his thumb on his eyes, gave them an instantaneous start from their sockets. The sufferer roared aloud.... The citizens again shouted with joy." These renowned local heroes hardened and sharpened their fingernails and oiled them for slickness.

The backcountry heroes bragged with great exaggeration about their abilities and accomplishments. Mike Finn, legendary boatman, daring hunter, and victorious gouger, boasted: "I'm half wild horse and half cock-eyed alligator....I can out-run, out-jump, out-shoot, out-brag, out-drink, an' out-fight, rough-an'-tumble. No holts barred, any man both sides the river...." This "spread eagle" rhetoric represented the young nation and its aggressive expansion.

The "rough and tumblers" lived in isolated, pre-modern areas in kin-based societies where subsistence agriculture was the norm. By the middle of the century eye gouging incidents began to decline as the modern world intruded on the backcountry. Bowie knives finished off more of the rough and tumbles. The invention of the inexpensive modern revolver that easily fit into a pocket changed the nature of frontier contests. Violence became neater and even more deadly.

In the growing cities organized spectator sports developed to counter the loneliness of urban life and preserve traditional pleasures. Steamboats and, later, railroads could carry fans to events and promote inter-city rivalries. Rising literacy and new printing technologies created the popular penny newspapers that reported sporting events. Despite the opposition of religious moralists, both workers and "slumming" upper class men flocked to "low sport" halls. There, they could watch and bet on a dog killing a pit full of rats or a sparring match between "two women who were nude above the waist."

Although it was illegal everywhere, during the 1840s and 50s, prize fighting became the most popular spectator sport. These bare-fisted matches were almost as brutal as the frontier rough and tumbles. In one epic 1842 contest, the two fighters thrashed each other for over two and a half hours until one collapsed and died when he drowned in his own blood. Irish working class men, who honed their skills in street survival, dominated boxing. (They would be replaced in the twentieth century first by Jews, then Italians, then blacks, as each group attempted to rise from the slums.) John "Old Smoke" Morrissey, an Irish immigrant, earned enough from his matches to open his own gambling house and was famous enough to win two terms in the House of Representatives. Newspapers publicized the 1860 match of his successor, John Heenan, against the English champion as the ultimate test of national superiority. (The match ended in a bloody two-hour draw.) The event stirred up wider publicity than the growing sectional conflict.

Organized team sports also began to capture the public fancy. Cricket clubs, spurred by English immigrants, grew rapidly. Over 24,000 attended an 1859 cricket match in Hoboken, New Jersey between an all-star American team and touring professionals. Others argued that Americans should support "a game that could be termed a 'Native American Sport.'" Boys had long taken part in impromptu bat-and-ball games in empty lots. Lower middle class men began to form clubs to play baseball, touted as "the national game." When the Brooklyn all-stars met the New York all-stars in an 1858 series, excitement reached new heights. One newspaper reported that spectators included, "a galaxy of youth and beauty in female form, who...nerved the players to their task." (New York won two of three: 22-18, 8-29, 29-18.)

The new sports, like the old, tended to encourage drinking, betting, and an absence of self-restraint, much to the dismay of religious critics. These sports, however, reflected the important changes in northern American life at a time of urbanization, immigration, beginnings of industrialization, and increased population growth.

LIFE IN THE NORTH: 1840-1860

The changes in northern society were largely a result of the modernization process. The extraordinary mobility of the American people also added to the upheaval in northern life. An amazed foreign visitor commented, "If God were to suddenly call the world to judgment, He would surprise two-thirds of the American population on the road like ants." The rapid transformations in American life affected ordinary Americans in many different, often contradictory, ways.

Social Classes

Despite the substantial gains in living standards and real wages, economic inequality increased significantly. The poor were gaining income but not as fast as the rich and middle class, leading to a widening gap between rich and poor. As early as 1845, the richest 4 percent of New York's population had increased its share of the wealth by 17 percent in 17 years, owning two-thirds of the city's wealth. By 1860, the top 1 percent of Philadelphia's population possessed half the city's riches, leaving a mere 3 percent for the lower 80 percent of the city's people. Affluent families began to separate themselves from the urban masses. They lived in magnificent mansions where servants waited on them, drove in private carriages, and dined on imported delicacies served in exclusive private clubs.

American inequality was certainly no worse than that of Western Europe at the time. But Americans professed to embrace "equality of condition." American leaders, alarmed by class conflicts and revolution in Europe in 1848, argued that inequalities in America were only temporary. They agreed with Senator Henry Clay of Kentucky that the rich were "enterprising self-made men who have whatever wealth they possess by patient and diligent labor." In reality, the overwhelming majority of prosperous men came from wealthy families, lending truth to the saying that "the rich get richer." Increasingly, they cemented their elite status by conducting their social lives, business associations, and marriages only with each other.

The wage earning working class was on the other end of the scale. Even when adequate, the whole idea of "wages" ran counter to the old American belief in equality among white men. In an earlier world, most white males had been either small farmers or independent artisans, owning their means of production. With capitalist modernization, most working men owned only their labor and became dependent on the "boss" who paid them. Wages rose slightly—those of unskilled day laborers and male factory workers increased from 85 cents a day in the 1840s to slightly over a dollar in 1860. But they remained pathetically low in relation to prices. In 1851 the *New York Tribune* published a bare-bones budget for a family of five that came to $10.37 per week.

This meant that women and children had to help make ends meet. Female factory workers earned $1.50 a week, children even less. Peddling, foraging, stealing, and prostitution became methods of supplementing family income. In the 1850s reformers launched an ambitious campaign to eliminate poverty by ending working class street life. Reformers established the Children's Aid Society to "save" the "street rats," children who earned their living through shining shoes, selling newspapers, or stealing. The Society's first report warned that, "they will have the same rights as we ourselves, though they have grown up ignorant of moral principle, as any savage or Indian." The Society sought to solve the problem by removing the children from their homes and shipping boys off to farm labor and girls to domestic service. This "solution" increased cultural and class antagonism.

Transient unskilled day laborers, both male and female, drifted in and out of cities, generally inhabiting the most fearful slums. Their lives were not all entirely grim, however. Some were single men and women who occupied rooms in lodging houses, away from their families. They helped to create a dynamic working-class youth subculture in areas like New York's Bowery. There, on a Saturday night, dance halls "came alive with workingwomen, journeymen, and laborers looking for marital prospects, sexual encounters, and general good times."

A middle class also began to emerge in the cities. It included small storeowners, salaried clerks, and managers. Technological innovations added higher status wage earners like telegraphers, railroad engineers, and machinists. Men in the latter group could earn $12 a week or more. As a result of the economic instability of the period, people fell out of the middle class as quickly as they climbed into it. Despite this uncertainty, an urban middle class life style developed stressing family life, the work ethic, and an increased purchase of consumer goods.

Few unskilled workers were ever able to rise to a higher level of employment (much less going from "rags to riches"). By the 1850s many of their sons were able to move up to semiskilled factory work. Despite this limited social mobility, there was far less class conflict in the United States than in Europe. One reason was extreme geographic mobility that complemented the prevalent ideology of a society without limits. Perhaps that neighbor who left for another location had "made it" to the top. In addition, even factory workers who had stable jobs could see improvements in their lives when families pooled their incomes to buy homes. Books, newspaper articles, and countless speeches repeated the ideology of a "land of opportunity."

Children in the growing public school system learned these same ideas. By the 1850s, most northern and western cities and states were supporting public schools. These schools attempted to teach students punctuality, honesty, determination, and other character traits helpful to workers in the new capitalist industrial society. One school committee expressed the common belief that chil-

Schools served to provide literacy skills for Americanizing the immigrants and instilling patriotic values.

This illustration shows the hard life of New England factory workers.

dren "entered the race aware that the prize was equally before all and attainable only by personal exertion." The McGuffey readers, which sold more than 100 million copies, taught children to accept their position in life and avoid class conflict. When the good poor child sees others living in splendor, "he does not envy them, nor wish to be like them." He understands "that it is God who makes some poor and others rich; that the rich have troubles which we know nothing of; and that the poor, if they are good, may be very happy."

Free Blacks in Northern Cities

A free black community was a relatively new part of urban life. African Americans competed with immigrants and other poor whites for employment and housing in the cities. Successful antislavery campaigns after the American Revolution brought freedom to blacks in the North. By 1860 there were more than 250,000 in the North. Legal freedom did not lead to any real equality. Whites passed laws segregating blacks, restricting their economic opportunities, and barring them from serving on juries or voting. Whites drove blacks out of Cincinnati for the third time in 1841. In 1842 a mob of Irishmen attacked a black temperance procession. In the following three days, according to one observer, "the Negroes were beaten, their houses torn to pieces and two of their churches were burnt down in spite of the police, and when it was all over & the rascals had done all they wished, the troops were called around."

Despite the hostility and restrictions, opportunities for jobs drew ex-slaves to the cities. The concentration of free African Americans in communities provided chances to find marriage partners, start families, and participate in communal life. Black men worked as laborers or mariners in northern seaports. Others were able to become low status artisans such as butchers or barbers, considered to be uniquely black fields. Women worked mainly as domestic servants or laundresses. A few ran boarding houses or small shops. Some turned to prostitution to earn a living. Most African-American men and women were stuck in poorly paid menial jobs. Nevertheless, a black elite gradually arose from members of the community who had achieved some education and modest wealth. They helped to establish community institutions including mutual aid societies, newspapers, and, most importantly, churches. The first independent black denomination was the African Methodist Episcopal (AME) Church. African-American Baptist churches were organized a few years later. The churches became the centers of community life, promoting educational and fraternal programs, and developing leaders. (This continued in the modern era with such influential figures as Martin Luther King Jr. and Jesse Jackson.)

Some freed or escaped slaves achieved national recognition. Harriet Tubman was a tiny woman who suffered from sudden fainting spells as a result of an overseer's blow to her head when she was a teenager. In 1849 she escaped from slavery in Maryland to Philadelphia. But she fearlessly returned to the South nineteen times to guide hundreds of slaves to freedom in the North or Canada. She became the

In northern cities, African Americans created their own African churches.

Harriet Tubman (far left) and fellow escapees

most famous "conductor" of the Underground Railroad, a living legend. Eventually, the price on the head of the "Moses of her people" rose to an astounding $40,000, but she always eluded capture. When one of the escaping slaves panicked, endangering the others, she would point her ever-ready pistol to his head and announce, "Dead niggers tell no tales; you go on or die." She credited God for her exceptional courage and luck, "Jes so long as He wants to use me, He'll take ker of me, and when He don't want me any longer, I'm ready to go."

Sojourner Truth, freed from slavery in the North, was one of the most popular and compelling speakers for antislavery and women's rights groups. The tall, gaunt Sojourner impressed Harriet Beecher Stowe with her dignity and demeanor: "I do not recall ever to have been conversant with anyone who had more of that silent and subtle power which we call personal presence than this woman." Both Truth and Tubman were Christian mystics who spoke in a language of sin and redemption that would resonate with their audiences.

Frederick Douglass was the most celebrated of all, probably the most important black leader of the nineteenth century. With some limited white aid, he had taught himself to read and write. He escaped from slavery and, in 1841, began to lecture for the Massachusetts Anti-Slavery Society. An extremely talented man, he rapidly became one of the most popular abolitionist lecturers, wrote a widely read autobiography, and edited his own newspaper, *The North Star*. He was an eloquent advocate of women's rights as well as racial equality. His oratorical skills were so extraordinary that many believed he was an impostor, arguing that no ex-slave could be so brilliant.

Sojourner Truth (left) and Frederick Douglass (right) became two of the outstanding black lecturers for the abolitionist movement.

Despite the efforts of these free blacks and many others, the conditions of African Americans had declined considerably since the signing of the Constitution in the supposedly progressive North. One British observer wrote: "Singular is the degree of contempt and dislike in which free blacks are held in all the free states of America....In fact in the United States, a Negro, from...his colour alone is a degraded being. Is not this extraordinary in a land which professes universal liberty, equality, and the rights of man?"

The Lives of Women

In the rapidly changing world of the mid-nineteenth century city, the home became a refuge from competition and disorder, a haven of stability, particularly for the middle class. Both middle class men and women increasingly viewed the home as an institution presided over by women where children lived and men visited. The home took on new significance as an idealized center of feminine morality and devotion, qualities sorely lacking in the outside world. *Godey's Lady's Book*, one of the most popular magazines, asked, "Our homes—what is their cornerstone but the virtue of a woman, and on what does our social well-being rest but in out homes? Must we not trace all other blessings of civilized lives to the doors of our private dwellings?"

In an earlier America home and work, the orbits of men and women, had intermingled. By the middle of the nineteenth century, the patterns of men and women's lives had differentiated. The growth of urban capitalism sent men, still considered heads of families, out into the world to make the money on which their families' status would rest. Their realm was now entirely separate from the female "chaste circle of the fireside." A perceptive English traveler, Frances Trollope, commented that, "in America, with the exception of dancing which is almost wholly confined to the unmarried of both sexes, all the enjoyment of men are found in the absence of women." The women, she noted, were restricted to "the sordid offices of household drudgery." It seemed to her that the spheres of men and women were so separate that they barely spoke to each other. It was also true, however, that if the woman's sphere seemed to be limited to the home, she now ruled that sphere. The father left home each day to go to his own sphere at work. Some have argued that, though the space left to women was restricted, it was better than no space at all.

Popular literature and the views of clergymen promoted the doctrine of women's sphere. Unlike aggressive men whose morality was suspect, society expected women to be pure, pious, loving, gentle, self-sacrificing, delicate, and dependent. One popular manual for "young ladies" informed its readers that, "the possession of even an average share of vitality and animal spirits is something less than fashionable and more than feminine." The multiple layers of garments ending in whalebone or metal "stays" to compress the waist and internal organs symbolized the constricted position of women. The "cult of true womanhood" provided a balance to the disorder and violence of a rapidly changing world. "We look to you ladies to raise the standard of character in our own sex," a New England minister admonished.

The stress on purity also led to greater female sexual control within marriage. Middle class families, particularly, had fewer children. In 1800 America's birthrate was the highest in the world. Between 1810 and 1860 the birth rate declined by 23 percent. The wives, now considered morally superior, were able to better control the number of children they had by asserting a right to limit sexual relations. Although the term "birth control" would have shocked Americans of this era, various other methods to limit family size were also used. Male withdrawal was a common, though widely condemned, method. Popular books advocated various dangerous chemical douches. Abortions, often performed by German immigrant practitioners, became more common among married couples until outlawed later in the century. A professor of medicine, writing about abortion, lamented that, "The contagion has reached mothers who are devoted with an ardent and self-denying affection to the children who already constitute their family." The limitation on the sexuality of "nice" women led to a substantial growth in prostitution, in spite of urgent medical warnings that sexual activities drained men of their limited supply of strength and energy.

The importance given to motherhood grew as family size declined. The nurturing and raising of children became the central focus of the family. Middle class

The women's sphere included housework and learning social skills. Men dominated the public sphere.

children no longer worked in a productive family unit. Childhood was now viewed as a separate stage of life. Mothers emerged as the main child rearers and motherhood as the ultimate role for women. Magazines and manuals stressed its significance. "How entire and perfect is this dominion over the unformed character of your infant," gushed one author. Northern state courts, considering the "good of the child" and "parental fitness," began to award custody to mothers in divorce cases. American mothers tended to reject the old belief in infant damnation. This led ministers to accept the idea that a good Christian upbringing could mitigate original sin. Mothers, rather than God, were in control of the souls of children.

The segregation of the spheres of middle class men and women led to the development of a self-contained women's world where women depended on each other for emotional support. Women in the nineteenth century developed long-lasting and intense relationships with other women that were central to their life experiences.

The constriction of clothes, sexuality, "animal spirits," and status caused a rise in female illnesses in the middle and upper classes. When the educator, Catherine Beecher, traveled around the country in the 1850s, she reported 8 of 10 women "ailing" or "in poor health" in one city, 3 of 4 over all. They had the "vapors," suffered from "neurasthenia," and complained of headaches and backaches. They turned to the newly licensed physicians for help. The role of midwifes, once a female monopoly, began to decline in the cities. Some women argued that females should be allowed to enter the medical profession to protect the purity of women. Only women could examine other women with propriety. This support led to the licensing of Elizabeth Blackwell, the first female medical college graduate.

Many doctors continued to follow the ideas of "heroic medicine" that called for massive bloodletting or dispensing enormous doses of purgatives to rid the body of disease. Alternative ideas surfaced, depending on botanical remedies or stressing nature and the body's ability to cure itself. Hundreds of new medical schools opened without any real standards. Thousands of new doctors were "turned loose on the community to cure or to kill as the case may be." Many women (as well as men) began to seek alternatives in patent medicines. Columns of advertisements for various miracle cures filled newspapers. Some patent medicine makers published almanacs. Others sent traveling shows around the country. Products were extolled as cures for virtually every ailment and were "guaranteed" to make a person feel better. Most were ineffective or even dangerous. Many were laxatives designed to purge the body of "agents of death." Others, such as Doctor Hostetter's Celebrated Stomach Bitters Tonic, contained one-third or more alcohol, leading to alcoholism. Some, particularly "nerve tonics," were laced with opium, causing an alarming rise in drug addiction among upper and middle class women.

The growth of the public education system in the North provided new opportunities for women. The acknowledged female mission of nurturing children could be expanded into the schools. Female teachers cost far less than male. Teaching rapidly became a feminine profession. By the 1850s almost three-fourth's of New England's public school teachers were women. The institution of "schoolmarm" was spreading throughout the North. Catherine Beecher crusaded for teacher training to attain "the elevation of my sex by the opening of a profession for them in the education of the young." While the pay was low and the conditions often difficult, teaching provided an honorable method of self-support.

Female teaches were far less costly than males and became a role for the better educated woman.

In addition, women had to be better educated to fill the role of teacher. By 1860, the United States was the first country in which literacy rates were about equal for the two sexes, since as many girls as boys attended school. Female academies or "seminaries" appeared throughout the North to train teachers. Oberlin College became the first coeducational institution in America. A teacher's letter of recommendation in support of a young middle-class woman's application to Antioch College illustrates the prevalent attitude toward female education. The applicant wrote "*well* for a girl" and, though spirited, was "*very governable.*" Her parents were sending her to a tutor "*to learn politeness and good manners*" before entering college. A Philadelphia editor believed that a girl should be taught to be "womanly" so that her husband would not be driven "to seek amusements elsewhere." She should learn to think, but, "she should not become mannish, or, as the world calls it, 'strong-minded!'"

As their educational levels increased, women came to the front in areas of popular communication. Women were the main contributors to the more than one hundred "ladies magazines" that flourished in this period. Sarah Hale, who was left with five children as a young widow, was the most successful of the editors of women's magazines. *Godey's Lady's Book*, her final publication, achieved a circulation of 150,000, far above that of other magazines. She was an ardent exponent of woman's sphere but also favored higher education for women. She was best known at the time for campaigning to get Thanksgiving recognized as a national holiday and for writing "Mary Had a Little Lamb."

Godey's Lady's Book **printed the latest fashions for the "well dressed" woman. These dresses were made of silk and muslin, trimmed with lace and other frills.**

Better-educated middle-class women, with increased leisure time, created a vast reading public. By the 1850s it was estimated that four-fifths of the nation's readers were women. Popular advice manuals and marriage guides featured the themes of "mother" and "home." Homemakers could learn about "domestic economy." Women also provided the main audience for novels. Women authors created heroines who triumphed over adversity created by unsavory or unsatisfactory men. Authors, who Nathaniel Hawthorne had dismissed as "those scribbling women," dominated the literary market in the 1850s with their sentimental fiction. One earned an astounding $10,000 a year through serial publications of her Gothic romances.

The changes in American industry that made mass publication possible also brought about new roles for women in manufacturing. The shift of production from the household to the factory created a need for cheap manageable labor. Employers, particularly in textile mills, found young unmarried New England farm girls an excellent source of labor for such towns as Lowell, Massachusetts. They lived in company-run boarding houses and were able to gain some personal autonomy by earning wages. By the 1840s, however, they organized a Female Labor Reform Association to agitate against grueling 14-hour workdays, wage cuts, and factory speed-ups. Mill owners quickly discovered that Irish immigrants were far more compliant. By the 1850s, temporary industrial work had disappeared as a means of upward mobility for northeastern farmwomen, but it was a major source of income for working class immigrants. By mid-century 10 percent of adult women, largely in cities, worked for pay. They made up one-quarter of the manufacturing labor force.

Other poor women, particularly immigrants and free blacks, worked as domestic servants. Seamstresses in cities competed for piecework in the home, where they could earn about half the wages of female factory workers. Crowds of poor women could be found in most cities, attempting to keep their families going by peddling such items as hot sweet potatoes or penny scrub brushes. Few of the occupations open to women allowed them to support themselves, let alone a family. As a result, widowhood could easily mean poverty. These working class women, faced with insecurity and possible destitution, had little time or energy to worry about women's sphere.

Domesticity or "true womanhood" also did not concern women who went with their families to the Great Plains or, even further, to California and Oregon. Men, "marching to the drumbeats of a song their women could not hear," initiated most westward treks. When they arrived at their remote and often desolate destinations, many agreed with the woman who felt "as if we had left all civilization behind." Everyday life in the West was similar to that of the colonial era when the family made up the basic unit of work. Women in the West struggled to recreate such communal institutions as schools and churches, bringing "civilization" to the West.

A Philadelphia editor, quite advanced for his times, pitied the thousands of "ill paid, overworked women, in our large cities, struggling in weariness and sorrow to earn a scanty pittance." He favored opening more fields at higher pay to them. But he warned that "much of the nonsense," expressed by those who could not accept that "women will still be women" who must remain in their "proper sphere," harmed their cause. They could not expect employment in intellectual pursuits, such as law or abstract science. Yet, if women were "deficient in the logical faculty," they were "superior to the other sex in many respects."

Life, Leisure and Popular Culture

The earlier focus of antebellum reformers on public education began to have a major impact in the decades from 1840 to 1860. Massachusetts pioneered in instituting the nation's first compulsory education law in 1852 and in extending public education to the secondary level. By 1860, most northern states had established public school systems to, at least, the eighth grade. Almost three-fourths of northern children between the ages of 5 and 16 attended school. (By contrast, the South did not have a public school system.) Northerners saw schools as agents of economic growth and greater equality of opportunity.

In addition to schools, other channels existed to spread ideas and information. A growing desire for adult education and "mutual improvement" increased attendance at lectures given in lyceums (public halls). Public fads tended to involve efforts to master the human mind. Mesmerists declared that they had found the laws of magnetism that governed relations between people. Spiritualists believed that they could communicate with the dead. The most popular "science of the mind" was phrenology. Phrenologists argued that they could determine human character by carefully measuring the form and shape of the head. Thousands of Americans attended lectures explaining the new "science," and others paid fees to have their characters examined through bumps on their heads. The *American Phrenological Journal* had a circulation of more than 50,000 in the mid-1850s. In a society in upheaval, phrenology was a means of setting fixed guidelines. Employers, who no longer had apprenticeships or personal relationships to rely on, could now use a phrenological examination to decide whether to hire a prospective worker. Criminologists could explain the basis of crime and identify likely criminals. Phrenology was only the first in a long line of American attempts to discover a popular science of human behavior.

The press was the most significant form of communication in the nineteenth century. Technology had an enormous impact upon newspapers. The telegraph made it possible to report news stories "instantly" from all parts of the country to newspaper offices. This led to the formation of the Associated Press in 1848. Newspapers could be produced faster and cheaper by the steam-driven rotary press that increased the capacity of a single press from 200 to 5,500 per hour. By the 1840s, some enterprising editors were able to reduce the price of their papers from six cents to a penny. The number of newspapers, which had doubled between 1825 and 1849, doubled again by 1860. The circulation of the 3,300 papers (one-fifth of which were dailies) grew twice as fast as the population. The weekly edition of Horace Greeley's *New York Tribune* boasted an astounding circulation of 200,000. The United States, the world's major newspaper-reading nation, had nearly one-third of all the newspapers in the world in 1860.

Popular papers lured readers with sensational stories, stressing "robberies, thefts, murders, awful catastrophes and wonderful escapes," much as the tabloids do today. Benjamin Day started this trend in his *New York Sun*, but James Gordon Bennett's *Herald* soon overtook him in its excesses. Other papers throughout the country rapidly adopted Bennett's circulation-building mixture of gossip, scandal, crime, and crusading. One observer, denouncing newspapers in which "crime and misery are concocted into melo-dramas," concluded sadly, "they may be regarded as representing to some extent the *general* mind; and certainly they are not calculated to convey a very high opinion of it."

The increase in crime and disorder, documented in the press, seemed to accompany the growth of cities and industry. Observers, while fascinated by such stories, lamented the evident decline in morals and law and order in language that seems surprisingly modern. A Chicago editor recalled that serious crimes once shocked the community, "Not so now...." This state of affairs revealed "a degeneracy truly deplorable and alarming." Another paper noted that murder, "in all its bloody variety of forms," was so common "that we have been obliged to let them pass without notice in our columns."

New York City, the commercial and cultural capital of the nation, also appeared to be its crime capital. Gangs of robbers, seemingly aided by corrupt public officials, unloosed an epidemic of street crimes, including many unsolved homicides. George Templeton Strong, a prominent New Yorker, noted that "'Garotting' and highway robbery" had become so common that, "Most of my friends are investing in revolvers and carry them about at night...though it's a very bad practice carrying concealed weapons." Two rival gangs, the Dead Rabbits and the Bowery Boys, started a riot in New York's notorious Five Points, firing on each other and the police from rooftops. They left a path of dead and wounded. When one observer asked why police had made no real effort to stop the carnage, he was told, "that the men of the Sixth Ward had vowed to kill them all, if they came there."

Many Americans worried about the causes of increasing crime. Their explanations sound very familiar today. Some believed that it was due to the declining importance of the father in the family and the resulting breakdown of disciplining children. Others felt it was a natural product of an excessively materialistic "money-worshipping...diseased society." Immigrant-haters charged that "criminals from abroad" committed most crimes. Some blamed lax law enforcement. The Chicago *Tribune* condemned the "squeamishness of jurors, the ingenuity of attorneys, and the carelessness of courts" for a 20-year lapse in hangings. Such "sentimentality" emboldened criminals. Southern commentators argued that the uncontrolled crime raging in northern cities was the result of "universal demoralization and anarchy" that arose from unlimited freedom and equality. This chaos in the North contrasted unfavorably with "the peaceful homes and pure hearths, the personal security and public tranquillity of Southern life."

To most Americans, sensational crime stories provided distraction. Entertainment infatuated Americans who could not seem to get enough of it. Public speaking, particularly formal oratory, was one of the major forms of popular amusement. Large audiences of people would sit, or even stand, enthralled by speeches that lasted from two to four hours. Great public speakers like Daniel Webster, who could go on for hours without formal notes, became folk heroes. The speeches provided opportunities for people to gather in crowds and share experiences. One English observer noted that Americans seemed to fear loneliness. "There is no part of the world, perhaps, where you have more difficulty in obtaining permission to be alone...than in America.... Everything is done in crowds, and among a crowd," he concluded.

Americans would go to see almost anything. Popular draws included such diverse attractions as the sporting events described in the section on rough and tumblers, Shakespeare's plays, Italian operas, Indians (such as Black Hawk), "freaks," beached whales, foreign revolutionaries, and tumblers and acrobats. The theater audiences were particularly passionate. Edwin Forest was America's leading Shakespearean actor. Forest and his main British rival, William Macready, appeared in competing productions of *Macbeth* in New York. Forest supporters showered Macready with rotten eggs and jeered at his performance, forcing the police to intervene. The ensuing riot required the dispatch of sixty cavalrymen and three hundred infantry. Twenty people were killed and hundreds wounded in the ensuing melee. Anti-British feelings of the lower classes, particularly the Irish, helped cause this extreme reaction. Their "betters" were Anglophiles who had contempt for the "vulgar" Forest and applauded his English rival. Other immense crowds came to Castle Garden in New York to see operas, watch Swiss Bell ringers, or experience the "liquid flow of melody" from the violin of a Norwegian virtuoso.

"Jim Crow" Rice and his "Ethiopian Operas" were even more popular. The success of this black-faced white Yankee created a minstrel tradition that spread throughout the country. Mesmerized audiences watched the exotic figures of swaying black-faced minstrels lighted by gas flames or candlelight on small country stages and large city theaters. The cast of characters always included "little limping Jim Crow," Zip Coon, a "very learned skoler," and the outcast, old Dan Tucker ("Git outen de way, ole Dan Tucker"). Minstrel performances ended with the "walkaround," competitive dancing within circular mazes, patterned on black plantation dancing. Ironically, minstrelsy, with its exploitation of the black as a comic figure, grew in popularity in the 1840s and 1850s just as the struggle for abolition of slavery gained support. Minstrel shows spread to California where Stephen Foster's "Oh Susannah," a minstrel song, became the anthem of the Western empire.

The county fair increasingly became a favorite form of entertainment. Although usually sponsored by agricultural societies, the crowds tended to flock to races, gambling, and "freak shows." Thirty thousand men, women, and children flocked to a "buffalo hunt" in Hoboken, New Jersey. Unfortunately, the buffaloes broke loose, becoming "the hunters instead of the hunted" and causing general mayhem.

The American fixation on entertainment helped make P.T. Barnum one of the leading men of the century. After some success exhibiting "George Washington's nurse," a "145-year old" black woman, he opened a museum of oddities. He earned a fortune promoting "General Tom Thumb," a two-foot tall, 20-pound man. He also brought the famous singer Jenny Lind, the "Swedish nightingale," to America, creating a mass outbreak of "Lindomania." The "wild man from Borneo," who was actually a disfigured black man from Paterson, New Jersey, was a less exalted popular attraction. Barnum's success illustrates the pleasure Americans took in being tricked, their admiration for hustlers. He placed a sign reading

"Egress" over the exit to his museum and charged visitors a nickel to see the Egress. The trick so amused them that they urged friends to be sure to see the Egress.

The Fourth of July celebration was the greatest entertainment of all. A good percentage of public oratory took place on this occasion, when speakers could embellish on the theme of the nation's glorious past and even more wonderful future. The exuberance of a day when "all America was in a blaze; and in addition to this mode of manifesting joy, all America was tipsy," astounded one British visitor. In cities, as well as small towns, inhabitants danced through the night and the skies were ablaze with fireworks. One onlooker noted in his diary, "A foreigner would put it in his book of travels as one of the marvels of New York, and compare it to a swarm of tropical fireflies gleaming in and out through a Brazilian forest."

The growth of middle and upper class incomes and living standards in northern cities led to increased demands for consumer goods. The expanded significance of the home had material, as well as social, consequences. The more substantial homes of the mid-century contained drawing rooms, carpeting, drapes, pianos, mirrors, and ornate furniture featured in *Godey's Lady's Book*, as well as a good supply of books and magazines. Downtown stores sparkled with expensive goods. A.T. Stewart's magnificent Marble Palace opened in New York in 1846. It featured six by eleven feet plate glass windows to display the store's merchandise to the public. The store, which employed four hundred clerks, was in a massive six-story white marble building. One woman described it as "spacious and magnificent beyond anything of the kind in the New World, or the Old either...." It was the model for the great downtown department stores, such as Macy's and Lord & Taylor, which were to follow.

Magazines and books often featured discussions of fashion and appearance. Some writers praised the newly stylish hoop skirt as a health improvement over

Phineas Taylor Barnum served as a member of the Connecticut legislature and was a temperance lecturer. However, his fame lay in his showmanship and his promotional ability. He read the times better than any promoter in American history. There was a need for mass amusements that would offer escapism but would be strictly moral. Barnum stepped into the center stage. His idea was to offer entertainment that would be educational, moral, and, of course, profitable.

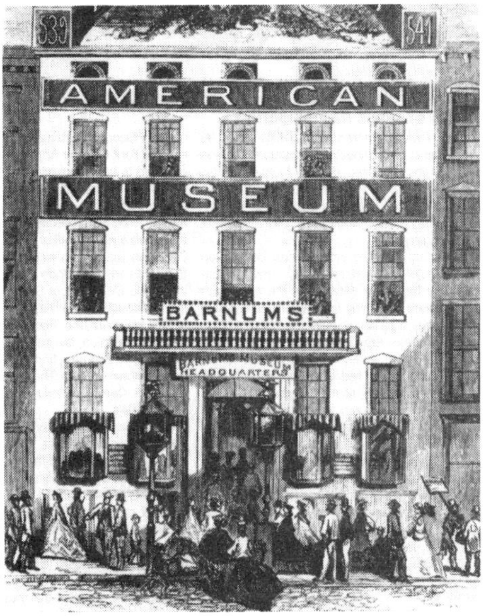

P. T. Barnum decided to collect real and fake oddities and display them to the public. People came from all over the United States and foreign countries to view his collection of freaks. Popular amusements were now becoming big business. The memory of P. T. Barnum as the "Father of Entertainment" will linger on.

the previously popular "ponderous bundle of individual skirts numbering twenty or more." Some worried that steel hoops, suggested as replacements for the overly expensive whalebone hoops, might attract lightening. The emphasis on female purity and respectability led to disapproval of such cosmetics as lip and cheek rouge. Women took to pinching their cheeks and biting their lips for color. Cosmetics were still sold but were endowed with health properties to avoid censure. "Tri-cosian Fluid," a hair dye, advertised itself as "highly beneficial in nervous headaches or weakness of the eyes." Women now compounded most cosmetics at home, however, following magazine beauty secrets.

Beards and mustaches supplied the fashion topic for men. American men had been beardless for two hundred years. In 1840, when one Massachusetts man dared to grow a beard, angry neighbors attacked him, and the authorities threw him in jail. But in the 1850s, for some unknown reason, facial hair sprouted all over the place, ranging from tidy goatees to long thicket-like beards. In 1853 the army, which had forbidden beards, gave up and decided that they were now within regulations. (President Lincoln's later decision to grow a beard ensured the continuing popularity of the new style.)

The vast quantities of food Americans consumed, particularly meat, constantly astounded Europeans. In Europe food was eaten slowly, conscientiously, and with an almost religious devotion. Americans seemed to devour their dinners in enormous haste. "Fast food" emporiums amazed European travelers. One such visitor compared "Americans at the dinner table to sharks." The reason for their hurry, he believed, was, "the desire to get down to business and not waste time." This was all part of the hustle and bustle of an increasingly dynamic northern society.

DOCUMENTS

FROM A BROKEN SAWMILL BLADE TO A STEEL PLOW:
The Story of John Deere's Invention, 1837

John Deere (1804-1886) was emblematic of those who used "Yankee know-how" to develop new products and ideas. He turned a sawmill blade into a plow that would conquer the tough prairie sod of the antebellum frontier. In 1848 he moved to Moline, Illinois, to establish a factory on the Mississippi River near the rapidly growing frontier where his business flourished. The following excerpt is based on an oral history account of what Deere did after he brought home a circular saw blade made of Sheffield steel broken and discarded at a sawmill.

"I cut the teeth off the mill-saw with a hand-chisel," John Deere said. "I cut a pattern out of paper for the moldboard and share." (One account says that he bent his first plow to a form which he carved out of wood.) "I laid the pattern on the saw and cut out around it with a hand chisel, with the help of a striker and a sledge. I then laid the piece on the fire of the forge and heated it, a little at a time, shaping it as best I could with the hand hammer." (According to one story, he used a wooden mallet to avoid denting the surface of the steel.)

"After making the upright standards out of bar iron," the account continues, "I was ready for the wood parts. I went out to the timber, dug up a sapling, and used the crooks of the roots for handles. I shaped the beam out of a stick of timber" (a fence rail, in one version) "with an axe and a drawing-knife. In this fashion, I succeeded in constructing a very rough plow." ... On that bright morning in 1837, when John Deere wiped the sweat from his brow with the back of his hand and said proudly, "She's finished"—it was an implement that caught and held the eye; new, sturdy, but light enough for a strong man to carry on his shoulder, the sun flashing from the polished steel as light from a mirror.

Farmers roundabout had heard what the blacksmith was up to. For the most part, they were skeptical, but willing to be shown. So, some of them, together with a number of villagers, assembled to watch John Deere's promised test of the new plow.... They climbed into the boat with John Deere and his precious plow, or followed in other boats, and rowed across to the far bank, calling jokes to one another, warning the curly-headed blacksmith not to be too down in the mouth when his plow proved itself no whit better than the plows brought from "back East." John was not given to light talk, but he sent as good chaff as he received; and, single-handed, he carried the plow across his shoulder to the field where Lewis Crandall was waiting with the necessary horse, and where it was said that no plow would ever scour.... Hitching up was no long process. In five minutes, all was ready.

"Want me to take her?" Crandall asked.

"I will," said John, "you drive."

Crandall slapped the reins on the horse's back. They were off. John Deere held the handles which he had fashioned from sapling roots and polished smooth. The plowshare bit deep into black soil. The horse put his withers into the pull. Soil began to cut and curl from the moldboard in a neat, smooth furrow. The spectators trudged behind, mostly silent, watching and wondering. After an eighth of a mile, they all stopped to appraise the performance.

"By cracky!" exclaimed one bystander, after a good look at the plow, "She's *clean*!"

There were several echoes of this approval—and some shouts of doubt.

"So *fur* she's clean," said one of the doubters, "but you wait!"

Crandall turned the horse, and they trudged back across the field, cutting another furrow. It was an ideal field, ideal weather for the test. The earth was still a little too moist; if ever it would stick to a plow, it should stick now. At the end of the second furrow, they stopped for a further examination. Moldboard was surprisingly clean. The gummy soil seemed unable to cling to it. A farmer turned to his neighbor:

"No need of your [cleaning] paddle with *that* plow!" he remarked triumphantly. "She moves right along, and polishes herself as she moves."

The one spoken to had broken many a prairie acre. "Aye," he said drily, "so it seems, but I *still* don't believe it!"

Round and round the field they went. Half a dozen times. A dozen. John Deere relinquished his place at the handles and let others take a turn at holding the plow. The worst pessimists finally had to admit that his plow scoured better than any plow they had ever seen. The optimists, on the other hand, were enthusiastic. John Deere himself was pleased; but not *too* pleased.

"I'm making you a present of this plow, Lewis," he said to Crandall, "for loaning the use of your land and the horse. But I'd like well to take it back with me to the shop for a few days. I doubt not I'll build another, and I will wish to study this. Maybe ways of improving it will occur to me."

So ended the test of John Deere's first steel plow.

Source: Neil M. Clark, *John Deere: He Gave to the World the Steel Plow* ([Moline, Ill.]: Priv. Print. [Desaulniers], [1937]), pp. 35-38.

1. What are the problems and advantages of the development of a steel plow?
2. What lesson about "Yankee know-how" and the ability to adapt can be found in this story of Deere's first plow?

"TRUE WOMANHOOD"

In times of rapid change, people often cling to stereotypes of the ideal society. In the antebellum era, one such stereotype that gained increasing public support was that of the "true" woman who always behaved like a perfect "lady." One historian has labeled this "the cult of true womanhood." Middle and upper class women of both the North and South accepted the virtues of chastity, piety, docility, and domesticity.

Social Expectations of White Women

Man is great in action - Woman in suffering.
Man shines abroad - Woman at home.
Man talks to convince - Woman to persuade and please.
Man has a rugged heart - Woman a soft and tender one.
Man prevents misery - Woman relieves it.
Man has science - Woman taste.
Man has judgment - Woman sensibility.
Man is a being of justice - Woman an angel of mercy.

Source: reprinted from the *North American Review* in the Charleston *Mercury* (October 10, 1837).

1. What are the main attributes of women according to the above source? How do women contrast with men?
2. To what extent are these views of women still accepted?

A VOICE OF PROTEST AGAINST TREATMENT OF FEMALE WORKERS

Despite the expectations that the woman's sphere would be in a sheltered home, the northern economy was rapidly modernizing. The ideas of a woman's place clashed with the economic need for a source of cheap labor. The development of the textile industry in New England in the 1830s and 1840s depended upon female workers in places like Lowell, Massachusetts. Lowell presented itself as a model environment for young women. The Lowell Female Labor Reform Association in its journal ***Voice of Industry*** *painted a far darker picture of the "slavery" of the factory girls.*

We were not aware, until within a few days, of the *modus operandi* of the factory powers in this village of forcing poor girls from their quiet homes to become their tools and, like the Southern slaves, to give up their life and liberty to become their tools and, like the Southern slaves to give up their life and liberty to the heartless tyrants and taskmasters.

Observing a singular looking "long, low, black" wagon passing along the street, we made inquiries respecting it, and were informed that it was what we term a "slaver." She makes regular trips to the north of the state (Massachusetts), cruising around in Vermont and New Hampshire, with a "commander" whose heart must be black as his craft, who is paid a dollar a head for all he brings to the market, and more in proportion to the distance—if they bring them from such a distance that they cannot easily get back.

This is done by "hoisting false colors," and representing to the girls that they can tend more machinery than is possible, and that the work is very neat, and the wages such that they can dress in silks and spend half their time reading. Now, is this true? Let those girls who have been thus deceived, answer....

Is there any humanity if this? Philanthropists may talk of Negro slavery, but it would be well first to endeavor to emancipate the slaves at home. Let us not stretch our ears to catch the sound of the lash on the flesh of the oppressed black, while the oppressed in our very midst are crying out in thunder tones, and calling upon us for assistance.

Source: *Voice of Industry*, January 2, 1846.

1. Why does the author of this article believe that women workers were being exploited?
2. How effective is the comparison to the issue of slavery?
3. Would the role of "true womanhood" play a part?

A MOTHER BEGGING HER MASTER NOT TO SEPARATE HER FROM HER CHILDREN

Chapter Two

THE AMERICAN SOUTH AND ITS SINGULAR SOCIETY

SOUTHERN "BACKWARDNESS"

The South did not share in the American passion for modernization and change. Although the southern economy grew, it never developed important commercial or industrial sectors. It remained as rural, agricultural, and labor-intensive as it had been in 1800. Educational reform barely touched the South, and almost half its population remained illiterate. A southern newspaper defiantly declared, "worst of all abominations is the modern system of Free Schools...the prolific source of infidelity and treasons...." The per capita circulation of newspapers and magazines among whites in the South was less than half that of the North. The two regions of the country had much in common: revolutionary and constitutional traditions; religious revivalism; the political party system; the preponderance of small, relatively self-sufficient farmers; and even anti-black racism. Northern racism, however, did not include justifying slavery. To Northerners, free labor, like free competition, was the basis of a modern society. They believed that slavery, a "relic of barbarism," would be eliminated by the power of progress.

Yet, reform movements, which had swept through the North, bypassed the South. Southerners stressed heritage and stability far more than progress or change. In the northern view, the South was an embarrassing, backward area, out of step with the forward march of the modernizing nineteenth century. Ralph Waldo Emerson, the famed philosopher, told an approving northern audience in 1844, "Slavery is no scholar, no improver; it does not love the whistle of the railroad;...it does not increase the white population; it does not improve the soil, everything goes to decay." But slavery was central to the Old South. It was a slave society at its very core.

"King Cotton" and the Southern Economy

The economic differences between the two sections increased in the years before the Civil War. "We are an agricultural people," a southern senator declared. "We want no manufactures; we desire no trading....As long as we have our rice, our sugar, our tobacco, and our cotton, we can command wealth to purchase all we want." By 1860, New York and Pennsylvania **each** manufactured more than twice as much as the eleven future Confederate states combined. New York alone had almost twice as much banking capital as all fifteen slave states. Since the South spent so much less on canals or railroads, it failed to develop a transportation network or unified market economy. Leading cities like Charleston or Richmond had only 5 percent of the population of New York (40,000 compared to 800,000) in 1860. Southerners were responsible for only 7 percent of the major inventions from 1790 to 1860. Eli Whitney, a New Englander who had

Eli Whitney's cotton gin increased the productivity of cotton plantations and the need for field hands.

gone South in 1792 to work as a tutor, invented even the cotton gin, which recast the southern economy.

Whitney's revolutionary invention made possible the successful commercial growth of short-staple cotton. It was a simple ingenious device that separated the fiber from the seed, a task once performed unprofitably by hand. The Industrial Revolution, based on the textile industry in Britain and, later, New England, created an ever-increasing demand for cotton. The climate and soil of the South were ideal for the cultivation of cotton. The growing use of the steamboat made it feasible to transport cotton from the inter-connecting southern rivers to domestic and international markets. The shortage of white labor caused greater dependence on the supply of black slave labor (unlike the North where the problem led to invention of labor-saving machines and encouragement of immigration). Slavery, which had appeared to be doomed to extinction after the American Revolution, was reinvigorated. The unparalleled natural increase of the southern slave population from 1.5 million in 1820 to almost 4 million in 1860 aided this process. (In contrast, slavery in Latin America depended on continued importation from Africa.)

As production moved steadily westward, the Cotton Kingdom, by 1835, spread more than 1,000 miles from South Carolina and Georgia through Alabama, Mississippi, Louisiana, Arkansas, and East Texas. Cotton output doubled each decade from 1800 to 1860. The South produced almost two-thirds of the world's cotton, and cotton accounted for more than half of America's exports in the antebellum years. Much of the capital and business know-how to market southern crops came from northern or British firms. Cotton exports paid for the largest share of the nation's imports, stimulated northern industry, and contributed to New York City's rise as a center of marketing and export. Southerners complained that, "the North fattens and grows rich on the South." Southerners firmly believed that northern industries would shrivel up and banks fail without a continuous supply of southern cotton.

The slave economy was, in fact, profitable for the large planters. Their investment returns equaled that of northern industrialists. Since slaves were counted as wealth, the per capita wealth of southern whites was double that of Northerners in 1860. Almost two-thirds of the richest men in America lived in the South, which contained only 30 percent of the nation's free population. The problem was that slaves were both labor and capital in the southern economy, the keys to prosperity. Most plantation owners invested more in slaves than in land and machinery combined. The aim of the cotton planter, as one contemporary observer noted, was, "to sell cotton in order to buy negroes—to make more cotton to buy more negroes, ad infinitum...." The prices of slaves soared, as higher cotton prices in the 1850s increased demand. By 1859 a prime field hand cost $1700 ($20,000 in current dollars). The plantation frontier accelerated its westward movement. Slave owners in the Upper South met much of the demand for new slaves in the fertile black-belt cotton growing area. Many of them shifted from struggling with soil exhaustion to profiting from the sale of excess slaves. Virginia, "the mother of presidents," became the prime breeder of slaves, earning more from that than any other commodity. The southern economy grew, but it failed to develop, lacking cities, skilled workers, an entrepreneurial middle class, or any kind of diversified economy.

A new method of curing led to a comeback in tobacco production after 1850. Sugar cane planting, requiring expensive machinery, was profitable on large plantations in southern Louisiana. Rice, grown in South Carolina, Georgia, and Louisiana, also utilized large gangs of slave labor. The value of cotton production, however, was greater than that of all other crops combined. The phenomenal demand for cotton in the 1850s made the southern economy even more narrowly specialized on a single staple crop and promoted a dangerous dependence on the world's demand for cotton.

The Lives of Southern Whites

Slave holding determined the social position of whites. It was at the foundation of the social order. Southern society was more complex than its image of privileged aristocratic planters, "poor white trash," and slaves. Only one-third of southern white families owned any slaves at all. One historian has pointed out that this was really a comparatively widespread distribution of such expensive property. (A

Unlike the wealthy aristocrats, the majority of southern white farmers lived in humble homes.

hundred years later only 2 percent of American families held stocks of similar value.) Of the slave owners, half possessed fewer than five, and only 12 percent owned more than twenty (although more than half the slaves belonged to this group). Thus, the average slaveholder was a farmer of rather humble origins, rather than an aristocrat. The true "planter aristocracy" consisted of the eight thousand families who held more than fifty slaves, in a white population of eight million.

This small group dominated the political and social life of the South, as well as its economy. These planters justified their supremacy by creating a paternalistic ideology in which they were the benevolent rulers of their inferiors, including blacks, other whites, and all women. They portrayed themselves as living graciously, following codes of chivalry, and exhibiting kindness to all. Honor was far more important than the money-grubbing that characterized the North. It was a romantic illusion that appealed to the American psyche (as shown by the popularity of *Gone With the Wind* many years later).

The lives of this ruling class centered on an elaborate social life and extended family. Kinship ties extended to distant cousins, who often intermarried. The "benevolent despot" was the oldest male, the leader of a patriarchal society far more extreme than elsewhere in America. "All the comfort of my life depends on his being of good humor," one southern woman wrote of her husband. Violence was a troubling undercurrent to the code of honor. Lesser whites, as well as blacks, were expected to yield the narrow sidewalks of southern towns to their betters and descend to the muddy, manure-filled streets. Failure to do so could cause the aggrieved party to "shoot at sight." The code of duels, disappearing in the North, remained in force in the South. When a North Carolina planter publicly whipped a lawyer, William Avery, Avery responded to this challenge to his honor by killing the planter in a courtroom at point-blank range. A jury acquitted Avery in ten minutes and greeted him with a standing ovation. Excessive drink, opium dependency, and a widespread addiction to gambling helped cause the large numbers of nervous breakdowns among the upper classes. Private asylums sprang up to discretely handle the afflicted.

Despite these problems, most southern aristocrats believed in "living well." They danced, flirted, hunted, and ate enormous quantities of food at splendid banquets. They constantly moved their families and retinues to city "town houses" in the unhealthy humid summers or to other plantations they owned. Above all, they were convinced that their life style and culture easily surpassed the North. "The South honestly believed," one writer noted, "in its innate superiority over all other races and peoples. It did not doubt, that, man for man, it was braver, stronger, better than the North."

Most southern whites were yeoman farmers, frontier individualists who owned their land, had few or no slaves, and strove for self-sufficiency. Unlike northern

In a duel each man stood back to back, paced to a measured distance, turned, drew his gun, and shot at one another.

farmers, they had little contact with the market, due to the lack of transportation. They lived in isolated rural communities where house-raisings, corn-shuckings, and quilting bees provided amusement, and religious revivals at camp meetings were the most important events. They may have grown a bale or two of cotton that they ginned at the nearest plantation. A few in this group were able to rise in class. One example was the family of Jefferson Davis, later president of the Confederacy. His father was a humble frontier farmer, but his brother prospered in the rich farm lands of Mississippi, rapidly adding land and slaves. The brother was able to obtain a West Point appointment for his younger brother, Jefferson, and supplied him with a large plantation. In a single generation, the Davis family had become aristocrats. Most yeoman farmers, however, remained in their own class

The 25 percent of southern whites who were landless best fit the traditional image of poor whites. They owned only a few meager household possessions and a few animals, generally pigs. They worked for others or rented patches of land. They scrimped, saved, and struggled to become yeomen. A few succeeded.

Small farmers in the South suffered in competition with slave holding plantation owners. As the cost of slaves rose, the ability of yeoman farmers to own slaves and ascend in status declined. By 1860 slave holding had declined to 25 percent of white families, but they controlled 95 percent of the South's agricultural wealth.

In spite of this, to the dismay of many Northerners, most whites seemed to support the slave system. Southern whites were bound together by ties of race—a white skin granted instant status. Frederick Law Olmstead, the architecture of Central Park who visited the South, perceptively remarked, "from childhood, the one thing in their condition which has made life valuable to the mass of whites has been that the niggers are yet their inferiors." All whites could consider themselves equal in their superiority over blacks. "Break down slavery," the Governor of Virginia warned, "and you would with the same blow destroy the democratic principle of equality among men." Ironically, southern whites saw slavery as the basis of liberty and equality.

The Lives of Southern Blacks

In the eyes of the law, slaves were forms of property. They had no right to marry, testify in court, or hold property. In most states it was illegal to teach them how to read and write. The masters possessed virtually unlimited power to buy and sell slaves as chattel property, to separate families, and to punish and physically abuse them. State laws protecting slaves from torture and murder and setting

Slave trading in the South

minimal living standards were, in practice, never enforced. The only real limits on the master's power were his sense of paternalism and, even more, his economic self-interest. As the value of slaves kept rising, it made sense to keep them in reasonable health and continued productivity. After all, dead or mutilated slaves could not grow cotton.

The slave system reached its height in the United States after Congress officially banned the African slave trade in 1808. This also affected the physical treatment of slaves. In Latin America extreme physical cruelty was far more common since planters could work slaves to death and easily import replacements from Africa. In the United States, natural reproduction was the means of replenishing the "slave stock." The slave population in America increased by about 27 percent per decade after 1810, virtually the same natural increase as that of the whites. (The slave population was unable to even maintain itself, much less increase, in any other country in the Americas.) Unlike other nations, the sex ratio among slaves in the United States was just about equal after 1820, allowing slaves to create families and raising the reproduction rate.

This does not mitigate the inherent cruelties of slavery. The lives of slaves involved unending toil, physical coercion, poverty, and resentment. Though terrible abuses were not as common as abolitionists charged, they did occur. While "bad" owners "whipped till he's bloodied you and blistered you," even good owners who did not "whip too much" used the threat of physical punishment to keep slaves in line.

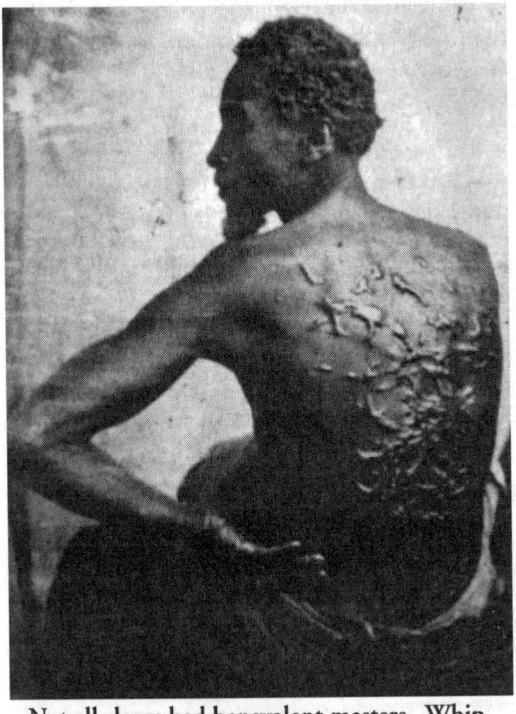

Not all slaves had benevolent masters. Whippings were common on many plantations.

Treatment varied with the personality of the owner and, on large plantations, the overseer. In general, most slaves were field hands who worked from "sun to sun," clearing the land, plowing behind a mule, chopping the unending rows of cotton, and picking the white fiber from the bolls.

The slaves lived packed into small one-room cabins with dirt floors. Diseases and infections, such as intestinal parasites, typhoid fever, lice, and dysentery, quickly spread through the crowded slave quarters. Few starved, but their diet consisted of cornmeal, pork fatback, and molasses, supplemented by sweet potatoes and greens from the tiny gardens most masters allowed them to have. The one or two changes of clothing were usually made of a coarse cotton fabric known to whites as "nigger cloth." Women worked as hard as men. Children carried water and food to the fields or did lighter fieldwork. The few older people cared for the youngest children and worked in gardens and stables.

The strength of the slaves' community and culture sustained them through their bondage. As a result of the end of the Atlantic slave trade, the proportion of native born blacks steadily increased, reaching 96 percent by 1850. They were African American, rather than African. Certainly, strong African influences remained. These included such diverse things as hair and head cover styles, musical instruments, drumming and dancing patterns, oral traditions, belief in the spirit world, and kinship patterns. These intermingled with American culture to create a unique African-American culture within the constraints of slavery.

The masters pushed Christianity in an effort to keep their slaves submissive. White preachers taught them to be obedient and accept their role in life. Slaves created their own form of Christianity, stressing personal and community salvation. In secret prayer meetings late at night in the woods, they prayed for deliverance from slavery. They did not envision a heaven in which slaves continued to wait on white masters. Instead, the slave owners would be "broilin' in hell for their sin," when the day of reckoning came. As an anthropologist has commented, "The ante-bellum Negro was not converted to God. He converted God to himself."

Their music, often derived from African forms, became an integral part of the slaves' religion, providing an outlet for individual feelings and connections to the community. Although whites frequently told them that they were unworthy or depraved, spirituals reaffirmed their sense of chosenness, "de people dat is born of God." Most songs, despite some sadness, expressed confidence that, like the Hebrews in the Bible, they too would be saved. After all, if the Lord "delivered Daniel from de lion's den," then the slaves logically inquired in song, "why not every man?" Some songs were more specific in describing escape routes: "Follow the drinkin' gourd." Nonreligious folk tales revolved around the image of the trickster, like "Br'er Rabbit," who triumphed over his more powerful opponents through his own cunning. Remarkably, whites remained oblivious to the true nature of the songs and tales.

Families provided the most important support system for the slaves. Slaves followed African kinship patterns in naming children for revered grandparents and in avoiding marriage between cousins (a common practice among southern whites). Although the law did not recognize slave marriages, most masters permitted and even encouraged them to stabilize their workforces. The master was usually present for wedding ceremonies and often presided over them. They generally culminated with the jumping over a broomstick as a symbol of commitment. The thousands of slaves who ran away to search for spouses and children who had been sold demonstrated the power of family attachments. After the Civil War, masses of freed men and women eagerly searched for their mates and were anxious to legalize their marriages. Despite its surprising strength, the slave family was vulnerable to the whims and economic needs of the owners. Families could be broken up when one or more members were sold to pay debts, settle estates, or even given as wedding presents. It has been estimated that about one-quarter of slave marriages suffered this fate. Families might also be disrupted by the sexual exploitation of slave women by white owners or overseers. Often extended families or strangers functioning as "aunts" and "uncles" took on the necessary role of preserving family responsibilities. In spite of all the obstacles, the black family exhibited remarkable tenacity.

Contrary to fictional images and the face they showed whites, most slaves mistrusted and resented their owners. As Frederick Douglass suggested, "Give him a bad master and he aspires to a good master; give him a good master, and he wishes to become his own master. Such is human nature." The preservation of a unique African-American culture in the dehumanizing institution of slavery was the most important form of slave resistance. But there were more direct forms of fighting back as well. Slaves tested the system and their masters' wills by slacking off when they weren't watched, feigning ignorance of instructions, pretending to be ill, breaking tools, stealing food, and maiming themselves. Slave owners argued over whether rewards or punishments were more effective in overcoming this behavior. Some slaves, particularly in the upper South, ran away. There were individual episodes of violence involving arson, poisoning, or the murder of a harsh overseer (usually reported as an "accident").

Armed rebellions were far less common than in Brazil and other slave societies. There were many reasons for this. Whites outnumbered blacks, owned the weapons, and had all the power. There were few areas of jungles or mountains in the South where rebels could hide. The pull of family life and the precepts of Christianity also operated against violence. Slavery did, however, produce some fearless revolutionaries in America and some violent conspiracies. A free black, Denmark Vescey, organized a large-scale rebellion in Charleston in 1822, involving the most trusted servants of leading members of the white establishment. "You are in God's eyes equal to your masters; will you fight for that principle?" he challenged his followers. He was betrayed before he could implement his plans, and forty public hangings ensued. Nat

Turner, a mystical and eloquent Virginia slave preacher who could read and write, led the most famous slave uprising. In 1831 he and his band of rebels went from farm to farm, butchering sixty-one white men, women, and children. Whites quickly suppressed the rebellion. Some two hundred blacks, many totally innocent, were killed in retaliation, "without trial and under circumstance of great barbarity," including "decapitation."

The South felt the impact of Nat Turner's revolt almost immediately. The uprising, coming in the midst of the emergence of the abolitionist movement, increased white southern fears of a slave rebellion. On the one hand, many planters attempted to improve the living conditions of the slaves, and their living standards did rise after 1830. On the other, however, tighter controls accompanied this improvement. Laws made manumission (the freeing of slaves) much more difficult, prohibited teaching slaves to read or write, and strengthened slave patrols. The largest item in most municipal budgets in the South was the cost of police and patrols for "keeping down the niggers," as one visitor reported. Most states limited freedom of speech. Louisiana mandated penalties of 21 years of hard labor for any public expression of ideas "having a tendency to promote discontent among free colored people, or insubordination among slaves." African Americans understood the message given by the bloody retaliations and the increased suppression. There were no other slave revolts, but the other forms of resistance continued.

Despite the irritation expressed by slavery's apologists against "the superstitious weakness of dying men" that "induces them, in their last moments, to emancipate their slaves," manumissions continued even in the face of "insuperable obstacles." The 1860 census reported three thousand manumissions, double the number of the previous census. There might have been more as a result of increasing concern about the propriety of buying and selling human beings if the laws had been more lenient.

"Free people of color" increasingly fell under suspicion. There were almost 250,000 of them in the South by 1860. Most were descendants of those freed by their owners in the idealism following the Revolution. New laws after the Nat Turner uprising limited their freedom of movement, prohibited association with slaves, denied them rights to testify in court, assemble or own guns, and required them to work at authorized jobs. A handful managed to prosper and even own slaves (although most of these were their wives and children who could not be freed). In the Deep South, particularly in New Orleans, there was a population of mulattos, children of some wealthy planters who freed and supported their offspring. They aspired, not always successfully, to a status above that of other freedmen.

The Old Plantation and the Modern World

Natchitoches, Louisiana is a town of 17,000 divided into separate black and white worlds of roughly equal size. In modern times they have gotten along by avoiding discussions about race, much like antebellum America attempted to avoid the issue of slavery. The old Magnolia Plantation along the Cane River was decaying, and its owner, Betty Hertzog, was struggling to maintain it. Friends convinced her to agree to the creation of Cane River Creole Historical Park, which would preserve her family's stories and teach visitors about the agriculture of the era when cotton was king.

At the south edge of the plantation stood eight modest cabins with whitewash peeling from mud-brick walls and gaping holes where there had once been windows and doors. These cabins, hidden from the main house by trees, had been largely forgotten. Only the stories of some of the 260 slaves who once lived in them remained. When the park service held hearings to find out what kind of programs it should offer in the new park, people were enthusiastic about restoring old buildings but unwilling to discuss slavery. Mrs. Hertzog, dressed in a Civil War-era pink satin gown, escorted visitors around the big house but avoided issues of slavery. She admitted that it was wrong for people to own others as property but argued, "A lot of people have put slavery behind them. It's a part of the history here....But I don't want them to talk about slavery and get stuck on that." She further maintained that blacks should stop complaining or demanding reparations. "I think they should be grateful they got their freedom....I think they ought to be glad they are Americans living in a free country. The more of that stuff that gets stirred up, the more hate there will be on both sides."

An early black visitor whose family had once been sharecroppers on Magnolia felt cheated, however, by Mrs. Hertzog's tour. "All I kept thinking was that they accumulated all this wealth because of the blacks who worked here," he complained. "But there was nothing on the tour about black people. It's as if their place in history was erased."

Eventually, the park service restored the slave cabins and hired a black park ranger and historical interpreters to bring the slaves' stories to life for the tourists. Even if reluctantly, the whites of Natchitoches came to accept the recreations of slave life on the plantation. After all, this was a town that tended to avoid confrontation. In 1927 a plantation owner gave the town a statue of a bowing slave, tipping his hat. The plaque declared that it had been erected "in grateful recognition of the good darkies of Louisiana." In 1968, as civil rights protests swept the country, young blacks denounced the statue as a symbol of servitude. Late one September night local officials quietly removed the Good Darkey.

The difficulties of coming to grips with slavery and its consequences remain 135 years after its demise. Perhaps, a new generation signals a shift in attitudes. A young relative of Betty Hertzog now acts as family liaison to the park. "It is not a comfortable thing for me to come out and say that my relatives owned slaves, but it is important that we all acknowledge where we came from so we can start to work through the problems that were created in the past," she said. "Racism is a difficult thing to deal with because it runs so deep. To me, this park offers a chance to at least help start a dialogue that doesn't exist right now."

Southern Women: White and Black

The emphasis on paternalism by the upper class in the South had a great impact upon women, as well as slaves. One woman observed darkly, "there is no slave like a wife." As in the North, the feminine ideal of dependency, piety, innocence, morality, and charm was widely promoted. The South, however, was unaffected by the middle-class transformations sweeping northern society where women were, at least, gaining influence within the home. Men, who stressed subordination, shaped the southern feminine ideal. "Women, like children, have but one right, and that is the right to protection," one author admonished, adding, "the right to protection involved the obligation to obey." The chivalrous protection of delicate "Southern womanhood" became a preoccupation of men and of the entire social order. Upper class women did manage the house, supervise the children, and attend sick slaves. But they were often isolated on large plantations, limited in their education, and excluded from public life. Unlike their northern counterparts, they rarely wrote books or articles, confining their literary output to letters and diaries. There, they frequently expressed opposition to slavery, particularly to miscegenation (sexual relations between white men and black slave women). "Like patriarchs of old, our men live all in one house with their wives and concubines," lamented Mary Chestnut in her diary. She vividly sketched the dilemma of these privileged women. "Any lady is ready to tell you who is the father of all the mulatto children in everybody's household but her own. These, she seems to think, drop from the clouds." The growing intolerance of any dissent in southern society prevented these women from airing their grievances about slavery. Many directed their anger at the women slaves, rather than their unfaithful husbands.

Most southern white women lived on small farms and lived a life that had barely changed since colonial times. Only 35 percent of white girls attended school at all, and 25 percent of white women over 20 were completely illiterate. Their birthrate was about 30 percent above the national average. As late as 1860, the average southern white woman bore six children. Early marriages and large families were common among women of all classes. Twice as many women died in childbirth in the South as in the Northeast. Those who survived often had to overcome the death of their children; 5 of 10 southern children died before reaching the age of five.

Life was even more difficult for African-American women. Slave women worked in the fields like slave men. Only 5 percent on large plantations attained the more privileged status of house servant. Like white women, slave women had their first children in their late teens. A mother was usually excused from fieldwork for a month before and after giving birth. Fertility rates were very high, but the combination of hard field labor and frequent pregnancies led to large numbers of miscarriages and stillbirths. Slave women worked hard to preserve the family and to maintain traditional gender roles within it, despite the blurring of these roles by the equal hard labor imposed by slavery. To black women, the greatest crime of slavery was the separation of mothers and children. Standards of sexual morality in the slave community differed from that of the prevailing white norms. There was little emphasis on female "purity" and premarital sex, even pregnancy did not lead to condemnation. The community, however, expected fidelity after marriage and denounced adultery. Southern white women complained about the supposed "loose" morals of black slave women. Antislavery women stressed the exploitation vulnerable and powerless slave women were subjected to by white men. Although it may not have been as widespread as abolitionists suggested, coercive sex was certainly a part of slavery. Harriet Jacobs, a fugitive slave, vividly described her master's abuse that began when she was 15: "He told me I was his property: that I must be subject to his will in all things. My soul revolted against the mean tyranny. But where could I turn for protection?"

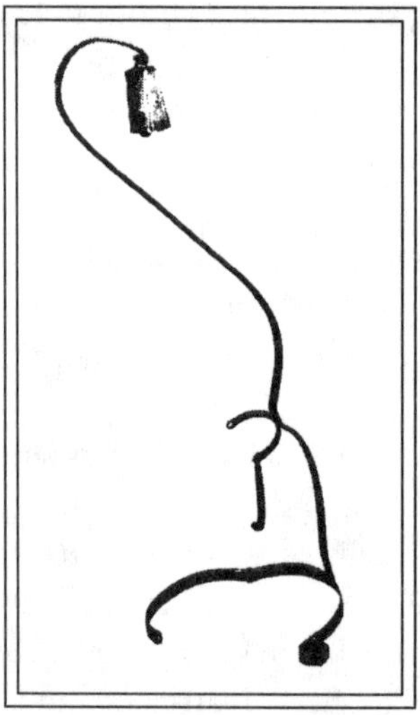

This harness was designed to keep track of a slave's movements. The bell was above the wearer's head where it could not be reached.

The Case of the White Slave

James White, a New Orleans slave trader, bought Jane Morrison in the slave market in Jefferson Parish in January 1857. Shortly thereafter, she ran away, and White did not see her again until October of that year when he encountered her in a courtroom in answer to her suit for freedom. Her case, considered by three juries and the Louisiana Supreme Court, created an enormous stir and shook the foundations of race and slavery in the South. The reason for this was that the fifteen-year-old girl, who claimed her real name was Alexina, had blond hair and blue eyes. She claimed that she was from Arkansas and had "been born free and of white parentage" and was "entitled to her freedom and that ***on view this is manifest.*** *" She was white, her lawyers argued, because she clearly looked white. The slave trader countered that she was a runaway who had been "harboured" and encouraged by abolitionists. The case brought up the troubling question, in the words of one historian, "Could slaves become white? And could white people become slaves?"*

Slave buyers looked for "blackness" in their agricultural laborers, since they believed that dark skin provided immunity to disease. They also probed for strength in men and the ability to bear children in black women. There was a premium, however, on light-skinned, slender women who could serve in the households of the wealthy or fulfill the sexual fantasies of the masters. The trade of "fancy girls" in New Orleans was notorious throughout the country. Still, it was believed that "black blood" could distinguish "nearly white" woman from genuinely white women. Louisiana, like many slave states, attempted to define suppositions of freedom by fractions of "black blood," down to one-sixteenth. If the slave was "too white," however, she (or he) might be tempted to escape to freedom and cross over the color line. Perhaps with that in mind, James White had curled the girl's hair and died it black when he first brought her home from the slave market

The witnesses for Alexina Morrison testified that the "flaxen haired blue eyed" young woman "conducted herself as a white girl. She is so in her conduct and actions. She has none of the features of an African." Southern racial ideology held that there were demonstrable behavioral differences between white and black women. Others contended that they could spot the race of a person, even in "the fourth or fifth degree," but there were no such telltale signs in Morrison.

The witnesses for the slave trader tried to convince the jurors that they could not believe their own eyes. A few argued that "she has African Blood," judging by "the shape of her cheek Bones." Her lawyers, pointing to spectators in the court, implied that if Alexina Morrison was black, it was possible that almost anyone else could also be so. James White's lawyers responded that "black blood" could disappear into ostensible whiteness without an obvious trace but still be there. They also tried to establish her extramarital sexuality to place her in the category of "quadroon mistress."

The jury was largely composed of nonslaveowners. Some came from the class of white laboring men who did such hard work as draining swamps, digging canals, and laying railroad tracks, work usually considered too dangerous for valuable slaves to do. Their wives and daughters often worked in the homes of prosperous neighbors. Morrison's lawyers were able to paint for them the alarming image of a defenseless white servant sold as a slave. This jury was unable to reach a verdict.

James White later claimed that, when he rode out with one of his witnesses to look at Alexina Morrison, he was "surrounded by a lawless mob" that threatened "personal violence because he dared to assert his property in his own slave, who said mob declared to be a white person." The court convinced that White could not find an unbiased jury in Jefferson Parish, transferred the case to New Orleans. In May 1859, a jury there unanimously declared Morrison free. The Louisiana Supreme Court overturned the verdict. A third jury in 1862 failed to agree but announced it had voted 10 to 2 in her favor. White's lawyers appealed once again, but the case was delayed during the Civil War and never considered again. Alexina Morrison and her little daughter, Mary, listed as a free white woman and child in the 1860 census disappeared in the 1870 census.

The case had raised troublesome issues in a society predicated on racial slavery. Could a slave act so white that she became white? Did that mean that there was no inherent difference and that distinctions were rather products of education and socialization? Could the whiteness of workers and their wives and daughters really protect them from being enslaved? Could slaveholders be sure that their property rights would always be protected? The case of ***Morrison v. White*** *demonstrated the complexity of slavery and its alliance with white supremacy.*

South vs. North

In 1832, the winter after the Nat Turner rebellion, a remarkable debate took place in the Virginia legislature. Non-slave owners who lived west of the Blue Ridge Mountains supported the argument that slavery was "ruinous to whites." Governor John Floyd vowed, "I will not rest until slavery is abolished in Virginia." Not a single voice was raised to justify the morality of the institution of slavery. The motion favoring eventual emancipation, however, lost by the relatively close margin of 73 to 58. This would be the last public debate about slavery in the South. Intimidation and legal prosecution silenced any white Southerners who opposed slavery or drove them North. Books and pamphlets criticizing slavery were impounded and destroyed. By the 1840s, southern apologists had moved from a genteel dislike of the "necessary evil" of slavery to an aggressive affirmation of slavery as a "positive good." They disdained laissez-faire northern capitalism that exploited the working masses and caused social revolution. They wrote endless pamphlets to "prove" that plantation slaves benefited from higher living standards than factory "wage slaves." One supporter of slavery actually wrote that, "the average condition of the slave at the South is infinitely superior, morally and materially, in all respects, to that of the labouring class under any circumstances in any other parts of the world."

Defenders of the slave system had to face the argument that slavery was an economic disaster for non-slaveholders who were unable to compete with planters. They claimed that manual labor was demeaning and, thus, suitable for blacks. A South Carolinian illustrated this attitude when he declared, "Any man is a doggone fool to work, when he can make a nigger work for him." Modernization, as it occurred in the North, required a work ethic. When manual labor is considered servile, the work ethic is seriously undermined. Most southern whites, in fact, had to perform physical labor. Writers assured them that their demeaning work would be temporary. They would one day become masters themselves. The steep rise in the price of slaves in the 1850s made this increasingly unlikely. Some slavery advocates even proposed reopening the African slave trade to drive down prices. This, however, would hurt those whose wealth was based on their slave ownership and would further depress the wages of free white workers.

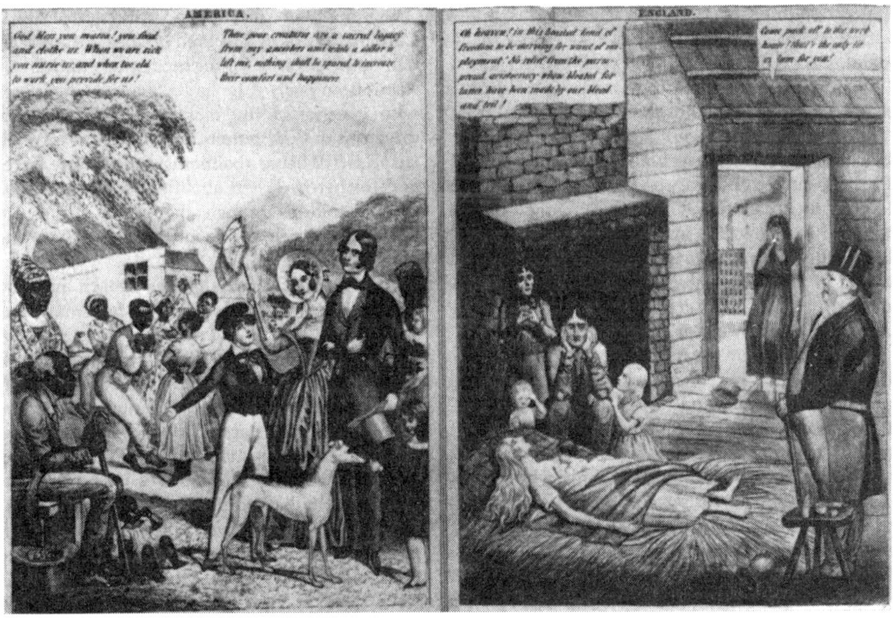

This proslavery cartoon shows that the black slave in America had a better life than the working-class white in England.

Unlike the North, which boasted about its "go-ahead" spirit, the South prided itself on its unchanging conservative society. Southerners believed that the money-mad North was "rotten to the core." The North was being torn apart by various horrible "isms," such as abolitionism, feminism, utopianism, transcendentalism, and many others. Southerners argued that all great civilizations had rested on the foundation of slavery. In contrast to the "ism-smitten people of Massachusetts," one southern editor declared, "the bondsmen, as a lower class...constitute an always reliable, never wavering foundation whereon the social fabric rests securely...entirely beyond the reach of agitation."

The dynamic modernizing North with its passion for "progress" seemed increasingly to be in a different world from the slave society of the South. One Northerner confided pessimistically to his diary in 1844: "Every day the difference between the North & South is becoming more prominent and apparent. The difference exists in everything which forms the life of a people—in institutions, laws, opinions, manners, feelings, education, pursuits, climate & soil.... A union...between two people who, in fact, in all important characteristics are broadly contrasted, must be a weak one, liable to be broken when at all strained."

DOCUMENTS

WHITE VIEWS ON SLAVERY

Plantation Song: "My Old Kentucky Home, Good Night!" 1853

Stephen Foster, a popular songwriter from Pennsylvania, wrote this plantation song. Although Foster originally intended the song as a reaction to the popular antislavery novel, ***Uncle Tom's Cabin,*** *it became symbolic of the happy days of slavery. The Kentucky legislature adopted it as a state song in 1928 and the maintained old mansion of Foster's slave owning cousin in Bardstown, Kentucky as an official state shrine to the song. In recent years, "old folks" have been substituted for "darkies," but the racist assumptions of the song's original story remain obvious.*

The sun shines bright in the old Kentucky home
'tis summer, the darkies are gay,
the corn top's ripe and the meadow's in the bloom
while the birds make music all the day.
The young folks roll on the little cabin floor
all merry, all happy, and bright.
By'n by hard times comes a-knocking at the door,
then my old Kentucky home, good night.

Chorus:
Weep no more, my lady,
oh weep no more today.
We will sing on song for the old Kentucky home,
for the old Kentucky home far away.

They hunt no more for the 'possum and the coon
on meadow, the hill and the shore.
They sing no more by the glimmer of the moon
on the bench by that old cabin door.
The day goes by like a shadow o'er the heart
with sorrow where all was delight.
The time has come when the darkies have to part
then my old Kentucky home, good night.

The head must bow and the back will have to bend
wherever the darky may go.
A few more days and the trouble all will end
in the field where sugar-canes may grow.
A few more days for to tote the weary load.
No matter, 'twill never be light.
A few more days till we totter on the road,
then my old Kentucky home, good night.

Source: A Treasury of Stephen Foster (New York: Random House, 1946), pp. 95-97.

1. What are "the hard times" that "Old Tom," the narrator, laments in the first verse (*Note the second verse, second to last line)*?
2. Who do you think is "my lady" and why is she weeping?
3. How is the slave experience in Kentucky portrayed, and how does it differ from slavery in the Deep South?
4. The plantation song was popular among white middle-class audiences throughout the country. How does this sentimental portrayal of Kentucky slavery reflect racist assumptions that were shared by most white Americans, North and South?

Slavery as a "Positive Good," Speech by John C. Calhoun in the U.S. Senate, 1837

I do not belong, said Mr. C., to the school which holds that aggression is to be met by concession... If we concede an inch, concession would follow concession—compromise would follow compromise, until our ranks would be so broken that effectual resistance would be impossible. We must meet the enemy on the frontier, with a fixed determination of maintaining our position at every hazard. Consent to receive these insulting petitions [from anti-slavery associations], and the next demand will be that they be referred to a committee in order that they may be deliberated and acted upon... We are now told that the most effectual mode of arresting the progress of abolition is, to reason it down; and with this view it is urged that the petitions ought to be referred to a committee. That is the very ground which was taken at the last session in the other House, but instead of arresting its progress it has since advanced more rapidly than ever. The most unquestionable right may be rendered doubtful, if once admitted to be a subject of controversy, and that would be the case in the present instance. The subject is beyond the jurisdiction of Congress—they have no right to touch it in any shape or form, or to make it the subject of deliberation or discussion....

As widely as this incendiary spirit has spread, it has not yet infected this body, or the great mass of the intelligent and business portion of the North; but unless it be speedily stopped, it will spread and work upwards till it brings the two great sections of the Union into deadly conflict.... They who imagine that the spirit now abroad in the North, will die away of itself without a shock or convulsion, have formed a very inadequate conception of its real character; it will continue to rise and spread, unless prompt and efficient measures to stay its progress be adopted. Already it has taken possession of the pulpit, of the schools, and, to a considerable extent, of the press; those great instruments by which the mind of the rising generation will be formed.

However sound the great body of the non-slaveholding States are at present, in the course of a few years they will be succeeded by those who will have been taught to hate the people and institutions of nearly one-half of this Union, with a hatred more deadly than one hostile nation ever entertained towards another. It is easy to see the end. By the necessary course of events, if left to themselves, we must become, finally, two people. It is impossible under the deadly hatred which must spring up between the two great nations, if the present causes are permitted to operate unchecked, that we should continue under the same political system. The conflicting elements would burst the Union asunder, powerful as are the links which hold it together. Abolition and the Union cannot coexist. As the friend of the Union I openly proclaim it,—and the sooner it is known the better. The former may now be controlled, but in a short time it will be beyond the power of man to arrest the course of events. We of the South will not, cannot, surrender our institutions. To maintain the existing relations between the two races, inhabiting that section of the Union, is indispensable to the peace and happiness of both. It cannot be subverted without drenching the country or the other of the races.... But let me not be understood as admitting, even by implication, that the existing relations between the two races in the slaveholding States is an evil:—far otherwise; I hold it to be a good, as it has thus far proved itself to be to both, and will continue to prove so if not disturbed by the fell spirit of abolition. I appeal to facts. Never before has the black race of Central Africa, from the dawn of history to the present day, attained a condition so civilized and so improved, not only physically, but morally and intellectually. In the meantime, the white or European race, has not degenerated. It has kept pace with its brethren in other sections of the Union where slavery does not exist. It is odious to make comparison; but I appeal to all sides whether the South is not equal in virtue, intelligence, patriotism, courage, disinterestedness, and all the high qualities which adorn our nature.

But I take higher ground. I hold that in the present state of civilization, where two races of different origin, and distinguished by color, and other physical differences, as well as intellectual, are brought together, the relation now existing in the slaveholding States between the two, is, instead of an evil, a good—a positive good. I feel myself called upon to speak freely upon the subject where the honor and interests of those I represent are involved. I hold then, that there never has yet existed a wealthy and civilized society in which one portion of the community did not, in point of fact, live on the labor of the other. Broad and general as is this assertion, it is fully borne out by history. This is not the proper occasion, but, if it were, it would not be difficult to trace the various devices by which the wealth of all civilized communities has been so unequally divided, and to show by what means so small a share has been allotted to those by whose labor it was produced, and so large a share given to the non-producing classes. The devices are almost innumerable, from the brute force and gross superstition of ancient times, to the subtle and artful fiscal contrivances of modern. I might well challenge a comparison between them and the more direct, simple, and patriarchal mode by which the labor of the African race is, among us, commanded by the European. I may say with truth, that in few countries so much is left to the share of the laborer, and so little exacted from him, or where there is more kind attention paid to him in sickness or infirmities of age. Compare his condition with the tenants of the poor houses in the more civilized portions of Europe—look at the sick, and the old and infirm slave, on one hand, in the midst of his family and friends, under the kind superintending care of his master and mistress, and compare it with the forlorn and wretched condition of the pauper in the poorhouse.

But I will not dwell on this aspect of the question; I turn to the political; and here I fearlessly assert that the existing relation between the two races in the South, against which these blind fanatics are waging war, forms the most solid and durable foundation on which to rear free and stable political institutions. It is useless to disguise the fact. There is and always has been in an advanced stage of wealth and civilization, a conflict between labor and capital. The condition of society in the South exempts us from the disorders and dangers resulting from this conflict, and which explains why it is that the political condition of the slaveholding States has been so much more stable and quiet than that of the North.... Surrounded as the slaveholding States are with such imminent perils, I rejoice to think that our means of defense are ample, if we shall prove to have the intelligence and spirit to see and apply them before it is too late. All we want is concert, to lay aside all party differences and unite with zeal and energy in repelling approaching dangers. Let there be concert of action, and we shall find ample means of security without resorting to secession or disunion. I speak with full knowledge and a thorough examination of the subject, and for one see my way clearly.... I dare not hope that anything I can say will arouse the South to a due sense of danger; I fear it is beyond the power of mortal voice to awaken it in time from the fatal security into which it has fallen.

Source: *Register of Debates in Congress...1824-1837,* Vol. 14, 24th Cong. 2nd Sess. (1837).

1. Mr. Calhoun predicts that, if left unchecked, the present course of events would lead to civil war. Who in his scenario would have started this war and for what reason?
2. What are Calhoun's arguments for keeping the institution of slavery intact in the South?
3. How does Calhoun contrast the conditions of southern slaves with European poor people?
4. Why does he feel the South is more orderly and stable than the North?

BLACK VIEWS OF SLAVERY

African-American Spirituals

Most slaves could not have directly expressed their thoughts and feelings. They usually hid their true meanings through symbols and allegories. Their songs were often religious, filled with Biblical imagery. They also concerned the day-to-day lives of the slaves who created and sang them. While whites perceived their message as merely religious, black views of liberation might include freedom from slavery as well as religious redemption.

Nobody Knows the Trouble I've Had

Chorus:
Nobody knows de trouble I've had [or, I've seen],
  Nobody knows but Jesus
Nobody knows de trouble I've had
  Glory hallelu.

One morning I was a-walking down,
  O yes, Lord!
I saw some berries a-hanging down,
  O yes, Lord!
Chorus

I pick de berry and I suck de juice,
  O yes, Lord!
Just as sweet as the honey in de comb,
  O yes, Lord!

Chorus
Sometimes I'm up, sometimes I'm down,
Sometimes I'm almost on de groun'.
Chorus

What make ole Satan hate me so?
Cause he got me once and he let me go.
Chorus

Deep River

Deep river, my home is over Jordan, Deep river,
Lord, I want to cross over into campground,
Lord, I want to cross over into campground,
Lord, I want to cross over into campground.
Oh, chillun, Oh, don't you want to go to that gospel feast,
That promised land, that land, where all is peace?
Walk into heaven, and take my seat,
And cast my crown at Jesus feet,
Lord, I want to cross over into campground,
Lord, I want to cross over into campground.
Deep river, my home is over Jordan, Deep river,
Lord, I want to cross over into campground,
Lord, I want to cross over into campground,
Lord, I want to cross over into campground, Lord!

Go Down, Moses

When Israel was in Egypt's land,
  Let my people go;
Oppressed so hard they could not stand,
  Let my people go.

Chorus:
Go down, Moses, way down in Egypt's land;
Tell old Pharaoh, to let my people go.

Thus saith the Lord, bold Moses said,
  Let my people go;
If not I'll smite your first born dead,
  Let my people go. *Chorus*

No more shall they in bondage toil,
  Let my people go;
Let them come out with Egypt's spoil,
  Let my people go. *Chorus*
O 'twas a dark and dismal night,
  Let my people go;
When Moses led the Israelites,
  Let my people go. *Chorus*
The Lord told Moses what to do,
  Let my people go;
To lead the children of Israel through,
  Let my people go. *Chorus*
O come along, Moses, you won't get lost,
  Let my people go;
Stretch out your rod and come across,
  Let my people go. *Chorus*
As Israel stood by the water side,
  Let my people go;
At the command of God it did divide,
  Let my people go. *Chorus*
And when they reached the other side,
  Let my people go;
They sang a song of triumph o'er,
  Let my people go. *Chorus*
You won't get lost in the wilderness,
  Let my people go;
With a lighted candle in your breast,
  Let my people go. *Chorus*
O let us all from bondage flee,
  Let my people go;
And let us all in Christ be free,
  Let my people go. *Chorus*
We need not always weep and moan,
  Let my people go;
And wear these slavery chains forlorn,
  Let my people go. *Chorus*
What a beautiful morning that will be,
  Let my people go;
When time breaks up in eternity,
  Let my people go. *Chorus*

Daniel

He delivered Daniel from the lion's den,
Jonah from de belly ob de whale,
And de Hebrew children from de fiery furnace,
And why not every man?

Source: *Slave Songs of the United States.* William Francis Allen, et al., comp. New York, A. Simpson, 1867.

NARRATIVES AND FOLK TALES

In the 1930s the government-financed Federal Writers' Project collected more than two thousand narratives from ex-slaves and placed them in the Library of Congress. Most of the interviewees were in their eighties or nineties at the time. They had been children in 1860. Most of the interviewers were white. Despite these limitations, their narratives reveal a great deal about their views of slavery. Often they told stories, true or not, that showed, often indirectly, their thoughts and feelings.

The Coon and the Dog

Every time I think of slavery and if it done the race any good, I think of the story of the coon and the dog who met. The coon said to the dog, "Why is it you're so fat and U am so poor and we both is animals?" The dog said, "I lay round Master's house and let him kick me and he gives me a piece of bread right on." Said the coon to the dog, "Better, then that I stay poor." Them's my sentiment.

The Rabbit and the Tortoise

I want to tell you one story 'bout the rabbit. The rabbit and the tortoise had a race. The tortoise git a lot of tortoises and put 'em 'long the way and the rabbit say, "How you now Br'er Tortoise?" And he say, "Slow and sure, but my legs very short." When they git tired, the tortoise win 'cause he there, but he never run the race, 'cause he had tortoises strowed out all 'long the way. The tortoise had other tortoises help him.

Papa's Death

My papa was strong. He never had a licking in his life. He helped the master, but one day the master says, "Si you got to have a whopping," and my poppa says, "I never had a whopping and you can't whop me." And the master says, "But I can kill you," and he shot my papa down. My mama took him to the cabin and put him on a pallet. He died.

Prayers

My master used to ask us children, "Do your folks pray at night?" We said, "No," 'cause our folks had told us what to say. But the Lord have mercy, there was plenty of that going on. They'd pray, "Lord deliver us from under bondage."

Marrying

After while I taken a notion to marry and Massa and Missy marries us, same as all the niggers. They stands inside the house with a broom held crosswise of the door and we stands outside. Missy puts a little wreath on my head they kept there, and we steps over the broom into the house. Now, that's all they was to the marrying. After freedom, I gits married and has it put in the book by a preacher.

Solomon in Hell

We was scared of Solomon and his whip, though, and he didn't like frolicking. He didn't like for us niggers to pray either. We never heard of no church, but us have praying in the cabins. We'd set on the floor and pray with our heads down low and sing low, but if Solomon heared he'd come and beat on the wall with the stock of his whip. He'd say, "I'll come in there and tear the hides off you backs." But some the old niggers tell us we got to pray to God that he don't think different of the blacks and the whites. I know that Solomon is burning in hell today, and it pleasures me to know it.

Source: B.A. Botkin, Federal Writers' Project, *Lay My Burden Down: A Folk History of Slavery* (Chicago, 1945).

1. Spirituals sung by slaves often depicted a Christian redemption and deliverance from the earthly life into paradise. How would slaves have used these messages? Why were Biblical heroes like Moses and Daniel popular?
2. How much can historians learn about slave communities by studying these songs? What were the hidden messages?
3. Why did many of the ex-slaves give indirect reactions to slavery?
4. How did slaves feel about their masters or mistresses? Their families? Their religion? Freedom? Themselves?
5. What do these songs and narratives and the white reactions in the first part reveal about the differences between white and black views of slavery?

HARRIET TUBMAN

Chapter Three

THE AGE OF REFORM

AN ERA OF REFORM

Excited gatherings of fervent believers were commonplace in an era when armies of reformers earnestly sought to transform American character. They sincerely believed in a nation in which continuous progress was ensured by the absence of barriers such as fixed social classes. As in contemporary America, these activists were troubled by what they saw as the American preoccupation with the pursuit of wealth and influence. The growing disparity between great wealth and grinding poverty, between religious revival and moral decline, and between freedom and slavery disturbed them.

Despite their concerns, most of these reformers were optimists who believed that human nature could be molded like potter's clay. If society was degraded, it could be uplifted by crusades to recreate a moral social order. The Northeast, particularly New England and northwestern New York State, was "burnt over" by the fires of reformist sentiment. Saints and missionaries have appeared throughout human history. The development of highly organized reform associations that stirred up popular opinion and influenced government actions, however, was an innovation of the pre-Civil War era. These groups pursued clear objectives such as banning alcoholic beverages, building public schools, aiding widows, orphans and the mentally ill, and even abolishing slavery.

Middle class women formed many of these voluntary associations. What had begun as charitable and religious societies in the early 1800s had expanded to the broader goals of eliminating social evils. In the first third of the nineteenth century religious revivals, like the Second Great Awakening, led to the formation of female associations dedicated to Sunday schools, charity, and missionary work. Eventually, members began to "visit" the poor to distribute aid. This led to the development of institutions to help the "worthy poor," such as widows and orphans. Although these pious activities never challenged the boundaries of women's proper sphere, they led inevitably to wider social activism.

Most reformers continued to believe in the possibility, indeed certainty, of human progress. The Benevolent Empire was the name given to an informal association of missionary and reform societies that shared a common goal: to reestablish "the moral government of God." Wealthy humanitarians, who funded these organizations, looked with alarm on the "lawless multitude" with its unbridled appetite for violence, sex, liquor, and coarse amusements. Public morals seemed to these reformers to be in great need of purification. Crusades were required to create a chaste, sober, and responsible society.

Revivalism and the Second Great Awakening

A major source of the impetus for reform came from Protestant revivalism that began with the Second Great Awakening. The leaders of this movement in the North stressed that anyone could choose salvation. God's grace could come to all who rejected and fought against sin. Foreign commentators like Alexis de Tocqueville noted that in the 1830s there was no other nation in which the Christian religion held "a greater influence over the souls of men." Throughout the nation, people flocked to revival meetings to declare their repentance for their

Camp meetings brought religion to the frontier.

sins, their rebirth, and, in the words of a popular hymn, to "stand up, stand up for Jesus."

The leading evangelical preacher of the Second Great Awakening was the charismatic, spellbinding Presbyterian minister, Charles Grandison Finney. Each person, he thundered, possessed within him or herself the ability to achieve personal salvation and spiritual rebirth. Finney argued that the "great political and other worldly excitements" of the time distracted Americans from achieving true soul searching. Those excitements could "only be counteracted by religious excitements." The expanding economy and its accompanying materialism gave the evangelists an obvious target to attack. The resulting growth of methods of communication and transportation—the railroad, steamship, and telegraph—also, however, made it possible to spread evangelical ideals more rapidly through the country and the world. Revivals, in the words of another preacher, prepared the nation "to lead the way in the moral and political emancipation of the world."

The great economic depression of 1857 led to "the event of the century," a massive wave of urban revivals in 1857 and 1858. In cities throughout the Northeast, workers and wealthy businessmen sat side-by-side in spontaneous midday prayer. Public high schools held exuberant revival meetings. Northerners experienced a new sense of unity in helping to bring about a better world.

The wealthy merchant bankers, Arthur and Lewis Tappan, were among Finney's most ardent followers. They became the major financial supporters of the Benevolent Empire. Finney also had great success appealing to women who found his message of personal control and responsibility to be liberating. Finney's revivalism evolved into activism in the form of a crusade against immorality. "The church," he declared, "must take the right ground on the subject of Temperance, the Moral Reform, and all the subjects of practical morality which come up for decision from time to time."

Moral Reform

The moral reform movement that swept the nation from the 1830s to the early 1840s was basically a woman's campaign. By 1840, the American Female Moral Reform Society had 555 chapters and thousands of members. Its goal was to end the sexual double standard by enforcing a single standard of moral purity on both men and women. The reformers sought to end prostitution by gathering in front of brothels where they sang hymns, prayed, looked for runaways, and threatened to publicize the names of patrons. They founded homes and employment services for "fallen women." They even lobbied, with some success, for laws that made seduction a crime. Eventually the movement sputtered out. It fell apart over the issues of the propriety of public discussions of sexual matters and of militant women moving beyond the sphere of their homes.

Sabbatarians

When Congress passed a law to deliver mail seven days a week to meet the needs of business interests for better communication, a movement developed to enforce the Christian Sabbath. The "serious Christians" involved in this crusade had gone from distributing Bibles and building Sunday schools to involvement in direct political action. Not only did they attempt to boycott businesses that opened on Sundays, they also launched a giant petition drive to convince Congress to end Sunday mail. "If this nation fails in her vast experiment, the world's last hope expires; and without the moral energies of the Sabbath, it will fail," one earnest supporter warned.

The Sabbatarians did not succeed at that time. Congress accepted a report of a Kentucky senator declaring that it was not "a proper tribunal to determine the laws of God." Many Americans were suspicious of people who claimed to know the will of God. In addition, divisions over slavery shattered the united front of evangelical reformers.

Temperance

The temperance crusade was the largest reform movement by far. Drunkenness, reformers argued, was responsible for poverty, crime, and abuse of wives and chil-

The reformers felt it was their duty to save these "fallen women."

The temperance movement, the largest reform movement, launched an enormously effective propaganda campaign that preached that drinking ruined families, caused poverty, and led to an inevitable death.

THE MARCH OF DEATH.

This March of Death is respectfully dedicated to the Temperance Societies thro'out the United States by their Obt. Servt. the Publisher

dren. Businessmen worried that alcohol misuse lowered workers' productivity. One evangelical preacher declared, "Intemperance is a sin upon our land and with boundless prosperity is coming in upon us like a flood."

In fact, alcoholism was a real social problem. The supply and demand for whiskey, hard cider, beer, and rum grew rapidly. Drinking eased the loneliness of farm life and was the principal pastime of most city workingmen. It has been estimated that, by 1830, the average American male consumed about three times as much alcohol as his modern counterpart.

Temperance societies used the techniques of religious revivalism to persuade people to abstain from alcohol consumption. Reformed alcoholics organized "Washington Societies" to urge people to "take the pledge" of total abstinence. They drew huge crowds to dramatic meetings where they described their past sins and even re-enacted the miseries of delirium tremens before enthralled audiences. Their efforts resulted in more than a million pledges to forgo alcohol.

Reliance on "moral suasion" to solve this problem, however, was undermined by the influx of hundreds of thousands of Irish and German immigrants who disdained these moralistic appeals. The reformers feared these new populations caused the disorder they believed to be prevalent. Some began to demand legislation to restrict alcohol or even prohibit it entirely. In 1851, Maine passed a law that banned the manufacture and sale of alcoholic beverages. Faith in individual moral self-improvement gave way to attempts to remove the temptation through legislation. One temperance advocate noted sadly that the only force that drunkards could understand was "the instrumentality of the law."

Rehabilitation

The same impulse that tried to restrain "the passions of men" through public schools, moral reform, and temperance led to another effective reform movement to create institutions for criminals, the mentally ill, and the handicapped. The Benevolent Empire was active in establishing such charitable institutions as the Perkins School for the Blind in Boston, the first such school in the nation. When he visited the school, the great English novelist, Charles Dickens, was impressed to learn about a blind, deaf, and mute girl who had been taught to communicate through sign language. Her teacher noted that, though the "darkness and silence of the tomb were around her, the immortal spirit which had been implanted within her could not die, nor be maimed nor mutilated." Other such institutions were built to provide education and moral structure for orphans, "friendless" women, and other disadvantaged members of society.

One of the most conspicuous evils of society was throwing criminals, debtors, mentally retarded, mentally ill people, and even senile old people together in overcrowded jails. Some of these facilities were quite literally holes; one Connecticut prison was an abandoned mineshaft. As early as the 1820s, some states began replacing these dilapidated facilities with new "penitentiaries," so named since they were to provide an opportunity for inmates to do penitence for their crimes. Reformers succeeded in gradually ending imprisonment for debt or poverty. Public hangings became increasingly rare.

Dorothea Dix, teaching a Sunday school class for prisoners in 1841 in Massachusetts, was appalled to discover the insane mixed in with, and often mistreated by, the other inmates. In the next eighteen months, she surveyed most of the jails and almshouses in the state. She recorded the terrible conditions in which she found "lunitics" and "idiots" restrained "in cages, closets, cellars, stalls, pens! Chained, naked, beaten with rods, and lashed into obedience." She presented her findings about "the condition of the miserable, the desolute, the outcast" to the Massachusetts legislature. The result was increased funding for "asylums" to treated the mentally ill and retarded.

Her success led her to travel 30,000 miles through the United States investigating facilities and presenting her well-known "memorials" to state legislatures. She was directly responsible for the creation of thirty-two state mental asylums and influenced the founding of many more in America, Europe, and even Japan. Eventually, unfortunately, most penitentiaries and many mental institutions became overcrowded and more like warehouses than facilities for rehabilitation or treatment.

Public Education

Both male and female reformers believed that education was the key to molding American character. Teaching the Bible to the uneducated poor and the immigrants would help create a moral and virtuous society. One missionary preacher passionately declared: "We must educate! We must educate! Or we must perish by our own prosperity." This rationale was reinforced by the Jeffersonian idea that education was essential to maintain and extend democracy. Only an educated populace could protect true democracy.

Despite the fact that literacy rates were far higher in America than Europe, educational reformers worried about the state of American education. In rural areas, the one-room schoolhouse, the subject of much romantic nostalgia in a later era, was overcrowded, dirty, ill heated, and undisciplined. Unruly older children occasionally beat up male teachers, and some women teachers kept pistols in their desks. In the rapidly growing northern cities, middle-class citizens could not help noticing growing armies of child beggars, gangs of juvenile delinquents, and increasingly younger prostitutes. Workingmen's parties, representing skilled workers, demanded more equal educational opportunities. Reformers argued that free tax-supported schools would make it possible to tap the innate capacity of even the lowliest person. Others maintained that schools could inoculate students with desirable social values to prevent the lower class disease of disorder and rebelliousness. Nevertheless, as of 1830, no state had instituted a system of universal public education.

Many parents who were wealthy enough to be able to afford private education for their children were hostile to the idea of paying taxes to educate poor children. Many working class parents worried that they could not afford to sacrifice the income that their children added to families that barely were able to make ends meet. One historian studying working-class families in a Massachusetts town of that era has shown that children under fifteen earned 20 percent of these families' incomes. In addition, by the 1840s, these workers in the northeastern cities were increasingly Roman Catholic, as Irish immigrants poured in. They resented the Protestant nature of public schools where Protestant hymns were sung and Protestant prayers recited. The New York Catholic Church even decided to build its own religious school system.

Public school reformers were successful in overcoming these obstacles. Horace Mann, the first secretary of the Massachusetts Board of Education, established in 1837, was the most influential of these reformers. He believed that the public school was "the greatest discovery ever made by man." Schools, more effectively than even the home or church, could preserve the precious values of American democracy. Mann and other reformers contended that women were best suited to inculcate such values as cooperation, righteousness, and deference. Since women worked for wages well below those paid to male teachers, local school boards accepted that point of view, and women soon dominated the field of elementary school teaching. Some observers have argued that the availability of large numbers of "cheap" women teachers made the extraordinary growth of the public school system possible.

Public school curriculum was designed to encourage those character traits (responsibility, honesty, punctuality, and obedience to authority) most valued by the leaders of a newly competitive capitalist society. The unleashing of the human talent inherent in all had its limitations. Most Americans, even reformers, were unconvinced that those in society who were not white Christian males could benefit from the advances of education. Even in the North, most public schools excluded African Americans. When Prudence Crandall opened her Female Boarding School in Canterbury Connecticut to "young ladies and little misses of color" in 1833, a storm of controversy erupted. The state responded with a "Black Law," making it a crime to teach or board "any colored person who is not an inhabitant of any town" of Connecticut. Eventually, a mob, under cover of night, completely destroyed the school. The local authorities refused to investigate or guarantee future protection. Reluctantly, the courageous Ms. Crandall was forced to close her school. A few cities, such as New York and Boston, established substandard segregated schools for African Americans. Massachusetts in 1855 became the only state to declare that no child could be excluded from public schools because of "race, color, or religious opinions."

Gradually, and with some reluctance, girls were included in the new formal public education system. Some reformers argued that the young republic required an educated, informed, and moral citizenry. The young men who would become the leaders in the great experiment of liberty would be raised and nurtured by their mothers. How could women fulfill this important role if they were ignorant? Secondary academies or "seminaries" for women began to appear in New England in the 1820s and spread to other parts of the nation, largely in the North, in the next forty years. Emma Willard opened the successful Troy (New York) Female Seminary in 1821. She asserted that advanced education, including science, mathematics, history, and languages, as well as domestic science, would enable women to achieve "the greatest possible use to themselves and others." Her seminary not only catered to the ambitious middle class, it also became a leading institution in the new field of teacher training. Mary Lyon founded the Mt. Holyoke Female Seminary in 1837. She included selective admission standards and course offerings that reflected the curriculum of men's colleges. Her institution later became a full-fledged college, the first women's college in the nation.

Mount Holyoke Female Seminary was chartered in 1836. Funds were raised by Mary Lyon, who solicited her first donations from Massachusetts housewives.

In 1837, Oberlin College in Ohio became the first coeducational college in America, although women were not given a completely equal education. Oberlin, as well as Harvard, Dartmouth, and a few other private colleges, also admitted a handful of African-American students. The number of colleges grew from 16 in 1799 to 182 in 1860. A system of informal educational institutions known as "lyceums" also flourished. They sponsored public lectures on a dizzying variety of topics ranging from the scientific to the philosophical to the practical. By 1860, more than three thousand lyceums flourished, mainly in the Northeast.

Despite the many limitations, school reformers had made remarkable strides by the end of the 1850s. Massachusetts had developed the parts of a modern educational system all the way up to "normal schools" for the training of female teachers. A boy in New York City could go from elementary "infant" school all the way through college without having to pay tuition. The United States had the highest literacy rate in the world: 94 percent of the population of the North and 58 percent of the South could read and write. More than half of all American women were literate, in startling contrast to the rest of the world of that era. The public school movement strengthened the American ideal that determined effort and democratic morality could eliminate the flaws that remained in American society.

WRITERS, THINKERS, AND DISSENTERS

In the forty years before the Civil War, an enormous growth in serious American literature took place fueled, at least in part, by the dramatic increase in literacy. The growing democratization of American culture led many to question the dependence upon European cultural life. In spite of this, many American artists and writers continued to be fascinated by European sophistication and romance. Others found Europe to be a refuge from the ills of an American society they believed to be obsessed by the search for material rewards and personal power. By the end of this era, a true American literature had been created. The remarkable artistic output of the 1850s has led some historians to describe the decade as the "American Renaissance."

Emerson and the Transcendentalists

More than any other single individual, Ralph Waldo Emerson was America's unquestionable philosopher of the nineteenth century. His essays and lyceum lectures had an enormous influence on American culture and ideas and helped activate the literary rebirth of the 1850s. His essays inspired a generation of reformers and ordinary people.

Emerson was an idealist who was drawn to humanitarianism and a philosophy that would bridge the gap between mind and matter. He introduced Americans to German idealist philosophy known as Transcendentalism. He defined the latter as a search for "perfect freedom...for progress in philosophy and theology" that appealed to those "who sympathize with each other in the hope that the future will not always be as the past." He proclaimed that "who so would be a man, must be a nonconformist." He criticized Americans' quest for material things, fame, and power. The American people, according to Emerson, were most endangered by a fragmentation within each individual soul: "The reason why the world lacks unity and lies broken in heaps is because man is disunited with himself." Self-reliance (one of Emerson's favorite concepts) meant that man could stand up against the tyranny of public opinion and achieve a wholeness flowing from unity with God, "the Oversoul." Americans were inspired by Emerson's view that ordinary people could demonstrate unlimited and godlike potential.

Henry David Thoreau, like Emerson, a Harvard man from Massachusetts, carried the ideas of the transcendentalists to their extreme in rejecting social conformity. As an abolitionist and advocate of self-improvement, he considered the state a threat to individual independence. In *Civil Disobedience* (1849), he argued that the just man would refuse to pay taxes to support an unjust government (in this case the United States of the time, which was fighting, in his view, the repre-

Thoreau went to live in solitude in the woods.

hensible Mexican War). In *Walden or Life in the Woods* (1854), he described his decision to live by himself to achieve self-improvement, free from the distraction of an artificial society where most men were uncertain about life, "whether it is of the devil or of God." Little known in his own lifetime, Thoreau has come to be regarded as one of the most original minds produced by the literary flowering of the nineteenth century.

Walt Whitman: Songs of America and the Self

Emerson had once decried the lack of a true American poet. "Yet America is a poem in our eyes; its ample geography dazzles the imagination," he maintained, "and it will not wait long for metres." Walt Whitman, a New York editor, journalist, and printer, became the poet Emerson hoped for. Whitman's first book of poetry, *Leaves of Grass*, first appeared to great controversy in 1855. Like Emerson, Whitman embraced human progress and celebrated the unlimited possibilities of America. He also defied the traditional limits on poetic language and espoused "what is vulgar," a frank celebration of his own body and sexuality. This led to attacks by conservative critics who characterized him as the "dirtiest beast of his age." Emerson, however, recognized in Whitman's poems "incomparable things, said incomparably well."

The Skeptical View: Hawthorne and Melville

Both Emerson and Whitman had a basically optimistic view of American society, despite any criticisms they made. Whitman declared that the American people

Walt Whitman (left) in the "carpenter portrait" that appeared in the first edition of his great work, *Leaves of Grass*, in 1855. *Tanglewood Tales* (right) was a collection of children stories by Nathaniel Hawthorne.

retained "a miraculous wealth of latent power and capacity." Other American authors of the period were far less certain.

Nathaniel Hawthorne, who made his living as a government employee while "scribbling women" wrote best selling romances, depicted a somber world in his short stories and novels. In *The Scarlet Letter* (1850), *The House of the Seven Gables* (1851), and *The Blithedale Romance* (1852) human progress is undermined by human vice, and the dreams of reformers are nothing more than illusion.

Herman Melville, Hawthorne's friend, rejected transcendental optimism even more powerfully. After writing two best sellers based on his adventures in the South Pacific, Melville destroyed his popularity by turning to studies of the nature of good and evil. Although he celebrated "the great democratic God," Melville described the destruction that results when humans reject boundaries on their actions. In *Moby Dick* (1851), the greatest American novel of the era, Captain Ahab relentlessly pursues a great white whale, a symbol of the beautiful, evil, and ultimately unfathomable forces of life. Ahab cannot admit that there are forces beyond his control or that he might be wrong. His obsession dooms himself and his ship to annihilation. Transcendentalists contended that humans were close to divine, and most Americans were firmly convinced that God would guarantee the inevitable triumph of democracy. Melville warned of the disaster Americans might face if they ignored limits in a quest to penetrate the unknowable.

RADICAL DISSENTERS

Some critics of American society despaired of its future. Simple reforms did not appear to them to be an adequate response to the evils of unbridled capitalism. Far more radical solutions seemed to them to be in order.

Communitarians

The horrors of the early Industrial Revolution led some Americans to search for the same kind of cooperative alternatives that European reformers were proposing. Robert Owen, a Scottish manufacturer and reformer, had built an industrial cooperative in New Lanark, Scotland. He came to America in 1825 and founded a utopian cooperative community in New Harmony, Indiana. His socialist community attracted some outstanding European scholars, as well as nine hundred Americans in search of a more perfect life. Within two years, the Owenite experiment had failed. Owen's attacks on "marriage...private or individual property...and absurd and irrational systems of religion" contributed to its decline by antagonizing the American public and its faith in social norms.

A young Scottish Owenite, Frances Wright, used part of her inheritance to buy 320 swampy acres in Tennessee to carry out an ambitious cooperative experiment. The new community, called Nashoba, a "city of refuge in the wilderness," would be a model of shared labor for white idealists and slaves gradually earning their emancipation. Frances Wright gave lectures to the slaves to explain Owenite philosophy and to "develop their sense of individual responsibility." The slaves, however, found it difficult to differentiate between their former slavery and the forced labor at Nashoba. One of her supporters published an account of the community's "free love" relationships in a popular magazine. To the reading public, Nashoba seemed to be nothing more than a "great brothel." They were not reassured when Wright defended "unlegalized connections" and the rights of unmarried mothers. She went on to denounce matrimonial law as a form of tyranny that kept women in servitude. She further scandalized the public by declaring that her commune was committed to racial amalgamation.

Wright turned to lecturing as a means to further her ideals. Her free lectures and eloquence attracted huge crowds. But, since public speaking was considered deviant behavior for a woman, many came out of curiosity to view the "female monster whom all decent people should avoid." Her denunciation of organized religion, espousal of women's rights, and plans for universal free boarding-school education brought a cascade of public criticism. One newspaper declared that she was "a bold blasphemer and a voluptuous preacher of licentiousness." She eventually ran out of most of her money and ruined her reputation, while demonstrating a singular example of sexual emancipation. One perceptive listener noted, "Simple minded men were out of their wits lest their wives should learn from her example...to question male supremacy." Eventually, Frances Wright abandoned both her lecture career and Nashoba. She chartered a ship and brought the thirty-four Nashoba slaves to freedom in Haiti where they were given land by the government.

Other communal projects drew on the beliefs of the French philosopher, Charles Fourier. Fourier assumed that the wasteful and humiliating competition of capitalism could be replaced by communal "phalanxes." New England transcendentalists were particularly attracted by the idea of combining idealistic co-operation and the dignity of labor. More than forty phalanxes were set up between 1840 and 1850. The most famous was Brook Farm, immortalized in Nathaniel Hawthorne's *Blithedale Romance*. Despite attracting more than four thousand admiring visitors a year, the community was abandoned by 1847.

The most successful communities were run by religious sects like the Shakers or under the discipline of strong leaders like John Humphrey Noyes. There were more than twenty Shaker communities with six thousand members in the 1840s. Their name came from a rapturous dance-like ritual in which chanting members could "shake" themselves free of sin. Shakers were committed to a simple life-style, sexual equality, and total celibacy. They tried to create a disciplined society, immune to the unbridled disorder they felt was characteristic of American life.

Ritualized dances were part of the Shakers' spiritual preparation for the Second Coming.

Noyes espoused "perfectionism," declaring that the time had come for "renouncing all allegiance to the government of the United States and asserting the title of Jesus Christ to the throne of the world." Americans, he believed, were enslaved by the possessiveness of private property and monogamous marriage. Noyes set up a community in Oneida, New York that owned property cooperatively and practiced "nonexclusive" plural marriage and "mutual criticism." The radical Oneida alternative to accepted economic and sexual norms lasted from 1847 to 1879. Ultimately, however, it failed just like the earlier attempts at cooperative communities. Perhaps Americans were too individualistic to be able to sustain these group ventures.

The Mormons

Mormonism, founded in New York in 1830 by Joseph Smith Jr., was America's first native religion. The Church of Jesus Christ of Latter Day Saints (the Mormons) attempted to create a new, more orderly society. In many ways it was also an extreme example of radical dissent, of people who believed in a higher moral law and resisted the secular and religious society of the time.

Smith, the son of a family of poor drifters, was only twenty-four when he published an extraordinary document—the Book of Mormon. It was the translation of golden tablets whose location had been revealed to him by an angel of God in one of his many religious visions. The book contained the history of an ancient Christian civilization in America whose vanished empire was the model for a new Kingdom of Christ in the United States. It also foretold the coming of an American prophet who would re-establish that kingdom with his community of "saints." Mormonism appealed to people who had been left out of the social and economic changes sweeping through America and England at the time. Most were small farmers and artisans whom expanding capitalism had bypassed. The poet, John Greenleaf Whittier, commented that Mormon services "speak a language of hope and promise to weak, weary hearts, tossed and troubled, who have wandered from sect to sect, seeking in vain for the primal manifestation of the divine power."

In the face of persecution, Smith attempted to find a sanctuary for his saints where he could build a "New Jerusalem." They were driven out of settlements they attempted to set up in Ohio and Missouri. In Missouri a band of vigilantes massacred nineteen of them. Smith escaped, although he was convicted of treason and sentenced to be executed. Finally, he and some fifteen thousand of his followers built the model city of Nauvoo in Illinois.

Its carefully laid out squares, spacious streets, mills, factories, schools, and hotel, as well as its magnificent, almost completed, stone temple, impressed visitors to the city in the 1840s. Smith dressed as a general and commanded a legion of two thousand troops. He had a revelation justifying polygamy (the right of a man to have more than one wife). He also established a secret Council of Fifty to prepare for the Kingdom of Christ. These actions led to public suspicions about Mormon international conspiracy and sexual depravity. Neither the state nor the federal government would defend the Mormons against Missouri outlaws who seized many of their buildings. Instead, Illinois charged Joseph Smith with treason and imprisoned him and his brother in the Carthage jail. In 1844, an angry "mob," created from a state militia group and including many leading non-Mormon men, stormed the jail and murdered the two Mormon leaders.

A new leader arose to replace the martyred prophet. He was Brigham Young, like Smith, a product of a modest New England family. Although he had limited education, he was an outstanding leader and organizer. He evacuated Nauvoo, selling Mormon property at below bargain prices. He traveled across prairies and desert with 3,700 wagon teams containing 12,000 of his followers. The weary voyagers finally settled in their new Zion in the Great Salt Lake Valley of Utah. There, they created the State of Deseret, which had its own army and even currency. Although they declared their loyalty to the United States, they tended to ignore federal government attempts to control their actions. Scandalized ministers and reformers denounced polygamy and declared that the Mormons were a menace to society. In 1857, President Buchanan actually sent a 2,500-man regular army force to put down the "rebellion." The troops were delayed by winter storms in the Rockies. They finally entered a Salt Lake City that had been evacuated by the Mormons. After an indecisive confrontation with squads of Mormon police, the troops were withdrawn. A few years later, when Abraham Lincoln was asked what he proposed to do about the Mormons, he responded, "I propose to let them alone."

Like other dissenters, the Mormons believed in human perfectibility. Since God had once been a man, every person could aspire to become a kind of god. The Mormons rejected American secular values of individualism and permissiveness. Against disorder and uncertainty, they created an organized, centralized structure, resting on absolute confidence in divine authority. Although they followed such accepted Protestant ideals as a strong work ethic and temperance, they seemed to represent a radical challenge to American secular ideals. Even worse, they threatened to resist persecution with force. They sorely tried American tolerance and were only able to find their refuge of security and order by moving to the outer edge of America's geographic frontier. They eventually did achieve respectability and grudging acceptance by compromising to accommodate the larger civilization.

THE STRUGGLE AGAINST SLAVERY

The issue of black slavery exposed the limitations of the work of the Benevolent Empire. By 1830, the gap between the optimism of humanitarian reformers' belief in inevitable human perfectibility and hard realities of human slavery had become apparent. Although federal law prohibited the African slave trade after 1808, the unexpected natural increase of America's slave population made the problem ever more noticeable. In the decade from 1820 to 1830 alone, the slave population grew from 1.5 million to more than 2 million. From the early 1830s on, the crusade against slavery increased in significance until it occupied the center stage in the reform movement.

The Early Antislavery Movement

Before the eighteenth century, few whites had challenged the morality of enslaving blacks. By the end of that century, however, antislavery sentiment emerged in the United States and Europe. One base for this movement was the growth of radical Protestant denominations that opposed slavery, particularly the Quakers. As early as 1775, the Quakers founded the first American antislavery society. Other Protestant sects, such as the Congregationalists and the Methodists, turned the

Women were encouraged to speak out in Quakers' meetings. The Quakers believed that all people were equal.

traditional view of sin as a kind of slavery (in which the sinner was enslaved by his own moral limitations) to the idea that slave ownership was a sin. New secular philosophies produced by the Enlightenment also led to questioning the basis of slavery in terms of social justice and economic viability.

The Age of Revolutions in America and France reinforced beliefs in human equality (at least, in equal opportunity). As a result, slavery was abolished in the states north of Maryland, in the French West Indies, and in most of the Latin American countries that won their independence from Spain. In 1808 Britain joined the United States in prohibiting the international slave trade and was active in utilizing its naval power to enforce this restriction. In 1833 Britain abolished slavery in its West Indian colonies. These efforts succeeded in limiting the slave trade and led to the freedom of almost 2 million slaves in the world. Increasing production of cotton, coffee, and sugar, however, entrenched slavery even more solidly in the southern United States, Brazil, and Cuba. Illegal slave ships continued to do a flourishing business in Brazil and Cuba and even smuggled some African slaves into the United States after 1808.

Colonization

As the ideals of the Revolution receded, the push to end slavery on the part of southern Jeffersonians began to lose steam. Many feared that "letting loose" great numbers of black slaves with their "savage instincts" would pose a menace to an orderly society. Jefferson himself remarked in 1820 that the South had "the wolf by the ears" and could not let go. In 1817, a group of prominent Virginians, including Henry Clay and George Washington's nephew, organized the American Colonization Society. The Society proposed gradual emancipation of slaves with masters receiving compensation from private charities or state legislatures. The newly freed blacks would be transported out of the country in order to prevent racial war in the North and terror in the South. "We must save the Negro," remarked one adherent of colonization, "or the Negro will ruin us."

The Society bought land in West Africa. There, they established the nation of Liberia to be a refuge for free American blacks whose transportation and settlement they had underwritten. Liberia did become an independent republic in 1847. Colonization societies, however, succeeded in sending fewer than ten thousand freed slaves there by 1860. This was only a small percent of the increase in the population of American blacks over that time period.

Proslavery advocates in the lower South resented even this modest effort to interfere with their "peculiar institution." African Americans, themselves, resisted the Society's efforts. Many were generations removed from Africa and insisted that they were Americans, not Africans. Another source of opposition came from newly militant abolitionists who denounced as racist the preconception that

William Lloyd Garrison, the leader of the militants, proposed the unconditional, universal, and immediate abolition of slavery. He founded the abolitionist newspaper, the *Liberator*.

America's race problem could only be solved by shipping black people out of the country.

Militant Abolitionists

The crusades against "sin," arising from the Second Great Awakening, led many to believe that each man was, indeed, his brother's keeper. It seemed obvious to these reformers that black slavery was, by far, the greatest national sin. As long as any American held slaves, all Americans must be held accountable for this sin. Followers of the preacher Charles Grandison Finney, such as the wealthy Tappan brothers and the brilliant lecturer Theodore Weld, along with the uncompromising William Lloyd Garrison, helped found the American Anti-Slavery Society in 1833. By 1838, it had 1,350 chapters and 250,000 members. The society and its auxiliaries launched an activist campaign against slavery. They sponsored lectures, published newspapers and books, and collected signatures for anti-slavery petitions that were sent to Congress.

These younger abolitionists rejected the moderation of the earlier anti-slavery groups. Colonization, they argued, was nothing more than a trick to strengthen slavery by ridding the country of free blacks. Compromise with slavery was impossible since the righteous person does not compromise with sin, but rather destroys it. William Lloyd Garrison, the leader of the militants, proposed a simple but genuinely revolutionary solution: the unconditional, universal, and immediate abolition of slavery. In 1831 Garrison founded an abolitionist newspaper, the *Liberator*. In its first issue, he announced the manifesto of the new militancy: "I will be as harsh as truth, and as uncompromising as justice. On this subject, I do not wish to think, or speak, or write with moderation.... I am in earnest—I will not equivocate—I will not excuse—I will not retreat a single inch—AND I WILL BE HEARD."

Old South Leaflets.

No. 78.

The Liberator.

Vol. I. No. 1.

WILLIAM LLOYD GARRISON and
ISAAC KNAPP, *Publishers.*

BOSTON, MASSACHUSETTS.— Saturday, January 1, 1831.

Our Country is the World — Our Countrymen are Mankind.

THE SALUTATION.

To date my being from the opening year,
I come, a stranger in this busy sphere,
Where some I meet perchance may pause and ask,
What is my name, my purpose, or my task?

My name is 'LIBERATOR'! I propose
To hurl my shafts at freedom's deadliest foes!
My task is hard — for I am charged to save
***Man from his brother!* — to redeem the slave!**

Ye who may hear, and yet condemn my cause,
Say, shall the best of Nature's holy laws
Be trodden down? and shall her open veins
Flow but for cement to her offspring's chains?

Art thou a parent? shall thy children be
Rent from thy breast, like branches from the tree,
And doom'd to servitude, in helplessness,
On other shores, and thou ask no redress?

Thou, in whose bosom glows the sacred flame
Of filial love, say, if the tyrant came,
To force thy parent shrieking from thy sight,
Would thy heart bleed — *because thy face is white?*

Art thou a brother? shall thy sister twine
Her feeble arm in agony on thine,
And thou not lift the heel, nor aim the blow
At him who bears her off to life-long wo?

THE LIBERATOR is published weekly at No. 6 Merchants' Hall. WM. L. GARRISON, *Editor*. STEPHEN FOSTER, *Printer*. Terms, two dollars per annum, payable in advance.

The *Liberator* became a standard-bearer for radical abolitionists.

Garrison **was** heard, despite the fact that the *Liberator* had only a small number of largely black subscribers in the Northeast. Southerners published impassioned rebuttals. The Georgia legislature even offered a $5,000 reward to anyone who would capture Garrison and bring him south to be tried. The new steam printing press and other technological advances made mass publications possible. The abolitionists were among the first to realize the potential for mass communications. In 1835 alone, the Anti-Slavery Society distributed 1.1 million pieces of literature. Angry mobs stormed southern post offices and set fire to the *Liberator* and other abolitionist tracts. Declaring that abolitionist books and pamphlets might lead to a slave rebellion, President Andrew Jackson ordered the postmaster general to prevent them from being delivered through the mails. Abolitionists found other ways to spread their propaganda. These included posters, candy wrappers, children's books, medals, and songs.

Abolitionists did not think of themselves as advocates of violence or civil conflict. They viewed their societies as part of the reform movement. Surely slavery and racial prejudice were at least as harmful to the community as drunkenness. Just like other reformers, they were trying to encourage the potentials of the human spirit. Who could possibly be more in need of help in fulfilling their possibilities as human beings than slaves? Theodore Weld clearly stated this position. Slavery, he wrote, was a terrible sin because, "no condition of birth, no shade of color...can annul the birthright character, which God has bequeathed to every being upon whom he has stamped his own image, by making him a free moral agent."

Anti-Abolitionists in the North

Most Northerners did not accept this abolitionist message. In a deeper sense, abolitionists seemed to be at war with the established values and institutions of American life. They were a more radical threat to the social order than even the Mormons were. Abolitionists, it seemed to many, were ignoring the rights of private property by urging uncompensated emancipation of the slaves. If the state could do that, whose property would be safe? Their crusade might lead to greater conflict between the sections. Newly freed blacks might flood the northern cities where black men would intermingle with white women. This was yet another threat to the order and stability of society at a time of great disorienting social change.

Anti-abolitionist violence and riots spread through the North in increasing waves in the 1830s. A Philadelphia mob in 1834 burned down the abolitionist headquarters and launched a murderous attack on free blacks. The wealthy Tappan brothers were widely condemned by other businessmen for encouraging radicals like Garrison with their financial support. A crowd of prominent New Yorkers laughed and cheered as they watched a mob of laborers demolish Lewis Tappan's house and burn his belongings

Garrison, himself, barely escaped lynching by an angry crowd in Boston. Three times, enraged mobs in Alton, Illinois smashed the printing presses of abolitionist editor, Elijah Lovejoy. Each time, he rebuilt his newspaper. In 1837, in a fourth attack, Lovejoy tried to defend his press. This time the mob set fire to the building and murdered Lovejoy. Most of this mob violence was carefully planned and organized. While the mobs consisted largely of lower class whites who feared job and social competition from freed blacks, some, particularly the leaders, included "gentlemen of property and standing." These leading citizens felt they were protecting the social order. They also used their influence to insure that the forces of law and order did nothing to protect the besieged abolitionists and free blacks.

Political Abolitionism

Garrison, as a result of all this violence, came to believe that American society itself was fatally infected with the virus of brutality. The entire body of the nation was contaminated. The only sane response was to repudiate all coercion represented by the oppression of nonwhites, women, and dissenters. Majority rule simply enforced repression, so Garrisonians withdrew from all political activities. In one of his more dramatic gestures, Garrison would set fire to the Constitution in front of shocked audiences. The Constitution, with its protection of slavery, was nothing more, in Garrison's estimation, than "a covenant with death, and an agreement with Hell."

Most other abolitionists, however, did not agree with Garrison's total moral withdrawal from a corrupt society. They hoped that they could achieve their goals through political action. They collected thousands of antislavery petitions against the slave trade in the District of Columbia and for the abolition of slavery. In 1836, southern congressmen, with the support of many northern sympathizers, passed the "Gag Rule," ordering any petitions relating to slavery "in any way" to be tabled and, therefore, ignored. The petitions were an effective way of challenging this rule. John Quincy Adams, the only former president to become a member of the House of Representatives, led an energetic campaign against the gag rule. Since the First Amendment of the Constitution guaranteed "the right of the people...to petition the government for a redress of grievances," the rule seemed a clear example of southern attempts to tyrannize free white Northerners just like slaves. To many Northerners, the gag rule provided further evidence that slavery was a danger to the rights of all Americans. In 1844, the resolution was repealed.

Some abolitionists decided that it was essential to enter politics directly. In 1840, they formed the Liberty Party and nominated James G. Birney, a reformed slaveholder, for president. The Libertymen attributed the depression of 1837 to machinations by the "Slave Power." This initial attempt had minimal impact since Birney only got seven thousand votes—a mere 0.3 percent of the votes cast. The Liberty Party was ultimately successful, however, in getting the idea of Slave Power conspiracy imprinted on the consciousness of northern public opinion.

Garrisonians rejected the efforts at political action, arguing that it would lead to compromising basic principles. They also attacked organized religion as a "den of thieves" for its refusal to unequivocally condemn slavery. This angered religious abolitionists. Other supporters were upset at the Garrisonian advocacy of equal rights for women. The consequence of these actions was a split in the Anti-Slavery Society. The Tappan brothers and others who withdrew from the society founded the Liberty Party and set up other political antislavery efforts. The most famous of these was the successful struggle to gain freedom for the Africans who had revolted and won control of the *Amistad*, a ship taking them to slavery in Cuba. John Quincy Adams actually represented the rebellious Africans in their victorious appeal to the Supreme Court.

Despite this split, the antislavery movement continued its varied activities after 1840. Political abolitionists narrowed their focus to restricting the spread of slavery in the territories, rather than calling for its immediate abolition throughout the nation. They believed that, as new territories entered the union, preventing the expansion of slavery would cause its inevitable collapse. This political push became most evident in the formation of the Free-Soil Party in 1848 and, more importantly, in the Republican Party in 1854. Now, however, more concern was expressed for the rights of free white men who had to compete with slaves than for the rights of black people. Free Soilers insisted that, "slavery withers and blights all it touches.... It is a curse upon the poor white laboring men." A Free Soil newspaper announced, "We are opposed to the extension of slavery because it diminishes the productive power of its population." The antislavery movement became more acceptable to northern voters by accommodating itself to white racism. Garrison contemptuously described free-soilism as "white-manism." But the free-soil argument was finally able to achieve what abolitionism could never manage: to gain the support of large numbers, eventually the majority, of white northern voters.

The Proslavery Justification

For some time after the Revolution, many planters in the Upper South followed the Jeffersonian tradition of aristocratic distaste for the institution of slavery. They expressed the cautious hope that some way could one day be found to rid the South of its "burden" or "curse." Some non-slaveholding whites seemed to agree that slavery was "ruinous to the whites." Even many supporters apologetically characterized slavery as a "necessary evil" that would one day, in the distant future, disappear.

The 1830s, however, seriously undermined this genteel viewpoint. The extraordinary growth of the cotton kingdom, coupled with a defensive reaction to the increasingly active antislavery movement, led to a defensive counterattack by Southerners. They argued that slavery was, in fact, a "positive good." All great societies of the past, from Biblical Israel and ancient Greece to the medieval empire of Charlemagne, they declared had rested on a foundation of slavery. The South, in their estimation, was superior to a chaotic North like the "ism-smitten people of Massachusetts" prey to such heresies as feminism and utopianism. In the South, society was stable as women and slaves alike understood their established places.

Black Abolitionists

The racism inherent in the arguments of the supporters of slavery and the hypocrisy of many antislavery reformers in accepting the racism of northern society increased the appeal of militant abolitionism to free blacks in the North. These free blacks, numbering around 250,000 by 1850, often lived under conditions of misery and intolerance. The bigotry directed at these African Americans in the North led Tocqueville to observe that "the prejudice which repels the Negroes seems to increase in proportion as they are emancipated." Most worked as domestics or in menial jobs. It was difficult for them to get any kind of formal education. Only a few states granted the vote to black citizens. Nevertheless, these blacks were very conscious of the importance of their freedom and of the danger slavery posed to their precarious position in society.

From the earliest days of organized abolitionism, blacks worked with antislavery groups. The lectures and printed accounts of the lives of escaped or freed slaves like Sojourner Truth, Solomon Northrup, and Frederick Douglass put a human face to northern images of slavery. Their dramatic accounts succeeded in weakening any feeling there may have existed in the North that slaves were carefree "darkies" who were well treated by kindly masters. Their intelligence and eloquence undermined stereotypes of black inferiority.

Black abolitionist speakers endured far more harrowing dangers on the lecture tours than whites. They were continually threatened, harassed, insulted, humiliated, and attacked. Most of the conductors on the "Underground Railroad" were black. They succeeded in aiding a relatively small number of fugitive slaves in escaping to the North or the greater security of Canada. Black abolitionist groups also hoped to secure the repeal of discriminatory laws in the North. Outside of Massachusetts, they had little success in challenging northern racism. Their white abolitionist allies urged them to remain in the role scripted for them in dramatic shows designed to attack slavery in the South while remaining quiet about discrimination in the North. Abolitionist leaders felt that it was important not to frighten northern audiences with talk of violence or racial equality.

Many northern blacks supported Garrison. But militant black leaders developed who asserted their own authority. David Walker, a Boston free man, as early as 1829, expressed a combativeness that terrified many whites. In his pamphlet: "Walker's Appeal...to the Colored Citizens," he proclaimed, "America is more our country than it is the whites—we have enriched it with our blood and tears." Whites who wanted to keep blacks as slaves "will curse the day they ever saw us." Walker counseled slaves to cut their masters' throats, to "kill or be killed."

By the 1840s, other black leaders began to affirm their own leadership and ideas. At a Convention of Free People of Color held in Buffalo in 1843, Henry Highland Garnet, an articulate activist, endorsed slave rebellion. He maintained that it was a sin to passively surrender to the bonds of slavery. Another black militant, Charles Lenox Remond, to the deep regret of the pacifist Garrison, openly declared "that slaves were bound, by their love of justice, to RISE AT ONCE, en masse, and THROW OFF THEIR FETTERS."

Most black antislavery leaders, however, were far less fierce in their orations. The greatest of these leaders was Frederick Douglass, one of the most thrilling speakers of an era renowned for its eloquence. Douglass was born a slave in Maryland where he illegally learned to read and write and taught himself intellectually challenging subjects like higher mathematics and Greek. In 1838, he escaped to Massachusetts where he became an outstanding lecturer for the abolitionist movement. He mesmerized audiences with his descriptions of his life under slavery. He published one of the great American autobiographies, *Narrative of the Life of Frederick Douglas.* After that, he spent two years lecturing widely throughout Britain where he was glorified by that nation's flourishing antislavery movement. On his return to the United States in 1847, he continued to speak throughout the North. Although an advocate of nonviolent resistance, Douglass broke with many white abolitionists by demanding full civil, political, and economic rights, as well as freedom for slaves. In 1847, he split with Garrison over his idea of founding a black abolitionist newspaper, *The North Star.* Douglas continued his battle for reform, supporting women's rights, as well as black equality.

Many black abolitionists believed gaining the right to vote would be the best route to greater influence and freedom. They, therefore, supported the efforts of the Liberty and Free-Soil Parties in the 1840s. Unfortunately, antislavery politics seemed to be increasingly focused on partitioning off western territories. The partition would keep out free blacks, as well as slaves. By the 1850s some disillusioned black leaders were talking of creating a separate black nation or even of voluntarily emigrating to Haiti or Africa.

By this time, however, increasing numbers of northern whites had become convinced that there was a Slave Power conspiracy. Enforcement of the Fugitive Slave Act, including seizing blacks in the streets of northern cities, led to growing anger, demonstrations, and civil disobedience. Moderates grew more receptive to Garrisonian militants. Wendell Phillips, the most electrifying abolitionist speaker, exulted that, "every five minutes gave birth to a black baby." In that infant's cry he detected a voice that would "yet shout the war cry of insurrection; its baby hand would one day hold the dagger which should reach the master's heart." Thus, black and white antislavery groups both came to an understanding that only extreme measures could destroy the "Slave Power."

Sojourner Truth

At the anti-slavery meeting in Indiana in 1858, she was a very imposing figure—a tall (almost six foot) gaunt black woman. Despite being illiterate, Sojourner Truth spoke with eloquence and passion. Her voice was powerful and low, almost masculine. As usual, she accompanied her talk with songs, pleasing to her audience.

As the meeting drew to a close, however, a sizable group of pro-slavery hecklers charged that Truth was, in reality, a man in a dress. They demanded that she show her breasts to the women in the audience who would verify her sex. After much "confusion and uproar," one particularly obstreperous man expressed loud doubts about her sex. Truth responded with words and actions that shamed her questioners. She informed them that "her breasts had suckled many a white babe, to the exclusion of her own offspring." Then, "in vindication of her truthfulness," she uncovered her breast to the entire audience. After asking her astounded tormentors whether "they too wished to suck," she concluded, "it was not to her shame that she uncovered her breast before them, but to their shame."

Sojourner Truth was born in the 1790s as Isabella, a slave in rural New York. When New York ended slavery, she heard the voice of God in 1826 urging her to live as a free woman. She had been overworked, beaten, and even sexually abused when she was a slave. Now she turned to an evangelical Christianity that made her feel sanctified, a woman with a friend in Jesus who she compared to "a soul-protecting fortress." She became a dynamic and moving preacher.

In 1843 she experienced a rebirth. She believed that the Holy Spirit wanted her to become Sojourner Truth—a seeker after truth who, in the words of a popular spiritual, "ain't got long to stay here." In her new persona, she was an enormously effective witness to the evils of slavery on the abolitionist circuit. She also became active in the inter-related struggle for women's rights. "If colored men get their rights and not colored women theirs," she told one gathering, "the colored men will be masters over the women, and it will be as bad as it was before."

THE RISE OF THE WOMEN'S RIGHTS MOVEMENT

Women had played a crucial role in many of the reform movements of the era. They were particularly involved in abolitionism. Women gained useful experience in public speaking, organizing, and raising funds in hundreds of female charitable and reform associations. As they labored to correct the ills of an imperfect society, they became increasingly aware of the problems that they, themselves, faced in a male-dominated community. This led to the founding of America's first feminist movement and the beginning of a prolonged struggle for women's rights.

Women and the Antislavery Crusade

Female antislavery societies began forming almost immediately after William Lloyd Garrison launched his movement in 1831. By 1838, there were over one hundred such associations throughout the Northeast and Midwest. At first, they devoted themselves to raising funds for the cause with "antislavery fairs" where homemade goods were sold. Soon, however, they became involved in more activist and controversial ways. Since middle-class women had more time to devote, they were the ones who canvassed door-to-door to collect signatures for abolitionist petitions in the drive to challenge the gag rule. This meant moving out of their traditional sphere—the home.

Their role as antislavery speakers on public platforms was even more problematic. This included speaking to "mixed" or "promiscuous" audiences, an activity considered totally improper for a respectable woman. In the face of mounting criticism, a women's national antislavery convention resolved: "The time has come for woman to move in that sphere which providence has assigned her, and no longer remain satisfied in the circumscribed limits which corrupt custom and a perverted application of scripture have encircled her."

Sarah and Angelina Grimké, two of Garrison's most important converts, best exemplified this exciting new role for women. They were the daughters of an eminent slave-holding South Carolina family whose members included judges and legislators. They deserted their father's plantation to move to Philadelphia where they converted to the Quaker faith, which preached human equality. They then embraced the ideals of abolitionism and became the first official female antislavery agents. As such, they launched a lecture tour, speaking at first to female audiences. Soon, however, they were shamelessly addressing mixed audiences. These clearly upper class and "proper" southern women, who could lecture about the evils of slavery from personal experience, quickly became a sensational attraction for the abolitionists. They drew crowds of thousands of curious spectators, converting many to the antislavery cause.

Clergymen and conservative reformers were outraged! Here were two women who had usurped "the place and role of man as public reformer." One minister charged that the Grimkés had abandoned "that modesty and delicacy...which constitutes the true influence of women in society." He implored them to return to "the appropriate duties and influence of women."

Sarah Grimké responded with an attack on the male domination of society, drawing an analogy between the treatment of women and that of slaves. "Men and women are CREATED EQUAL. They are both moral and accountable beings," she declared. "All I ask our brethren is that they take their feet from off our necks and permit us to stand upright on the ground which God destined for us to occupy."

This stand angered those abolitionists who believed that the spectacle of women challenging their traditional roles would harm the antislavery cause. Garrison became the main defender of the Grimkés. He drew a parallel between the condition of women and slaves, announcing in the *Liberator*: "As our object is universal emancipation, to redeem women as well as men from a servile to an equal condition—we shall go for the rights of women to their utmost extent." Garrison had persuaded the Grimkés that Christian "principles of peace" were the heart of all reform. In turn, the Grimkés convinced Garrison and his followers that these principles applied to the "domestic slavery" of women as well.

A number of black women were also actively involved in the abolitionist movement. Both the Boston and Philadelphia Female Antislavery Societies had black women as members, and even one officer. In general, however, northern racial segregation led most black women abolitionists to form their own societies. Once women began to speak in public gatherings, African-American women who had once been slaves proved to be particularly effective in describing the harmful effects of slavery on black family life. Sojourner Truth and, somewhat later, Harriet Tubman were especially popular speakers.

The controversy over women's participation caused a final split in the American Anti-Slavery Society. The more conservative faction left the Society to Garrison and his radicals and founded its own organization. The issue spread to the World Antislavery convention in London in 1840. The men who controlled the proceedings refused to allow female American delegates to actively participate. Relegated to the balcony as observers (accompanied by a supportive William Lloyd Garrison), Lucretia Mott and Elizabeth Cady Stanton came to the conclusion that improving the status of women should become their major goal as reformers.

The Struggle for Legal Rights

During the 1840s, a sustained campaign was launched to end legal discrimination against wives. Under the law, in all states, married women were considered legal possessions. They could not control their own property and had no rights to their own earnings or even to their children. Attempts to remedy this situation met with some success in the 1840s. Some state legislators, who owned property themselves, reacted favorably to measures to preserve their estates from the hands of greedy sons-in-law when daughters were the sole heirs.

In New York a women's pressure group was formed under the leadership of the fiery Ernestine Rose. She was the daughter of a Polish rabbi who fled the restrictions of her home to go to England. There, she became a follower of Robert Owens. Rose had recently immigrated to the United States. Her group argued that married women should be allowed to keep their own property and earnings and should be given joint guardianship over their children. In 1848, New York passed a bill providing married women with some control over their property. Gradually, other states passed similar legislation. To some extent, these laws were designed to provide a legal loophole to protect property from husbands' creditors. As one historian notes, however, "In the context of the nineteenth century, the right of wives to own property entailed their right not to be property."

The Women's Rights Movement

After 1848, the battle against legal inequality continued increasingly under the standard of the women's rights movement. After their disillusioning experience at the world antislavery convention, Elizabeth Cady Stanton and Lucretia Mott resolved to convene a convention to call for action to eliminate the many inequities women faced.

This first women's rights convention was held in 1848 in Seneca Falls, New York (Stanton's hometown). The manifesto that emerged from this meeting was called the "Declaration of Sentiments and Resolutions." It was patterned on the Declaration of Independence, proclaiming that "all men and women are created equal," and that women also have certain inalienable rights to life, liberty, and the pursuit of happiness. Just as the original Declaration listed grievances against the King of England, the women's Declaration identified the adversary as the "absolute tyranny" of man and then listed "his repeated injuries and usurpations." These included exclusion of women from better jobs, higher education opportunities, and the professions; the deprivation of property rights; and the imposition of a sexual double standard. In oppressing woman, man had also tried "to destroy her confidence in her own power, to lessen her self respect, and to make her willing to lead a dependent and abject life." After a list of demands to rectify these grievances, the declaration concluded with a claim that women were entitled to the right to vote, a major assault on the long-cherished view that women did not belong in the public sphere.

The Seneca Falls meeting launched America's women's rights movements.

This demand for women's suffrage was the most controversial of all. Even women's rights activists were unsure. At Seneca Falls, the call for the vote was the only resolution not approved unanimously by the delegates. It only gained a slim majority after Frederick Douglass gave it his eloquent endorsement. Women who were willing to sign petitions calling for legal rights refused to support petitions demanding the right to vote. One woman wrote her suffragist sister, "I am sure I do not feel burdened by anything man has laid upon me, to be sure I can't vote, but what care I for that, I would not if I could." In spite of these difficulties, the struggle for women's suffrage continued until women finally gained the constitutional right to vote in 1920.

The Seneca Falls meeting led to a whole series of conventions throughout the North and Midwest to restate and embellish its sentiments. The press greeted these meetings with animosity and ridicule. Despite this, Elizabeth Cady Stanton, joined by Susan B. Anthony, persisted in her efforts. Although Stanton and Anthony pressed for more radical changes, most of the conventions held in the 1850s emphasized legal and economic inequality. Many directly challenged the statements of clergymen that the Bible decreed that the "weaker sex" remain in a dependent "sphere." Lucy Stone, a militant feminist, told them, "Leave woman to find her own sphere."

Only moderate progress was made in meeting the goals of women's rights activists by the 1850s. Limited advances occurred in the area of legal rights for married women. Some individual women, like Elizabeth Blackwell, the first licensed female physician, began to break down some barriers to advancement. Blackwell's sister-in-law, Lucy Stone, took the radical step of keeping her maiden name after marriage. (For years after, women who followed her lead were known as "Lucy Stoners.") Some women demonstrated their feminism in their choice of

Many people ridiculed women who wore bloomers. Some men and boys threw eggs at women who wore bloomers in public.

clothing. They wore an outfit that combined a short skirt with long pantaloons. Although a famous English actress first introduced the costume to Americans, it came to be called "bloomers," after Amelia Bloomer, its most ardent advocate. In the face of a rising turmoil over women seeking to "wear the pants" in the family, leading feminists abandoned it. They worried that the bloomer issue was overshadowing their more serious activities.

Attempts to enlarge the following of the women's rights movement by combining with the much larger, more conservative, temperance community did not succeed. In New York State, a Women's Temperance Association with Elizabeth Cady Stanton as president quickly split up over Stanton's idea that drunkenness should be grounds for divorce.

In many ways feminists benefited from their association with other reform movements, particularly abolitionism. These reform groups provided women's rights advocates with a ready-made sympathetic audience and conduits to communicate their ideas. On the other hand, this relationship could also be a hindrance. Women's rights, even in the eyes of most of the women involved in both abolitionist and feminist movements, was always secondary to the more pressing need to emancipate the slaves. Until the slave had achieved his or her freedom, the women's rights movement could not advance due to its dependence on an antislavery foundation.

The Impact of Reform

The antebellum (pre-Civil War) period was characterized by an unprecedented burst of reformist sentiment. Organizations struggled to tackle all the perceived

Elizabeth Cady Stanton was the intellectual leader of the women's rights and suffrage movement, in addition to raising seven children.

ills of society including alcoholism, prostitution, moral laxity, violation of the Sabbath, oppression of women, and, above all, enslavement of human beings. It is important to remember that reform, like dynamic economic changes, was basically a product of northern life. Southerners were largely untouched by the push to create a better society. Although relatively few Americans shared the abolitionist view that slavery must be immediately and completely eliminated, the struggle over slavery ultimately dominated American political life before the Civil War settled the issue once and for all. While some reform goals, such as ending all consumption of alcohol and making seduction illegal, may seem extreme and puritanical to us today, others including racial and sexual equality eventually became the shared ideals of most Americans.

DOCUMENTS

PROTESTING THE "GAG" RULE IN THE U. S. HOUSE OF REPRESENTATIVES AND MAIL CENSORSHIP

From 1836 to 1844, the House of Representatives adopted a number of procedural rules to exclude any petitions asking for the abolition of slavery from consideration by the House of Representatives. Southern congressmen and some northern representatives supported the rules since they regarded the antislavery petitions as inflammatory. The former president of the U.S., John Quincy Adams, then a member of the House from Massachusetts, led the fight to rescind the gag rules. At the beginning of each session, Adams moved to strike the offending gag rule. Finally, on Dec. 3, 1844, he was successful. The following is from a speech given before the House by Judge William Jay, a founder of the American Bible Society and ally of the philanthropist reformers, the Tappan brothers.

"Address to the Friends of Constitutional Liberty, on the Violation by the United States House of Representatives of the Right of Petition, 1840."

To the Friends of Constitutional Liberty: —

There was a time, fellow citizens, when the above address would have included the People of the United States. But, alas! the freedom of the press, freedom of speech, and the right of petition, are now hated and dreaded by our Southern citizens, as hostile to the perpetuity of human bondage; while, by their political influence in the Federal Government, they have induced members at the North to unite with them in their sacrilegious crusade against these inestimable privileges.

On the 28th of January last, the House of Representatives, on motion of Mr. Johnson, from Maryland, made it a standing rule of the House that "no petition, memorial, resolution, or other paper, praying the abolition of slavery in the District of Columbia, or any State or Territory of the United States, in which it now exists, shall be received by the House, or entertained in any way whatever."

Thus has the right of petition been immolated in the very Temple of Liberty, and offered up, a propitiatory sacrifice to the demon of slavery. Never before has an outrage so unblushingly profligate been perpetrated upon the Federal Constitution. Yet, while we mourn the degeneracy which this transaction evinces, we behold, in its attending circumstances, joyful omens of the triumph which awaits our struggle with the hateful power that now perverts the General Government into an engine of cruelty and loathsome oppression.

Before we congratulate you on these omens, let us recall to your recollection the steps by which the enemies of human rights have advanced to their present rash and insolent defiance of moral and constitutional obligation.

In 1831, a newspaper was established in Boston, for the purpose of disseminating facts and arguments in favor of the duty and policy of immediate emancipation. The Legislature of Georgia, with all the recklessness of despotism, passed a law, offering a reward of $5000, for the abduction of the editor, and his delivery in Georgia. As there was no law by which a citizen of Massachusetts could be tried in Georgia, for expressing his opinions in the capital of his own State, this reward was intended as the price of BLOOD. Do you start at the suggestion? Remember the several sums of $25,000, of $50,000, and of $100,000, offered in Southern papers for kidnapping certain abolitionists. Remember the horrible inflictions by Southern Lynch clubs. Remember the declaration, in the United States Senate, by the brazen-fronted Preston, that, should an abolitionist be caught in Carolina, he would be HANGED. But, as the slave-holders could not destroy the lives of the abolitionists, they determined to murder their characters. Hence, the President of the United States was induced, in his Message of 1835, to Congress, to charge them with plotting the massacre of the Southern planters; and even to stultify himself, by affirming that, for this purpose, they were engaged in sending, by *mail*, inflammatory appeals to the *slaves*—sending papers to men who could not read them, and by a conveyance through which they could not receive them! He well knew that the papers alluded to were appeals on the immorality of converting men, women, and children, into beasts of burden, and were sent to the masters for *their* consideration. The masters in Charleston, dreading the moral influence of these appeals on the conscience of the slaveholding community, forced the Post Office, and made a bonfire of the papers. The Postmaster-General, with the sanction of the President, also hastened to their relief, and, in violation of oaths, and laws, and the Constitution, established ten thousand censors of the press, each one of whom was authorized to abstract from the mail every paper which *he* might think too favorable to the rights of man.

For more than twenty years, petitions have been presented to Congress, for the abolition of slavery in the District of Columbia. The right to present them, and the power of Congress to grant their prayer, were, until recently, unquestioned. But the rapid multiplication of these petitions alarmed the slaveholders, and, knowing that they tended to keep alive at the North, an interest in the slave, they deemed it good policy to discourage and, if possible, suppress all such applications. Hence Mr. Pinckney's famous resolution, in 1836, declaring, "that all petitions, or papers, relating *in any way, or to any extent* whatever to the *subject of slavery*, shall, without being printed or referred, be laid on the table; and no further action whatever shall be had thereon!"

The peculiar atrocity of this resolution was, that it not merely trampled upon the rights of the petitioners, but took from each member of the House his undoubted privilege, as a legislator of the District, to introduce any proposition he might think proper, for the protection of the slaves. In every slave state there are laws affording, at least, some nominal protection to these unhappy beings; but, according to this resolution, slaves might be flayed alive in the streets of Washington, and no representative of the people could offer even a resolution for inquiry. And this vile outrage upon constitutional liberty was avowedly perpetrated "to repress agitation, to allay excitement, and reestablish harmony and tranquillity among the various sections of the Union!!"

But this strange opiate did not produce the stupefying effects anticipated from it. In 1836, the petitioners were only 37,000—the next session they numbered 110,000. Mr. Hawes, of Kentucky, now essayed to restore tranquillity by gagging the uneasy multitude; but, alas! at the next Congress, more than 300,000 petitioners carried new terror to the hearts of the slaveholders. The next anodyne was prescribed by Mr. Patten, of Virginia, but its effect was to rouse from their stupor some of the northern Legislatures [Massachusetts and Connecticut, in April and May 1838], and to induce them to denounce his remedy as "a usurpation of power, a violation of the Constitution, subversive of the fundamental principles of the government, and at war with the prerogatives of the people."

Source: William Jay, *Miscellaneous Writings on Slavery* (Boston: John P. Jewett & Co., 1853), pp. 397-400.

1. What action of the Postmaster General does Jay find objectionable?
2. According to Jay, what was the "particular atrocity" of the gag rule?
3. What do you think would be the impact of abolitionist arguments against the gag rule?
4. What arguments do you think abolitionists gave in particular about the institution of slavery in the District of Columbia?

ON THE WAY TO LIBERIA, a Letter to a Former Mistress (1833)

The widow Mary Owen "Polly" Todd Russell Wickliffe, a wealthy Kentucky slave owner, who remarried, insisted on the emancipation of several slaves to carry out her missionary goals for Africa. Milly Crawford and her son, Alfred, were house servants who learned to read and write. Polly Wickliffe hoped that Milly would become a teacher and Alfred would become a minister in Africa. In March of 1833, Milly and Alfred finally left for Liberia with their cousin, Lucy Russell, and her children. Milly wrote a long letter of thanks from their first stop in Frankfort. They then traveled to New Orleans where other emigrants joined them. They boarded the brig "Ajax" on April 20, 1833, with white missionaries. The American Colonization Society paid for the expedition. Disease claimed the lives of 30 (mostly children) during the passage. On July 11, 1833, 146 new settlers (31 men, 42 women, 74 children age 12 & under, mostly farmers) arrived in Liberia after 3 months aboard the brig.

Milly Crawford and Lucy Russell on their way to Liberia from Lexington Kentucky

A letter to Mary Owen Todd Russell Wickliffe*** [the letter is transcribed as written without any changes in punctuation or spelling] ***

March 10 1833 Saterday night

My Dear Misstress we have all arrived at frankfort in safety and health little George Lucy and all the children are well. My dear Misstress how shall we thank you for all your kindness too us. We sometimes despond being all females and children haveing no male protecter of our own. but we try to put our trust in the Almighty and go on in his srength. whatever betide us.

My Dear Mystress you have done your whole duty. and may the [Almighty] bless and reward you a thousand fold.

[this section is from] Lucy all love and thanks to you for your goodness care and kindness to us all. the children all desires me remember them to Mystress.

Mystress we all desire you thank Mayster for his goodness and kindness to us.

I hope the Lord will bless him give our love to miss Margaret miss Mary Mys Sally Wooly [Robert Wickliffe's three living white children] and all our friends. the Lord has raised up manny friend to us in fankford we are treated with so much kindness by all who see us. the gentleman at whose house we now lodge Mr Gray trets us with the utmost kindness—he had us all in his dining room prayed with and for us—the gentleman you wrote too received your letter recommending us to him he took us home with him gave us supper and we returned again mr grays you will hear again from us att Louisville May the [Lord] bless preserve and reward you for all kindness is the prare of your unworthy but affecunate servant

Milly C

Source*:* Wickliffe-Preston Family Papers, Box 39, University of Kentucky Special Collections and Archives, Lexington, Kentucky.

1. Re-read the letter and identify examples of Christian piety. This language is similar to that used by many teachers in the U.S. (of any color) at this time. Why is Milly so grateful to her master and mistress? What kind of lessons do you think Milly will teach her students in Liberia?
2. How successful do you think efforts to send American blacks "back" to Africa would prove to be?

PART II

THE ROAD TO WAR

MANIFEST DESTINY

Chapter Four

STORM CLOUDS GATHER: Manifest Destiny, Expansion, and Division

MANIFEST DESTINY AND EXPANSION

The era that ended in irrevocable division began in a spirit of triumphal nationalism. The Missouri Compromise of 1820 had settled the potentially explosive issue of slavery in the Louisiana Purchase territory. Under its terms Missouri was admitted to the Union as a slave state while Maine was created out of Massachusetts' territory as a free state, preserving the balance of slave and free states in the Senate. A line was drawn across the remainder of the Louisiana Purchase at the 36° 30′ parallel. Slavery would be prohibited North of the line and permitted South of it, thus settling the nettlesome issue of slavery in the territories. Congress had seemed to accept the northern view that the federal government had jurisdiction over slavery in the territories. Although former President Jefferson warned that the issue was a "firebell in the night" filling him "with terror," most Americans believed that the controversy had been put to rest.

By the 1830s, a two-party system of Democrats and Whigs had developed, providing a relatively balanced nation-wide competition and contests in virtually all the states. The Whigs followed the old Federalist belief in nationalism and strong government. They became the party of modernization, favoring government promotion of economic growth through tariffs, bank charters, and aid to such internal improvements as railroads. The Democrats followed Jeffersonian views of states' rights, limited government, and suspicion of urbanization and industrialization. This led them to oppose the economic program of the Whigs.

The Whigs appealed to those who profited by change or hoped to do so. The Democrats' constituency tended to be "have-nots," such as small backcountry farmers and unskilled laborers.

Both parties, however, were active in all sections. In northern cities evangelical Protestants, who favored such reforms as temperance, public schools, and limitations on slavery, dominated the Whig Party. Democrats in these cities appealed to poor people, workers, immigrants, and Catholics who resented efforts to reform and order their lives. In farm areas Whigs attracted dynamic cash crop growers who believed that they would benefit from transportation improvements. Democratic farmers tended to be smaller, more self-sufficient, and outside the market economy. They preferred government to leave them alone. In the South, both parties supported slavery, but the Whigs tended to be wealthier slaveholders, professionals, and town merchants. Under the loose federal system the Whigs could be proslavery in the South and antislavery in the North. The slow communications of the era before the telegraph helped make this seeming contradiction possible.

The two-party system facilitated national unity by blurring the potentially dangerous issue of slavery and offering the voters choices based on competing views about governmental activism. In addition, both parties offered nationalistic versions of American expansionism. The Whigs believed in progress through economic growth and modernization. The Democrats favored the Jeffersonian vision of territorial expansion that would extend freedom and the possibilities for the self-reliant farmer, the foundation of American society. If America failed to expand, its population would eventually, in Jefferson's graphic words, pile "upon one another in large cities, as in Europe, and go eating one another as they do there."

The Election of 1840

In view of the hard times caused by the national depression under the Democrats, the Whigs had good reason to feel confident in the election of 1840. To ensure their triumph, they turned from Senator Henry Clay, their logical choice, to rally behind an elderly military "hero," William Henry Harrison, the "victor" over the Shawnees in the 1811 Battle at Tippecanoe Creek. Harrison's strongest point seemed to be that he stood for almost nothing and, thus, would not antagonize any of the Whig's varied voters. John Tyler of Virginia, who had left the Democratic Party in opposition to Andrew Jackson, was picked for vice president to add to the ticket's strength in the South. The glum Democrats renominated President Van Buren and were unable to agree on a vice-presidential candidate. The Whigs took a leaf from the Democrats' book by portraying Harrison, a speculator, descended from plantation aristocracy, as a simple frontiersman. They used the symbols of a log cabin and a barrel of cider in raucous rallies for "Tippecanoe and Tyler Too." They characterized Van Buren, a man of far more modest origin, as an Oriental potentate who wore purple satin underwear, ate French food from golden plates, and rested on a "Turkish divan" in the "President's Palace." Whether as a result of this unashamedly misleading campaign or the belief that their votes would make a real difference, almost 80 percent of the eligible electorate voted, a record in American history. Although Harrison's popular vote margin was narrow, he won an overwhelming 234 to 60 victory in the electoral college.

An enormous flood of triumphant Whigs descended on Washington for Harrison's inauguration. The new president was quite elderly by the standards of the time. (He was 68.) His inauguration speech, delivered in bad weather, was very lengthy and difficult to hear. Feeling rather ill and faint, the president greeted thousands of well wishers, confiding to his aide that he did not even have time to do "the necessary functions of nature." A month later, the exhausted and overwhelmed old general was dead. He was honored by a spectacular funeral and extended mourning period.

John Tyler became the first "accidental president," a vice president who rose to the office of president as a result of the death of the incumbent. Whig leaders like Henry Clay had expected to be the real powers in a Harrison administration. Tyler, however, was more of a Democrat than a Whig in his view of the proper role of government. He vetoed key parts of the Whig economic program including internal improvements, higher tariffs, and the re-establishment of a national bank. The disillusioned Whigs read Tyler out of the party and all of his inherited cabinet resigned except for Daniel Webster, the Secretary of State.

Webster remained only to conclude negotiations with Britain to defuse a series of dangerous disputes that seemed to many to foreshadow an inevitable war. These included confrontations over American aid to Canadian rebels, a border "war" in Maine, and American anger over safe haven given by the British in the Bahamas to slaves who had taken control of an American slave ship. The Webster-Ashburton Treaty settled the disputed American-Canadian borders and smoothed over the other conflicts, providing a model for future compromises with Britain. That accomplished, Webster promptly resigned. An ardent defender of slavery replaced him. In fact, for the first time, vehement proslavery advocates controlled an entire administration.

Both Democratic and Whig Party leaders had attempted to keep the explosive and divisive issue of slavery out of national politics. Tyler, a president without a party, tried to find an issue to save his presidency. The issue he seized upon was the immediate annexation of Texas. That annexation and the resulting war with Mexico propelled the issue of the expansion of slavery into the center of national politics. The division of the two national parties along sectional lines was the inevitable consequence.

The Saga of the Amistad

On February 22, 1841, the Supreme Court began hearing arguments in a remarkable case involving mutiny on a Spanish slave ship, **Amistad***, off the coast of Cuba. Although the African slave trade was illegal, the ship held fifty-three captives, including four children and a 26-year old man from Sierra Leone who had been given the name Joseph Cinque. Cinque led a brief, bloody struggle on the ship, killing its cook and captain. After 60 days sailing up and down the Atlantic coast of the United States, American sailors seized the ship. They found forty-three malnourished Africans (the others had died of disease or exposure) and two Spanish officers who demanded the return of their "property."*

Louis Tappan and other abolitionists saw the case as an opportunity to expose the slave trade and its brutality. They even found two Africans working on the docks in New York who could translate the language of the mutineers, enabling them to tell their side of the story. Roger S. Baldwin, the Africans' lawyer, argued that they had been illegally kidnapped from their homeland and, thus, were entitled to resist their abductors by any means necessary. Observers were divided into those who saw Cinque as a strikingly handsome black folk hero and others who felt he was a murderous barbarian who deserved to be executed.

The Van Buren administration, citing diplomatic necessities, attempted to return the Africans to Spanish Cuba. Van Buren's blatantly pro-southern **Amistad** *policy may well have contributed to his defeat in the 1840 election by alienating northern Democrats. Meanwhile, the case worked its way to the Supreme Court. Abolitionists persuaded the cranky, nearly deaf 73-year old former president, John Quincy Adams, to take the case. The cause became a crusade for the crusty old congressman when he received a powerful letter from Kale, one of the children who had learned English and served as the groups' spokesperson. The letter concluded with the eloquent words, "All we want is to make us free."*

After Adams' passionate eight-hour argument, Justice Joseph Story read a decision that freed the mutineers on the grounds that they were "kidnapped Africans" who possessed the innate right of self-defense according to the "eternal principles of justice." Eventually, abolitionists raised funds that enabled the captives, on November 25, 1841, to return to Sierra Leone. What happened to each of them thereafter is not certain. But what is certain is that this was the only time in American history that Africans captured by slave dealers and shipped to the Americas won their freedom in the American courts. This contributed to the continuing struggle against slavery.

Manifest Destiny and Texas

Many Americans fervently believed that American expansion to occupy the entire continent was preordained by God to spread a uniquely American system of democracy and Christianity. A Democratic editor popularized this view. He used the phrase "Manifest Destiny" to urge that Americans must "overspread the continent allotted by Providence for the free development of our yearly multiplying millions." By 1860, more than half of the population was already living west of the Appalachians. The public believed in continued expansion that would sweep aside Indian "savages" and "inferior" Mexicans incapable of making proper use of the land. Many believed that a larger stronger America was essential as protection against looming external enemies, particularly the British.

The Republic of Texas (which also included parts of modern Oklahoma, Kansas, Wyoming, New Mexico, and Colorado) had originally been a part of Mexico. When Mexico gained its independence from Spain in 1821, the Mexican government sought to encourage settlers in these northern provinces. It offered large land grants at low prices to settlers who agreed to become Catholics and Mexican citizens. By the 1830s there were some thirty-five thousand Americans in Texas, many of whom were slaveholders. The Mexican government, increasingly alarmed by the settlers' willful disregard of Mexican laws, attempted to halt further immigration and importation of slaves. (Slavery had been abolished in Mexican provinces, although a loophole had been included for Texas.) British anti-slavery reformers and American abolitionists hoped that Texas could demonstrate the possibility of growing cotton with free labor.

Attempts by Mexican strongman General Santa Anna to tighten control over Texas, including abolishing slavery, led Americans there to rebel. In early 1836 they declared their independence and set up a provisional government with a constitution that protected slavery. At the Alamo mission in San Antonio less than 200 Texans held off 3,000 Mexicans under General Santa Anna for two weeks. All the defenders, including legendary frontiersmen Davy Crockett and James Bowie, were killed and their bodies stripped and burned. This Mexican victory united American public opinion against them and "Remember the Alamo" became the Texas rallying cry. (The heroic stand at the Alamo became such a part of American myth that it was the subject of a film more than 100 years later with John Wayne as one of the heroes. The film never mentions the desire to protect slavery as one of the freedom fighters' motives.) Under the inspired leadership of Sam Houston, the Texans were able to defeat a much larger Mexican army a month after the Alamo debacle. They captured Santa Anna and forced him to sign a treaty recognizing the independence of Texas.

Many Americans, particularly in the South, saw the victory as the triumph of white freedom-loving Protestants against backward dark skinned inferior Catholics. They welcomed the efforts of the new "Lone Star Republic" to be admitted into the United States. Whigs, particularly antislavery Northeasterners, bitterly opposed annexation, viewing it as a plot by slave owners to add five to seven new slave states to the union. John Quincy Adams, who served in the House of Representative for 17 years after he left the presidency, was untiring in his eloquent speeches denouncing the southern "Slave Power" conspiracy to annex Texas. In view of its political explosiveness, both Presidents Jackson and Van Buren avoided the issue.

The new Republic then began to openly talk about strengthening ties with Great Britain. The British, naturally, were receptive to the idea of an independent Texas that would export cotton to them and buy British manufactured goods, while serving as a barrier to further American expansion. They were also, however, committed to opposition to slavery, so the treaty of trade and recognition they offered to Texas included a secret clause to ban the slave trade. Southerners firmly believed that the British were plotting to control Texas, make it a haven for fugitive slaves, and subvert the Union. The publicizing of a private diplomatic note stating that the British government "desires and is constantly exerting herself to procure the general abolition of slavery throughout the world," further inflamed southern public opinion and increased "Texas annexation fever." John C. Calhoun, who had become Secretary of State in 1844, submitted an annexation treaty to the Senate. He informed the British that such a step would protect slavery, which was "essential to the peace, safety and prosperity" of the United States. This avowed proslavery purpose, combined with an unwillingness even by southern Whigs to provoke war with Mexico, led the Senate to decisively reject the treaty.

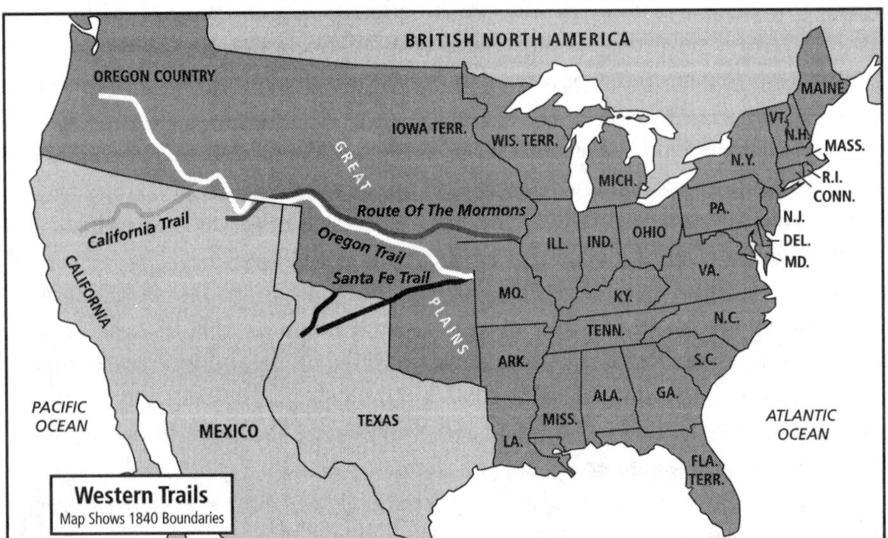

Calhoun had suggested linking the issue of Texas with that of Oregon to gain northern support. Oregon Country had been the site of active competition among the Russians, British, and Americans. When the Russians agreed to give up claims below 54° 40′, it left the British and Americans to struggle for supremacy in the region. American traders had long challenged the authority of the powerful British Hudson Bay Company that ruled the area. But the issue did not become pressing until American Methodist missionaries arrived to convert the Indians. They quickly became enthralled by the beauty and fertility of the Willamette Valley. The enthusiastic reports they sent back, particularly to the farmers of the Old Northwest, led to an epidemic of "Oregon fever." In May of 1843 over a thousand pioneers set off from Independence, Missouri on the 2,000-mile Oregon Trail, a grueling journey of six months or more. Despite the hardships, five thousand settlers arrived within a few years. Demands for "All Oregon" grew to a clamor. The expansionists adopted the slogan, "Fifty-four Forty or Fight."

Expansionism and the Election of 1844

The two leading presidential contenders in 1844, Henry Clay, the Whig, and Martin Van Buren, the Democrat, had, by mutual agreement, simultaneously published letters in opposition to the annexation of Texas. They, thus, had hoped to keep this inflammatory issue out of the national campaign. This stand was acceptable to the Whigs who unanimously nominated Clay. Van Buren's letter and his antislavery stance, however, angered southern Democrats. They used a newly adopted two-thirds rule to block Van Buren's nomination, even though he had a majority of delegates on the first ballot. By the ninth ballot, exhausted Democratic delegates turned to James K. Polk of Tennessee, the Speaker of the House, as their candidate, the first "dark horse" presidential candidate in American history. Polk, a protégé of Andrew Jackson, was such a good orator that he was known as the "Napoleon of the stump." He was an ardent expansionist who ran on the connected slogans of "reannexation of Texas," and "reoccupation of Oregon," implying that these two territories were once part of the United States. Democrats also attacked Clay for "his blasphemy...his gambling propensities...his debaucheries and midnight revels...too shocking, too disgusting to appear in public print."

Henry Clay, known as the man who "would rather be right than president," decided that, in fact, he would rather be president than right. Alarmed by defections by southern Whigs, Clay hedged on his opposition to the annexation of Texas by declaring, "I should be glad to see it without dishonor, without war, with the common consent of the Union." Clay's retreat won few southern votes but angered thousands of antislavery Whigs who voted for James Birney, the candidate of the abolitionist Liberty Party. Although the Liberty Party succeeded in

Henry Clay (left) and James K. Polk (right)

winning only a small portion of antislavery votes, it did succeed in popularizing the image of a Slave Power conspiracy. It was an extremely close election. (Polk won the popular vote by a mere 38,000 votes and the electoral vote by 170 to 105.) Birney's 16,000 votes, drawn away from Clay, gave New York's 36 key electoral votes and the election to Polk.

Despite Polk's paper-thin victory, President Tyler and the victorious Democrats chose to interpret the election as a mandate for immediate annexation of Texas. Since he realized that he could never win the two-thirds majority required for approval of a treaty, Tyler proposed that Texas be annexed by a joint resolution of Congress. This required only a simple majority of both houses. Despite the dubious constitutionality of the measure, it passed through the votes of Democratic congressmen of both sections. President Tyler signed it three days before he left office in March 1845. Mexico severed relations with the United States, making war far more likely. Texas was admitted to the union as a slave state in December 1845.

In his message to Congress, Polk created his own addition to the Monroe Doctrine, declaring that, "The people of this continent alone have the right to decide their own destiny." (He meant the right to be annexed by the United States.) He added that European interference would not be tolerated. He was committed to an American expansionism that would spread "from sea to sea" all the way to the Pacific.

Northern Democrats had accepted the swallowing of Texas because they expected reciprocal southern support for acquiring the whole Oregon territory in the Pacific Northwest. Polk, however, while willing to incite war with Mexico to gain the Southwest, was wise enough to avoid conflict with Britain over Oregon.

The 54° 40′ slogan had served its purpose of helping to elect Polk. He began to back down, asserting, without any evidence, that the land north of the 49th parallel was unsuited to agriculture. In 1846 both nations compromised by agreeing to divide the territory at the 49th parallel to the dismay of many northern expansionists. As a result of the Oregon Treaty, the United States did gain uncontested control over present-day Oregon, Washington, Idaho, and parts of Wyoming and Montana.

The Mexican War

Relations between Polk's administration and the Mexican government rapidly disintegrated. Mexican anger over the annexation of Texas was compounded by the claim by Texans and the American government that the Rio Grande River was the southern border of Texas. When Texas was a Mexican province, the Nueces River had been the southern boundary. The disputed area would double the size of Texas. Polk also wanted to obtain as much of New Mexico and California as possible. He authorized a "scientific expedition" to California by the gallant "Pathfinder," Captain John C. Fremont and his band of well-armed "engineers." Before long, Fremont began encouraging American settlers to rise up in "self-defense."

The president sent a secret minister to Mexico at the end of 1845 to offer up to $30 million for the territories Polk coveted and to agree to assume the debts Mexico owed American citizens in return for acceptance of the Rio Grande boundary. The deeply resentful Mexican government refused to even receive Polk's envoy. In one of Mexico's numerous revolutions, a militantly nationalist regime came to power promising to regain the "stolen province" of Texas. Mexicans did not believe that the United States was much of a military threat. They saw the North Americans as a group of undisciplined small farmers who lacked any military tradition or leadership. In contrast, the Mexican army consisted of professional soldiers trained and led by generals in resplendent uniforms.

When he learned of the failure of his representative, Polk was anxious for an excuse to go to war and seize California. In January 1846, he ordered General Zachary Taylor to occupy the area of the Rio Grande while American ships blockaded the river. Polk drafted a declaration of war and waited impatiently for an incident to justify it. He was about to send the war message without any provocation when word arrived in May of a minor scuffle between American and Mexican patrols. "Notwithstanding our efforts to avoid it," Polk indignantly informed Congress, war "exists by the act of Mexico itself." Mexico, he declared, "invaded our territory and shed American blood on American soil."

Since Mexico's claim to the disputed area was probably stronger than that of the United States, it might have been fairer to say that Americans had shed Mexi-

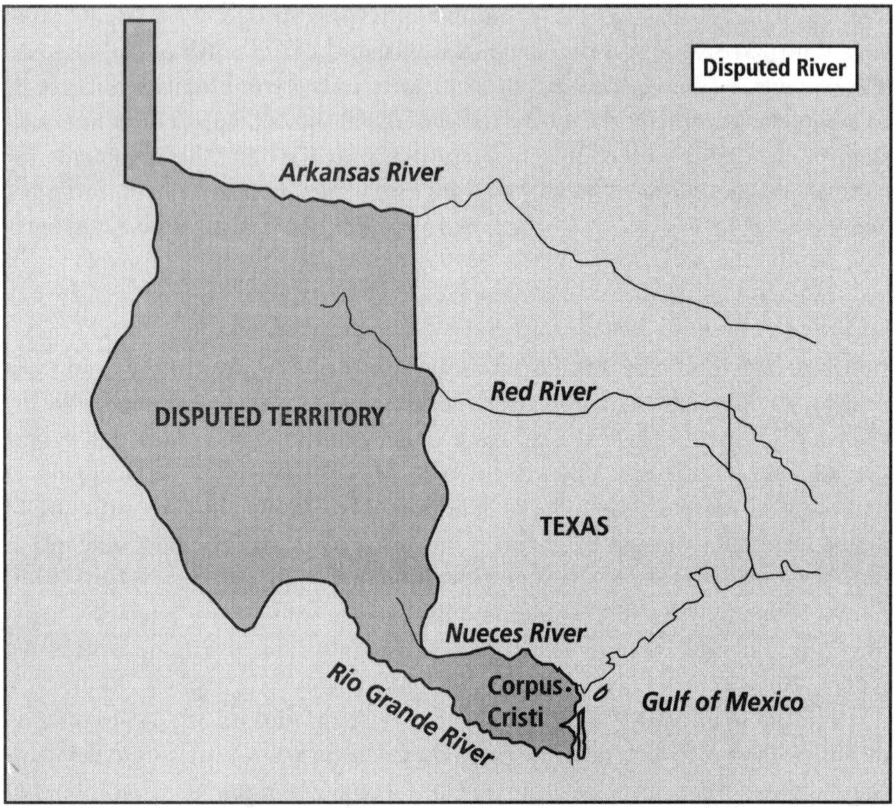

can blood on Mexican soil. This certainly was the view of abolitionists and most antislavery Whigs. They denounced "Mr. Polk's War" as brutal aggression caused by the evil "slave power conspiracy." The Massachusetts legislature even proclaimed that the war was "unconstitutional" with the purpose "of extending slavery, of strengthening the slave power, and of obtaining control of the free states." Few congressmen, however, were willing to risk their futures by voting against a war that appealed to American patriotism. Those who did demonstrate such political courage included the old warrior, John Quincy Adams, who died minutes after casting his vote against the war, and a tall young Illinois Whig, Abraham Lincoln, whose promising political career seemed over as a result. (Lincoln described the war as one "of conquest brought into existence to catch votes.") A less daring antiwar faction did emerge in Congress. It might have become more effective if the American army had not won such remarkable victories.

The army was a rather undisciplined mixture of regulars and volunteers. They were led by two stout and relatively elderly, but effective, generals: Zachary Taylor, affectionately known by his troops as Old Rough and Ready and Winfield Scott, who bore the less flattering nickname of Old Fuss and Feathers. Taylor defeated an army twice his size when he crossed the Rio Grande and occupied the important town of Monterey. Later, in February 1847, he demolished an army three times as large as his in the Battle of Buena Vista. West Point-trained officers used American artillery with deadly effectiveness. The Mexicans, who courageously advanced with flags flying, bands playing, and magnificently colorful cavalry brandishing swords and lances, were ruthlessly mowed down. Despite the heavy casualties (almost seven hundred Americans killed or wounded and twice that number of Mexicans), Buena Vista was considered a splendid victory. In California, a small detachment of regular army troops joined Fremont and rebellious settlers to win American supremacy. General Scott invaded central Mexico with fourteen thousand men and a fleet of warships. Despite disease, guerrilla warfare, the unruliness of his troops, and Mexican bravery, Scott captured the capital of Mexico City in September 1847. Polk's joy at these successes was tempered by the fact that both Taylor and Scott were Whigs.

The brilliant performances by the West Point officers saved the military academy from Democratic attempts to abolish it as an elitist and militarist institution. The war provided training for young officers who later led both Confederate and Union forces in the Civil War. These included Lee, Grant, Sherman, Meade, Thomas, McClellan, Beauregard, Stonewall Jackson, and Taylor's dashing young son-in-law, Jefferson Davis, who distinguished himself in combat. Europeans, who had not been involved in major conflict for over 30 years, were astounded by the overwhelming American victories. One British paper commented that American triumphs were unequaled, "except in that of Alexander the Great through Persia....or Napoleon over the Alps into Italy."

Southerners had provided two-thirds of the volunteer soldiers, most of the officers, and both commanding generals who had won the war. They expected to gain at least a third of Mexico as an area for further extension of slavery. Polk had sent a colorful and self-important commissioner, Nicholas Trist, to negotiate a treaty with Mexico. When Trist seemed too willing to compromise, Polk angrily recalled him. Trist, however, blithely ignored the president's communiqué and concluded the totally unauthorized Treaty of Guadalupe Hidalgo in February 1848. In the treaty, Mexico gave up all claims to Texas north of the Rio Grande and agreed to relinquish New Mexico and California in return for $15 million and the assumption of Mexican debts to Americans. (Mexico would receive another $10 million in 1853 for an additional tract of land in southern Arizona and New Mexico, the Gadsden Purchase.) These terms, virtually the same as those offered by the American government before the war, did not exploit American military victories. A furious Polk reluctantly submitted the treaty for Senate approval, fearing that any attempt to renegotiate would split his party in an election year. Polk's only recourse was to fire his envoy and denounce him an "impudent and unqualified scoundrel." The Senate ratified the treaty in March 1848.

The United States had gained an enormous territory, over a half million square miles, fulfilling the dreams of the believers in "Manifest Destiny." The costs, however, were high. These included the deaths of 13,000 Americans (11,000 from disease) and 50,000 Mexicans. Relations with Mexico and the rest of Latin America became increasingly distrustful. The domestic cost was even higher: an escalation of the bitterness between the North and the South.

Many Northerners considered the war a southern conflict whose purpose was the extension of slavery. Even as American troops were winning their victories, the great essayist, Ralph Waldo Emerson, confided to his journal: "The United States will conquer Mexico, but it will be as the man who swallows arsenic which brings him down in turn. Mexico will poison us." One of the most memorable

This cartoon displays the pride most Americans felt over Mexico's humiliating defeat in 1848.

protests against the war was Henry David Thoreau's refusal to pay taxes and his imprisonment that followed. This led to his writing of "Civil Disobedience," a great essay on the preeminence of individual conscience. Governments, he argued, are subject to injustice, "Witness the present Mexican war, the work of comparatively few individuals using the government as their tool...."

The Wilmot Proviso

The new territories in the West rapidly became the testing grounds for the competing visions of the pro and antislavery forces. In 1846, when the Mexican War was a mere three months old, Congressman David Wilmot of Pennsylvania offered an amendment to a pending bill stating "that as an express and fundamental condition to the acquisition of any territory from Mexico...neither slavery nor involuntary servitude shall ever exist in any part of said territory." The Wilmot Proviso surprised and frightened Southerners because Wilmot was not an ideological antislavery Whig. Rather, he was a northern Democrat who described himself as having, "no squeamish sensitiveness on the subject of slavery—no morbid sympathy for the slave." He favored manifest destiny but believed that the new territories must be places "where the sons of toil of my own race and own color can live without the disgrace which association with negro slavery brings upon free labor."

Northern Democrats had become increasingly resentful of southern domination of their party and control of the national government. The House of Representative approved the Wilmot Proviso several times, as all but four northern Democrats joined the unanimous northern Whigs to vote for the measure. Every northern state legislature but one endorsed the proviso. The measure lost in the more closely divided Senate. The principle, however, became the center of sectional division for the next 15 years.

Southern congressmen also united across party lines on this issue. The normal party division dissolved into sectional discord. Southerners fervently believed that slavery must continue to expand to survive. If slavery was limited to a fixed area, arable plantation land would be exhausted, and slavery would become unprofitable as the black population continued its natural growth. Iowa, Wisconsin, and, shortly thereafter, Minnesota were about to enter the union as free states. These, added to the free states carved out of this vast new territory, would overwhelm the South and destroy its ability to defend slavery. John C. Calhoun presented radical resolutions that declared that the territories were the "common property" of all the states and, therefore, Congress could not prevent the spread of slavery there. In fact, he argued, Southerners had a constitutional right to bring slaves anywhere in the territories. Clearly, this argument reversed history in which the Founding Fathers had barred slavery from the Northwest Territory, and the Missouri Compromise had excluded slavery from the larger part of the Louisiana Purchase. This sectional split posed a serious danger to a political system that had reconciled sectional differences by avoiding the issue of slavery.

The Election of 1848

In the 1848 presidential election, both major parties continued their efforts to evade the perilous issue of slavery in the new territories. President Polk, having accomplished his goals of expansionism, lower tariffs, and economic prosperity, made political history by declining to seek renomination. The Democrats nominated Senator Lewis Cass of Michigan, known for his poorly-fitting red wig and his proposal of "popular sovereignty" in the territories. This deceptively simple idea called for the settlers in each territory to decide whether it should be slave or free. This concept seemed to fit in with democracy and local self-government and would move the issue of the extension of slavery from the national to the local level. The proposal, however, was deliberately ambiguous in its details, since it never specified at which point the people in the territory could regulate slavery. Northern Democrats believed that early territorial legislatures could choose to prohibit slavery. Southerners interpreted popular sovereignty to mean that the issue of slavery could be decided only when the territory was ready to apply for statehood. The Democrats, hoping to appeal to both sections, resolutely ignored this issue and published separate versions of the Cass campaign biography in the North and South.

The Whigs went even further in avoiding the slavery issue. They adopted no platform at all. In nominating a presidential candidate, they passed over party leaders like the great senators, Henry Clay and Daniel Webster, and chose a nonpolitician, Mexican War hero and Louisiana slaveholder, General Zachary Taylor. Taylor had never even voted and only declared himself a Whig in 1848. The nation was treated to the strange sight of the antiwar party nominating a general (although one who had initially opposed the war). The stout, disheveled "Old Rough and Ready" with his tattered straw hats had been popular with his soldiers and seemed the model of democratic simplicity. His insistence that he was above party politics led to comparisons with George Washington.

The not-so-subtle evasions by both parties disturbed many antislavery people. Northern Democrats who favored the Wilmot Proviso split from their party to support Van Buren, a political opponent of Cass. (They were known as Barnburners because they were willing to destroy the Democratic barn to eliminate the proslavery "rats.") "Conscience" Whigs were unhappy to see a slaveholder at the head of their party's ticket. They saw Taylor's nomination as the result of a conspiracy between "the Lords of the Lash" (slaveholders) and "the Lords of the Loom" (textile manufacturers). The two groups, together with supporters of the Liberty Party, joined to form the Free-Soil Party. They nominated Van Buren for president and Charles Francis Adams, the son of John Quincy Adams, as his running mate. Their slogan was "Free Soil, Free Speech, Free Labor and Free Men," as they pledged an absolute ban on slavery in the territories.

The entry of the Free-Soilers into the campaign upset the two major parties' strategy of avoiding the slavery issue. Instead, both adopted an antislavery stance in the North and a proslavery one in the South. Northern Whigs pointed to their support for the Wilmot Proviso, while northern Democrats declared that popular sovereignty would enable territorial legislatures to keep slavery out. At the same time, southern Democrats emphasized their support for territorial expansion and protection of slavery. Southern Whigs stressed that a slaveholder (Taylor) could be trusted to protect southern interests far more than a Midwesterner (Cass).

Taylor won a relatively easy victory, increasing Whig support in the South and holding on to 7 of the 15 free states. Although the Free-Soilers did not win a single state, they did very well for a new third party, gaining 14 percent of the northern popular vote (10 percent overall). They also elected about a dozen congressmen who might be influential in a closely divided House. Most of the defectors reluctantly returned to their respective parties. The two-party system had survived. Underneath the surface, however, the shaky coalitions holding each party together were starting to disintegrate.

The Gold Rush and the Westward Migration

The issues became more acute as a result of events in California in 1848. A carpenter, building a sawmill for a Captain Sutter, discovered "something shining in the bottom of the ditch." He later recalled, "I reached my hand down and picked it up; it made my heart thump, for I was certain it was gold." He retrieved several nuggets and showed them to the other workers, announcing, "Boys, I believe I found a gold mine!" Sutter and the small group of men who knew about the find tried to keep it secret. According to the story, however, one of them could not resist riding into San Francisco waving a bottle of nuggets and shouting, "Gold! Gold on the American River!" The response was a wave of "gold fever" that swept the country like "wildfire," leading to one of the greatest movements of people in history. The trickle of pioneers trekking across the continent had become a flood.

Those who had more funds took the 18,000 mile six-month trip from Atlantic ports around South America to the West coast. (The trip cost $600 per person, a year's salary for a workingman.) Many of the ships crowded in far more passengers than they could accommodate. The food, disagreeable at the beginning, grew steadily worse as the voyage dragged on. Cholera, dysentery, and scurvy spread among the passengers, making the thousands of arrivals in California all the more remarkable. Others sailed to Panama where they disembarked, crossed the isthmus by land, and continued by sea. The cholera that had killed one-quarter of the native population afflicted many of the adventurers. Most, however, went overland on five- to six-month voyages across the Great Plains and over the formidable obstacles presented by the Rockies and Sierra mountain ranges. They had to overcome the ravages of cholera, conflicts with Native Americans, fatigue, and internal strife among the wagon train members to reach their final destination. Although four people could make this trip for the same financial outlay as one by ship, the cost was within the means of middle-class Americans only, well beyond the possibilities of the poor. In spite of this, some 350,000 came to California or Oregon by the overland trails between 1841 and 1867. Thousands of others journeyed part of the way to places such as Utah and Colorado.

Generous government land policies to establish farms attracted many emigrants. This was particularly true in Oregon where single men were granted 320 acres of free land and married men 640 acres if they made improvements and lived on the land for four years. These settlers set up familiar institutions such as courts, elections, schools, churches, and newspapers. By 1848, Oregon had achieved territorial status and, following the pattern of the Old Northwest, had adopted measures to bar both slavery and free black settlers. Events in California increased demands for the products of Oregon farms and forests, further stimulating the growth of Oregon.

Thousands of others sought instant riches in the gold fields of California. Few of them succeeded in making any money. Few were even able to break even. Some made fortunes that they gambled, dissipated, or speculated away. A handful became fabulously wealthy, usually by exploiting the labor of others. These capitalists eventually transformed mining into corporate industry with expensive machinery and wage laborers. Other migrants tried to make their fortunes as shopkeepers and merchants, or even washerwomen and prostitutes, determined "to prospect the miners rather than the mines." Boom towns and cities rose rapidly, though many decayed and died when the gold ran out. Racial antagonisms grew in the disorderly mining towns, directed against foreigners, particularly Mexicans ("greasers") and Chinese ("chinks"). Special taxes were levied against foreign miners in an attempt to drive them out. White miners were even more hostile to the small number of slaves brought by southern masters and free blacks, said to be "proverbially lucky" in finding gold. Whites believed that it was unfair and humiliating "to swing a pick side by side by the Negro," slave or free.

The Gold Rush had many positive and negative consequences for the nation. Forests were heedlessly stripped and rivers diverted and polluted. The national economy received an enormous stimulus. The world's gold supply doubled. The gold built cities (particularly San Francisco), harbors, and railroads. The West became a permanent part of the American imagination. "Manifest Destiny" had truly been realized. (If God did not favor America's ultimate triumph, reasoned many, why did He wait until we owned California to reveal its gold?)

Within a year, the population of California grew from 15,000 to 100,000. By 1852 it was over 220,000. Clearly, it was ready for statehood. Like most of the West, however, California, though racist, was unlikely to allow slavery. California's admission as a free state would destroy the balance of slave and free states in the Senate. And what about the rest of the Mexican Cession? Some Southerners suggested extending the Missouri Compromise line to the Pacific coast. But Northerners, determined to prevent the further extension of slavery, rejected this division of California. The very success of the new territories made the issue of slavery all the more intense.

POLITICAL EFFORTS TO DEAL WITH THE ISSUE

The Compromise of 1850

President Zachary Taylor quickly shocked his southern supporters. He had gained a national outlook from his forty years in the army. He branded proslavery extremists as "intolerant and revolutionary." In his State of the Union address Taylor urged Americans to "abstain from the introduction of those exciting topics of

Migrants streamed to California from Australia, Europe, and Latin America as well as from the eastern states. There was the hope of becoming rich overnight.

sectional character...." Any other course, he warned, would endanger the Union. "In my judgment its dissolution would be the greatest of calamities...Upon its preservation must depend our own happiness and that of countless generations to come." Taylor even declared to a startled fellow Southerner that if Congress passed the Wilmot Proviso, "I will not veto it." Southerners complained that "a Southern president with northern principles" had fooled them

The solution seemed simple to the blunt old soldier. His proposal was to bypass Congress and the problem of slavery in the territories by admitting California and New Mexico immediately as **states**. Since Mexican law had barred slavery from these territories, they would be free states. At the president's urging, California drafted a state constitution barring slavery and applied for admission to the union. To make matters worse, from the southern point of view, the free state of New Mexico would include an area claimed by Texas, a slave state.

The increasingly heated controversy set the stage for marvelous political theater featuring the three great senators of the 1830s, Calhoun, Clay, and Webster. All three were old and ill. (All would be dead by 1852.) Clay, a Whig from the border state of Kentucky, seeking to recreate his 1820 role as the Great Compromiser, proposed a comprehensive bill in January 1850 to settle all the issues dividing the country. His measure included admitting California as a free state, applying popular sovereignty to the rest of the Mexican Cession, and strengthening the Fugitive Slave Act. A seven-month debate, featuring some of the most eloquent speeches in the history of the Senate, followed Clay's articulate argument on behalf of compromise.

In March, a grim Calhoun, too ill to deliver his own speech, sat wrapped in a blanket and watched with burning eyes as a fellow Southerner delivered his prepared address. In opposing any compromise, Calhoun gravely warned that the Union was in danger. If something was not done quickly to protect southern "property" (slaves) everywhere, "the South will be forced to choose between abolition and secession." Already such bonds of Union as political parties and Christian churches had been snapped over the issue of slavery. The only way to avoid the inevitable break-up of the Union was a constitutional amendment to return to the South "the power she possessed of protecting herself before the equilibrium between the sections was destroyed." This could be achieved by having two presidents, one from each section, each having a veto over legislation. Calhoun was dead before the end of the month.

Three days later, Daniel Webster, a Whig from New Hampshire and renowned orator, replied with an anguished plea for the preservation of the Union. "I wish to speak today," he declared, "not as a Massachusetts man, nor as a northern man, but as an American...." Both sections should reject extremists. Nature and God assured that slavery could never take hold in the parched Southwest, so why offend southern honor by banning slavery there? Webster particularly condemned the idea of secession: "to break up this great government! To dismember this glorious country!.. No, Sir! There will be no Secession!" Despite this eloquence, Webster's willingness to give up the Wilmot Proviso and to endorse a strengthened fugitive slave law angered antislavery forces. Horace Mann, the great education reformer, described Webster as a "fallen star." The poet John Greenleaf Whittier best expressed the distress of many Northerners in his poem, "Ichabod":

All else is gone, from those great eyes
The soul has fled:
When faith is lost, when honor dies,
The man is dead!

Daniel Webster

Millard Fillmore

A few days after Webster's three-hour speech, Senator Seward of New York reaffirmed the antislavery opposition to any compromise that strengthened or extended slavery. Emancipation "is inevitable," he asserted, because "there is a higher law than the Constitution," the divine law under which all men were both free and equal. Southern rhetoric became even more extreme in response to Seward's declaration. Violent language led to physical clashes. Fistfights broke out on the floor of Congress and one southern senator even pulled a revolver on a colleague. In this poisonous atmosphere, the Senate voted down the compromise. An exhausted and disillusioned Clay withdrew from Washington.

News from New Mexico added fuel to the fires of controversy. Following the lead of President Taylor, that territory had drafted a free state constitution that included the area in dispute with Texas. Texans threatened a civil war over the issue. Taylor, in a very Jacksonian response, promised to use federal troops to stop any Texas invasion of New Mexico and to lead the troops himself. The crisis was defused when Taylor died suddenly of typhus fever, after having consumed gallons of ice water at a hot July 4th celebration. Millard Fillmore, who succeeded to the presidency, like many of those picked to be vice-president, had few qualifications for the highest office. As a seasoned politician, unlike Taylor, however, Fillmore did support Clay's compromise. He also quietly shelved the New Mexico constitution.

In Clay's absence, the job of managing the compromise fell to Senator Stephen Douglas, a Democrat from Illinois. Douglas, at 37 the youngest man in the Senate, was a perfectly self-confident leader with great parliamentary skills. He was also a political realist who later admitted that he did not care whether slavery in the territories was voted up or down. His strategy involved dividing Clay's combined compromise bill into five separate pieces of legislation. Each could be passed by congressmen of the section that benefited and the one-quarter of congressmen, mainly northern Democrats and border and Upper South Whigs, who would vote for both northern and southern measures in the compromise. Douglas also won some support by encouraging congressmen to invest in Texas bonds, selling for 45 cents on the dollar. These bonds would then rise to full value when Congress voted to redeem them as part of the compromise, enriching Texas bondholders, including many in Congress.

The five bills that comprised the Compromise of 1850 passed by mid-September. Two measures favored northern interests: the slave trade (although not slavery) would be prohibited in the District of Columbia, and California would enter the Union as a free state. The South gained a much more stringent fugitive slave law, and Texas got federal money for its bondholders and an adjusted boundary with New Mexico that included additional territory. The fifth bill attempted to settle the issue of slavery in the rest of the Mexican Cession that had precipitated the crisis. It divided the area into the territories of New Mexico and Utah and provided that they "shall be received into the Union, with or without slavery, as their constitution may prescribe at the time of their admission." This seeming acceptance of "popular sovereignty" was deliberately vague. It avoided the southern view that slave property must be protected in the territories, at least, until statehood. But, it also did not endorse the northern view that territorial legislatures could bar slavery. While the door may have been left open for its possible expansion, the central issue of slavery in the territories was far from settled.

In 1850 the crisis was, at least, postponed. Most Americans joyously celebrated the "final and irrevocable settlement" (in the words of President Fillmore) of their differences. In fact, however, there had been no real compromise. Majorities of northern and southern congressmen had voted against those measures they considered to be against the interests of their section. Few were willing to compromise with the views of their opponents. Perhaps the term coined by a later historian, "the Armistice of 1850," was more accurate.

The Fugitive Slave Law

The passage of the Fugitive Slave Act, little debated at first, turned out to be the most significant part of the Compromise of 1850 and the most revealing of its essential fragility. The law, that southern congressmen insisted upon, probably did more to stir up northern antagonism towards slavery than any other event. Southerners were angry about abolitionist publicity given to heroic escapes from slavery and the romanticized "Underground Railroad" (which was never as widespread as the legend implied). Although probably fewer than one thousand slaves

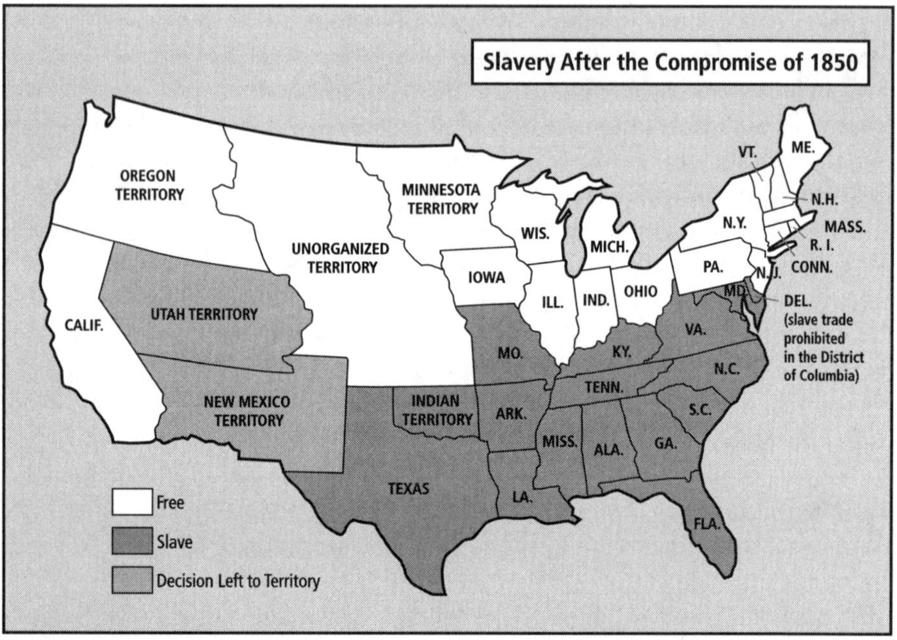

escaped to the North in a year, their symbolic importance increased through abolitionist circulation of the autobiographies of some of them and the success of others as effective orators on the antislavery circuit. (Frederick Douglass was the most famous.) Northern Personal Liberty Laws in the 1840s prevented state authorities from taking part in the arrest or imprisonment of suspected fugitive slaves. Southerners demanded tough federal legislation, willingly abandoning their supposed devotion to states' rights when their interests were at stake.

Under the new law, federal commissioners were given total authority to issue warrants for the arrest and return of runaway slaves. A class of professional slave catchers arose to take advantage of the law. The slave owner or his agent had only to present an affidavit claiming ownership. The fugitive had no right to testify in rebuttal, and there was no jury trial. The slave commissioner would receive a $10 fee if he ruled in favor of the claimant but only $5 if he freed the accused fugitive. (One antislavery commentator noted that a slave was worth $1000 but the soul of a Yankee only $5.) The commissioner could force bystanders to assist or to take part in local posses to round up fugitives, with stiff penalties for refusal. Southerners believed that this act would lessen antislavery agitation by involving Northerners in supporting the institution. Obviously, the opposite occurred. Many Northerners agreed with Ralph Waldo Emerson that it was "a filthy law" that no one could obey "without loss of self-respect."

Rather than remaining an abstract institution that existed in the distant South, slavery developed a human face for many Northerners. Professional slave catchers arrived in northern cities where they were denounced as criminal "kidnappers." In several northern cities, particularly Boston, angry mobs harassed slave hunters and attempted to rescue their quarry. Most "vigilance committees" favored non-violent resistance, but others agreed with Frederick Douglass' argument in favor of the "rightfulness of forcible resistance." Douglass, whose concerned friends purchased his freedom, suggested that perhaps the best way to make the Fugitive Slave Act a dead letter was "to make a dozen or more dead kidnappers." Blacks in Christiana Pennsylvania resisted a posse formed to return four runaways to a Maryland owner. Singing, "I will die on the field of battle/Die on the field of battle,/With glory in my soul," they drove the posse away, killing the slave owner and wounding his son. No jury could be found to convict them. An influential Boston paper commented on the incident, "All the natural rights...are on the fugitive's side. He did only what any white man would be applauded for doing."

The most distressing fugitive slave case of the 1850s was that of Margaret Garner and her four children. The family had escaped to Cincinnati in 1856. The owner traced them, and a U.S. marshal's posse came to arrest them. Margaret Garner resolved to kill her children rather than allow them to be sent back into slavery. She slashed her daughter's throat but was prevented from doing the same

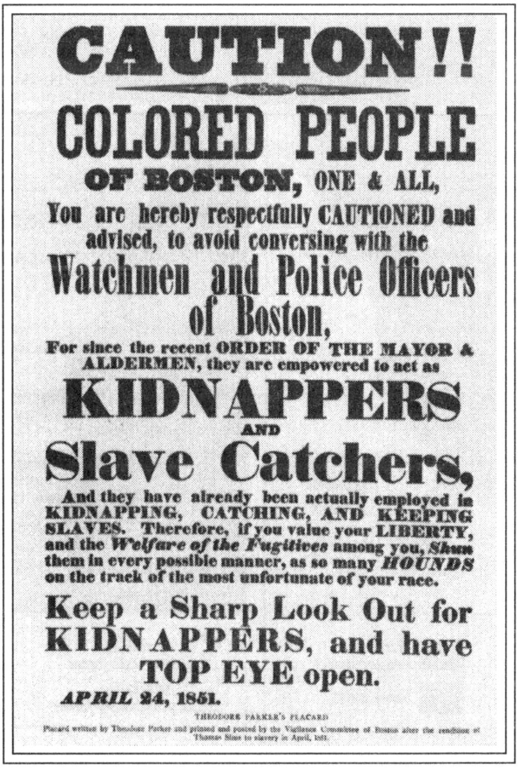

Professional slave catchers arrived in northern cities where they were denounced as criminal "kidnappers." In several northern cities, particularly Boston, angry mobs harassed slave hunters and attempted to rescue their quarry.

to her sons. Despite efforts by Ohio courts to keep her and try her for murder, she and her surviving children were returned to their owner. Her baby was killed in a steamboat accident on the way to the New Orleans slave market. There, she and her two remaining sons were sold to a new master.

Abolitionists received a propaganda bonanza as appalled northern whites witnessed the return to slavery of hard working people who had lived among them as good citizens for many years. After a few successful rescues in Boston, the local vigilance committee was ready in 1854 when slave catchers suddenly seized Anthony Burns, an escaped Virginia slave, from the clothing store where he worked. The federal government resolved to make an example of this case after repulsing an assault on the federal courthouse. Federal troops marched Burns to a ship waiting to carry him back to slavery. Tens of thousands of distraught Bostonians bitterly looked on as flags flew at half-mast and the bells of the city's churches "tolled the death of liberty" in the place that had given birth to the Revolution. A conservative attorney, who had earlier opposed defiance of the law, wrote that when it was all over and he was alone, "I put my face in my hands and wept. I could do nothing else." It had cost $100,000 (equal to more than $2 million today) to restore this one black to slavery.

Anthony Burns was the last fugitive returned from New England. (A Boston committee later purchased his freedom.) Thousands of northern blacks made their way to Canada to avoid being captured. New personal liberty laws made it much more difficult and costly to catch runaways. In the states where these new laws were passed, only twenty-seven slaves were returned after 1854. In total, at great expense in time and money, perhaps three hundred blacks returned to slavery under the act. This was about the same number as one fugitive slave, Harriet Tubman, had led to freedom. In 1859, the Supreme Court, in *Ableman v. Booth*, ruled that the Fugitive Slave Law was constitutional, and any state interference with exacting compliance was illegal. The irony of this decision was that the South, supposed supporters of states' rights, cheered this assertion of the supremacy of federal law in the face of northern support for state sovereignty. Clearly, slavery was a far more fundamental issue than that of states' rights.

Uncle Tom's Cabin

The publication of one of America's all-time best-sellers, Harriet Beecher Stowe's *Uncle Tom's Cabin,* both illustrated and intensified northern loathing of slave hunting. The book, written as a result of Stowe's anguish at the passage of the Fugitive Slave Act, was first published in serial form in 1851. Packed with marvelous characters and breath-taking dramatic events, each month's episode ended with a suspenseful gripping situation. The following year it was published in full. Within nine months, 300,000 copies were sold, a million by the following year. For the

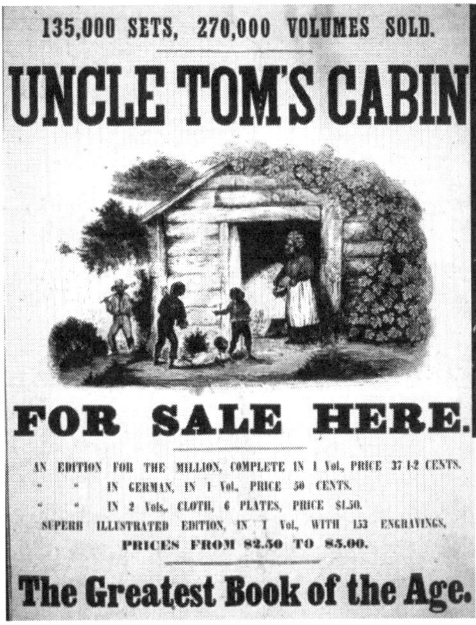

Harriet Beecher Stowe, author of *Uncle Tom's Cabin*

first time in American literature, black characters were real people who suffered the agonies of slavery. The book quickly became a play. There were productions in virtually every northern city and town where even illiterate people could cheer a slave mother fleeing across a frozen river with her baby and hiss the classic villain, Simon Legree. The vivid depiction of slavery's destruction of the purity of family life and the saintly character of Uncle Tom stirred northern evangelical Protestants. The novel indicted both Northerners and Southerners for their willingness to compromise with an immoral institution. Its emotional impact was enormous. Southerners felt the need to respond with novels showing the happy life enjoyed by "darkies" under slavery. Only Thomas Paine's *Common Sense* of the Revolutionary era made an equivalent impression on American public opinion. Ten years later, President Lincoln reportedly, and perhaps unfairly, remarked when he was introduced to Mrs. Stowe, "So you're the little woman that wrote the book that made this great war."

While politicians congratulated themselves on the apparent success of the Compromise of 1850, the passions aroused by the Fugitive Slave Act and the popularity of *Uncle Tom's Cabin* revealed the shaky foundations of compromise. As Northerners found slavery increasingly distasteful, Southerners went to greater extremes in its defense. A few went as far as to argue that slavery was not merely a "positive good" in its paternalistic protection of slaves but that it was such a perfect system of labor management that the North should adopt it for the factory system!

The Election of 1852

The Whig Party was in serious trouble. Southerners believed that they could no longer trust northern Whigs to be their allies. Northern anger at the Fugitive Slave Act had reinforced the antislavery wing of the party in the North. The hurt from President Taylor's "betrayal" remained strong. In addition, the country experienced an economic boom fueled by spending during the Mexican War, the gold pouring in from California, and the surge of cheap labor from Ireland. This undercut the traditional Whig appeal for government intervention in the economy that had once won the support of commercially oriented Southerners.

Hoping to replicate their success of four years earlier, the Whigs turned to another hero of the Mexican War, General Winfield Scott. Clay and Webster, the old lions of Whig leadership, both died, and the party rejected its own prosouthern president, Millard Fillmore, after a bruising 52-ballot struggle. The Democrats, following an equally lengthy convention, came up with a "dark horse." He was their own less-distinguished Mexican War general, the colorless Franklin Pierce, a proslavery Yankee from New Hampshire. Both parties carefully avoided any clear-cut issues and emphasized personalities in another of the many "dirty" campaigns of the era. Whigs attacked Pierce, who had left the Senate because of a drinking problem, as a drunkard. Democrats mercilessly ridiculed Scott, the old hero once known as "Old Fuss and Feathers," for his appearance and vanity. The voters were so turned off by all of this that one observer reported that "General Apathy" was the main candidate in his state.

The Whigs suffered a disastrous defeat, as Scott won only 42 electoral votes to Pierce's 254. Although the popular vote was closer, the Whigs lost all the slave states of the Deep South. Their popular vote in the South fell from 50 to 35 percent in four years. One former southern Whig leader ruefully declared that in the South, "the Whig party is dead." The Whigs had become a squabbling northern party. The two-party system that had once held the forces of disunion in check was on the verge of total collapse.

The Rise of the Know-Nothings

The refusal of political parties to take stands on issues of significance to the public led to the voters' growing disgust. As evidence increased that politicians were openly selling their votes, public anger over corruption grew. Many native-born Protestants believed that foreign-born Catholics caused the overwhelming dishonesty infecting the body politic. More than three million immigrants entered the United States in the decade before 1855, the largest proportional increase in American history. More than half of these immigrants were Catholics, largely unskilled laborers. Protestant workers were convinced that the Catholic "men-

Know-Nothings often charged that immigrant voters were stealing American elections. This cartoon depicts German and Irish immigrants, represented by German beer and Irish whiskey, stealing a ballot box.

ace" harmed hard-working people by flooding the market with cheap labor. They blamed Catholics for drinking alcohol freely and openly, increasing crime and poverty, and following strange rites in their churches. In deeply Protestant America, large numbers of people had arrived whose way of life threatened American individualism by their subordination to the absolute authority of a foreign "monarch," the Pope. When the Catholics pushed to prevent the reading of the Protestant Bible in public schools and to gain public funds for their parochial schools, it seemed further evidence of a Catholic plot to destroy American democratic institutions. In addition, increasing numbers of the new immigrants were able to vote by the 1850s, and they supported a Democratic Party that seemed more tolerant of differences in religion and personal behavior. Anti-immigration nativists were certain that these Catholics slavishly obeyed the dictates of their priests.

In response to this perceived danger, many nativist Protestants turned to secret anti-immigrant, anti-Catholic organizations such as the Order of the Star Spangled Banner, which eventually became the American Party. When asked by outsiders about the party or its organization, the members were supposed to respond, "I know nothing." In state and local elections of 1854, secret Know-Nothing tickets swept to victory in Massachusetts and other areas on an unprecedented tide of write-in votes, dumbfounding old-time party leaders with its "hurricane" force. By 1855, the Know-Nothings won control of most of New England and were the main opposition to the Democrats in the Middle Atlantic states, California, the border states, and the Upper South. They became the political wild card, providing the final blow in the collapse of the Whigs. (They appealed to the very middle-class and skilled working-class voters who had been the backbone of the Whig Party.)

Some antislavery leaders refused to succumb to the tide of nativist sentiment. In Illinois, Abraham Lincoln, an antislavery Whig, declared his opposition to the Know-Nothings, "How can any one who abhors the oppression of negroes, be in favor of degrading classes of white people?" he asked. In office, the Know-Nothings failed to achieve their goals of restricting immigration or even of lengthening the five years residency required for citizenship. Their lack of political savvy led to their eventual absorption by the new Republican Party by 1856. Their greatest significance was in helping to destroy the discipline of the existing party system that had restrained sectional conflict. The Kansas Nebraska Act provided the final blow in the destruction of that system, increasing the likelihood of sectional strife.

DOCUMENTS

THE MEXICAN WAR

James K. Polk, who was elected president in 1844, was a firm believer in Manifest Destiny. He was committed to obtaining American territory in the Southwest to the Pacific Ocean. After the failure of his efforts to purchase this land from Mexico, he was willing to use other methods to achieve his goals. He ordered American troops into a disputed region between the Rio Grande River, which the U.S. claimed constituted the southwestern boundary of the new state of Texas, and the Nueces River, Mexico's stated boundary. Shots were fired in the disputed area, and Polk used the clash as a pretext to declare war.

While most Americans enthusiastically supported the war, many Whigs and northern antislavery advocates were vocal in their opposition. The poet James Russell Lowell was one of the latter. Lowell wrote many poems in a rural Yankee dialect spoken by a fictional spokesman, Hosea Biglow.

Polk's War Message

The strong desire to establish peace with Mexico on liberal and honourable terms, and the readiness of this Government to regulate and adjust our boundary and other causes of difference with that power on such fair and equitable principles as would lead to permanent relations of the most friendly nature, induced me in September last [1845] to seek the reopening of diplomatic relations between the two countries. Every measure adopted on our part had for its object the furtherance of these desired results. In communicating to Congress a succinct statement of the injuries we had suffered from Mexico, and which have been accumulating during a period of more than twenty years, every expression that could tend to inflame the people of Mexico or defeat or delay a pacific result was carefully avoided. An envoy of the United States John Slidell repaired to Mexico with full powers to adjust every existing difference. But though present on Mexican soil by agreement between the two Governments, invested with full powers, and bearing evidence of the most friendly dispositions, his mission has been unavailing. The Mexican Government not only refused to see him or listen to his propositions, but after a long-continued series of menaces have at last invaded our territory and shed the blood of our fellow-citizens on our own soil ....

Thus the Government of Mexico, though solemnly pledged by official acts in October last to receive and accredit an American envoy, violated their plighted faith and refused the offer of a peaceful adjustment of our difficulties. Not only was the offer rejected, but the indignity of its rejection was enhanced by the manifest breach of faith in refusing to admit the envoy who came because they had bound themselves to receive him....

In my message at the commencement of the present session [of Congress] I informed you that upon the earnest appeal of the Congress and the convention of Texas I had ordered an efficient military force to take a position between "the Nueces and the [Rio Grande] Del Norte." This had become necessary to meet a threatened invasion of Texas by the Mexican forces, for which extensive military preparations had been made. The invasion was threatened solely because Texas had determined, in accordance with a solemn resolution of the Congress of the United States, to annex herself to our Union, and under these circumstances it was plainly our duty to extend our protection over her citizens and soil....

The movement of the troops to the Del Norte was made by the commanding general under positive instructions to abstain from all aggressive acts toward Mexico or Mexican citizens and to regard the relations between that Republic and the United States as peaceful unless she should declare war or commit acts of hostility indicative of a state of war. He was specially directed to protect private property and respect personal rights.

The Army moved from Corpus Christi on the 11th of March, and on the 28th of that month arrived on the left bank of the Del Norte opposite to Matamoras, where it encamped on a commanding position, which has since been strengthened by the erection of fieldworks. A depot has also been established at Point Isabel, near the Brazos Santiago, 30 miles in rear of the encampment. The selection of his position was necessarily confided to the judgment of the general in command.

The Mexican forces at Matamoras assumed a belligerent attitude, and on the 12th of April General Ampudia, then in command, notified General [Zachary] Taylor to break up his camp within twenty-four hours and to retire beyond the Nueces River, and in the event of his failure to comply with these demands announced that arms, and arms alone, must decide the question. But no open act of hostility was committed until the 24th of April. On that day General Arista, who had succeeded to the command of the Mexican forces, communicated to General Taylor that "he considered hostilities commenced and should prosecute them." A party of dragoons of 63 men and officers were on the same day dispatched from the American camp up the Rio del Norte, on its left bank, to ascertain whether the Mexican troops had crossed or were preparing to cross the river, "became engaged with a large body of these troops, and after a short affair, in which some

16 were killed and wounded, appear to have been surrounded and compelled to surrender."

The grievous wrongs perpetrated by Mexico upon our citizens throughout a long period of years remain unredressed, and solemn treaties pledging her public faith for this redress have been disregarded. A government either unable or unwilling to enforce the execution of such treaties fails to perform one of its plainest duties.

Our commerce with Mexico has been almost annihilated. It was formerly highly beneficial to both nations, but our merchants have been deterred from prosecuting it by the system of outrage and extortion which the Mexican authorities have pursued against them, whilst their appeals through their own Government for indemnity have been made in vain. Our forbearance has gone to such an extreme as to be mistaken in its character. Had we acted with vigor in repelling the insults and redressing the injuries inflicted by Mexico at the commencement, we should doubtless have escaped all the difficulties in which we are now involved.

Instead of this, however, we have been exerting our best efforts to propitiate her good will. Upon the pretext that Texas, a nation as independent as herself, thought proper to unite its destinies with our own, she has affected to believe that we have severed her rightful territory, and in official proclamations and manifestoes has repeatedly threatened to make war upon us for the purpose of reconquering Texas. In the meantime we have tried every effort at reconciliation. The cup of forbearance had been exhausted even before the recent information from the frontier of the Del Norte. But now, after reiterated menaces, Mexico has passed the boundary of the United States, has invaded our territory and shed American blood upon the American soil. She has proclaimed that hostilities have commenced, and that the two nations are now at war.

As war exists, and, notwithstanding all our efforts to avoid it, exists by the act of Mexico herself, we are called upon by every consideration of duty and patriotism to vindicate with decision the honor, the rights, and the interests of our country.

James D. Richardson ed., *A Compilation of the Messages and Papers of the Presidents* (New York: Bureau of National Literature 1896), vol. 5, pp. 2287-93.

1. Do you think Polk was sincere in his list of grievances against Mexico? Which argument was most convincing?
2. Do you believe Polk really wanted "to establish peace with Mexico on liberal and honorable terms"? Or was he merely using this as an excuse to fulfill his territorial goals?
3. How would this message have been received in the United States? In Mexico?

The Mexican War is on Behalf of Slavery
by James Russell Lowell

'T would n't suit them Southun fellers,
They're a dreffle' graspin'set,
We must ollers' blow the bellers'
Wen they want their irons het';
May be it's all right ez preachin ;
But my narves it kind o'grates,
Wen I see the overreachin'
O' them nigger-driven' States . . .

Ez fer war, I call it murder,
There you hev it plain an' flat;
I don't want to go no furder
Than my Testyment fer that;
God hez sed so plump an' fairly,
It's ez long ez it is broad,
An' you've gut to git up airly
Ef you want to take in God ....

Wut's the use o'meetin-goin'
Every Sabbath, wet or dry,
Ef it's right to go amowin'
Feller-men like oats an' rye?
I dunno but wet it's pooty
Trainin' round in botail coats,
But it's curus Christian dooty
This 'ere cuttin' folks's throats.

They may talk o'Freedom's airy'
Tell they're pupple in the face,
It's a grand gret eemetary
For the barthrights of our race;
They jest want this Californy
So's to lug new slave-states in
To abuse ye, an' to scorn ye,
An' to plunder ye like sin.

Aint it cute' to see a Yankee
Take sech everlastin' pains,
All to get the Devil's thankee
Helpin' on 'em weld their chains!
Wy, it's jest ez clear ez figgers,
Clear ez one an' one make two,
Chaps thet make black slaves o' niggers
Want to make wite slaves o' you.

James Russell Lowell, *The Biglow Papers* (Boston, 1891), pp. 64-70.

1. What theory about the real cause of the Mexican War is advanced by "Biglow"? Who would have agreed with that theory?
2. What do the last two lines tell you about the reasons for northern opposition to new slave territory?
3. What does the use of the word "nigger" by a fervent antislavery supporter tell you about racism in America at the time?

JOHN BROWN

Chapter Five

THE STORM CLOUD BURST

TERRITORIAL ISSUES AND KANSAS-NEBRASKA

Although continued American expansionism had not been an issue in the presidential election of 1852, the new president, Pierce, was determined to duplicate the accomplishments of Polk in adding American territory. While attempts to buy large sections of northern Mexico failed, the Gadsden Purchase did gain a strip of desert on the southwestern border. This facilitated the building of a transcontinental railroad linking the South to the Pacific Coast. American adventurers, known as "filibusterers," were encouraged by southern support to stage raids into Mexico and Central America with the purpose of adding slave territories (in addition to personal wealth and glory). The most famous, William Walker, became a southern hero by launching three invasions of Nicaragua with southern backing. After some brief successes, his storybook career was ended by a firing squad.

More realistic expansionist hopes focused on Cuba, which had been shaken by unrest. Proslavery expansionists longed to acquire the slave-holding island that might be divided into several more slave states. When Spain refused to sell its possession, American ministers to Spain, France, and Britain met and drafted a memorandum declaring that Cuba "belongs naturally" to the United States. They added that, if Spain continued its opposition, "by every law, human and Divine, we shall be justified in wresting it from Spain." This "Ostend Manifesto" was leaked to the press and confirmed northern belief in the Slave Power's conspiratorial expansionism. Southern attempts to gain new slave territory helped to further undermine the "Armistice of 1850."

The passage of the Kansas-Nebraska Act confirmed the worst suspicions of Northerners. Stephen Douglas, who opened this pandora's box of sectional hostilities, was largely uninterested in the issue of the expansion of slavery. He was, however, a great believer in Manifest Destiny, which, he believed, could be most completely fulfilled by the building of a transcontinental railroad. As a senator from Illinois, he expected Chicago to become the hub of this development. He counted upon the railroad to create a tremendous economic boom that the nation would credit to Democratic policy. He also had speculated in Chicago real estate and in railroad stock, both of which would benefit. The plan, however, depended upon congressional approval of a bill to organize the Nebraska territory through which the railroad would run. That part of the Louisiana Purchase was north of the 36 30' line where slavery was forbidden. Southerners would never agree to the creation of more free territory. Douglas' bill divided the area into two territories: Kansas and Nebraska. Both would be subject to popular sovereignty in the same vague language used in the Compromise of 1850. To further placate Southerners, the bill declared that the Missouri Compromise was "inoperable and void." Douglas did not consider this important, since he felt that the climate and soil of the territories would keep slavery out.

To the astonishment of Douglas and his supporters, an angry storm swept through the North. Free Soil and other antislavery members of Congress quickly published an "Appeal of the Independent Democrats," denouncing the Kansas-Nebraska Act as part of "an atrocious plot" by the Slave Power to turn the West into a "dreary region of despotism inhabited by masters and slaves." It was an enormously effective piece of political propaganda that convinced many Northerners that the Slave Power was breaking its "sacred pledge" (the Missouri Compromise) and violating America's God-given mission to be a light of freedom to the world.

Douglas, using all of his considerable political skills, did succeed in gaining the passage of the Kansas-Nebraska Act after a three-month struggle. With the help of President Pierce, Douglas persuaded forty-four reluctant northern Democrats in the House to vote with the Southerners to pass the bill. The very triumph that he had hoped would win him a presidential nomination in 1856 turned into a disaster for northern Democrats. To Douglas, the issue had been one of economics rather than righteousness. But many Northerners believed basic morality had been violated. They spoke of Douglas as "the Benedict Arnold of 1854." One incensed group of citizens sent him thirty pieces of silver. As Douglas traveled home, he spotted so many likenesses of himself hanging from trees and lamp posts and set on fire that he commented wryly, "I could travel from Boston to Chicago by the light of my own effigy." One observer later declared that the bill created more abolitionists in two months than 20 years of struggle by the movement's leaders had produced.

The transcontinental railroad bill that had been the final objective of all of Douglas' maneuvers remained bottled up in congressional committees for the rest of the decade. This was a result of the sectional rivalries aggravated by the Kansas-Nebraska Act. By the summer of 1854, coalitions were forming against "the Nebraska outrage." In the congressional elections that fall, an astounding 66 of 91 northern Democrats went down in defeat, including all but 7 of the 44 who had voted for the Kansas-Nebraska Act. In addition, the Democrats lost all but two of the legislatures in the North. The Democrats had become a largely southern party and remained so for many years to come.

The Rise of the Republican Party

The main beneficiary of the Democratic catastrophe was the new Republican Party, which had been formed by anti-Nebraska Whigs, Democrats, and Free Soilers. That was not totally clear at first, since the Know-Nothings had won more votes in several states. (Most northern congressmen elected in 1854 were both Know-Nothings and Republicans.) By 1856, however, the Republicans had absorbed the northern Know-Nothings. The Republicans combined opposition to both slavery and Catholicism, labeling both examples of backwardness and subjugation. They included the dynamic capitalist ideology of the Whigs and Protestant reformist views. They revived the principle of the Wilmot Proviso as their primary doctrine: no slavery in any territory and no more slave states. Alarmed Southerners saw them as "Black Republicans," the nation's first purely sectional major party.

The election of 1856 took place barely two years after the Republicans' first appearance as a party. The Republicans nominated Colonel John C. Fremont, the adventurous young "Pathfinder," renowned for his exploits in the conquest of California. Their platform called for a free Kansas and reaffirmed the need "to prohibit in the territories those twin relics of barbarism—Polygamy, and Slavery." They marched in giant torchlight parades, chanting their slogan, "Free Soil, Free Labor, Free Men, Fremont."

The Democrats tried to avoid any candidate too closely associated with the Kansas-Nebraska Act. They settled on the undistinguished party regular, James Buchanan of Pennsylvania, a "northern man with southern principles." Buchanan had the added advantage of having been out of the country as minister to Britain during the Pierce administration and was, thus, untainted by the Kansas controversy. What was left of the American Party, supported by last-ditch Whigs, selected ex-president Millard Fillmore, the third candidate. In addition to endorsing popular sovereignty in the territories, the Democrats sought to exploit the issues of racism and fear of disunion in the lower North. The election, they declared, would show whether Northerners preferred "niggers...to their own race and color and the Union and all its countless blessings." Buchanan won with 45 percent of the popular vote. He carried 14 of the 15 slave states (Fillmore took Maryland), but Fremont won 11 of the 16 free states. The American Party vote in the lower North cost Fremont the election. The Republican showing was remarkable for a new party. Buchanan's election was a southern victory, but it ultimately led to a strengthening of the antislavery forces in the North.

"Bleeding Kansas"

One of the most explosive issues in the campaign had been the situation in Kansas. Senator Seward of New York accepted the challenge of his southern colleagues "in behalf of the cause of freedom," to compete "for the virgin soil of Kansas." Free Soilers quickly organized the New England Emigrant Aid Society to encourage antislavery settlement of Kansas. The 1,200 or so New Englanders sent by this organization were only a small fraction of those who had settled in Kansas by 1856. Most genuine settlers were Midwesterners more concerned with grabbing land titles, speculating, and defrauding Indians than with slavery. They did not like the idea of blacks, whether slave or free, in their state. One such emigrant declared, "I kem to Kansas to live in a free state and I don't want niggers a-trampin' over my grave." Southerners, however, believed that a "vast moneyed corporation" was recruiting abolitionist hordes armed with "Beecher's Bibles" (so-called because noted antislavery minister Henry Ward Beecher had suggested that

"Border Ruffians" headed for Kansas from Missouri to cast ballots with rifles in hand.

Sharp's rifles might be of greater use than Bibles to those fighting for the Lord in Kansas). In response, thousands of "border ruffians" crossed into Kansas from Missouri to harass free-staters and to fraudulently cast ballots for a proslavery legislature in 1855. The "bogus" legislature then passed laws depriving antislavery Kansans of any rights. (Distributing abolitionist literature became a capital offense.) These actions served to confirm northern fears of the Slave Power conspiracy. Angry free-state settlers, by now a substantial majority, held their own extra-legal elections and drew up a constitution that banned both slavery and free blacks. Kansas now had two governments—one supposedly legal but fraudulent, the other illegitimate but clearly representative of most of the settlers.

Scattered violence erupted as the two "governments" attempted to enforce their rule. On May 21, 1856, a proslavery force sacked the free-state town of Lawrence, destroying its two newspapers and burning down its hotel and some of the houses of free-state leaders. On the following day, southern Congressman Brooks bashed northern Senator Sumner on the floor of the Senate. These incidents strengthened the image of the barbarous Slave Power, reinforced by reports from Kansas by northern correspondents. Republican banners in the 1856 elections coupled "Bleeding Kansas" with "Bleeding Sumner."

In Kansas an abolitionist named John Brown saw himself as an instrument of God's vengeance. He was ready to "fight fire with fire" when he learned about Lawrence, and word of the caning of Sumner sent him into a "frenzy." On the evening of May 24, Brown and his small band (including four of his sons) arrived at Pottawatomie Creek. They dragged five supposedly proslavery settlers out of their beds and split their skulls open with broadswords. The northern press largely ignored this bloody massacre, but it did lead to full-scale conflict in Kansas. Although the national press exaggerated the scale of the "battles," continued skirmishes caused some two hundred deaths. Eventually, a more effective governor succeeded in bringing about a troubled peace in the territory.

Preston Brooks entered the Senate chamber and grasped his golf-headed walking stick and beat Senator Sumner over the head with it until the caner broke.

John Brown, believing with messianic zeal that slavery could be ended only by the sword, massacred five southern sympathizers in Kansas.

By 1857, it was clear to any impartial observer that the overwhelming majority of settlers in Kansas opposed slavery. The Pierce administration had originally recognized the proslavery "legislature." The new Buchanan administration, believing that it must placate its southern supporters, compounded the earlier miscalculations. Buchanan supported the pro-slavery Lecompton Constitution that had been drawn up by a convention chosen by a small minority of eligible voters. Stephen Douglas saw this as a travesty of the idea of popular sovereignty on which he had staked his political career. Buchanan was a lonely bachelor who devoted himself to the Democratic Party and believed unquestioned loyalty was the greatest virtue a politician could have. He tried to pressure wavering Democrats, leading to a bitter split with Douglas. (When the president noted that the great Andrew Jackson had crushed all Democrats who opposed him, Douglas replied that Jackson was dead now.) Revolvers were openly flashed and, during one all-night debate, a wild fistfight broke out among thirty congressmen. Buchanan ultimately suffered a shattering defeat. Northern Democrats forced a compromise that sent the Lecompton Constitution back to Kansas for a popular vote. The voters rejected it by a 6 to 1 margin, even though the price was postponing statehood. Eventually, Kansas did enter the union as a free state in 1861. The Democratic Party suffered an irreparable split from which it never recovered. Despite this, Buchanan assured the nation that he did not regret his decision to support the Lecompton Constitution. "In the course of my long public life," he insisted, "I have never performed any official act which in the retrospect has afforded me more heartfelt satisfaction." That could be the measure of his administration.

The Crime Against Kansas / The Crime Against Sumner

On May 19, 1856, Senator Charles Sumner of Massachusetts, a leader of the anti-slavery forces, rose on the floor of the Senate to deliver a passionate speech he called, "The Crime Against Kansas." He decried, "the rape of a virgin territory, compelling it to the hateful embrace of slavery...." to a gallery crowded with anti-slavery representatives from the House as well as the Senate. "Even now while I speak," he warned darkly, "portents lower in the horizon, threatening to darken the land, which already palpitates with the mutterings of civil war." During his tirade, which lasted two days, Sumner reserved some of his strongest language for Senator Andrew Butler of South Carolina. Butler's mistress, he charged, was the "harlot slavery." All decent and just men must work "to dislodge from the high places that tyrannical sectionalism of which the Senator from South Carolina is one of the maddest zealots." Sumner concluded his "last appeal" in the name of "the Constitution outraged, of the laws trampled down...of humanity degraded...of freedom crushed to earth," and, finally, "in the name of the Heavenly Father whose service is perfect freedom...."

Even in an era of unrestrained oratory, Sumner's speech was unusually bitter and provocative in its sexual allusions in a prudish age. Northern Democrats, like Stephen Douglas, rose to denounce Sumner's words as "unfit for decent young men to read." "Is it his object," Douglas inquired, "to provoke some of us to kick him just as we would a dog in the street, that he may get sympathy upon just chastisement?" The speech, however, was rapidly reprinted for distribution in the North where it gained the admiration of many. The poet, Henry Wadsworth Longfellow, for one, wrote to Sumner to congratulate him on his "brave and noble speech," which was "the greatest voice on the greatest subject, that has been uttered since we became a nation."

Preston Brooks, a young congressman from South Carolina, who was a relative and protégé of Senator Butler, resented the personal attacks upon the older man. Brooks, a tall handsome man with "sparkling eyes," was considered "amiable and friendly" by his colleagues. But he decided that "family honor" demanded that he "punish" Sumner. On May 22, he entered the Senate chamber and came up behind Sumner, denouncing the "libel on South Carolina and Mr. Butler." He grasped his gold-headed walking stick and beat Sumner over the head with it until the cane broke. Unable to defend himself because his legs were pinned under his desk, Sumner slumped to the floor, bleeding and unconscious, seriously injured.

Not a single southern Senator condemned the attack. The vote to expel Brooks from the House failed to receive the necessary two-thirds majority when the South-

erners all voted against it. Brooks resigned but was unanimously reelected by his district and exultantly returned to Congress. The South rejoiced in Brooks' defense of southern honor, showering him with praise and hundreds of new walking sticks sent by admiring constituents to "whip some more Yankees."

The North, however, saw the incident as evidence of southern brutality rather than nobility. The New York ***Evening Post*** *bitingly asked, "Are we too, slaves, slaves for life, a target for their brutal blows, when we do not comport ourselves to please them?" George Templeton Strong, a conservative New Yorker who believed "antislavery agitators" to be "wrong in principle and mischievous in policy," nevertheless added, "But the reckless, insolent brutality of our Southern aristocrats may drive me to abolitionism yet." Northerners, he noted, were busy making money and were "law abiding and peace loving." Southern aristocrats claimed to be highly civilized, gallant, chivalrous gentlemen, "whereas I believe they are in fact a race of lazy, ignorant, coarse, sensual, swaggering, sordid, beggarly barbarians...."*

The distaste generated in the North, in reaction to Brooks' assault, drove thousands of undecided voters into the fold of the new Republican Party. In the 1856 election campaign the party's banners included "Bleeding Sumner" alongside "Bleeding Kansas." In January 1857, the Massachusetts state legislature unanimously reelected Sumner as Senator and party martyr. For three years, as he slowly recovered, his Senate seat remained empty, a mute reminder of the nation's bitter divisions and a valuable addition to the anti-slavery cause. Sumner was eventually able to return to the Senate and to continue his fight for racial justice until his death in 1874. Ironically, it was the 37-year-old Brooks who died seven months after the attack of suffocation caused by "acute inflammatory sore throat." While Southerners eulogized the "gallant defender" of southern rights, less charitable northern correspondents saw Brook's death as evidence of God's judgment and quoted scripture, "Vengeance is mine saith the Lord: I will repay."

The Dred Scott Decision

The events in Kansas dramatically demonstrated the inability of Congress to settle the issues of slavery in the territories. The vague terms of popular sovereignty did not resolve the key question of whether a territorial legislature could ban slavery before statehood. The formulations offered in the Compromise of 1850 and the Kansas-Nebraska Act stirred up, rather than calming, emotions. In 1857, the Supreme Court stepped in, intending to end the controversy with a definitive decision in the Dred Scott case. Instead, it succeeded only in further inflaming sectional conflict and in convincing Northerners that the southern plot to spread slavery was a reality.

Dred Scott (left) and Chief Justice Roger Taney (right)

Dred Scott was a Missouri slave who sued for freedom in 1846 on the grounds that his late master, an army surgeon, had taken him to the free state of Illinois and to Wisconsin Territory where slavery had been forbidden by the Missouri Compromise. For eleven years the suit had slowly worked its way through state and federal courts. Despite its seeming complexity, the case boiled down to three issues. (1) Did a lengthy stay in a free state or territory make a slave a free man? (2) Was Scott, a slave and black man, an American citizen who could sue in federal courts? (3) Could Congress constitutionally, in the Missouri Compromise or any other law, prohibit slavery in the territories? The Court could have avoided the explosive second and third questions by upholding the Missouri court's opinion on the first issue. The state court ruled that Scott remained a slave since he had been only a "sojourner" in the free state and territory. There were many precedents for such a decision. Generally, the Supreme Court prefers to issue opinions on the narrowest grounds possible and to avoid sweeping, politically charged decisions. In this case, however, the Court, under the domination of Southerners and southern-sympathizers, issued the broadest possible decision in its determination to resolve all controversies by embracing the proslavery viewpoint.

Chief Justice Roger Taney, the spokesman of the Court, ruled that, as a slave and a black, Scott could not be a citizen of the United States and, therefore, could not sue in federal courts. At the time of the Constitution, he wrote, blacks had been "regarded as beings of an inferior order...so far inferior that they had no rights which the white man was bound to respect." In a concurring opinion, another justice went even further, stating that the "African Negro race" did not even belong "to the family of nations" and was rightly the object of "commerce or traffic." This argument, which would deny even free blacks any rights of American citizenship, distorted history. In a powerful dissenting opinion, Justice Benjamin Curtis showed that blacks were, in fact, legal citizens of several states in 1787. Constitutional provisions granted citizens of each state all the rights of U.S. citizens.

Taney's racist argument, though troubling to free blacks and many abolitionists, would not have so completely divided the nation had he stopped there. After all, most white Americans, North and South, including many abolitionists, agreed with his views about racial inferiority. The real political bombshell was the ruling that slavery, as a recognized form of property, could not be excluded from federal territories. Just as it was illegal to prevent a farmer from bringing his horse into the territories, neither Congress nor territorial legislatures could deny any citizen "enjoyment" and use of his slave property without due process of law. The Missouri Compromise, which prohibited slavery north of the 36° 30′ line, was, thus, unconstitutional. Popular sovereignty or any other compromise that allowed people in a territory to exclude slavery was also unconstitutional. Only the states themselves had any authority to deal with slavery within their borders. (Even that might have been endangered by a case working its way through the New York courts challenging the power of free states to ban slave property.) The decision was so one-sided in accepting southern arguments that it could have been written by John C. Calhoun. A southern newspaper exulted, "Southern opinion upon the subject of southern slavery...is now the supreme law of the land."

Legal scholars agree that the *Dred Scott* decision was poorly constructed and an example of "unmitigated partisanship...more like an ultimatum than a formula for sectional accommodation." It is difficult to understand how anyone could have believed that this finding would settle the sectional conflict over slavery in the territories. President Buchanan had welcomed the verdict as a solution of the controversies in Kansas. He failed to understand that the Democratic Party could only remain united when its northern and southern wings could each interpret the vague idea of popular sovereignty in accordance with sectional interests. The Court's mandate that slavery was protected in all territories destroyed that fragile balance and ensured the ultimate division of the Democratic Party. The decision settled nothing. Rather than weakening the Republican Party, it lent weight to the charges that a southern conspiracy was growing bolder in its plots to nationalize slavery in all the states.

Stephen Douglas, the leading exponent of popular sovereignty, well understood the dangers posed by the *Dred Scott* decision to his political career. Douglas agreed with the denial of citizenship to blacks, but he realized that his view that inhabitants of a territory could pass laws barring slavery if they wished was no longer legal. Resourceful as always, Douglas sought to resolve the contradiction in an important speech in June 1857 in Springfield, Illinois. There he acknowledged that a territory could not **actively** ban slavery, but it could accomplish the same ends **passively** by refusing to enact slave codes and necessary police measures. The right to bring in slaves was "practically a dead letter" without "appropriate police regulation and local legislation." In this way, popular sovereignty could be salvaged. Douglas may have saved his northern base, but he enraged southern Democrats. Two weeks later, on the same stage, a Republican politician named Abraham Lincoln announced his unequivocal opposition to the *Dred Scott* decision and methodically tore apart Douglas' arguments. In spite of this, Douglas' principled opposition to the Lecompton Constitution in Kansas restored his reputation in the North, particularly in Illinois where he faced reelection. Some eastern Republicans even suggested endorsing Douglas as a reward for his opposition to Buchanan and a method of broadening the antislavery coalition.

Lincoln, Douglas and Their Debates

Illinois Republicans, led by Abraham Lincoln, rejected any suggestion that they support Douglas. It was Douglas, they noted, who had pushed to repeal the Missouri Compromise. He had often repeated that he did not care whether slavery was voted up or down. Such moral blindness was abhorrent to Illinois Republicans who considered slavery evil and immoral. In 1858, a Republican state convention unanimously nominated Abraham Lincoln to challenge Douglas for his senate seat. In his great acceptance speech of June 1858 Lincoln proclaimed: "A house divided against itself cannot stand. I believe this government cannot endure, permanently half *slave* and half *free*...I do not expect the Union to be dissolved...but I do expect it will cease to divided. It will become *all* one thing or *all* the other." Under the Democrats, it might well become all slave. But the Republicans, just like the Founding Fathers, were committed to stop the spread of slavery and put it on "the course of ultimate extinction." Lincoln was, thus, opening public debate on the meaning, morality, and impact of slavery on American life.

Although Lincoln was virtually unknown in the East, he was widely respected in his own state as a top lawyer and shrewd politician. Unlike most politicians who claimed lowly backgrounds, Lincoln really was born in a rough log cabin in rural Kentucky in 1809. His antislavery feelings came directly from his parents who belonged to a religious sect that barred slaveholders from membership. Aided by a sympathetic stepmother, Lincoln developed a craving for self-education and social ambition that enabled him to rise above his crude origins. (He tended to be embarrassed by his humble beginnings until they became a political benefit.) His social status rose with his often-stormy marriage to Mary Todd, the daughter of a socially prominent Kentucky family. He served several terms as a Whig state legislator and one as a congressman and established a successful corporate law practice, including the position of counsel for the Illinois Central Railroad. He believed in rigid self-control, abstained from alcohol, and was a fervent adherent of progress and self-improvement. He was a legendary storyteller with an endless supply of jokes and folk humor. As a lawyer, he had also learned how to persuade backcountry juries by stripping complicated issues down to their essentials. He was a complex man whose extended periods of introspection at times turned into manic depression. His talents as a speaker and debater were widely acknowledged in Illinois. In fact, Douglas recognized Lincoln as the strongest Republican, "the best stump speaker, with his droll ways and dry jokes, in the West."

At that time, state legislatures elected senators. (Direct election of senators began in 1913 with the passage of the Seventeenth Amendment.) Douglas and Lincoln each appealed to the voters to elect a legislature of his party, committed to choose him as Senator. In view of Douglas' national reputation and his wariness of Lincoln's skills, his best policy would appear to have been to avoid Lincoln and rely on his own prestige to bring about his reelection. But when Lincoln issued a challenge to debate, Douglas, for personal reasons and ego gratification, could not resist agreeing to seven face-to-face debates. The two candidates crisscrossed Illinois for four months, traveling nearly 10,000 miles. After bands, parades, and fireworks, thousands of people crowded into each of the seven towns to listen intently to three hours of debate in weather that ranged from suffocating heat to chilly rain. Press representatives came from all over the nation to report on the encounter between the famed national leader and the gawky unknown. It seemed to be a case of David against Goliath (except that the six feet four inches David (Lincoln) towered by at least a foot over Goliath).

Douglas attempted to paint Lincoln as a radical abolitionist who would break up a union that had always been, and could continue to be, half slave and half free. He also repeatedly and shamelessly played the card of racism. "Do you desire to turn this beautiful state into a free negro colony," he asked receptive audiences, particularly in southern Illinois. "I do not believe the Almighty ever intended the negro to be the equal of the white man. He belongs to an inferior race," Douglas declared. "Those of you who believe that the nigger is your equal...socially, politically, and legally have a right to entertain those opinions, and of course will vote for Mr. Lincoln." His listeners responded, "Down with the negro."

These tactics put Lincoln on the defensive. Particularly in the southern counties, Lincoln assured his audience that he did not favor the social or political equality of the races. These comments are sometimes cited to prove that Lincoln was just as racist as Douglas. They prove only that he was a shrewd politician who wanted to win in a race-conscious state. At other times, Lincoln ridiculed the

Though Lincoln lost the contest for the Senate seat in 1858, he received national prominence.

Democrats' assertion that, "because I do not want a black woman for a *slave*, I must necessarily want her for a *wife*. I need not have her for either. I can just leave her alone." At times in the debates, he reached higher levels of eloquence. Whether or not the black man was intellectually equal to the white, he maintained, "in the right to eat the bread, without leave of anybody else, which his own hand earns, he is *my equal and the equal of Judge Douglas, and the equal of every living man.*" While Lincoln accepted the moderate position that the federal government could not interfere with slavery in existing states, he insisted that it was an evil that must be restricted until it ultimately withered away, as the original founders intended. In the last debate, Lincoln stressed his ethical distance from Douglas' amorality on the issue of slavery, "It is the eternal struggle between these two principles—right and wrong—throughout the world."

Lincoln succeeded in intensifying the gap separating Republicans from Douglas Democrats. He also reinforced the split between Douglas and southern Democrats by posing the question, in view of the *Dred Scott* decision, "Can the people of the United States territories in any lawful way...exclude slavery from their limits prior to the formation of a state constitution?" To preserve his integrity as an exponent of popular sovereignty and to win the election, Douglas was forced to answer that they could, "for the reason that slavery cannot exist a day or an hour anywhere unless supported by local police regulations." Lincoln cleverly pointed out that this was saying, "A thing may be lawfully driven away from a place where it has a lawful right to stay." Although Douglas was only repeating the view he had espoused right after the *Dred Scott* decision, the national publicity engendered by the debates added to his breach with bitter Southerners.

In the election, the voters of Illinois were evenly divided. Republican legislative candidates actually won slightly more votes than Democrats, but Douglas supporters won a narrow majority of seats. Although Lincoln lost the election, the debates vaulted him into national prominence. Elsewhere in the North, in the 1858 congressional elections, the Democrats suffered another calamity. They lost 21 of their already reduced 53 free state seats.

Sectional Division Increases

The Democrats were hurt not only by Dred Scott and the events in Kansas but also by the Panic of 1857, which had shaken the northern economy. Eastern banks suffered as a result of speculative excesses, and Midwestern farm prices collapsed. Southerners exulted that only their cotton economy remained unscathed, demonstrating the superiority of "King Cotton." Every society, one southern senator argued, must have a class "to perform the drudgery of life...the very mud sill of society." The South had a race of slaves for that purpose, "Yours are white." At the Lincoln-Douglas debates, Republicans in the audience had held up banners defiantly declaring, "MUD SILLS OF SOCIETY, GREASY MECHANICS FOR A. LINCOLN."

By the later 1850s a serious drive was underway to reopen the African slave trade. Its supporters included the governor of South Carolina and Jefferson Davis who argued that the 1808 law banning slave importation was both unconstitutional and an insult to the South. The price of slaves had escalated rapidly in the 1850s, and many believed that lower prices would lead to more widely dispersed slave ownership and greater loyalty to the institution of slavery. Although this campaign did not realize its practical goals, it did seem to lead to an increase in smuggling of slaves. Southern juries acquitted illegal traders who were caught by federal authorities. Northern outrage at this led to southern accusations of hypocrisy. A Mississippi newspaper asked, "What is the difference between a Yankee violating the fugitive slave law in the North, and a Southern man violating… the law against the African slave trade in the South?"

Two books published in 1857 reflected the bitterness of the division. George Fitzhugh's *Cannibals All* argued that slavery was "a glorious thing." The North's problems stemmed from its foolish insistence that men were born entitled to equal rights. "It would be far nearer to the truth to say that some were born with saddles on their backs, and others booted and spurred to ride them; and the riding does them good," he contended. "Slavery is the natural and normal condition of the laboring man, whether white or black."

Hinton Rowan Helper's *The Impending Crisis of the South*, published at the same time, was at the opposite end of the spectrum. Helper, who came from the class of yeoman farmers in North Carolina, insisted that slavery caused the stagnation and backwardness of the South. By monopolizing the land and resources, "Slavery lies at the root of all the shame, poverty, ignorance, tyranny and imbecility of the South." Even though Helper was a racist who wanted to see slaves shipped to Africa, he favored abolition of slavery and the organization of nonslaveholding whites to overthrow the rule of the plantation aristocracy. Although Helper had to move North to get his book published with the aid of Republican contributions, southern leaders were infuriated by its "incendiary, insurrectionary" potential.

During a tour of the South in 1859, Douglas was dismayed by his encounters with those young "fire-eaters" who favored reviving and protecting the African slave trade. In the Senate, although he had been removed from his position as chairman of the Committee on Territories, Douglas led a successful fight against southern insistence on a federal slave code to protect slavery in all territories. Southern demands had become much more extreme. In the new House, there was an eight-week struggle to elect a new Speaker. Tempers flared between northern and southern congressmen who brought arms to the sessions. "The only persons who do not have a revolver and a knife are those who have two revolvers," one reporter noted. A shoot-out in Congress seemed likely until the deadlock ended, despite a southern walkout.

THE MARCH TO WAR

Less than two months before that explosive session in Congress, John Brown's raid on Harper Ferry increased anxieties. It began a year in which possibilities for compromise seemed more remote than ever. The political system was disintegrating as sectional tensions increased.

John Brown's Raid

Since his bloody exploits as an antislavery guerrilla in Kansas, John Brown had been working on a plan to strike against slavery in the South itself. He was an austere Calvinist who was convinced that a wrathful God had appointed him the instrument to atone in blood for the sin of slavery. He secured the financial support of a secret group of wealthy abolitionists for his plan to seize the federal arsenal at Harper's Ferry, Virginia (now West Virginia). He planned to distribute its arms to slaves who would join him in rebellion. Brown also had close contacts with free black communities in the North. He sought to convince their leader, Frederick Douglass, to take part in his wild scheme. But Douglass, realizing its hopelessness, tried to talk "the dear old man" out of the plan, warning that Harper's Ferry was "a perfect steel trap and that once in he would never get out alive." Despite this, Brown proceeded with his "army" of nineteen white and black recruits and seized the unguarded arsenal on the night of October 16, 1859. From a military point of view, his raid was unbelievably amateurish. He brought no rations or supplies and ignored an opportunity to escape with his weapons into the nearby mountains. Instead, he waited in Harper's Ferry until a marine detachment, under the command of Colonel Robert E. Lee, stormed the arsenal and killed or captured all the remaining raiders.

John Brown's battle to liberate the slaves was over 36 hours after it began. Not even one slave had voluntarily joined the insurrection. To many, the raid seems a tragic failure by an unstable, possibly insane, man. If Brown's real aim, however, was to cause a violent showdown that would ultimately free the slaves, he succeeded beyond all expectations. He seems to have understood this after his capture when he steadfastly accepted moral responsibility for his acts, rejecting plans to save his life by attempted rescues or insanity pleas. He insisted that he was fulfilling God's will that he die for human freedom. "I am worth inconceivably more to *hang* than for any other purpose," he told admirers. He faced his death with calm and dignity. When he walked to the gallows, he handed a jailer a note proclaiming, "I John Brown am not quite *certain* that the crimes of this *guilty land* will never be purged *away*; but with Blood."

Brown's courage and his execution turned him into a saint and martyr among northern armchair antislavery reformers. On the day he was hanged, sympathizers held prayer meetings, church bells tolled, and canons boomed in northern cities. Louisa May Alcott (the author of *Little Women*) reflected the sentiments of many when she wrote this verse:

> No breath of shame can touch his shield
> Nor ages dim his shine.
> Living, he made life beautiful
> Dying, made death divine.

This outpouring of grief showed the depth of antislavery feelings in many parts of the North. It also sent shock waves of fear and revulsion through the South. Despite disavowals of Brown's act by northern Republicans and denunciations by northern Democrats, Southerners saw Brown's raid as proof of a northern conspiracy to destroy the South by fomenting slave rebellion (always a fear among slaveholders). In their frenzy to head off any such insurrection, Southerners strengthened slave codes and patrols. Violence erupted against blacks and any whites who showed less than absolute support for slavery. Stories about these atrocities reached the northern press and reinforced antislavery feelings. John Brown's "martyrdom," thus, cast a long shadow on America in 1860. It was not surprising that Union troops in the Civil War marched to the strains of "John Brown's Body." The rousing refrain repeated that, while John Brown's body "lay a'moldering in the grave," his "truth goes marching on."

The Election of 1860

The confrontational atmosphere strengthened the positions of Republicans and southern zealots who seemed to agree that slavery would survive only if it could expand under federal protection. Both rejected popular sovereignty for opposite and irreconcilable reasons: the Southerners that slavery must be protected property and the Republicans that it must be banned in all territories. The northern Democrats held the only possibility for compromise—Stephen Douglas may well have been the last national leader with any chance of winning support in both sections. Southern Democrats, led by Senator Jefferson Davis of Mississippi, followed a rule or ruin strategy that insisted on federal protection of slavery and a federal slave code. Douglas, pledged to popular sovereignty, realized that acceptance of the southern demands would ensure defeat in the North.

With emotions at their height, the Democrats held their nominating convention in April 1860 in Charleston, South Carolina, a hotbed of "fire eating" sentiment. Douglas Democrats were in the majority, but they lacked the two-thirds vote needed for nomination. Southern Democrats from eight states walked out to try and force a slave code platform. Instead, the exhausted delegates adjourned and agreed to try again six weeks later in Baltimore. After some more bitter fighting, the Democratic Party self-destructed in Baltimore. Southern Democrats bolted and nominated Buchanan's vice president, John C. Breckinridge of Kentucky, on an extreme proslavery platform. The remaining loyalists nominated Douglas and reaffirmed their support of popular sovereignty. The divided and disheartened Democrats faced a campaign against a confident, united Republican Party.

The Republicans, meeting in Chicago in May, were in a buoyant mood, as victory seemed assured. The leading candidate was Senator William Seward of

New York, but his long years in politics had created many enemies. In addition, his famous speeches proclaiming a "Higher Law" for the emancipation of slaves and warning of "Irrepressible Conflict" gave him an undeserved reputation for radicalism. Abraham Lincoln, less well known, had made fewer enemies. While condemning slavery, he seemed more moderate. He also had the appealing image of a man of the people, "honest Abe," the humble rail-splitter. After much shrewd political wheeling and dealing, Lincoln overtook Seward to win the nomination on the third ballot. In addition to opposing any extension of slavery, the Republican platform sought to appeal to northern economic interests by favoring protective tariffs, government aid for a transcontinental railroad, and a Homestead Act, granting free land to farmers in the West.

A fourth party, the Constitutional Union Party, largely moderate and conservative former Whigs in the border states and Upper South, nominated John Bell of Tennessee. The party based its appeal on opposition to extremism and support for the Constitution and the Union, both in deep danger.

The momentous four-party election quickly resolved into two sectional contests: Lincoln against Douglas in the North and Bell versus Breckinridge in the South. Only Stephen Douglas insisted on bravely conducting the first nationwide speaking campaign by a presidential candidate, repeating his urgent message of the jeopardy the Union was facing in both the North and South. His tireless, exhausting effort was his noblest hour. (He was dead in less than a year at the age of 48.) Less virtuously, northern Democrats tried to exploit racism, claiming a Republican victory would bring "nigger equality" and featuring cartoons of a grinning Lincoln watching black men kiss white women.

Although he won only 40 percent of the total popular vote, Lincoln won a substantial majority of electoral votes (and would have done so even if his opposition had combined against him). Lincoln carried every free state, except New Jersey where he won 4 of 7 electoral votes. In ten of the slave states, Lincoln did not receive a single popular vote! Douglas ran second to Lincoln in the North and won a half million more popular votes than Breckinridge but was only able to win 12 electoral votes (Missouri and part of New Jersey). Bell carried Tennessee, Kentucky, and Virginia, while Breckinridge won the rest of the South. The sectional division was complete, even though Bell and Douglas, both of whom opposed disunion, had together won more southern votes than the extremist Breckinridge. A northern Republican jubilantly celebrated "the great revolution" whereby "the country has once and for all thrown off the domination of the Southerners." A Virginia paper agreed more darkly that a party dedicated to "hatred of African slavery, is now the controlling power...No clap trap about the Union...can alter this or weaken its force."

Republicans had always refused to take threats of secession seriously. One leader recalled that during the 1859 struggle over Speaker of the House, southern congressmen had stormed out, taken a drink, and then returned. After Lincoln's election, he quipped, they would take two drinks before they came back. William Cullen Bryant, an editor and poet, remarked genially, "I am sorry on their own account that the people of South Carolina are making such a fuss about their defeat, but I have not the least apprehension that anything serious will result from it."

Secession and the Fall of the House Divided

As soon as word of Lincoln's election arrived by telegraph, the legislature of South Carolina, where secessionist sentiment was strongest, voted to convene a convention to leave the union. On December 20, 1860, an ordinance of secession passed unanimously. Within six weeks Mississippi, Florida, Alabama, Georgia, Louisiana, and Texas, the six other Deep South states, had also called conventions and voted to secede. Although each convention voted overwhelmingly for secession, the margin of victory for secessionists in the elections for convention delegates had been surprisingly narrow. Support for secession was weakest in hill and backcountry areas where there were few slaves. Considering the significance of the issues involved, voter apathy was also astonishing, as turnout fell by more than one-third from the presidential election vote.

Secessionists won support by painting a frightening picture of the consequences of Republican victory. The worst fears of the South had come to pass with the election of a "Black Republican." Despite Lincoln's reassurances that he would not interfere with slavery in existing states and his willingness to guarantee that with a constitutional amendment, he and his party believed slavery was morally wrong. For the first time in American history the federal government would be committed to the ultimate extinction of slavery. Southern fears were not as irrational as some historians have suggested. The South, as a result of political skills and dominance in the Democratic Party, had controlled the national government for most of the 72 years of its existence. For 60 of the years, the president had either been a Southerner or southern sympathizer. The South had always had a majority in the Supreme Court. Lincoln's election signaled a crucial change in which the North would be ascendant. Exclusion of slavery from the territories would bring in new free states, overwhelming the South in Congress. Lincoln would appoint Republican justices to the Supreme Court, ending its role as protector of southern interests. Republicans might eventually win the votes of nonslaveholders in the South by cleverly using patronage to appoint supporters to key postal, military, and judicial positions. One secessionist somberly noted, "we live in desperate times. Not only our property but our honor, our lives and our all are involved."

The states of the Lower South acted swiftly and decisively, setting up a government of the Confederate States by February 1861, with Jefferson Davis of

Mississippi as president. But the eight states of the Upper South, where slavery was declining, refused to join the Confederacy. In the crucial time period from December 1860 until Lincoln would take office on March 4, 1861, the national government was unwilling or unable to act. (The Twentieth Amendment changed inauguration day to January 20 in 1933.) President Buchanan, discredited and weary, eloquently argued that secession was illegal but simultaneously declared that the government had no power to "coerce" a seceding state to return to the Union. Seward quipped that the president believed, "no state has a right to secede unless it wishes to" and that he had a "duty to enforce the laws, unless somebody opposes him." At the same time, for several weeks, Lincoln and Seward believed in "masterly inactivity" to allow secession fever to dissipate and the "erring sisters" to return.

As it became obvious that such a scenario was unlikely to occur, Congress set up committees to consider numerous compromises suggested generally by border and Upper South members. Nearly all of these would have required the North to make all the concessions and the Republicans to renounce their intentions of barring slavery in the territories. This was the very basis of Republican ideology and its electoral victory. Republican votes defeated compromises that would have protected the interstate slave trade and slavery in all present and *future* territories south of the 36° 30′ line through unrepealable amendments. Although Lincoln

"Our new government is founded upon exactly the opposite idea:...its cornerstone rests upon the great truth that the negro is not equal to the white man; that slavery...is his natural and normal condition. This, our new government, is the first in the history of the world based upon this great physical, philosophical, and moral truth."

made no public statements, he was instrumental in advising Republicans to "entertain no proposition for a compromise in regard to the *extension* of slavery." Indeed, it is difficult to imagine any compromise that could undo the simple fact that Lincoln referred to in a letter to his old friend Alexander Stephens of Georgia (soon to become vice president of the Confederacy): "You think slavery is *right*

This Matthew Brady photograph was taken when Lincoln arrived in Washington for his inauguration.

and ought to be extended; while we think slavery is *wrong* and ought to be restricted. That I suppose is the rub."

As Lincoln prepared to take office, the key issue seemed to involve the important states of the Upper South, still in the Union. Seward urged Lincoln to be "conciliatory, forbearing and patient." In his inaugural address, the most significant one in American history, Lincoln attempted to balance his assertion of national authority in the South with reassurance that his government had no intention of interfering with slavery where it existed. In his eloquent conclusion, Lincoln declared, "In *your* hands, my dissatisfied fellow countrymen, and not in *mine*, is the momentous issue of civil war. The government will not assail *you*...*You* have no oath registered in Heaven to destroy the government, while *I* have the most solemn one to 'preserve, protect, and defend' it."

Lincoln's main objective in this message was to gain time to allow Seward's idea of voluntary reunion to occur and to avoid confrontation. On the day after his inauguration, however, he received troubling news that would force him to change his course. Major Robert Anderson sent word that the garrison at Fort Sumter in Charleston harbor would have to evacuate in a few weeks unless its dwindling supplies were restocked. Since the secessionists had already seized federal installations throughout the Lower South, Sumter had become

The Stars and Bars replaced the stars and stripes above Sumter.

a symbol of Union presence and resolve in the South out of proportion to any real military significance. At first, Lincoln appeared to waver, suggesting that he might be willing to leave Sumter in exchange for firm commitments from the remaining slave states, particularly Virginia, to remain in the Union. A meeting with a representative of Virginia unionists seems to have convinced Lincoln of the futility of such hopes. Later that day (April 4), he decided to proceed with an expedition to bring relief to Sumter. To avoid antagonizing the Upper South, Lincoln notified Governor Pickens of South Carolina that "an attempt will be made to supply Fort Sumter with provisions only; and that if such an attempt be not resisted, no effort to throw in men, arms, or ammunition will be made without further notice, or in case of attack upon the fort." If the South fired on the unarmed supply ships, it would be responsible for starting the war. The Confederates, to whom Sumter was a symbol of their national sovereignty, demanded the surrender of the fort and opened fire when they received an unsatisfactory response from Anderson. On April 14, after 33 hours of bombardment, the Union garrison surrendered. To the wild cheers of Charlestonians, the Confederate stars and bars replaced the stars and stripes. The next day Lincoln issued a call for 75,000 state militiaman to put down the "insurrection" in the South. The Confederate Congress quickly declared that a state of war existed. Within the next five weeks, Virginia, Arkansas, Tennessee, and North Carolina, declaring solidarity with their southern cousins against federal force, joined the Confederacy. The bloodiest war in American history had begun.

The founders of the United States had seen slavery as an unpleasant and undesirable inheritance from the British that they expected would eventually disappear. But slavery had demonstrated unexpected staying power with the growth of the Cotton Kingdom. Southerners began to see slavery as the essential foundation of their freedom. Northerners, on the other hand, increasingly regarded slavery as a challenge to the basic principles of freedom. Each section believed that the other was betraying America's fundamental principles of liberty. Each detected evidence of conspiracy in the actions of the other. For 40 years the nation had expanded, gaining new territories, building new cities and industries, and welcoming new people. Most Americans believed that God had given the American people the ingenuity and means to overcome all obstacles to their "manifest destiny." But the one dilemma that American resourcefulness could not solve was black slavery. As Americans expanded into the territories, the issue of slavery continually arose, allowing the nation no breathing spells. Both sides believed that slavery must expand to survive—confining the institution to a limited area would mean its inevitable extinction. The issues became ones of life and death to a society and way of life. In the end, even those opposed to war could not come up with a way to prevent it.

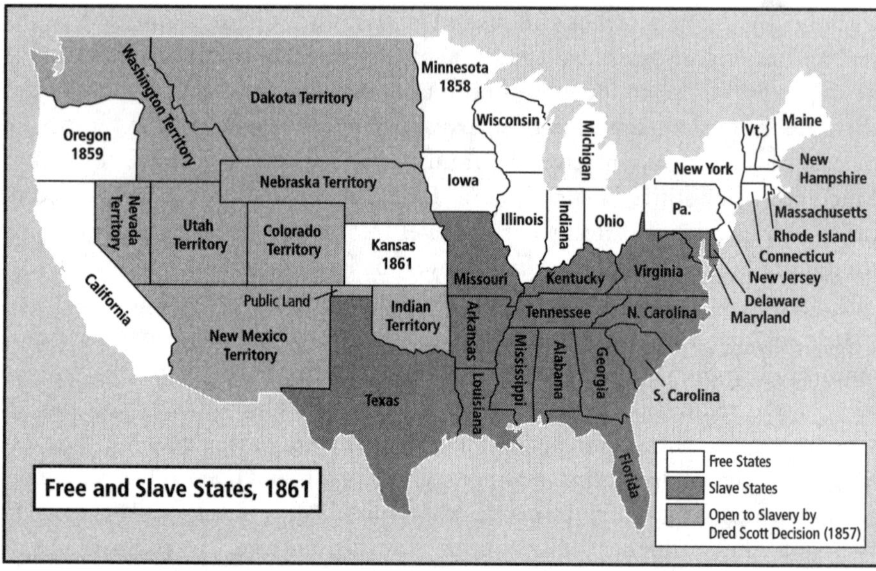

Free and Slave States, 1861

In March 1861, Confederate Vice President Stephens declared that ideas of equality, like those in the Declaration of Independence, were mistaken. "Our new government," he proudly proclaimed, "is founded upon exactly the opposite idea:... its cornerstone rests upon the great truth that the negro is not equal to the white man; that slavery...is his natural and normal condition. This, our new government, is the first in the history of the world based upon this great physical, philosophical, and moral truth." On the other side of the great American divide, the abolitionist, Lydia Maria Child, wrote three months later, "God grant that all the slave-holders may rebel, and remain in rebellion, till the emancipation of their slaves is accomplished." At the end of the bloody and brutal conflict, her wish would be granted and his "truth" would be in tatters.

DOCUMENTS

LETTERS FROM THE CONFLICT IN KANSAS

It had seemed, for a while, that the Compromise of 1850 had settled the issue of whether slavery would be allowed to expand into the western territories. When Senator Stephen Douglas of Illinois introduced the Kansas-Nebraska Act in 1854 to organize the territories of Kansas and Nebraska, he reopened the issue by providing that the settlers themselves, through "popular sovereignty," would decide the status of slavery. The unintended result was that Northerners and Southerners rushed into Kansas and sought to implement the decision by means of rifles. The continuing conflict led people to describe the territory as "Bleeding Kansas." Eventually, after a bitter struggle, the antislavery forces won, and Kansas finally entered the Union in 1861. The authors of these letters from Kansas eventually fought on opposite sides in the Civil War. While John Lawrie survived, Axalla John Hoole died at Chickamauga in 1863.

LETTER FROM JOHN LAWRIE: A NORTHERNER'S VIEW

Wolf Mound Farm, White Co., Indiana
Apl. 16th, 1857
Dear Art,

After an absence of ten months I now find myself again at home, and surrounded by old associations, among which prominently stands my long-neglected correspondence with you. It was my hope on my way home that when I reached it I would find you with Bob and Lizzy of the Georgian block house, yet some twenty-five miles distant, and met with no incidents worthy of note until we reached the vicinity of the block house, where we were all rather anxious to see how the boys would behave under fire, many of them never having as yet heard singing lead. The night was rather dark, and the enemy showed no light and made no noise. Our captain (who by the way was an old man of wars man) reconnoitered the ground and concluded to lead us right on to the place and take it by assault as we had no artillery to storm the place with. The battalion was divided into two platoons, and the block house approached from toward its front and left so that in case we found it necessary to fire we could give them a destructive cross-fire. We went up as well as old veterans ever dared to go; and if there was any disorder at all whatever, it was occasioned by some of the boys rushing ahead too fast. The sound of our steady tramp! tramp! was too much for the garrison and they incontinently fled. We found about ten hundred pounds of bacon, some meal, several sacks of flour, a barrel of sugar, [and?] various articles recognized by many of our men as having been taken from Lawrence on the 21st of May, besides a number of letters written by Free-State men to their friends in the states which had been mailed in U. S. post offices, and probably had been abstracted in Missouri and forwarded to the Robbers of the Blue Lodge in order to give them whatever information they might possess of the prospects and conditions of their writers. After taking out all the provisions and military stores, we fired the block house and started home again by the light of it. On our return we had a most fatiguing time, but reached Lawrence without any incident occurring worthy of note ....

I found all our people well. I shall remain here until the middle of June when I intend returning to Kansas.

Your affectionate brother
John Lawrie

LETTERS FROM AXALLA JOHN HOOLE: A SOUTHERNER'S VIEW

Kansas City, Missouri,
Apl. 3d., 1856
My Dear Brother

It has cost me over $102 to get here, besides about $25 which I have spent for necessaries, &c. We have been quite well since we left-with the exception of one day that I had a headache and fever, caused I guess from losing so much sleep, and the fatigue of travelling. We did not get to Nashville until Sunday evening; we left that place Monday about 12 o'clock and went down the Cumberland river on the steamer City of Huntsville to Cairo, at the junction of the Mississippi and the Ohio rivers, where we changed boats and went up to St. Louis, Mo., where we arrived Friday morning about 8 o'clock. We remained there about two hours, in which time I purchased a six-shooter for $20, and some other things. We then changed boats and sailed up the Missouri river to this place. The boats travel very slow up this river at this time, as it is very low and swift.

I have seen none of the country except along the banks of the river, which is, with very little exceptions, nothing but lofty, rugged rocks, sometimes two or three hundred feet high. It was quite a sight to me at first, but I got very tired of looking at them. I saw thousands of wild geese in the Missouri river; I shot at them once about 200 yards, and of course missed. I saw duck also in abundance....

The banks of the river were low and I could see for miles, but there were houses scattered all over the prairie. I fell in company with a young man who had just married, from Georgia, who said he was going to Kansas, but there were other families along from Georgia, who were going to Missouri, and when they left the boat about 60 miles from here, he left with them and I was not sorry for it, as I did not fancy him much; neither did I fancy his wife. I would have but little to do with them—one objection I had to him was, he drank liquor

The Missourians (all of whom I have conversed with, with the exception of one who, by the way, I found out to be an Abolitionist) are very sanguine about Kansas being a slave state & I have heard some of them say it shall be. I have met with warm reception from two or three, but generally speaking, I have not met with the reception which I expected. Everyone seems bent on the Almighty Dollar, and as a general thing that seems to be their only thought—There was a large box on one of the boats about a week ago coming up the river, which some of the Missourians thought contained Sharp's Rifles, so they sent a deputation to its destination, which was at this place, to have it opened. When they arrived here the person to whom it was consigned refused to let them open it, where-upon they opened it by force—when lo! it contained nothing but a piano. There was a box containing a cannon which a confounded Yankee opened, but closed it up again before any of them could examine it, saying that it was nothing but some cartwheels. His daughter-in-law told me this this morning, hesitatingly, as if her father-in-law had done a smart trick. If she had been a man, I don't know what I should have said, but she was a pretty young woman.

Well, dear brother, the supper bell has rung, so I must close. Give my love to [the immediate family] and all the Negroes .... Excuse bad writing for I am very nervous. I am anxious to hear from home...direct to Lawrence City, Kansas Territory, as I shall leave word there for my letters to be forwarded to whatever place I go.

Your ever affectionate brother,
Axalla.

Douglas, K. T., July the 5th., 1857

Dear Sister

I fear, Sister, that coming here will do no good at last, as I begin to think that this will be made a Free State at last. 'Tis true we have elected Proslavery men to draft a state constitution, but I feel pretty certain, if it is put to the vote of the people, it will be rejected, as I feel pretty confident they have a majority here at this time. The South has ceased all efforts, while the North is redoubling her exertions. We nominated a candidate for Congress last Friday—Ex-Gov. Ransom of Michigan. I must confess I have not much faith in him, tho he professes to hate the Abolitionists bitterly, and I have heard him say that Negroes were a great deal better off with Masters. Still, I fear him, but it was the best we could do. If we had nominated a southern man, he would have been sure to have been beaten, and I doubt whether we can even elect a Northerner who favors our side.

One of our most staunch Proslavery men was killed in Leavensworth a few days ago. It is hard to ascertain the facts in relation to the murder correctly, but as far as I can learn, there was an election for something. The man who was killed (Jas. Lyle) went up to the polls and asked for a ticket. An Abolitionist handed him one which he, Lyle, tore in two. The other asked him why he did that; he replied he did all such tickets that way. The Abolitionist told him he had better not do so again, when Lyle told him if he would give him another he would. It was given him, and he tore it also, at which the Abolitionist drew a bowie knife and stabbed Lyle to the heart, then ran a few paces, drew a revolver, and commenced firing at the dying man. The fellow was taken prisoner and eighty men were sent from Lawrence that night, by Jim Lane, to keep Lyle's friends from hanging him. Gov. Walker put out for Leavensworth on Friday to have the prisoner carried to the fort, in order to keep the Abolitionists from rescuing him, or prevent Lyle's friends from hanging him by mob law.

There was a big ball in Lecompton on the night of the 3d., but they had no celebration there yesterday. The Abolitionists had a barbecue at Bloomington, about 8 miles south of this, but it was a party thing, I hear. There was a big celebration at Tecumseh and all were invited to attend, tho it was given by Proslavery men. Judge Cato was the orator of the day. I celebrated the day by hard work...so you may guess I felt like sleeping last night....

You must give my love to all....Tell all the Negroes a hundred Howdies for us .... Your Affectionate Brother, Axalla.

P. S. 6th. Mr. Smith, the man engaged with me in work, was bit by a rattlesnake last night about midnight. He got up to give his child a drink of water, & stepped on the snake on the floor. He drank a pint of whiskey and got drunk. He has the Doctor with him this morning, and I hope he will be up in a day or two.

V. E. Gibbons (editor), "Letters on the War in Kansas in 1856," In *Kansas Historical Quarterly,* 1941, 10: 370-373.
William Stanley Hoole (editor), "A Southerner's Viewpoint of the Kansas Situation, 1856-1857," In *Kansas Historical Quarterly,* 1934, 3: 43-45; 64-65; 164-166.

1. How do the views of the two men differ about conditions in Kansas?
2. Why do think Axalla Hoole's view of which way Kansas would go changed so much between April and July?
3. How did events in Kansas reflect the conditions in the rest of the country?

LINCOLN AND DOUGLAS DEBATE

After President Buchanan sought to bring Kansas into the Union as a slave state, against the clear mandate of its settlers, the Supreme Court issued the ***Dred Scott*** *decision, which declared that Congress had no right to bar slavery from the territories. These two events put Senator Douglas's cherished idea of "popular sovereignty" in serious jeopardy. Against this background, Senator Douglas ran for re-election in 1858. His opponent, a shrewd Republican lawyer, Abraham Lincoln, argued that Douglas's policy could lead only to chaos. The two men had a series of intense and well-attended debates.*

SOME OF THE DEBATE

Lincoln, at Springfield

"A house divided against itself cannot stand." I believe this government cannot endure permanently half slave and half free....I do not expect the house to fall; but I do expect it will cease to be divided. It will become all one thing, or all the other.

Douglas, of Chicago

Mr. Lincoln advocates boldly and clearly a war of sections, a war of the North against the South, of the Free States against the Slave States....He objects to the Dred Scott decision because it does not put the negro in the possession of citizenship on an equality with the white man. I am opposed to negro equality....I am in favor of preserving, not only the purity of the blood, but the purity of the government from any mixture or amalgamation with inferior races.

Lincoln, at Chicago

I protest, now and forever, against that counterfeit logic which presumes that because I do not want a negro woman for a slave, I do necessarily want her for a wife. My understanding is that I need not have her for either, but, as God made us separate, we can leave one another alone, and do one another much good thereby....The Judge regales us with the terrible enormities that take place by the mixture of races....Why, Judge, if we do not let them get together in the Territories, they won't mix there.

From *Political Debates between Abraham Lincoln and Stephen A. Douglas in the Celebrated Campaign of 1858 in Illinois* (Cleveland, Ohio: The Arthur H. Clark Company, 1902), pp. 1, 14, 18, 33.

1. Douglas won re-election. Do you feel he won the debate? Why or why not?
2. How did the two men differ on issues like slavery, race, and the possibilities of war?
3. Some modern commentators have argued that Lincoln was a racist. If that is so, how would you describe Douglas?

JOHN BROWN'S RAID: TWO VIEWS OF AFRICAN AMERICANS

While Southerners saw John Brown as an evil dangerous abolitionist, northern abolitionists, particularly African Americans, thought of Brown and his raiders as heroes. A northern black woman sent the first letter to Brown. The second came from John Copeland, a fugitive slave who was one of Brown's men. He was later executed.

Although the hands of Slavery throw a barrier between you and me, and it may not be my privilege to see you in the prison house, Virginia has no bolts or bars through which I dread to send you my sympathy. In the name of the young girl sold from the warm clasp of a mother's arms to the clutches of a libertine or profligate,—in the name of the slave mother, her heart rocked to and fro by the agony of her mournful separations—I thank you that you have been brave enough to reach out your hands to the crushed and blighted of my race. You have rocked the bloody Bastille; and I hope from your sad fate great good may arise to the cause of freedom. Already from your prison has come a shout of triumph against the giant sin of our country....

We may earnestly hope that your fate will not be a vain lesson, that it will intensify our hatred of Slavery and love of Freedom, and that your martyr grave will be a sacred altar upon which men will record their vows of undying hatred to that system which tramples on man and bids defiance to God. I have written to your dear wife, and sent her a few dollars, and I pledge myself to you that I will continue to assist her....

Letter to John Brown, in prison, from a free black woman,
FRANCES ELLEN WATKINS,
Kendallville, Indiana, November 25, 1859

Dear Brother:

...It was a sense of the wrongs that we have suffered that prompted the noble but unfortunate John Brown and his associates to attempt to give freedom to a small number, at least, of those who are now held by cruel and unjust laws, and by no less cruel and unjust men. To this freedom they were entitled by every known principle of justice and humanity, and for the enjoyment of it God created them. And now, dear brother, could I die in a more noble cause? Could I, brother, die in a manner and for a cause which could induce true and honest men more to honor me, and the angels more readily to receive me to their happy home of everlasting joy above...? And were it not that I know that the hearts of those to whom I am attached by the nearest and most enduring ties of blood relationship—yea by the closest and strongest ties that god has instituted—will be filled with sorrow, I would almost as [soon die now as at any time, for I feel that I am now prepared to meet my maker....

JOHN A. COPELAND,

sentenced to death for participating in the Harpers Ferry Raid, in a letter to his brother,
December 10, 1859

1. Why did John Brown seem to strike such an emotional chord among African Americans?
2. What reaction do you think Southerners would have to his exploits?
3. Why did this man excite such emotion among his opponents and defenders?

SLAVERY IS THE CORNERSTONE OF THE CONFEDERACY

by Alexander H. Stephens

In many ways, slavery was the key to southern secession. Both sides acknowledged its importance. In his 1861 speech, Alexander Stephens, vice president of the Confederate States of America, describes the Confederate constitution and compares it to the Constitution of the United States. He reaffirms the total commitment to slavery in the Confederate Constitution.

But not to be tedious in enumerating the numerous changes for the better, allow me to allude to one other—though last, not least. The new constitution has put at rest, *forever*, all the agitating questions relating to our peculiar institution—African slavery as it exists amongst us—the proper status of the negro in our form of civilization. This was the immediate cause of the late rupture and present revolution. Jefferson in his forecast, had anticipated this, as the "rock upon which the old Union would split." He was right. What was conjecture with him, is now a realized fact. But whether he fully comprehended the great truth upon which that rock *stood* and *stands,* may be doubted. The prevailing ideas entertained by him and most of the leading statesmen at the time of the formation of the old constitution, were that the enslavement of the African was in violation of the laws of nature; that it was wrong in principle, socially, morally, and politically. It was an evil they knew not well how to deal with, but the general opinion of the men of that day was that, somehow or other in the order of Providence, the institution would be evanescent and pass away. This idea, though not incorporated in the constitution, was the prevailing idea at that time. The constitution, it is true, secured every essential guarantee to the institution while it should last, and hence no argument can be justly urged against the constitutional guarantees thus secured, because of the common sentiment of the day. Those ideas, however, were fundamentally wrong. They rested upon the assumption of the equality of races. This was an error. It was a sandy foundation, and the government built upon it fell, when the "storm came and the wind blew."

Our new government is founded upon exactly the opposite idea; its foundations are laid, its corner-stone rests upon the great truth, that the negro is not equal to the white man; that slavery—subordination to the superior race—is his natural and normal condition.

This, our new government, is the first, in the history of the world, based upon this great physical, philosophical, and moral truth. This truth has been slow in the process of its development, like all other truths in the various departments of science. It has been so even amongst us. Many who hear me, perhaps, can recollect well, that this truth was not generally admitted, even within their day. The errors of the past generation still clung to many as late as twenty years ago. Those at the North, who still cling to these errors, with a zeal above knowledge, we justly denominate fanatics. All fanaticism springs from an aberration of the mind—from a defect in reasoning. It is a species of insanity. One of the most striking characteristics of insanity, in many instances, is forming correct conclusions from fancied or erroneous premises; so with the anti-slavery fanatics; their conclusions are right if their premises were. They assume that the negro is equal, and hence conclude that he is entitled to equal privileges and rights with the white man. If their premises were correct, their conclusions would be logical and just—but their premise being wrong, their whole argument fails. I recollect once of having heard a gentleman from one of the northern States, of great power and ability, announce in the House of Representatives, with imposing effect, that we of the South would be compelled, ultimately, to yield upon this subject of slavery, that it was as impossible to war successfully against a principle in politics, as it was in physics or mechanics. That the principle would ultimately prevail. That we, in maintaining slavery as it exists with us, were warring against a principle, a principle founded in nature, the principle of the equality of men. The reply I made to him was, that upon his own grounds, we should, ultimately, succeed, and that he and his associates, in this crusade against our institutions, would ultimately fail. The truth announced, that it was as impossible to war successfully against a principle in politics as it was in physics and mechanics, I admitted; but told him that it was he, and those acting with him, who were warring against a principle. They were attempting to make things equal which the Creator had made unequal.

In the conflict thus far, success has been on our side, complete throughout the length and breadth of the Confederate States. It is upon this, as I have stated, our social fabric is firmly planted; and I cannot permit myself to doubt the ultimate success of a full recognition of this principle throughout the civilized and enlightened world.

As I have stated, the truth of this principle may be slow in development, as all truths are and ever have been, in the various branches of science. It was so with the principles announced by Galileo—it was so with Adam Smith and his principles of political economy. It was so with [William] Harvey, and his theory of the circulation of the blood. It is stated that not a single one of the medical profession, living at the time of the announcement of the truths made by him, admitted them. Now, they are universally acknowledged. May we not, therefore, look with confidence to the ultimate universal acknowledgment of the truths upon which our system rests? It is the first government ever instituted upon the principles in strict conformity to nature, and the ordination of Providence, in furnishing the materials of human society. Many governments have been founded upon the principle of the subordination and serfdom of certain classes of the same race; such were and are in violation of the laws of nature. Our system commits no such violation of nature's laws. With us, all of the white race, however high or low, rich or poor, are equal in the eye of the law. Not so with the negro. Subordination is his place. He, by nature, or by the curse against Canaan, is fitted for that condition which he occupies in our system. The architect, in the construction of buildings, lays the foundation with the proper material—the granite; then comes the brick or the marble. The substratum of our society is made of the material fitted by nature for it, and by experience we know that it is best, not only for the superior, but for the inferior race, that it should be so. It is, indeed, in conformity with the ordinance of the Creator. It is not for us to inquire into the wisdom of his ordinances, or to question them. For his own purposes, he has made one race to differ from another, as he has made "one star to differ from another star in glory."

The great objects of humanity are best attained when there is conformity to his laws and decrees, in the formation of governments as well as in all things else.

Our confederacy is founded upon principles in strict conformity with these laws. This stone which was rejected by the first builders "is become the chief of the corner"—the real "corner-stone"—in our new edifice.

I have been asked, what of the future? It has been apprehended by some that we would have arrayed against us the civilized world. I care not who or how many they may be against us, when we stand upon the eternal principles of truth, if we are true to ourselves and the principles for which we contend, we are obliged to, and must triumph.

Thousands of people who begin to understand these truths are not yet completely out of the shell; they do not see them in their length and breadth. We hear much of the civilization and christianization of the barbarous tribes of Africa. In my judgment, those ends will never be attained, but by first teaching them the lesson taught to Adam, that "in the sweat of his brow he should eat his bread," and teaching them to work, and feed, and clothe themselves.

Henry Cleveland, *Alexander H. Stephens in Public and Private* (Philadelphia: National Publishing Company, 1866), pp. 721-23.

1. What great truth does Stephens say is the "corner-stone" of the new government?
2. What arguments does Stephens give to support the institution of slavery?
3. Do you think that slavery was the basic cause of the Civil War? Why or why not?

PART III

THE CIVIL WAR

ABRAHAM LINCOLN

Chapter Six

THE CIVIL WAR BEGINS

THE WAR BEGINS

Immediately after the surrender at Fort Sumter, Lincoln had called upon state and territorial governors to supply the government with seventy-five thousand militiamen to serve for ninety days to quell an insurrection "too powerful to be suppressed by the ordinary course of judicial proceedings." The response was instantaneous and overwhelming. After the continuous accumulation of tensions through the 1850s and the unbearable suspense of the previous six months, the outbreak of war seemed almost to be a relief. "Civil war is freely accepted everywhere," one Bostonian announced a week after the war began. War fever swept through both the North and the South.

An amazed Bostonian, watching flags waving, bands blasting, and orators declaiming, wrote, "I never before knew what popular excitement can be." Even sophisticated New Yorkers mounted huge Union rallies. People rushed to enlist. "War! and volunteers are the only topics of conversation and thought," an Oberlin college student remarked. "I cannot study. I cannot sleep, I cannot work, and I don't know as I can write." Ohio had been expected to contribute thirteen regiments, but there were so many volunteers that the Governor notified the Secretary of War that, "owing to an unavoidable...enthusiasm of our people," he could not "stop short of twenty regiments. The lion in us is thoroughly aroused."

A divided North was united by the assault on Fort Sumter. An 1843 West Point graduate, Ulysses S. Grant, who was working as a clerk, after drink and apathy had forced him from the peacetime army, volunteered and became a mustering officer handling the flood of enlistments. "There are but two parties now," he declared, "traitors and patriots, and I want hereafter to be ranked with the latter." The same view could be seen all across the North as Lincoln's opponent, Stephen Douglas, came to the White House to personally pledge his support.

Wealthy men and leading politicians recruited volunteer regiments in their communities. Sometimes entire towns signed up. Men from Flint, for example, made up the 10th Michigan whose commander was the mayor. Each regiment had its own distinctive quality or insignia. The 6th New York had so many Bowery thugs that people said, "a man had to have served time in prison just to get in." In contrast, the aristocratic 7th regiment marched to Washington carrying sandwiches made by a fancy New York restaurant and a thousand velvet-covered stools on which to sit and eat. The Northern Zouave regiments dressed like French North African troops. Their magnificent red fezzes and baggy trousers, set off with blue sashes, might have been fine in a desert or in parades but were not nearly as effective when the men had to cross streams. Their puffy pants ballooned and caused them to float down the stream like some outlandish buoys. Immigrants also joined—Irishmen in the St. Patrick Brigade and the Irish Volunteers, among others; Italians in the Garibaldi Guards and the Italian Legion; Germans in the Steuben Volunteers and the German Rifles. Many of these immigrants could not even understand English. Each of these regiments, whether immigrant or native-born, was sent off to war with a colorful farewell ceremony including speeches, prayers, hand-sewn flags made by patriotic women, and a variety of home-cooked foods.

The same feelings gripped the South. A London *Times* reporter visiting the South commented on the huge crowds with "flushed faces, wild eyes, screaming mouths," whose curdling "rebel yells" competed with bands blaring "Dixie." It was an article of faith in the South that Southerners were invulnerable, while Northerners were greedy weaklings. Southern regiments, like those of the North, featured a variety of uniforms and weapons. A Louisiana battalion, for example, was made up of daring New Orleans dock workers who called themselves the Tigers. They wore scarlet skullcaps with slogans like "Tiger on the Leap" and "Tiger in Search of a Black Republican." The wives and sweethearts of these Confederate troops were as ardent in their support as the northern women were.

Both sides were equally convinced they were on a holy crusade for justice and honor. Each had a romantic image of a noble little war that would be rapidly completed. Each side was certain that the other would cave in within ninety days. It would not be long before they would be disillusioned.

The First Battle of Bull Run

The Confederates had moved their capital from Montgomery, Alabama to the busy commercial and industrial city of Richmond, Virginia, only a hundred miles

At the beginning of the war volunteers, like these Confederate soldiers, enlisted eagerly.

from Washington. This decision made northern Virginia the main battle center of the war. As the nearby rival capitals glowered at each other, civilians grew increasingly impatient. Lincoln was too. Irvin McDowell, the Union field commander, warned, "This is not an army. It will take a long time to make it an army." He was not ready to fight. "You are green, it is true," Lincoln responded, "but they are green also; you are all green alike."

The first significant battle took place on July 21, 1861—the Battle of Bull Run. (The North generally named battles after the nearest stream or other body of water, while the South preferred a nearby town or physical feature: in this case Bull Run or Manassas.) Neither side was really ready for a major engagement, but both hoped for a quick early victory. The plan by the elderly and ailing General in Chief Winfield Scott, to suffocate the Confederacy by blockading it on all sides and launching an invasion down the Mississippi to the Gulf, would take months to be effective. Northern newspapers ridiculed it as "The Anaconda Plan" and demanded immediate action. The influential *New York Tribune* added "Forward to Richmond" on its masthead and vowed to keep it there until a decisive operation was launched. In addition, the three-month enlistments were starting to expire, so a battle had to take place quickly or there would have to be a lengthy delay. In fact, on the day of the battle, Union troops moving forward actually

General Winfield Scott

passed regiments who, with their enlistment period over, were returning to Washington to be discharged.

In this battle, as in most others throughout the war in northern Virginia, generals on both sides tended to use the same strategic plans that they had learned at West Point. Based on theories advanced by European strategists, they emphasized the necessity to conquer territory, particularly the enemy's capital. In battle, the two armies were to be in opposing lines with victory determined by the concentration of a more powerful force on the enemy's weakest spot. Battles were, thus, visualized as a kind of elaborate game of chess, mastered by professional officers. Most of the early battles of the war illustrated these theories.

At Bull Run, both armies tried to carry out the same battle plan: attack the enemy's left flank, followed up by a lesser assault on the center and right. (If this had actually been accomplished by both, each army would have ended up in the enemy's original position!) The messy reality of poorly trained troops turned the neatly drawn-up plans into shambles.

Thousands of Union troops in crisp new uniforms, "arms gleaming in the sun," marched south to stirring martial music. Despite the oppressive heat, they seemed to be having a very good time, pausing every few minutes to pick blackberries or drink water from nearby streams. They took two and a half days to march 25 miles, a distance experienced troops covered in less than half that time later in the war.

Large numbers of civilian onlookers, including leading politicians, accompanied the forces, hoping to witness an entertaining victory. They brought binoculars, picnic baskets filled with goodies, and bottles of champagne to celebrate. The "French cooks and hotel-keepers," wrote one observer, tripled "the price of their wines and of the hampers of provisions which Washington people are ordering to comfort themselves at their bloody derby."

At first, the Union forces seemed to be carrying the day. Soldiers shouted, "We'll hang Jeff Davis to a sour apple tree...The war is over." The civilian sightseers, spread out on the green hills above the battlefield, waved their hats and handkerchiefs enthusiastically. However, at the center of the southern line, a Virginia brigade, led by Thomas J. Jackson, grimly held on. Another general exhorted his troops, "Look there is Jackson with his Virginians, standing like a stone wall!" The nickname, as well as the Confederate lines, held. As the fighting continued to seesaw, Confederate General Beauregard ordered a huge counterattack. At the urging of Jackson, southern troops began to "yell like furies," the famous high-pitched "rebel yell." Northerners began an orderly retreat, which turned into a rout. Some soldiers in their panic threw away their blankets, knapsacks, and even their muskets. Frightened civilian partygoers who rushed to get away increased the hysteria. One southern officer reported finding along the road, "parasols and dainty shawls lost in their flight by the frail fair ones who had seats in most of the carriages of this excursion." Actually, most of the Union troops were able to withdraw in fairly good order. Nevertheless, the Union forces remembered the Battle of Bull Run as "the great skedaddle."

The southern army, according to one of its generals, was "more disorganized by victory than that of the United States by defeat." In any case, a heavy rainstorm the next morning turned the roads to mud and made it impossible for the southern army to pursue the retreating Northerners. Although this was a relatively small battle compared to later Civil War encounters, it was the largest and deadliest battle in American history to that point: approximately 4,500 men were killed, wounded, or captured by the two sides. Americans were jolted and sobered by losses that seemed enormous to them. Horace Greeley, the editor of the *Tribune* who had been instrumental in pushing for the premature drive on Richmond that led to the defeat, now demanded an end to the war. "It is best for the country and for mankind," he argued, "that we make peace with the rebels, and on their own terms, do not shrink even from that."

The consequences of this Confederate victory were significant for the future of the conflict. Many Southerners were convinced that they had won the war and that one Rebel could easily whip ten Yankees (even though the actual numbers of fighting men in the battle were just about equal and the southern army had come perilously close to defeat itself). Some Confederate volunteers, anxious to return home for the fall harvest and confident of imminent victory, left the army. In that sense, the battle's result may have deluded Southerners into expecting easy victory while shocking Northerners into a more realistic view. Some historians feel, however, that this decisive win gave the Rebels an upper hand psychologically. It increased their confidence in future battles and, perhaps, created a feeling of inferiority among some Union troops.

Despite this, Southerners who expected the North to throw in the towel after one thrashing quickly learned otherwise. A grim resolve replaced the earlier easy optimism as huge numbers of three-year volunteers flooded Union recruiting officers. President Lincoln took firm control over the management of the conflict. He introduced the concept of simultaneous advances to better utilize the North's numerical advantage, an idea that became more significant as the war progressed. Lincoln also promoted a fresh man to head the newly named Army of the Potomac, George McClellan.

A Brothers' War

John and James Welsh were brothers, raised together in Virginia's beautiful Shenandoah Valley. In 1853, James, seeking more opportunities, moved to Illinois. There he became a Republican and supported Lincoln for president in 1860. When the southern states seceded after having fired on the American flag at Fort Sumter, James Welsh fired off a letter to his brother still in Virginia, declaring that, "Jeff Davis and his crew of pirates," were guilty of "treason and nothing more or less." John responded that he was "very much pained to find...that I have a brother who would advocate sending men here to butcher his own friends and relations." He also announced, "I don't intend to submit to black Republican rule." John angrily informed his brother that becoming a Republican meant renouncing, "home, mother, father and brothers...to sacrifice all for the dear nigger." James replied with equal venom that he never imagined a brother of his could "raise a hand to tear down the glorious Stars and Stripes, a flag that we have been taught from our cradle to look on with pride." He concluded by proclaiming, "I would strike down my own brother if he dared to raise a hand to destroy that flag. We have to rise in our might as a free and independent nation and demand that law must and shall be respected or we shall find ourselves wiped from the face of the earth...and the principles of free government will be dashed to the ground forever."

James and John Welsh never communicated with each other again. John volunteered for the Confederate army. He served with the 27th Virginia and was killed at Gettysburg. James marched in Sherman's campaign through Georgia as a member of the 78th Illinois. He survived. The Civil War has often been called a "Brother's War." In this case and many others, that was literally true. In a deeper sense, it was symbolically true as the now dysfunctional family of the Union had become, as Lincoln had suggested, a "house divided."

George McClellan: The Union's Hope

The press was virtually unanimous in greeting McClellan's appointment as the step that would save the Union. Although he was not yet 35 years old, admirers hailed him as "the Young Napoleon" who brought "an indefinable *air of success.*" A brilliant and hard-working man, he had been admitted to West Point at the age of fifteen and had graduated second in the class. He served with distinction in the Mexican War where he learned the value of avoiding unnecessary head-on assaults. He went on to become a skilled engineer and author of manuals on military tactics.

An excellent military administrator, McClellan quickly imposed order on what he found to be, "chaos...drunken officers and men absent from their regiments without leave—a perfect Pandemonium." He introduced rigorous discipline, staging grand reviews to help morale. His men, who adored him for giving them back their pride, dubbed him "Little Mac." "You have no idea," he told his wife, "how the men brighten up when I go among them...I can see every eye glisten." But all the praise went to his head. He began to see himself as the master of a president for whom he had nothing but contempt, rather than his subordinate. "The President," he wrote his wife, "is nothing more than a well-meaning baboon...the original gorilla." He developed a messiah complex: "I receive letter after letter, have conversation after conversation, calling on me to save the nation...God has placed a great work in my hands."

As summer turned to fall, however, the Army of the Potomac did not appear to be going anywhere. McClellan insisted that it was old General Scott who was responsible for the delays. His old hero was either "a *dotard* or a *traitor.*" Lincoln agreed to Scott's retirement and the promotion of McClellan to General-in-Chief. "I can do it all," McClellan insisted. In reality, however, he did nothing. He had created a magnificent army but seemed to have no plans to lead it anywhere. He tended to exaggerate the odds against his forces. His spies reinforced his natural caution by assuring him that Confederate forces were three times their actual numbers. He was embarrassed when it was discovered that the great cannons Confederates supposedly had trained on Washington were nothing but huge logs painted black, "Quaker guns," in the words of a mocking reporter. Still, he remained immobilized. He imitated the caution he had learned from General Scott in the Mexican War, but he lacked the audacity and remorselessness of the older man. This "problem child of the Civil War" did not have the courage to act at the moment of truth, which is the characteristic of great generals. In addition, as a proslavery-leaning Democrat, he allowed his politics to become intermingled with his military strategy. It took a while for a long-suffering Lincoln, who endured numerous slights and insults from his general, to lose patience.

Lincoln visited McClellan to urge the general to take action.

The Border States

Lincoln worried that the defeat at Bull Run would make it more difficult to keep the slaveholding border states in the Union. Virginia, Arkansas, Tennessee, and North Carolina had voted to secede almost immediately after the firing upon Fort Sumter and Lincoln's call for troops. In Indian Territory in the West (later Oklahoma), the Confederacy won the support of most of the Five Civilized Tribes, many of whom owned slaves. Most remained loyal supporters of the South, although a rival group of Cherokees and most Plains Indians sided with the Union. Elsewhere, the story was different. Delaware, in which slavery had declined to the point that only two of every hundred residents was a slave, never really considered secession. Missouri, Kentucky, and Maryland, however, seemed dangerously undecided. Missouri and Kentucky were first and third among slaves states in the size of their free white population. Confederate control of Missouri would have interfered with Union control of the upper Mississippi and cut Kansas and the Pacific coast off from the central government. Kentucky, with its access to the Ohio River, was a logistical key to campaigns in the West. Maryland was even more crucial since, if it seceded, Washington would have been surrounded by hostile states and would probably have been evacuated.

Although Maryland was probably largely Unionist, southern sympathizers were widespread in Baltimore and on the Eastern shore. A pro-secession mob had actually attacked a Massachusetts regiment on its way to Washington and cut off communications between Washington and the free states. Lincoln arranged for further reinforcements of Union troops to bypass Baltimore until passions cooled. The president threatened to use troops to storm any secessionist strongholds in the state. The legislature, meeting in the Unionist area of western Maryland, voted 53 to 13 to reject secession. To ensure the permanence of this action, Lin-

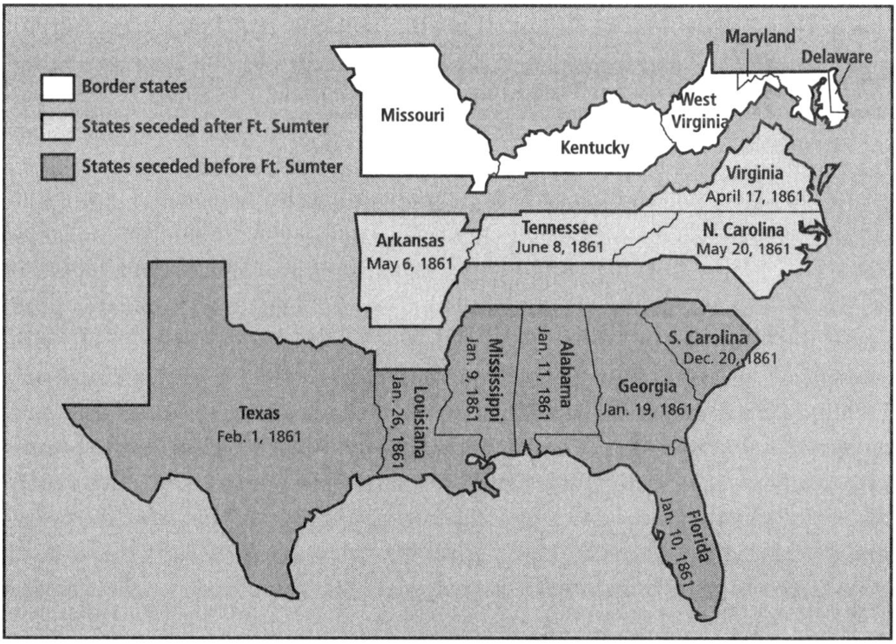

coln suspended the writ of *habeas corpus* in parts of Maryland, denying suspected secessionists the right to be brought before civilian judges. On the eve of a statewide election in the fall of 1861, the pro-confederate mayor of Baltimore and nineteen state legislators were arrested and imprisoned without trial. Confederate sympathizers were arrested when they tried to vote. Maryland held for the Union for the rest of the war, although a substantial proportion of its white male population fought for the Confederacy (20,000 compared to 30,000 for the Union).

The situation was far messier in Missouri. There, largely German-American volunteer regiments from St. Louis surrounded pro-southern militiamen, obtained their surrender, and marched them through St. Louis. An angry mob responded by throwing stones at the "Hessians" and shooting a Union officer. The soldiers then opened fire, killing twenty-eight civilians, including a baby in its mother's arms. Bloody riots followed. Eventually, the army was able to gradually extend the territory under Union control, and the state legislature voted to remain in the Union. During the following three years, however, guerilla warfare devastated the state. Confederate guerilla bandleaders included William Quantrill, a notorious horse thief and murderer, whose force contained such outlaws as the Younger and James brothers. The struggle left an unfortunate postwar legacy of violence arising from "the terrible grudges of neighbor against neighbor created in the guerilla conflict."

Kentucky, the native state of both Abraham Lincoln and Jefferson Davis, best illustrated the idea of "a brothers' war." Three of Henry Clay's grandsons enlisted in the Union army, while four fought for the Confederacy. Two sons of Senator John Crittenden (who had tried to bring about a compromise before the war broke out) became generals, one for the North and the other for the South. Four of Mrs. Lincoln's brothers and three brothers-in-law actually served in the Confederate army, creating suspicions on the part of northern public opinion. As a secessionist governor and Unionist legislature struggled for control, Confederate volunteers marched on one side of a Louisville street while Union troops paraded down the other. After a period in which both governments seemed to accept Kentucky's attempt to declare its neutrality, Unionists organized, keeping the state out of the Confederacy, while federal troops occupied three-quarters of the state. The Civil War itself created a fifth Union border state: West Virginia. The people in the western counties of Virginia had few slaves and had long resented the domination of their state by the "tidewater aristocrats." When Virginia seceded, many of the "up-country" delegates returned home resolved to remain in the Union. After a series of very complicated legal maneuvers, they created a new "reorganized" Virginia, which quickly gave its permission, required by the Constitution, for a new state to be formed from the counties west of the Allegheny Mountains in 1863.

These five border states were considered so important to the success of the Union that Lincoln believed that special efforts were needed to maintain their loyalty. Thus, he resisted pressure from abolitionists and Europeans to tamper with slavery.

THE TWO SIDES

It seemed to many that two irreconcilable nations had arisen. Increasingly, as the two governments built up their armies, raised funds to equip them, and sought diplomatic support abroad, the American people saw themselves as two enemy nations: the Yankees and the Rebels. The British foreign minister commented, "I do not see how the United States can be cobbled together by any compromise." Despite this, however, the two nations tended to face the same wartime problems and come up with remarkably similar solutions.

Northern Advantages

At least on paper, the North appeared to have all the advantages. It had two and a half times as many people (and almost three and a half times the white men of military age) as the South. This meant that a greater pool of manpower was available for the armies and industries of the North. It should be noted, however, that the half million people who lived in the Far West would not be able to contribute to the war effort. During the war, Union regiments had to be diverted to the West to fight Indians. There were thousands of people in border Union states and in southern Illinois, Ohio, and Indiana who supported or even fought for the Confederacy. There also were many Southerners who were loyal to the Union, particularly in backcountry areas, but far less than the reverse. Northern public opinion was more divided than that of the South, and support for the war seemed shakier. A significant southern victory at any of the war's key moments might well have broken the North's resolve to continue the conflict.

The Union had a far more advanced industrial system. The North actually possessed 90 percent of the nation's industry in 1860. Its superiority in military related industries was even greater. For example, it produced fifteen times as much iron and twenty-two times as many firearms as the South. By 1862, the North was able to manufacture virtually all of its war needs. Despite impressive attempts to develop its own munitions plants and other factories, like the huge Tredager Iron Works in Richmond, the Confederacy continued to rely on imports from Europe.

The North also had a far better transportation system than the South. It had twice the density of railroad mileage per square mile, several times the amount of rolling stock, and a much more integrated system. As the war dragged on, the already second-rate Confederate rail system continued to deteriorate until, by 1864, it was virtually non-existent.

One of the most serious deficiencies of the Confederacy was the lack of accessible capital. Southern capital was invested mainly in land and slaves and, thus, was not readily available. The Confederate Treasury Department, in the beginning, consisted of one dirty room in a bank, "without furniture of any kind...or other appliances for the conduct of business." The secretary of the treasury had to use his own money to purchase some dilapidated furniture. The financial structure of the federal government was also antiquated. There was no national bank or even a national currency. The nation's banking system and its supply of liquid capital, however, was concentrated in the cities of the Northeast.

Southern Advantages

With all those obvious disadvantages, how could Southerners have the slightest chance of winning? The most significant advantage for the South was the difference between war aims. The Confederacy did not have to invade the North or demolish northern armies. It had only to defend its own soil and avoid the annihilation of southern armies. In order to win, the North had to invade and conquer the South, a far more difficult task than to defend one's own land. The Crimean War, which had ended in Europe in 1856, showed that modern weaponry made armies almost invulnerable to destruction. They could certainly damage their enemies, but they could not totally eliminate each other. The weaker side had only to hold out, to cause what appeared to be an uneven contest to eventually end inconclusively. In addition, morale, a critical though intangible element, benefited an army fighting to defend its homeland. Confederate leaders commented, "We shall have the enormous advantage of fighting on our own territory and for our very existence." They could appeal to the ardent patriotism of Southerners who considered Yankee domination to be a kind of slavery. In contrast, a struggle to preserve the Union may have seemed far more abstract to the average Northerner.

Geography gave the South another important advantage. The Confederacy was a large territory: at 750,000 square miles, it was double the size of the American colonies in the Revolutionary War. Its topography also benefited the defense. This included the barrier of the Appalachians and heavily wooded areas that provided cover. Invading armies had to depend on railroads vulnerable to guerrilla attacks and on inferior roads. Southern roads were largely dirt tracks, lacking ditches to keep them from becoming virtually impassable in wet weather. Wagons would sink to the axles. One Union officer in Virginia claimed he saw an army mule sink out of sight except for its ears, although "it was a small mule."

Obviously, the roads were just as bad for the Confederate soldiers as they were for the Union forces. But the Southerners, in their own territory, required fewer wagons because they could gather food and supplies from the helpful countryside. In addition, many of these obscure southern roads were not on any map. Often, they ran through thick woodlands where troops could be concealed from the enemy, but a wrong turn could cause them to be hopelessly lost. This was a great advantage for the Confederates who could use these roads for surprise attacks on their enemy.

Since most of the war was fought in the South, Union soldiers had to operate amid an unfriendly population who sometimes brought military intelligence information to Confederate officers. Belle Boyd, who passed important information to Stonewall Jackson in the Shenandoah Valley campaign of 1862, was just one example of a successful southern woman spy.

As the Union army bore deeply into enemy territory, its supply lines grew longer and longer. It became vital to detach troops to defend those lines. Other troops had to be deployed to hold conquered cities and territory. As a result, the supposed numerical superiority of northern troops was, in reality, far less overwhelming than is often portrayed. The best calculation, based on sixty major battles, shows that the Union armies averaged about one-third more men than the Confederates did.

Another Confederate advantage involved the quality of its fighting men. For years, southern officers had dominated the U.S. army. The South seemed to have a better appreciation of military professionalism than the North and, in the earlier stages of the war, did a better job in identifying and promoting its abler officers, including its top echelons. The average Confederate was probably, initially, a better soldier than his Union counterpart. Southern boys almost invariably learned to ride, hunt, and shoot when they were growing up. While this was also true of many northern boys, others had to be taught to shoot. Martial values seemed to be a more central part of southern culture.

Many Southerners firmly believed in the primacy of "King Cotton." They were convinced that the reliance of the British and, to a lesser degree, the French textile industries on American cotton would cause an inevitable intervention by these nations on the Confederate side. (Four-fifths of Britain's cotton supply came from the South.) The North was equally fearful of foreign interference. For the first year and a half of the war, the Confederates continued to expect British and, possibly, French help. By 1862, British cotton imports from the South had fallen to about 1 percent of the 1860 level. By the fall of 1862, however, hopes for British intervention faded. Bumper crops in the late 1850s had created a cotton surplus that continued through 1861. By that time, the British had begun to develop alternate sources of cotton in India and Egypt.

In a shorter war, the southern advantages might well have been crucial. As the war dragged on and on, however, northern material and manpower superiority became increasingly decisive. The years enlarged such material advantages of the North as factories, food production, transportation, and capital.

Rival Governments

Both Abraham Lincoln and Jefferson Davis faced the problem of forming workable governments. The Union had the clear advantage of having a recognized government in place in the nation's capital, while the Confederacy had to begin everything from scratch. The new nation had to decide whether the laws and court decisions of the United States would apply. A new constitution was drafted, which was very similar to the Constitution of the United States. There were a few significant changes reflecting Confederate ideology. The preamble declared that the nation was established by "the people of the Confederate states, each state acting in its sovereign and independent character," rather than by, "We the people," as in the federal Constitution. There was no provision for congressional power to promote the "general welfare." As expected, the constitution "recognized and protected...the right of property in negro slaves." The new nation even had to choose a flag, although some Southerners claimed that they were better representatives of the real America and ought to keep the Stars and Stripes.

Davis was severely limited in choosing his cabinet. He could not pick any southern Unionists and also felt obliged to exclude the most extreme "fire-eaters" who might project an image of irresponsibility. He attempted to balance former Whigs and Democrats and to have one representative from each of the Confederate states. As a result, his cabinet consisted neither of compatible personal friends nor of distinguished southern political leaders. In a government that lacked resources and established procedures or routines, this second-rate cabinet created a serious problem.

Despite the Union advantage of an already existing system of laws, procedures, and flag, Lincoln's government also was initially quite disorganized. Lincoln had scarcely received a ringing mandate in the 1860 election in which he received less than 40 percent of the popular vote. The meager Union army of 14,657 men was experiencing daily defections of southern officers. The same situation plagued many Washington offices. Hundreds, possibly thousands, of eager Republicans flooded into Washington, demanding offices from a besieged president. Lincoln said he was like an innkeeper whose customers clamor for him to rent them rooms in one wing of the inn while he was attempting to douse a fire in his office.

Since Lincoln's cabinet was entirely Republican, none had ever held national executive office. Several had tried to win the Republican nomination in 1860 and continued their rivalries in office. Secretary of State William Seward believed only he could save the country from an inept and unschooled president. Salmon Chase, the egotistic Secretary of Treasury, who also hoped to be president and had an equally patronizing view of Lincoln, was Seward's main rival. Other cabinet members, who had been appointed for political reasons, were also questionable. Simon Cameron, the secretary of war, had received his position as part of a bargain to obtain the backing of Pennsylvania for Lincoln's nomination. His reputation was so unsavory that one observer remarked that the only thing he would not be willing to steal was a red-hot stove. Interested only in utilizing the immense patronage available to him to reward his supporters, Cameron turned the War Department into a mess of incompetence and corruption. In one instance, when a Union general in Missouri requested 411 horses for his cavalry, he was supplied with five dead animals and 350 who were old, blind, or otherwise totally unfit for service.

By 1862 both Lincoln and Davis realized that they needed better cabinet officers. Lincoln convinced Cameron to take the position of American minister to Russia. He then appointed Edwin Stanton, a blunt and domineering man, to reorganize the War Department and eliminate fraud and patronage. A confirmed workaholic, Stanton succeeded in minimizing corruption and assuring that the Union army was the most well equipped force in history up to that time. Davis also strengthened his War Department by appointing a hard-working secretary. His best appointment was the Chief of Ordinance, Josiah Gorgas, who created hundreds of factories to supply powder and ammunition. His unique innovations included an appeal to southern churches and plantations to donate their bells to be recast into cannon. Southern women were recruited to save the contents of their chamber pots to be filtered to extract niter that produced gunpowder. Army officers even searched battlefields to find lead to be recycled into bullets.

Both sides faced similar problems in raising money and troops. Neither knew what to do with the initial flood of volunteers. The twelve-month enlistment period for Confederate troops was about to expire in the spring of 1862, just as the Union army was advancing toward Richmond. Despite some discomfort about ignoring states' rights, the Confederate Congress passed a national conscription act on April 16, 1862. In theory, every healthy white male between the ages of 18 and 35 was eligible for this first draft in American history. In reality, there were many exemptions, including government officials and, in a later act, planters or overseers responsible for twenty or more slaves. This last provision created a great deal of animosity on the part of small farmers who complained, as did their northern counterparts, that it was "a rich man's war, but a poor man's fight." The law was designed more to encourage reenlistment than to raise troops. It stated that those who stayed could continue in their regiments and elect their own officers, while those who departed might be subject to draft and sent to any regiment that needed men.

The Union also moved to conscription, although somewhat more slowly. After the particularly ferocious battles in the summer of 1862, volunteering virtually ceased. In July Congress passed a vague authorization for the president to fix quotas of troops for each state to raise and to utilize a draft if these quotas were not met. This implied threat did not work. In March 1863, Congress passed a national draft law under which practically all young male adults were eligible. Unfortunately, a potential conscript could escape service by hiring a substitute or paying the government $300. This led to fierce opposition to conscription, particularly on the part of workers and immigrants who lacked the wealth to buy their way out. In the end, a relatively small number of men were actually drafted, as the law seemed to lead to more voluntary enlistments.

If raising troops presented a problem to both governments, raising funds to pay for and supply them was even more difficult. Taxes might have been one source of revenue, but Americans of that era were not accustomed to paying taxes. Both administrations feared that an imposition of taxes might kill their citizens' enthusiasm for the war effort. Americans, it seemed, were "more willing to die for their government than to pay for it." The Union Congress did take the unusual step of imposing an income tax of 3 percent on incomes over $800 a year (later increased to 5 percent). This was not collected until late in 1862 but eventually supplied about 21 percent of Union war finances. The Confederacy also imposed a 0.5 percent "war tax," but states' resistance made it impossible to collect. Taxation barely produced 5 percent of the total funds of the Confederate government. Neither side could realistically expect to borrow large sums of money to finance the war either. Americans of that era tended to stash away any extra money and were suspicious of pieces of paper promising future payment (bonds). Although the sale of war bonds got off to a very slow start, eventually Union Treasury Secretary Chase was able to organize an army of 2,500 agents to sell bonds throughout the North. Ultimately, close to a million Northerners, 1 out of 4 families, purchased war bonds. Borrowing was far less successful for the Confederacy. Attempts to sell bonds directly to the southern people were stymied by the lack of precious metals to pay for the bonds. Eventually, the Confederate government issued such large quantities of bonds that people lost what little faith they had and refused to buy them. Attempts to float bonds in Europe using cotton as security were equally unsuccessful.

As a result, both governments started to issue paper money, backed only by a promise to one day repurchase the notes with gold. Although he had once condemned "an irredeemable paper currency" that would result in "impoverishing the masses and discrediting the government," Treasury Secretary Chase came to feel that issuing paper money was "indispensably necessary." Early in 1862, Congress passed the Legal Tender Act authorizing the printing of $150 million in treasury notes, promptly called "greenbacks" because of their color. The Confederacy was far more dependent on paper currency to pay for the war. The national government, states, banks, and even cities all issued their own notes in the South, producing disorder and extreme inflation. The $1.5 billion in paper money printed by the Confederacy was more than twice the amount produced in the North. While prices in the North rose 80 percent, this was comparable to the inflation in World War I and II. By contrast, prices in the South rose a disastrous 9,000 percent.

The Two Leaders

Although it was not immediately apparent at the time, the character and ability of its president gave a clear advantage to the Union. Both presidents involved themselves in military strategy, a role that seemed better fit for the Confederate leader. Jefferson Davis was a West Point graduate who had commanded troops in the Mexican War. Despite this, he turned out to be very mediocre as a military strategist. He had a tendency to keep inept generals who were friends and to provoke quarrels with other generals and subordinates. A proud man, he tended to be aloof and inflexible and was plagued by poor health. He suffered from insomnia and a twitching cheek, a symptom of neuralgia that eventually caused him to lose his sight in one eye. He was so formal that he didn't even call his slaves by their first names. His adoring wife admitted that "he did not know the arts of a politician and would not practice them if understood." A good deal of his energy had to be expended in fending off ardent advocates of states rights who resisted almost every attempt to establish national authority. The governors of Georgia and North Carolina even tried to separate their forces from the Confederate army and to stash away extra supplies for their states' militias. Judah Benjamin, a brilliant and arrogant New Orleans lawyer who held a variety of cabinet posts including secretary of state, was the most capable member of the Davis administration. He was, however, constantly attacked by both newspapers and politicians as "the hated Jew" and was given only lukewarm support by Davis.

Abraham Lincoln had less experience in high political or military office than any chief executive. Many feared that the Illinois rail-splitter would not be up to the intimidating responsibilities he faced. But, in disposition and character, he was more fit to lead in a lengthy conflict than Davis was. He was tolerant, adaptable, untiring, and a shrewd politician. He endured savage attacks in the press, describing him as an ignorant clown, an "ape," a petty bumbling fool. Faced with the daunting task of molding opposing elements into a government capable of winning the war and defining the nature of its victory, he succeeded brilliantly in accomplishing this task. When Lincoln first took office, Seward seriously offered to take over most of the president's functions in view of his obvious superiority. But Seward quickly learned after a disagreement with Lincoln that "the President is the best of us. There is only one vote in the Cabinet, and it belongs to him. Executive ability and vigor are rare qualities, but he has them both." Lincoln combined firmness, tact, and humor in creating an effective team out of a divided cabinet. Each secretary was allowed to run his own department administratively, but the president always made the important policy decisions. Lincoln had the ability to dominate his subordinates without appearing to do so.

Lincoln seldom took action until he believed that public opinion would support him, enduring attacks for his incompetent leadership. Abolitionists insisted that he moved far too slowly, while conservatives criticized him for going too fast. He often responded to questions about what his policy was on a given issue by saying, "My policy is to have no policy." As a master of careful timing, he understood how to use a series of small decisions to lay the groundwork for a major policy like emancipation.

In addition to his political skills, Lincoln demonstrated generosity, great intelligence and an unparalleled ability to express his ideas in soaring prose. He understood that the war tested the very principle of democracy in an era when conservative Europeans believed that democratic governments were doomed to sink into anarchy. Despite his famous humor, he had a deep streak of melancholy and remained a mystery, even to those who were closest to him. His law partner, William Herndon, characterized him as a "sphinx…incommunicative—silent—reticent—secretive—having profound policies—and well laid—deeply studied plans." One commentator has described the curious ability of Lincoln to "remove himself from himself, as if he were looking at himself."

Lincoln had a remarkably broad view of presidential war powers: "I conceive that I may in an emergency do things on military grounds which cannot be done constitutionally by Congress." Since his whole presidency took place during an emergency, he claimed more power than any other American president had. This led opponents, with some justification, to call him "tyrant," "dictator," and "despot." Rather than call Congress into session after the bombardment of Fort Sumter, he proclaimed a blockade, in effect a declaration of war. Without any legislative authority, he issued a call on May 3, 1861, for forty new regiments of three-year volunteers. Despite the provision in the Constitution that, "No money shall be drawn from the Treasury, but in Consequence of Appropriations made by Law," he appropriated $2,000,000 for "military measures necessary for the defence and support of the government." (When Congress met that summer, it retroactively approved of these executive actions.)

Lincoln's trampling of some of the constitutional protections of personal rights and liberties was more problematic. Citing "the extremest necessity," the president gave military commanders the right to arrest people without warrants and suspended the writ of habeas corpus in some parts of the country, particularly in crucial border states. Approximately fifteen thousand Americans were imprisoned under these provisions, many of whom remained in jail without trial until the end of the war. Most were real Confederate sympathizers in or close to war zones, but some were men whose crime was to get drunk and shout, "hurrah for Jeff Davis." A few were even imprisoned for eliminating the established prayer for the president from church services. Despite this extreme assertion of executive authority, there is no evidence that Lincoln had any intention of continuing this expansion of executive power once the war ended.

EUROPE AND THE WAR

In the world of diplomacy large internal conflicts often escalate into international wars. The South had hoped for foreign intervention based on the "King Cotton" illusion. Northerners, knowing the strength of the anti-slavery movement in Europe, hoped for a condemnation of the slaveholding Confederacy. This was as much an illusion as the Confederate hopes had been, particularly since in the early years of the war the Union government took no steps towards emancipation and even proclaimed that it would not interfere with slavery where it existed. In a war whose purpose was declared to be the maintenance or break-up of the Union, European policy would be determined by their own self-interest. European powers quickly declared neutrality. They recognized the existence of a state of war between the Union and "the states styling themselves the Confederate States of America." They acknowledged the Confederacy as a belligerent but not as an independent nation. Although both the Union and the Confederacy considered this a great southern success, it was merely an impartial recognition of international law.

Seward's Early Ideas

William Seward, who eventually would rank as a great secretary of state, had some decidedly outlandish ideas in the early days of the crisis. In a private memorandum to Lincoln he urged a shifting of the issues before the public to "a question upon union or disunion." This would be achieved by provoking war with Great Britain, Russia, France, and Spain! Lincoln responded by quietly filing away this eccentric plan to start a world war and permitting Seward to recover his good sense. Nevertheless, word of Seward's aggressiveness leaked out and may well have encouraged European powers to be more cautious in any inclinations to recognize the Confederacy.

The best Union diplomatic appointment was Charles Francis Adams as minister to Great Britain. Adams proved to be a polished, tactful, and dignified am-

Jefferson Davis, President of the Confederacy, (left) and William H. Seward, (right) Secretary of State for the Lincoln administration.

bassador. His lineage as the son of President John Quincy Adams and grandson of John Adams appealed to the aristocratic British foreign ministry officials. By contrast, the first Confederate commissioner to Great Britain, William Yancey, was a well-known "fire-eater," who angered British anti-slavery forces.

The Blockade and Diplomatic Issues

Lincoln's proclamation of a blockade of southern ports was his first significant strategic decision. Lincoln understood that no matter how large the Confederate army was, they would still have to import huge amounts of military supplies from Europe in return for cotton exports. This was particularly true early in the war before they could develop their own sources of equipment. At the beginning, of course, the Union navy had too few ships to seal off a 3,550-mile Confederate coastline. Eventually, the number of Union warships grew from 42 to 700. The effectiveness of the Union blockade has been the subject of some dispute. Although most Confederate blockade-runners were able to get through in the early years of the war, they had to be fast, light vessels that had very limited carrying capacity. By the latter part of the war, the ocean trade of the South was cut by two-thirds. The greatest success was the prevention of the importation of heavy industrial equipment. This meant that the crumbling southern railroad system could not be maintained or replaced, which had an enormous impact on the ability of the Confederacy to supply its troops.

From a diplomatic point of view, Lincoln's blockade proclamation weakened his public position that the war was only a domestic uprising. In international law, a blockade is considered a weapon of war between sovereign states. The United States had insisted in the War of 1812 that a blockade was legal only if every enemy port was totally sealed off, an obvious impossibility. The British had always argued that a blockade was "physically effective" if patrolling warships attempted to stop vessels going to or from enemy ports. Now that the United States was at war and the British neutral, the Union adopted the traditional British stance. The British government accepted the legality of the blockade. The British navy, in the past, had also put forth the doctrine of "continuous voyage" to allow the seizure of cargoes going to neutral ports that might eventually end up in enemy hands. The United States now adopted this view when they seized British ships with war contraband headed for Mexican and West Indian ports. While the British press demanded retaliation against the "arrogant Yankees," the government tacitly accepted the American assertion of "continuous transportation." (Much later, in World War I, Britain used this same justification to intercept American exports to neutral nations that were ultimately bound for Germany.)

The Trent Affair

In November 1861 this neutrality was almost destroyed by the reckless act of Union naval Captain and Antarctic explorer Charles Wilkes. His warship, patrolling off the coast of Cuba, stopped the British steamship *Trent* and arrested two Confederate envoys, John Slidell and James Mason, on their way to Paris and London. Although Wilkes' action was a clear violation of international law, he was greeted as a national hero when he returned to Boston with his prisoners. The *New York Times* advocated that a second Independence Day be declared in his honor, and Congress voted him a special medal. The British were not amused. Prime Minister Palmerston informed his anxious cabinet, "You may stand for this but damned if I will!" The British fleet was put on war footing, and thousands of reinforcements were dispatched to Canada. It seemed to many that war was inevitable. Charles Darwin wrote to an American scientist, who was his friend, "When you receive this we may be at war, and we two be bound as good patriots to hate each other."

Neither side, however, would gain from such a "silly" conflict. When the British government prepared an uncompromising note demanding an apology and release of the Confederate agents, Prince Albert (Queen Victoria's husband), on his deathbed, softened its tone. He added the idea that Wilkes' action might have been unauthorized. This gave Lincoln a face-saving way of releasing the envoys. His cabinet wanted to hold the Confederate agents, but the president said they had become "white elephants" and a nation should fight "one war at a time." Mason and Slidell went on to London and Paris where they spent the next three years in a fruitless attempt to win European recognition and help.

In the end, Europeans continued their neutrality. Northern wheat had become crucial for European food supplies, more important than southern cotton. Although Napoleon III of France used the distractions of the war to attempt to gain a foothold in Mexico, most imperial powers believed it was against their interests to establish the precedent of supporting a war for political independence. The British government flirted with the idea of offering to mediate the conflict but ultimately backed away from the proposal. Only a series of decisive Confederate victories, assuring political independence, might have induced the British to recognize its nationhood. On the other hand, a Union unequivocally committed to ending slavery might neutralize pro-Confederate sentiment in Great Britain.

THE WAR STALLS

By December 1861, the Union had over 600,000 men in its armies and navies. Yet McClellan brought his great army into its winter quarters. He still blamed others for this hiatus. He had been "thwarted and deceived by...incapables at every turn," he informed his wife. "It now begins to look as if we are condemned to a winter of inactivity. If it is so the fault will not be mine." McClellan took great pride in marching his men smartly in parade but continued to be reluctant to risk his well-drilled troops in actual conflict. His chronic unwillingness to risk failure was compounded by a case of typhoid fever.

In the interim, Congress had reconvened. Radical Republicans, who opposed slavery and were angry about the returning of fugitives by generals "soft on the Negro question," established a Joint Committee on the Conduct of the War. The committee began to suspect that McClellan, known for his "softness" on slavery, was reluctant to fight the rebels. Radicals demanded that he be replaced. Even Secretary of War Stanton, a friend of McClellan's, wrote, "*The champagne and oysters on the Potomac must be stopped.* I will *force* this man McClellan to fight." Lincoln's patience also began to wear thin, and he issued General Order No. 1, designating February 22 (Washington's birthday) as "the day for a general movement of the land and naval forces of the United States against the insurgent forces." McClellan, however, paid little attention to this direct command. On February 13, 1862, he bragged, "In ten days I shall be in Richmond." In reality, Union troops did not enter Richmond until 1865. On March 11, McClellan was relieved of his post as general-in-chief of the Union armies so he could concentrate all his attention on the grand assault on Richmond.

DOCUMENTS

FIRST BATTLE OF BULL RUN

*When the war began, both North and South were overcome with enthusiasm. Each assumed the war would be over in a few weeks. The first battle and its unheard-of casualties, a decisive Union debacle that the Confederate army was unable to capitalize on, quickly sobered the public. William Russell, a well-known correspondent of the London **Times**, wrote this account of the battle that angered many Northerners, including President Lincoln.*

July 21, 1861
Manassas, Virginia

WILLIAM HOWARD RUSSELL

Centreville appeared in sight—a few houses on our front, beyond which rose a bald hill, the slopes covered with bivouac huts, commissariat carts, and horses, and the top crested with spectators of the fight.

The scene was so peaceful a man might well doubt the evidence of one sense that a great contest was being played out below in bloodshed....But the cannon spoke out loudly from the green bushes, and the plains below were mottled, so to speak, by puffs of smoke and by white rings from bursting shells and capricious howitzers....With the glass I could detect now and then the flash of arms through the dust clouds in the open, but no one could tell to which side the troops who were moving belonged, and I could only judge from the smoke whether the guns were fired towards or away from the hill. In the midst of our little reconnaissance Mr. Vizetelly, who has been living and, indeed, marching with one of the regiments as artist of the Illustrated London News, came up and told us the action had been commenced in splendid style by the Federalists, who had advanced steadily, driving the Confederates before them—a part of the plan, as I firmly believe, to bring them under the range of their guns. He believed the advantages on the Federalist side were decided, though won with hard fighting.

As I turned down into the narrow road, or lane, there was a forward movement among the large four-wheeled tilt waggons, when suddenly there arose a tumult in front of me at a small bridge across the road, and then I perceived the drivers of a set of waggons with the horses turned towards me, who were endeavouring to force their way against the stream of vehicles setting in the other direction. By the side of the new set of waggons there were a number of commissariat men and soldiers, whom at first sight I took to be the baggage guard. They looked excited and alarmed and were running by the side of the horses—in front the dust quite obscured the view. At the bridge the currents met in wild disorder. "Turn back! Retreat!" shouted the men from the front, "We're whipped, we're whipped!" They cursed and tugged at the horses' heads, and struggled with frenzy to get past. I got my horse up into the field out of the road, and went on rapidly towards the front. Soon I met soldiers who were coming through the corn, mostly without arms; and presently I saw firelocks, cooking tins, knapsacks, and greatcoats on the ground, and observed that the confusion and speed of the baggage-carts became greater, and that many of them were crowded with men, or were followed by others, who clung to them. The ambulances were crowded with soldiers, but it did not look as if there were many wounded. Negro servants on led horses dashed frantically past; men in uniform, whom it were a disgrace to the profession of arms to call "soldiers," swarmed by on mules, chargers, and even draught horses, which had been cut out of carts or waggons, and went on with harness clinging to their heels, as frightened as their riders. Men literally screamed with rage and fright when their way was blocked up. On I rode, asking all "What is all this about?" and now and then, but rarely, receiving the answer, "We're whipped;" or, "We're repulsed." Faces black and dusty, tongues out in the heat, eyes staring—it was a most wonderful sight.

All the road from Centreville for miles presented such a sight as can only be witnessed in the track of the runaways of an utterly demoralized army. Drivers flogged, lashed, spurred, and beat their horses, or leaped down and abandoned their teams, and ran by the side of the road; mounted men, servants, and men in uniform, vehicles of all sorts, commissariat waggons thronged the narrow ways. At every shot a convulsion as it were seized upon the morbid mass of bones, sinew, wood, and iron, and thrilled through it, giving new energy and action to its desperate efforts to get free from itself....The Federalists, utterly routed, had fallen back upon Arlington to defend the capital, leaving nearly five batteries of artillery, 8,000 muskets, immense quantity of stores and baggage, and their wounded and prisoners in the hands of the enemy!

Source: The London *Times*, August 6, 1861.

1. How does Russell characterize the actions of the "Federalist" (Union) army?
2. What impact do you think his report would have had in England?
3. How would the outcome of this first battle of the war have affected the attitudes and actions of both sides?

THE SIGNIFICANCE OF SLAVERY

Although Lincoln declared that the war was a "struggle to save the Union and is not either to save or destroy slavery," the issue of slavery, the basic cause of the war, continued to linger above the conflict. Early in the war, Southerners continued to argue that slavery was a source of strength to them. Northern officers increasingly noticed that the slaves were taking matters into their own hands by fleeing to Union lines.

A UNION GENERAL ON THE SIGNIFICANCE OF SLAVES

In September and October last, and perhaps as late as November (1861) in two or three instances, orders came from the headquarters of the army of the Potomac, directing that such and such persons naming them—claiming to have slaves in one of my camps...should be permitted to search the camp, and reclaim their slaves. I addressed a communication...stating that such steps would likely lead to disorder and mischief in the camps; because in several instances the sympathies of the men [Union soldiers] had been excited by seeing slaves, reclaimed under such circumstances, very harshly treated....

The most valuable and reliable information of the enemy's movements in our vicinity that we have been able to get derived [originated] from Negroes who came into our lines....

...They will submit to any privation, perform any duty, incur any danger. I know an instance in which four of them recently carried a boat from the Rappahannock River [Virginia], passing through the enemy's pickets successfully, to the Potomac and crossed over to my camp and reported themselves there. They gave us information of the enemy's force which was communicated to headquarters; a service upon which it would be difficult to fix a price. These services rendered by these men are known to the soldiers, and contribute, I presume, largely to the sympathy they feel for them....

...There was one case in the 5th regiment where a man named Cox claimed some slaves. He was very badly treated by the soldiers. He came there with an order from the division headquarters for two or three slaves. He pointed out who they were and undertook to take them away; but the soldiers pounced upon him and beat him severely....He went away without his slaves.

With our people there was a feeling of indignation against it, from the lowest to the highest; it was a universal feeling.

Testimony of GENERAL DANIEL E. SICKLES before the *Joint Committee on the Conduct of the War, 37th [U.S.] Congress, Third Session1862*

A SOUTHERN NEWSPAPER ON THE "ADVANTAGES" OF SLAVERY

The total white population of the eleven States now comprising the Confederacy is 6,000,000, and therefore to fill up the ranks of the proposed army (600,000) about ten per cent of the entire white population will be required. In any other country but our own such a draft could not be met, but the Southern States can furnish that number of men, and still not leave the material interests of the country in a suffering condition. Those who are incapacitated for bearing arms can oversee the plantation, and the Negroes can go on undisturbed in their usual labors. In the North, the case is different; the men who join the army of subjugation are the laborers, the producers and the factory operatives. Nearly every man from that section, especially those from the rural districts, leaves some branch of industry to suffer during his absence. The institution of slavery in the South alone enables her to place in the field a force much larger in proportion to her white population in the North....The institution is a tower of strength to the South, particularly at the present crisis, and our enemies will be likely to find that the "moral cancer" about which their orators are so fond of prating, is really one of the most effective weapons employed against the union by the South.

Editorial in the *Montgomery Advertiser*

Alabama, November 6, 1861

A NORTHERN GENERAL ON SLAVERY AS A MILITARY QUESTION

Sir:

Since I wrote my last dispatch the question in regard to slave property is becoming one of very serious magnitude. The inhabitants of Virginia are using their Negroes in the batteries, and are preparing to send the women and children South. The escapes [of slaves] from them are very numerous and a squad [of escaped slaves] has come in this morning to my pickets bringing their women and children.... Twelve of these Negroes I am informed have escaped from the erection of batteries on Sewall's Point which this morning fired upon my expedition as it passed by out of range. As a means of offense therefore in the enemy's hands these Negroes when able bodied are of... importance. Without them the batteries could not have been erected at least for many weeks. As a military question it would seem to be a measure of necessity to deprive their masters of their services. How can this be done? As a political question and as a question of humanity can I receive the services of a father and mother and not take the children? Of the humanitarian aspect I have no doubt. Of the political one I have no right to judge. I therefore submit all of this to your better judgement....

Letter from GENERAL BENJAMIN BUTLER to General-in-Chief Winfield Scott, May 27, 1861

1. What attitude towards slavery does General Sickles attribute to his men?
2. How would such an attitude affect the actions of Union troops and the treatment of slaves?
3. Why does the southern newspaper consider slavery to be an advantage for the South?
4. What flaws, if any, do you find in its argument?
5. What actions by slaves are reported by General Butler?
6. In the long run, how do you think slavery and the reaction of slaves would affect the outcome of the war?

THE STRUGGLE TO ALLOW BLACK TROOPS IN THE UNION ARMY

As the war dragged on with its appalling casualties, many people realized that there was a large source of manpower still unused: African Americans. However, allowing blacks to be soldiers would seem to suggest that white Northerners were willing to recognize them as equals. Blacks, like the great abolitionist leader, Frederick Douglass, argued passionately for the use of African-American soldiers. Many white Northerners were equally vehement in their opposition.

Newspaper Editorial by Frederick Douglass

Our Presidents, Governors, Generals and Secretaries are calling, with almost frantic vehemence, for men—"Men! men! send us men!" they scream, or the cause of the Union is gone;...and yet these very officers, representing the people and Government, steadily and persistently refuse to receive the very class of men which have a deeper interest in the defeat and humiliation of the rebels, than all others.... What a spectacle of blind, unreasoning prejudice and pusillanimity is this! The national edifice is on fire. Every man who can carry a bucket of water, or remove a brick, is wanted; but those who have the care of the building, having a profound respect for the feeling of the national burglars who set the building on fire are determined that the flames shall only be extinguished by Indo-Caucasian hands, and to have the building burnt rather than save it by means of any other. Such is the pride, the stupid prejudice and folly that rules the hour.

Why does the Government reject the negro? Is he not a man? Can he not wield a sword, fire a gun, march and countermarch, and obey orders like any other?...If persons so humble as we can be allowed to speak to the President of the United States, we should ask him if this dark and terrible hour of the nation's extremity is a time for consulting a mere vulgar and unnatural prejudice?...We would tell him that this is no time to fight with one hand, when both are needed; that this is no time to fight only with your white hand, and allow your black hand to remain tied.... While the Government continues to refuse the aid of colored men, thus alienating them from the national cause, and giving the rebels the advantage of them, it will not deserve better fortunes than it has thus far experienced.—Men in earnest don't fight with one hand, when they might fight with two, and a man drowning would not refuse to be saved even by a colored hand.

Source: *Douglass' Monthly*, September 1861.

PUBLIC OPPOSITION TO USE OF BLACK TROOPS

Letter to the Editor,

I am quite sure there is not one man in ten but would feel himself degraded as a volunteer if negro equality is to be the order in the field of battle.... I take the liberty of warning the abettors of fraternizing with the blacks, that one negro regiment, in the present temper of things, put on equality with those who have the past year fought and suffered, will withdraw an amount of life and energy in our army equal to disbanding ten of the best regiments we can now raise.

Source: *New York Tribune*, August 16, 1862.

1. What argument does Frederick Douglass put forward for using black troops in the war?
2. Why does the letter writer oppose the use of such troops?
3. Which argument do you think would win out in the long run? Why?

ANDERSONVILLE PRISONER

Chapter Seven

THE WAR INTENSIFIES

UNCONDITIONAL SURRENDER IN THE WEST

Although the nation's capital was preoccupied with the lack of action on the Potomac, good news began to arrive from the West. William Tecumseh Sherman once wrote, "Whatever nation gets…control of the Ohio, Mississippi, and Missouri Rivers will control the continent." These western rivers, which flowed north to south, cut into the heart of the Confederacy.

U.S. Grant, who had already seized Paducah, Kentucky in 1861, controlling access to the Tennessee and Cumberland Rivers, won two even more important victories. His troops, assisted by fleets of gunboats, captured **Fort Henry** on the Tennessee and **Fort Donelson** on the Cumberland. When the Confederate commander of the latter asked for surrender terms, Grant replied, "No terms except unconditional and immediate surrender can be accepted. I propose to move immediately upon your works." Nearly fifteen thousand Rebel soldiers surrendered. Northerners went crazy with excitement over "Unconditional Surrender Grant," who had forced the Confederates out of Kentucky and half of Tennessee. Grant was a modest 39-year-old who had graduated only twenty-first out of thirty-nine in his West Point class, left the army under a cloud, and had difficulty even getting a command in the war. Now he was promoted to the rank of major general. Newspaper stories, describing him coolly smoking under fire, led grateful admirers to send him hundreds of barrels of cigars. Although he had always smoked a pipe, he began smoking twenty cigars a day, a habit that probably led to his eventual death from throat cancer.

Even more important, with the Cumberland River under the control of the Union navy, Confederates were forced to abandon Nashville. It was the first Confederate capital to fall to Union forces. Grant, with about forty thousand men, continued to advance southward along the Tennessee River, hoping to gain control of railroad lines essential to the Confederacy. His men, excited by their recent victory at Fort Donelson, expected an easy victory. Grant, himself, underestimated the Confederate will to resist, writing to his wife, "'Sesesch' is...on its last legs in Tennessee." He predicted a big battle, which "it appears to me, will be the last in the west." He encamped near **Shiloh**, Tennessee, awaiting reinforcements for a prospective drive into the heart of Mississippi. Some of the men whiled away their time shooting at flocks of wild geese or even at civilians on the riverbanks. For almost a month, the soldiers shivered with anticipation as well as from the cold and wet and suffered from dysentery (called "the Tennessee Two-Step"). Albert Sidney Johnston, a general both Grant and Jefferson Davis considered the most accomplished southern officer, decided to attack before the fresh Union troops arrived. On the first day, April 6, Grant's troops were driven back two miles to the river. Amidst the piles of wounded and corpses, General Sherman, who had returned after shaking off severe depression that winter, came upon his commander getting ready to sleep under a tree. "Well Grant," Sherman declared, "We've had the devil's own day, haven't we?" Grant responded, "Yes. Lick 'em tomorrow." That kind of tenacious attitude was one element in Grant's greatness as a general. The South also suffered from what Jefferson Davis called an "irreparable" loss. General Johnston, after leading an exuberant charge on his horse, Fire-Eater, was hit by a Union bullet that severed an artery in his knee, and he died that afternoon.

The next day, the fresh federal troops arrived and the Union forces attacked. The outnumbered and bedraggled Southerners, drenched by a relentless night long rainfall, were forced to withdraw. The battlefield was so covered with corpses that Grant later recalled, "it would have been possible to walk across the clearing in any direction stepping on dead bodies without a foot touching the ground." One amazing sight was that of a large Northerner and young Southerner laying against each other, each with gun in hand. They had shot each other at point blank range, and their faces in their "death embrace" were virtually expressionless. Of the 100,000 men who fought at "Bloody Shiloh," almost 1 in 4 was a casualty. The 3,757 men who died exceeded the total of American soldiers killed in the Revolution, War of 1812, and Mexican War combined. One Union officer, the 32-year-old James A. Garfield (later to become President of the United States) wandered out beyond the Union lines where dead bodies were stacked in rows, and the stench was unbearable. He wrote home, "The horrible sights that I have witnessed on this field I can never describe. No blaze of glory, that flashes around the magnificent triumphs of war, can ever atone for the unwritten and unutterable horrors of the scene of carnage."

Some appalled Northerners called for the dismissal of the "butcher," Grant. The general, however, understood the real meaning of the carnage: "I gave up all idea of saving the Union except by *complete conquest.*" Despite the criticism, Lincoln still frustrated by the inactivity and failures of his eastern generals, declared, "I can't spare this man; he fights." The Battle of Shiloh may well have been the decisive conflict in the struggle to control the Mississippi Valley without which the Confederates could not really expect to win the war. Northern forces then marched into Corinth, Mississippi, a railroad center, and gained control of the Mississippi River to Memphis.

As the North celebrated the victories in Tennessee, word arrived of an astounding naval triumph—the capture of **New Orleans**. The Union fleet, commanded by a 60-year-old Southerner, David Farragut, slipped past forts and smashed barricades to seize the virtually undefended city without having to fire a shot. Farragut, who had served in his country's navy for fifty years, like most naval officers had a stronger feeling of nationalism than many Americans did. "You fellows will catch the devil before you get through with this business," he warned Southerners who joined the Confederacy. Farragut, who also captured Baton Rouge and Natchez, became a hero in the North and the country's first rear admiral. Only Vicksburg, high on a bluff, remained impregnable and kept the Union from having total control of the Mississippi River.

Naval Warfare: The Ironclads

The Confederacy was forced to take the lead in experimentation in the field of naval warfare. When the war began, the southern Secretary of the Navy had no navy whatsoever to command. "I regard the possession of an iron-armored ship as a matter of the first necessity," he wrote. He believed that, since the Confederacy could never construct as large a fleet as the Union, it could use iron ships to demolish wooden ones at will. The Confederacy actually built a number of these vessels. The most famous was the *Virginia,* originally the warship *Merrimack,* which had been scuttled when the Union abandoned the Norfolk naval yards. Since April 1861, Confederate workers had been bolting four-inch iron plates on its superstructure and a cast-iron battering ram on its front.

Union Secretary of the Navy Gideon Welles immediately understood the potential of the "monster." He begged the Swedish-born inventor John Ericsson, an eccentric, brilliant, and contentious man who had a running feud with the navy, to design a ship to counter the *Virginia.* Ericsson came up with an entirely new kind of ironclad, the *Monitor,* that he built in three months. It looked like "a tin can on a shingle." It had two guns to the *Virginia*'s ten, but they were mounted on a revolving turret. Many professional naval men had quarreled with Ericsson and remembered when an experimental gun he designed had blown up in 1844, killing the Secretaries of State and the Navy. They were skeptical about the ability of the odd-looking vessel to actually work. Lincoln overruled them, remarking, "All I can say is what the girl said when she put her foot in the stocking—I think there's *something* in it."

On March 8, 1862, washday for the blockading Union fleet, the *Virginia* headed for a Union gun sloop where she appeared "like a huge, half-submerged crocodile." The horrified Union naval officers watched as their bullets bounced off the *Virginia*'s side, "like India rubber balls." The *Virginia* went on to destroy two ships and run a third aground. It seemed as if the South had found the means of breaking the northern blockade. The next day, however, the odd-looking *Monitor* appeared to bar the way. The two ironclads hammered away at each other for more than three hours until the exhausted crews withdrew. Although the battle was a draw, the *Virginia*'s threat to the Union blockade ended, and the *Monitor*, faster and more maneuverable, proved to be the superior ship. Two months later,

The Monitor and the Merrimack

when Norfolk fell to the Union, the Southerners blew up the *Virginia* to prevent her capture. The Union went on to build fifty-eight more ironclads just like the *Monitor.* The nature of naval warfare had been altered forever as wooden ships became obsolete.

The Confederate navy also experimented with other new weapons. They were the first to use "infernal machines" (torpedoes created from cans or barrels filled with explosives) to sink Union vessels. They also were the first to test submarines. The most successful was the *H.L. Hunley.* It was driven under water by a crank turned by its crew. Four times, trial runs resulted in the death of all the crew. Finally, in 1864, the *Hunley* succeeded in sinking a Union warship in Charleston harbor, but the submarine also sank in the effort. In the end, no matter how innovative they may have been, Confederate naval officials could not keep up with the steady growth of the Union navy that made the increasing effectiveness of the blockade of southern ports possible.

They did have some success in commissioning British ship builders to construct conventional naval raiders to prey upon Union merchant shipping. The most notorious of these was the *Alabama.* From 1862 to 1864, it roamed the oceans destroying sixty-nine merchant ships, valued at $6 million before the Union navy finally sunk it. These raiders caused insurance costs to rise so much that most of the merchant marine stayed out of the ocean during the war. Two ships under construction in Liverpool, England represented a far greater menace. They were steam-powered, iron-plated, and outfitted with underwater ramming spikes. They would have been effective weapons against the wooden ships of the Union blockade. In September 1863, however, the British Foreign Office acceded to Union pressure and withheld these "Laird rams." This destroyed the last hope the Confederacy had of breaking the blockade.

Virginia: 1862

As events unfolded in the West and in the navy, Washington was preoccupied with its own protection and a great assault on the enemy capital, Richmond. McClellan had succeeded in creating a combat-ready army, the most formidable one in American history. Lincoln who, in exasperation with the slow pace had taken to studying books on military strategy, favored a massive frontal attack on Richmond. Despite, or perhaps because of its presidential backing, McClellan opposed this plan. Rather than heading overland directly to Richmond, he decided on a roundabout route to bypass Confederate defenses. In March 1862, an enormous flotilla of four hundred ships transported his troops down the Potomac to "the Peninsula," a strip of land east of Richmond between the York and James Rivers.

The General's Wife

One of the men leading the fight at Shiloh was 40-year-old Brigadier General William H. L. Wallace, the newly appointed head of the Second Division of the Union army. He wrote to his wife that he had been ill and prayed for the "strength and wisdom to enable me to do my whole duty toward the country in this her hour of peril." He also described his longing to see her and his family once again and his hope that the war would end. His wife, Ann, twelve years his junior, was so moved by his letters that she decided to go south from Illinois to visit him, despite warnings that she would not be allowed through.

She had known her husband since she was a child when, as a young lawyer, he visited her father, a very successful attorney. He had taken a lively interest in the bright little girl, suggesting books to read, watching her play, and chatting with her. When he returned from service in the Mexican War, he discovered that she had become a delightful young woman of fifteen. He announced his love to her and asked her to marry him when she was sixteen. They wed shortly after her eighteenth birthday. After so many years, it seemed to her that he should not face illness and danger alone. "It seems wrong to enjoy every comfort of a good home and you sick in a tent." She wrote him. "Is it indeed my duty to stay so far back and wait so anxiously?"

She arrived by steamboat on April 6, 1862. As she prepared to walk to her husband's headquarters, a captain suggested that he should go there first to see how great a distance it was. She could hear the increasingly loud sounds of firing. When the captain returned, he told her that the battle had begun, and she would not be able to see her husband until it ended. So she waited anxiously on the steamboat. Later that night, a friend from her home in Illinois came to see her. "It is an awful battle," he kept repeating. Finally, he revealed that her husband had been hit by enemy fire. Grief-stricken, she could not sleep and spent the night helping to take care of the many wounded she found all around her.

Her spirits revived the following morning when the news came that her "Will" had been found still alive. Despite a horrible wound on his head, she was able to squeeze his hand and detected a glimmer of recognition. She stayed by his side as he was sent to a hospital where, at first, his condition seemed to improve. Then he began to fail and, three days later, he died. Ann later wrote that she was grateful that at least he didn't die by himself on the battlefield and that she could spend his last few days with him.

By the beginning of April, McClellan had some 100,000 men facing 17,000 Confederates entrenched in the old Revolutionary battlefield, Yorktown. Instead of using his superior strength to smash the Confederate line, however, McClellan settled down for a month-long siege. He had been fooled by the Confederate commander, John Magruder, a lover of amateur theater, who paraded his men and artillery back and forth to give the illusion that he had more men than he did. A disappointed Lincoln warned McClellan that a lengthy siege would only reinforce suspicions that the general was unwilling to fight: "It is indispensable to *you* that you strike a blow…*you must act.*" McClellan informed his wife that the president had telegraphed that, "he thought I had better break the enemy's lines at once. I was much tempted to reply that he had better come and do it himself." Finally, when he had more than a hundred massive guns in place in early May, McClellan decided to begin his bombardment. But the Confederate forces had slipped away. Confederate General Joseph Johnston was thrilled with his good luck. "No *one* but McClellan could have hesitated to attack," he remarked. Nevertheless, McClellan declared victory, proclaiming, "Our success is brilliant."

As the two armies moved on toward Richmond, the city feared imminent disaster. The Confederate Congress and Jefferson Davis' family fled the city. But, once again, McClellan advanced at a snail's pace, convinced illogically that his forces were outnumbered. His subordinates began calling him, "the Virginia creeper." He refused to mount an assault unless he received reinforcements. An enraged Secretary Stanton commented, "If he had a *million* men, he would swear the enemy had two millions, and then he would sit down in the mud and yell for three."

The reinforcements did not come because they were occupied with Stonewall Jackson's brilliant campaign in the **Shenandoah Valley**. Jackson became a folk hero in the South as a result of this campaign, which is still studied in military schools as a model of how a small army can use mobility and geography to gain the advantage over larger, divided enemy forces. In one month, Jackson's 17,000-man army marched 350 miles, won four battles against much larger forces, captured large quantities of needed equipment, and pinned down almost 60,000 federal troops. Jackson was a religious man who would not even read his beloved wife's letters on Sunday but who felt little emotion about the deaths of the young men he led. His troops admired rather than loved him, but his "inner fire" inspired their intense effort.

While Jackson ran his circles around the Union army, McClellan split his army in two, giving the Confederates an opportunity to launch an offensive in an effort to destroy the detached Union units. In the **Battle of Fair Oaks (or Seven Pines)** Confederate forces fell on the exposed Union wing. Although they failed in their objective and lost General Joseph Johnston, who was severely wounded, it was McClellan who was intimidated by the sight of a battlefield strewn with corpses.

Robert E. Lee took Johnston's place as head of the Army of Northern Virginia (he had been chief of staff). "The shot that struck me down," General Johnston later declared, "was the best every fired for the Confederacy." Ordinary southern soldiers came to adore Lee and consider him a man who "communed with the angels of Heaven." The unsentimental Stonewall Jackson once said, "So great is my confidence in General Lee that I am willing to follow him blindfolded." Lee was an aristocratic Virginian whose father, "Light Horse Harry," had been a close friend and associate of George Washington. His wife was a granddaughter of Martha Washington. Lee was such an outstanding cadet at West Point that he did not get even one demerit, earning the nickname "the Marble Model." Unlike Grant, he had a distinguished military career and was considered the country's outstanding officer when the war began. Lee refused an offer to command the Union army, not because of devotion to the cause of slavery and secession but, because of his loyalty to Virginia. (In contrast, General George Thomas, also a Virginian, served with the Union because he felt it was indivisible.) Lee delighted in the attentions of worshipful women who struggled for locks of his white hair, but he maintained his dignity and his cold, hard stare when angry. Some observers consider him the greatest military genius of the Civil War. He certainly was daring and had an uncanny ability to read the minds of opposing generals. Less admiring military historians argue that Lee was too concerned with defending his native Virginia to develop a consistent overall strategy.

McClellan announced that he was pleased by Lee's promotion since Lee was "wanting in moral firmness when pressed by heavy responsibility and is likely to be timid and irresolute in action." In fact, this would have been a better description of McClellan himself. Lee decided to seize the offensive by attacking the

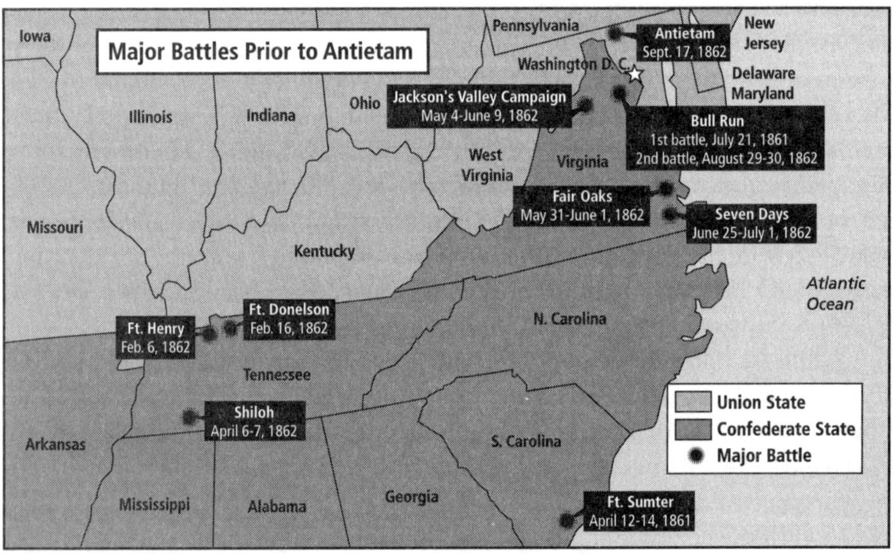

Union army as it withdrew across the peninsula. His plans, however, while admirable on paper, were far too complex for division commanders to carry out. In the **Seven Days Battle** between June 26 and July 2, McClellan was able to inflict heavy losses on Lee's advancing forces, winning all but one of the series of battles. Southern losses were nearly 20,000, compared to 11,000 for the North. Nevertheless, McClellan acted as though he had lost. Once again, John Magruder used his theatrical skills to fool McClellan into believing that an attack was imminent by marching his men back and forth and shouting orders to imaginary regiments. Although several of his generals recommended a counterattack, McClellan ordered a retreat. One division commander angrily denounced the order as one that "can only be prompted by cowardice or treason." McClellan sent a dispatch to Secretary of War Stanton that showed how much the battle had unbalanced him: "I have lost this battle because my force was too small… this Government has not sustained this army… If I save this army now… I owe no thanks to you or any other persons in Washington. You have done your best to sacrifice this army." Despite the failure of his tactical plans, Lee had saved Richmond. No Union forces would come so close to the Confederate capital for two more years.

Like Shiloh had in the West, the Seven Days showed the horrors of total war in the East. The "smart, well provided" Union soldiers returned, "sad, weary, covered with mud, with uniforms in rags." Soldiers wrote home about the horrors of their experience in seeing, "corpses swollen to twice their original size…burst asunder with the pressure of foul gasses and vapors…we all sickened and were lying with our mouths close to the ground, most of us vomiting profusely." But, eventually, the men hardened at the sight of death. One thoughtful Rebel wondered about when he had changed: "I know there is a change for I look on the carcass of a man now with pretty much such feeling as I would were it a horse or hog." McClellan's failure pushed northern public opinion from the elation of the spring to what one New Yorker described as an overwhelming "feeling of dispondency" in the summer.

When McClellan insisted to Lincoln that he had "*failed to win* only because overpowered by superior numbers" and demanded another fifty thousand men, the president's legendary patience finally ran out. He called off the peninsula campaign and replaced McClellan as commander of the Army of the Potomac with the reckless and self-glorifying John Pope. Pope, who could "talk a better battle than he could fight," was a decent general officer but totally over his head as an army commander. Sensing this weakness and realizing that a petulant McClellan would be very slow in sending his troops to reinforce his rival, Lee wheeled his army around, led by Jackson's corps, to strike at Pope. The **Second Battle of Bull Run** (August 29-30), like the first one, was an overwhelming Confederate victory. There were 25,000 casualties (16,000 of those Union); five times the number that had so shocked the nation in the first battle fought at Bull Run. This defeat was all the more appalling to the northern public because it came immediately following self-glorifying dispatches from Pope that he was ready to "bag" Stonewall Jackson. One New York Zouave regiment sustained the heaviest losses of any Civil War regiment on any day in the war. A Southerner recalled that the dead men in their colorful uniforms lay so closely together that they looked like a field of posies. Pope was sent west to deal with a Sioux uprising, a job for which he was suited. In desperation, a reluctant Lincoln replaced him with McClellan. "We must use the tools we have," Lincoln informed his astonished cabinet. "If he can't fight, he excels in making others ready to fight." When McClellan rode back to the troops, they gratefully cheered his return. "Again, I have been called upon to save the country," he informed his wife.

Antietam

Southern victories in the summer of 1862 had gained Europe's attention. One more great victory, Lee suggested to Jefferson Davis, might well lead Europe to recognize the Confederacy. Lincoln also needed a victory because he planned to strike at slavery by issuing a proclamation of emancipation, and Seward had convinced him to wait for a Union victory to do so. That way, it would not appear to be an act of desperation in a losing cause.

In September, Lee led a raid into Maryland. There, he expected to forage for fresh provisions for his army described by one local woman as "the dirtiest men I ever saw, a most ragged, lean, and hungry set of wolves." He also hoped to rally slaveholding Maryland to support the Confederate cause, even instructing his men to sing "Maryland, My Maryland" as they marched through small towns.

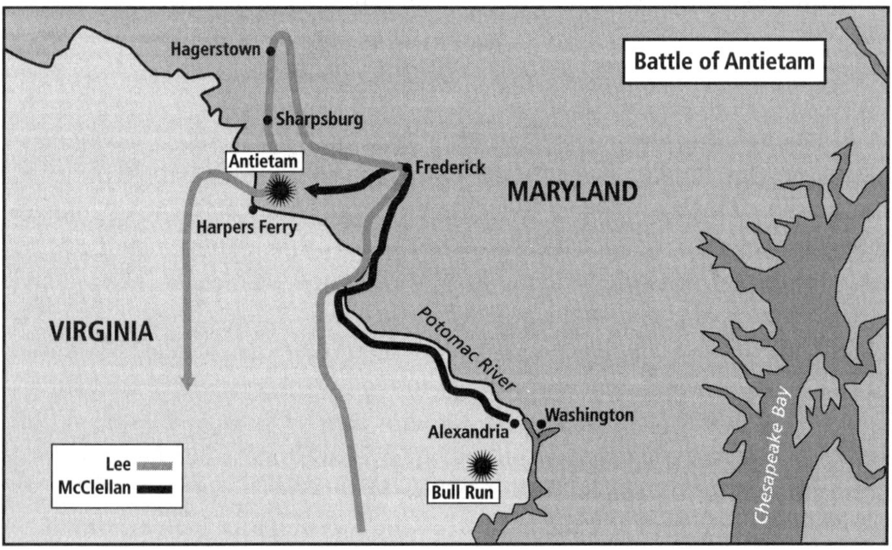

Most local residents, however, remained behind resolutely shuttered doors. He sent almost half his command under Jackson to capture Harper's Ferry where they seized thousands of weapons and captured 12,500 prisoners (the largest single surrender of American troops ever until World War II).

After this successful beginning, things began to fall apart for the Confederates. A Union corporal, searching for souvenirs in a field where the Rebels had camped, found three cigars wrapped in a piece of paper that, amazingly, turned out to be a copy of Lee's battle plans. McClellan now knew that Lee had dangerously divided his army. "Here is a paper," he gleefully remarked to his aides, "with which if I cannot whip Bobbie Lee, I will be willing to go home." Noted Civil War historian, Bruce Catton, has commented, "no Civil War general was ever given so fair a chance to destroy the opposing army one piece at a time." Had he attacked immediately with his overwhelming advantage, the main Confederate army would have been destroyed, and the war may well have ended shortly thereafter. Since, in his mind the tricky Rebels outnumbered him, however, he wasted more than three days assembling his men near Antietam Creek and preparing his attack. This enabled the Confederates to reassemble most of their forces. On

On the Antietam battlefield the bodies of the dead are strewn beside a fence.

September 17 both sides battered each other unmercifully, particularly along a sunken road later known as Bloody Lane where volleys "brought down the enemy," in the words of one officer, "as grain fall before a reaper" and the bodies lay two and three deep. By nightfall, the bloodiest single day of the Civil War was over, leaving more than twenty-six thousand casualties. The Union, alone, suffered double the losses of D-Day, more than 80 years later. The Confederates lost almost a quarter of their men. Photographers were able to reach the field before the dead were buried. Their all-too-vivid pictures were published widely in the North where they made a stunned public more aware of the horrors of the war.

As the sun rose over the battlefield on the September 18, Union reinforcements arrived, giving McClellan more fresh men than Lee had remaining in his entire army. Lee, now outnumbered almost 3 to 1, braced for the inevitable crushing Union attack. But it never came. Despite Lincoln's urgent wire, "Destroy the rebel army if possible," McClellan, as usual, squandered this opportunity. Lincoln finally removed McClellan for good in November. "He is an admirable engineer," the president noted, "but he seems to have a special talent for a stationary engine." McClellan never accepted this conclusion. Every year, he celebrated the anniversary of Antietam. "Those on whose judgment I rely," he declared, "tell me I fought the battle splendidly and that it was a masterpiece of art."

Despite the carnage and battlefield stalemate, the Union could claim victory since Lee's invasion had been repulsed, and he was forced to retreat back into Virginia. Lincoln used this "victory" to issue his Preliminary Emancipation Proclamation on September 22, 1862.

Fredericksburg

Ambrose Burnside, a Lincoln favorite, replaced McClellan. Burnside was a soft-spoken, good-natured, imposing-looking man. (His fluffy side-whiskers became popular as "sideburns," a play on his name.) But Burnside was in over his head. Indecisive and fearful, he was only too aware of his own failings. He knew that Lincoln expected an offensive as soon as possible, so he forged ahead, despite obvious holes in his strategy and delays when pontoons to bridge the Rappahannock River failed to arrive. At Fredericksburg, on December 13, his men valiantly assaulted entrenched Confederate positions on a hill called "Marye's Heights" fourteen times. Each time they were driven back at dreadful cost. A Confederate officer compared the federal troops toppling in the withering gunfire to "the steady dripping of rain from the eaves of a house." A reporter wrote, "It can hardly be in human nature for men to show more valor, or generals to manifest less judgment." The only positive in the futile bloodbath was a Confederate soldier who carried canteens of water to aid wounded Union soldiers and became known to both sides as "the Angel of Marye's Heights." The battle ended on December 15 with a northern retreat and over 12,000 Union casualties, compared to 5,000 Confederates. Watching the slaughter from a hill above the battlefield, Lee told an associate, "It is well that war is so terrible—we should grow too fond of it."

After weeping openly at the terrible costs his men paid, Burnside hoped to redeem himself by a rapid march to outflank Lee. But he was thwarted by torrents of icy rain that wiped out roads and created massive mud quagmires in which animals sank down to their bellies. One officer put in a requisition for "50 men, 23 feet high, to work in mud 18 feet deep." After seeing his men getting drunk and fighting each other in frustration, Burnside realized the hopelessness of this "mud march" and ordered a retreat. At his own request, he was relieved of his command.

In the west, Union forces fared somewhat better. The year (1862) ended with the Confederate presence being eliminated from Kentucky and pushed out of most of Tennessee. These modest victories, however, did not compensate for the debacle in the east in the minds of most Northerners.

THE HOME FRONT

The seemingly endless slaughter and inconclusive engagements hurt civilian morale on both sides. Northern despair was particularly intense. One of Lincoln's associates wrote that, "exhaustion steals over the country. Confidence and hope are dying." The impact of the war reverberated at home.

Politics During the War

Despite interference with civil liberties, in general the Lincoln administration was willing to tolerate widespread political dissent. Anti-administration newspapers and magazines criticized the president and his party in the harshest terms. A few pro-Confederate politicians (called "Copperheads), including Ohio congressman, Clement L. Vallandigham, were arrested for disloyal activities. But most "Peace Democrats" were able to express their views, run for office, and even hold seats in state legislatures and Congress. Democratic legislatures in Indiana and Illinois, elected in 1862, actually adopted resolutions calling for an armistice and urging the withdrawal of state troops from the war. The imprisoned Vallandigham was treated as a martyr by the Democrats and nominated for governor. The president cleverly undermined this stance by freeing the Copperhead leader from prison and banishing him to the South. Vallandigham fled to Canada from where he ran his Ohio gubernatorial campaign. (He lost.) Compared to the over-zealous enforcement of the sedition laws in World War I and the internment of Japanese-

Americans in World War II, the violation of civil liberties in this greatest-of-all crises seems relatively mild.

Even at the worst times, political partisanship remained vigorous. Congressional elections were held as scheduled in 1862 when the Union prospects seemed dim. Democratic orators declared that "every white man in the North who does not want to be swapped off for a free Nigger, should vote the Democratic ticket." Democrats succeeded in gaining 32 seats in the House and the key governorship of New York. The Republicans, however, did maintain control of Congress and even gained five seats in the Senate. After the terrible defeat at Fredericksburg, Republican senators demanded that Lincoln reorganize his cabinet to exclude Seward whom they considered "lukewarm" and responsible for the military failures. But Lincoln, without making any enemies, was able to use his considerable political skills to outmaneuver those who sought to limit his control of his own administration.

The Republican Congress did enact a number of significant measures unrelated to the war, in accordance with their economic goals. In 1861 tariff legislation raised duties considerably to aid American businessmen. Other pro-business legislation included the authorization of a transcontinental railroad to be heavily subsidized by public land grants and loans and the creation of a national banking system. This ultimately insured that a uniform national currency would replace the dozens of bank notes issued on state and local levels. Farm support was bolstered by the 1862 Homestead Act, which offered any citizen 160 acres of public land free if he cultivated and resided on the land for five years. The Morrill Act of 1862 donated large tracts of public lands to states that created colleges teaching agriculture. (This became the foundation of the large co-educational state universities.)

In the South, meanwhile, Jefferson Davis' support, both popular and political, continued to erode. The Confederate Congress became a forum for increasingly bitter attacks on his administration and its conduct of the war. By 1863, most southern newspapers expressed open opposition to Davis. One problem was that, unlike Lincoln, Davis did not have the assistance of an organized political party. The Confederacy never acquired a two-party system, making it particularly difficult for the president to organize support for disputed policies. Without parties, the opposition became increasingly personal and irresponsible.

Emancipation

At the beginning of the war, most Northerners believed that the struggle was one to preserve the Union, not to interfere with the institution of slavery, which continued to exist in slaveholding border Union states. The war was meant to be a white man's fight, and black volunteers were not accepted at first. Abolitionists, like Frederick Douglass, argued: "Teach the rebels and traitors that the price they are to pay for the attempt to abolish this Government must be the abolition of slavery." Lincoln advocated caution. He overruled Union commanders who freed slaves in areas occupied by their troops. He even proposed plans for gradual emancipation, including voluntary "colonization" of freed blacks outside of America. He did not want to alienate slaveowning Unionists and understood the prevalence of racial prejudice in the North. Emancipation, he informed antislavery subordinates, was an issue "which, under my responsibility, I reserve to myself."

The actions of the slaves themselves, however, began to influence Union policy. They were "voting for freedom with their feet" when as many as a half a million ran away from plantations to nearby Union lines. They offered themselves as a valuable source of labor to the army. Nearly 200,000 worked as laborers, cooks, nurses, fortification builders, carpenters, and teamsters in army camps. Many brought important information about the location of Confederate forces. Some of them were willing to serve as valuable spies or scouts, often becoming the eyes and ears of the Union army in important campaigns. A few came bearing useful supplies for the federal forces. Robert Smalls and his brother, Charleston slaves, boldly seized a Confederate ship and steered it through heavily armed Confederate defenses to the blockading Union navy. ("Captain" Smalls served as a navy pilot for the rest of the war and went on to a distinguished political career during Reconstruction.) Even less daring runaways had risked beatings, mutilation, or even death had they been recaptured, and they refused to return to slavery.

It also became increasingly obvious to Northerners that each slave behind federal lines working for the Union was one less laborer for the South. Northern army officers began to comment that these freedom-loving blacks hardly resembled the happy-go-lucky, submissive slaves of southern myth. Some of these observers even began to argue what had once been unthinkable: that ex-slaves might well become effective federal troops. The actions of the slaves and the army officers who championed their cause helped to redefine Union war aims to embrace emancipation.

In March 1862, Congress acted by forbidding the Union army to return fugitive slaves who were defined as "contrabands" (essential to the enemy war effort). That April, Congress, with the support of the president, abolished slavery in the District of Columbia, with compensation to the slaveholders. Two months later, Congress ended slavery in all federal territories without reimbursement. It then adopted a Confiscation Act, declaring that slaves belonging to anyone who supported the rebellion should be "forever free of their servitude." Although this was not enforced, it did demonstrate the changing tide of northern public opinion.

The border slave states lost their chance to stem that tide when they failed to endorse Lincoln's plan for gradual emancipation. Blacks were not interested in his colonization plans. One African-American newspaper suggested that *slaveowners*

Fugitive slaves—"Contrabands"—came into the union lines and were employed as laborers.

be colonized. Frederick Douglass protested, "We are *Americans*, speaking the same language, adopting the same customs...and shall rise and fall with Americans." As casualties rose, more and more northern soldiers, while still quite prejudiced, increasingly saw the logic of adding black troops. Others realized that a blow to slavery would be a blow to the South. Lincoln, after eighteen months of bitter combat, concluded, "We...must change our tactics or lose the war." Emancipation might well represent that decisive transformation.

After waiting for a Union "victory" at Antietam, Lincoln issued a preliminary emancipation proclamation on September 22, 1862. It was justified as an act of "military necessity" under the president's war powers, aimed at undermining enemy resources. It gave the Confederate states one hundred days to return to the union without losing their slaves. On January 1, 1863, when, as expected, no rebellious state had taken advantage of this offer, Lincoln issued his final Emancipation Proclamation. In it, he declared that "all persons held as slaves" in states or parts of states still in rebellion "are and henceforth shall be free." He also authorized that "such persons" could now "be received into the armed service of the United States." The War Department quickly began accepting thousands of additional black recruits to supplement the handful already in the Union army.

Critics noted that the document had "all the moral grandeur of a bill of lading." Southerners denounced the hypocrisy of "emancipating" only slaves beyond northern control and leaving the others in slavery. A London newspaper commented that the principle involved was "not that a human being cannot justly own another, but that he cannot own him unless he is loyal to the United States." Abolitionists, although disappointed by its seemingly limited scope, understood the ultimate significance of the proclamation. A huge crowd of black and white antislavery activists gathered in the Boston Music Hall on midnight of the new year, 1863, to celebrate the occasion. Harriet Beecher Stowe, her eyes filled with tears, waved to the cheering crowd from the balcony. After their chaplain read the proclamation to them, the newly formed black 1st South Carolina Volunteers regiment broke spontaneously into a rousing version of "My Country 'Tis of Thee." A former slave recalled hearing that "Lincoln gonna turn us free," but the mistress insisted this was false. Then a Yankee soldier told someone "that Lincoln done signed the 'Mancipation…everybody commenced getting ready to leave. Don't care nothin' about Missus—was going to the Union lines." The measure hastened the breakdown of slavery as an effective labor system. About one-quarter of the slaves were freed during the war under the proclamation, depriving the South of a substantial portion of its work force.

The Emancipation Proclamation brought about a new war aim. The Union army was transformed into an army of liberation, fighting to erect a new Union rather than merely restore the old one. Had the proclamation been submitted to a public referendum a year earlier, one newspaper noted, a majority would have opposed it. "And yet not a year has passed before it is approved by an overwhelming majority," the paper added after sweeping victories by antislavery Republicans in the 1863 elections. Maryland and Missouri actually added emancipation provisions to their state constitutions. The proclamation also guaranteed that antislavery Britain would never recognize the Confederacy. A dramatic growth in pro-northern opinion occurred as fifty-six large public meetings were held in Britain within three months after the proclamation was issued, to support the Union cause. The great English philosopher, John Stuart Mill, wrote that any Confederate triumph would be "a victory of the powers of evil." The Civil War, he concluded, was "destined to be a turning point for good or evil, of the course of human affairs."

The Wartime Economies

The huge military operations placed heavy burdens on the economic resources of the two sides. Many Confederate farmers, unable to sell their cotton or tobacco, turned to the production of foodstuffs. Unfortunately, the inadequacy of the internal transportation system in the South limited its ability to distribute food and other non-military supplies. Its unsatisfactory rail network connected plantations to ports rather than food suppliers to population centers. The intrusion of northern troops further disrupted this already limited system. The food that was raised did not get to the people who needed it. Southern soldiers, though relatively well armed as the war progressed, were increasingly malnourished, as were city dwellers. The Impressment Act of 1863 authorized Confederate government agents to seize food, horses, or other supplies needed by the army at below market prices. Farmers and local officials forcefully resisted this policy and hid their crops, causing even greater shortages.

As usual during a war, there were people in both sections who profited. Wartime demands helped pull the northern economy out of a depression. Farmers prospered from the demand for grain, and new industries, such as petroleum, boomed. The needs of the Union army led to the development of machine production of shoes (as opposed to hand craftsmanship) and ready-to-wear clothing. Although the Civil War did not begin the modernization of the American economy, it certainly accelerated its development. Many of the newly rich openly flaunted their wealth, building expensive mansions and throwing extravagant parties in the midst of the war. Because of inflation, wages of factory workers lagged 25 percent or more behind prices. Many of these workers were immigrants, largely Irish, who also disagreed with Republican economic policies and war aims. Their rising discontent led to strikes later in the war, demanding higher wages to pay for the rising living costs. The strikes of skilled workers generally were successful, enabling them to keep up with inflation.

Suffering, of course, was far worse in the South. There were some people who made huge profits in the face of all the misery. These included blockade-runners who felt their risks were better compensated by small costly items like jewels, rather than bulky military supplies. Speculators withheld necessary commodities to await price rises and instituted a profitable, if risky, trade with the enemy. (Cotton was exchanged in places like Memphis for coffee, cloth, and other northern luxuries.) On the eve of one major battle, Richmond merchants bought up all the coffins and mourning crepe and then jacked up the prices. At the same time, ordinary people made "coffee" out of okra seeds and sweet potatoes, spun their own cloth, and turned drapes and rugs into dresses and coats. Those in the paths of invading armies struggled to exist from day to day. Shortages in the cities were so severe that one government clerk wrote in his diary that Richmond was amazingly clean since "no garbage or filth can accumulate." The people had to be "such good scavengers" that there was "no need of buzzards." The runaway inflation compounded the suffering. In early 1864 it took $46 to buy what $1 bought in 1861. By the end of the war, a wagonload of money was needed to purchase even a small item.

Women on the Home Front

The impact of the war on the lives of women was far greater than merely making it more difficult to buy necessities. In the North, new jobs opened up, as well as

Many women replaced skilled male workers in the labor force. These women are filling cartridges in the Watertown Asenal.

new directions for community involvement. The U.S. Sanitary Commission was the chief agency through which northern women helped the war effort. Most of the volunteer workers were women who ran its thousands of auxiliaries collected clothing, food and medicine, and organized "Sanitary Fairs" to raise money. Elizabeth Cady Stanton and Susan B. Anthony founded the National Women's Loyal League, enabling them to continue the struggle for the abolition of slavery and women's rights in the context of the war effort. Northern women took over many of the remaining male jobs in teaching and, for the first time, gained positions in government offices and stores, as a result of the wartime manpower shortages. Many of these women, whose husbands and fathers were away in the army, would have been destitute without these new jobs.

Just like the women in the North, southern women formed patriotic societies and collected supplies for the soldiers. But they suffered far worse shortages and more severe losses of manpower, resulting in greater hardships. Many women had to manage farms and plantations in the face of disappearing supplies and crumbling equipment while their husbands were away at the front. Plantation mistresses often had to manage their slaves at a time when slavery was disintegrating. As stealing, dawdling, and even sabotage by restless slaves was increasing, soldiers exhorted their wives to take charge. "You may give your Negroes away," one weary mistress wrote her husband in 1864, "I cannot live with them another year alone." Many women, North and South, suffered the loss of their husbands, lovers, and sons and had to learn to make do without them. "I have not read my bible since Charlie died," one bereft southern woman wrote, "My tears and feelings seem frozen. I know, I feel but one thing, I am alone, utterly desolate."

Riots and Discontent

Food shortages in southern cities led to a series of riots by 1863. These bread riots were led by starving women, often wives of soldiers. The worst took place in Richmond where the angry crowd shouting "Bread or Blood!" smashed store windows and grabbed food, clothing, and even jewelry. Only Jefferson Davis' threat to order the militia to fire on them caused the sullen crowd to disperse. States began to distribute food to the poor and spent millions in direct relief. It has been estimated that toward the end of the war 20 to 40 percent of southern white civilians were receiving some kind of public relief.

In the North the new conscription law with its obvious class bias in its exemption and substitution clauses led to popular indignation. Although the poor and foreign-born did not, in fact, provide a disproportionate percentage of the fighting men, Democratic newspapers and politicians reinforced their suspicions about government policies instituted by the Negro-loving rich who could pay to avoid fighting. The first drawing of names for the new conscription, coming a few months after the Emancipation Proclamation, confirmed the feeling that blacks were to blame first for the war and now for the draft. Armed bands in "copper-

This drawing pictures the drawing of lots for the draft.

Rioters in New York City viewed African Americans as the cause of the war and were enraged that rich white men had been able to buy exemptions from the draft.

head" areas in the Midwest attacked and killed draft officials. Boston rioters were shot down after stoning troops. But the worst explosion erupted in New York City on July 13, 1863—one of the bloodiest riots in American history. Huge mobs of Irish working class men and women terrorized the city for four days. They burned the draft office and the homes of leading Republicans, looted stores, and even attacked elegantly dressed "swells." Fearful that freed slaves would come north and threaten their jobs, they vented most of their anger on blacks. Shouting, "kill the naygers," they lynched at least a dozen defenseless blacks and burned down the Colored Orphan Asylum, guarding the front door to prevent escape. (An alert employee was able to lead most of the children out the back way unharmed.) Eventually several regiments of federal troops had to be rushed to New York from Pennsylvania. They restored order by shooting down rioters "as coolly as they had shot down Rebels at Gettysburg." At least 120 people died, most of them rioters.

The Draft Riot underscored the racial, class, and ethnic tensions in American society. It also increased anti-Irish feelings among middle and upper class Northerners and led to a backlash against Peace Democrats. The draft continued without further disorder. Only 46,347 men actually served after being drafted. (About 80,000 paid the $300 commutation fee to be excused from service and another 116,000 furnished substitutes.) Others, however, enlisted before they were called to avoid the "stigma" of conscription.

Grant's Notorious Order #11

During the Civil War minorities living in the North sometimes felt the impact of the crisis. The Draft Riots and the public reaction to them revealed a great deal about attitudes towards blacks and Irish immigrants. Only 150,000 Jews lived in the United States at the time. They divided much like other Americans on the issues of slavery and secession. During the war, northern rabbis offered prayers for the Union and southern clergymen for the Confederacy. However, many Americans, like Europeans, believed negative stereotypes about Jews.

Speculators, who traded gold, merchandise, supplies, and even arms for cotton, had plagued General Ulysses Grant in his area of command in Tennessee and Kentucky. Some speculators were Jewish, but Grant identified the entire illegal traffic with Jews. Actually, very few of the merchants arrested for profiteering were Jewish. Nevertheless, on December 17, 1862, Grant issued the most sweeping anti-Jewish order in American history, General Order No. 11, that stated:

> *The Jews, as a class violating every regulation of trade established by the Treasury Department and also department orders, are hereby expelled from the department within twenty-four hours from the receipt of this order.*

As a result of this order, thirty families, including some of "the most respectable Union citizens of the city" were expelled from Paducah, Kentucky, even though none of the men were traders. Leaders of the Jewish community of Paducah sent letters and telegrams that aroused a storm of protest. Then one of them, Cesar Kaskel, went to Washington to bring their complaint to President Lincoln. The president, who knew almost nothing about the facts of the case, listened attentively. "And so the children of Israel were driven from the happy land of Canaan?" Lincoln responded. "Yes," replied Kaskel, "and that is why we have come unto Father Abraham's bosom, asking protection." "And this protection they shall have at once," Lincoln assured him. The order was quickly countermanded.

The whole "sensational" issue did lead to some expressions of support for the action of General Grant by a few Republican papers, couched in anti-Semitic language, such as that castigating Jews as "scavengers of commerce." Most, however, agreed with the **New York Times** *that it was an "odious principle" to condemn an entire group, "contrary to common sense and common justice." Loyal and orderly Hebrew citizens, the* **Times** *asserted, had been forced out of Paducah in a "revival of the spirit of the medieval ages." At least Lincoln had redeemed the nation from "the disgrace of a military assault" upon rights guaranteed to all Americans by the Constitution. No other incident arose during the war to make Jews feel uncomfortable in America.*

LIFE ON THE BATTLEFIELD

General Sherman once told a group of fresh, enthusiastic recruits, "There's many a boy here today who looks on war as all glory, but, boys, it is all hell." This was a lesson learned all-too-quickly by the soldiers on both sides of the Civil War. Still, one young Confederate soldier who was mortally wounded at Shiloh gazed into the eyes of his friend and asked as he was dying, "Johnnie, if a boy died for his country, the glory is his forever isn't it?"

Billy Yank and Johnny Reb

More than three million men, over half those of military age in the nation, served in the war. Of these, two-thirds were younger than 23-years-old and most came from rural America. Some were much younger. Confederate General Nathan Bedford Forrest's 15-year-old son fought at Shiloh and even captured some enemy soldiers as his father anxiously searched for him among the battlefield casualties. The youngest of all were the drummer boys. Johnny Clem, a ten-year-old who accompanied the Twenty-Second Wisconsin Infantry at Shiloh, and Chickamauga was particularly celebrated. (He stayed in the army until 1916 when he retired as a major general.) Despite the characterization of the war as a "poor man's fight," studies show that the soldiers were actually quite representative of all classes in the population.

These young recruits were not accustomed to the regimentation of army life. After the anarchy of the early battles, both sides decided to develop discipline in army training camps with their "50,000 pup tents and wigwams." There, raw novice soldiers got their first experiences with the boredom and hardships of army life. Noncommissioned officers from the peacetime army were the most effective in instilling discipline in the camps. Often established in swampy areas lacking sufficient fresh water, the camps were also responsible for thousands of deaths from water-borne diseases such as dysentery and typhoid fever. A great deal of army humor was directed at the food issued to the soldiers. One soldier said that his beef issue was carved from a bull "too old for the conscript law." The battlefield ration usually consisted of "hardtack and half-cooked beans" and the lack of fruits or vegetables led to such diseases as scurvy. As the war went on, Union soldiers were issued more and better food, while the Confederate diet worsened. The combat these men faced was particularly brutal. The weapons used were far ahead of the tactics. In past wars infantrymen would be massed in opposing lines, firing at each other with muskets that were reloaded twice a minute and had a range of 100 yards. Charging troops would rush forward with bayonets bared to break the defenders' line before they could reload. In the Civil War the rifles were not only loaded far more quickly, but they had a range of 800 yards. Generals lined their men up to march against an entrenched position and got their men blown away. (Nine of ten infantry assaults failed.) The bayonet was rarely used except as a spit to cook meat. Green troops often forgot the camp lessons when they experienced combat for the first time. One soldier admitted, "though i did not run i mite have if i had thought of it in time." One trooper wrote home, "I must say I have had enough of the glory of war. I am sick of seeing dead men and men's limbs torn from their bodies."

Troops regularly were sent on 25-mile marches. The shoes issued to Union soldiers did not have left or right feet; marching wore them into left or right-foot shoes. The Confederates did not even have that luxury. When they wore out their own shoes, they often had to march barefoot. One southern soldier wrote home that he had sadly learned, "the realities of a soldier's life." He slept on the ground "without regard to the weather" and learned to like raw bacon. "Without time to wash our clothes or our persons, and sleeping on the ground all huddled together, the whole army became lousy more or less with body lice."

Between the flashes of combat and the long marches, the armies waited. Boredom overwhelmed the men, particularly in the oppressive heat of summer. Sometimes, they would take a stick and ball and play an impromptu game of baseball. Occasionally a soldier would jump onto the parapets and direct insulting gestures to the other side, often getting shot in the process. Many soldiers would "go down the line," a term for visiting houses of prostitution that proliferated not far from the lines. Sometimes, when times were quiet, rival troops, who, after all, shared a common language and culture, would fraternize with each other. A southern private wrote about one such incident: "Our boys and the Yanks made a bargain not to fire at each other and went out in the field...and gathered berries together and talked over the fight, traded tobacco and coffee, and exchanged newspapers as peacefully and kindly as if they had not been engaged in the last seven days in butchering each other."

Black Troops

As soon as the war broke out, blacks had requested the right to fight for their freedom. At first, there was some reluctance at accepting them as soldiers. General Sherman was asked whether a "negro" was as good as a white man in stopping a bullet. Yes, he replied, "and a sand-bag is better." He felt that blacks could not skirmish and improvise like whites. Grant disagreed. He gave his "hearty support" to the arming of black troops. "By arming the Negro we have added a powerful ally. They will make good soldiers and taking them from the enemy weakens him in the same proportion they strengthen us." The decision to recruit black regiments led to vehement protests. A group of Democratic congressmen protested that the enlistment of black soldiers was an evil Republican plot to bring about "the equality of the black and white races." In one sense they were right. There is no question that one consequence of black soldiers fighting for the Union was to advance ideas of black equality. Frederick Douglass understood this when he told blacks, "This is your golden opportunity." Once the black man was in uniform, he believed, "there is no power on earth which can deny that he has earned the right to citizenship in the United States."

Black men responded to Douglass' challenge in extraordinary numbers. Free blacks in the North enlisted at a rate three times that of whites. Since enrollment in the army brought freedom to their families, enlistment was particularly high in areas like the loyal border states that were not covered by the Emancipation Proclamation. One former slave remembered. "This was the biggest thing that ever happened in my life. I felt like a man with a uniform on and a gun in my hand." By the war's end, 180,000 blacks were in the Union army and 10,000 more in the navy, which had always accepted black recruits. Their participation was a critical factor in the Union victory. By the beginning of 1865 one in eight northern soldiers was a black man. Their numbers approximately equaled the total number of Confederate soldiers still available for combat. By this time, many northern districts filled their troop quotas with southern blacks who had been recruited by

By the end of the war there were nearly 180,000 black men in the Union army and 10,000 in the Union navy. They played a crucial role in the ultimate Union victory.

state agents, substituting nonlocal blacks for local whites as combat soldiers. One popular song extolled "Sambo's Right to be Kilt" as an adequate excuse for the use of black troops.

Most black troops were used for debilitating garrison and rear guard duty, often in areas where white troops had been wiped out by yellow fever and malaria. As a result, they suffered high disease rates typical of soldiers limited to one spot where the water supply had become polluted and disease-ridden. They also received poorer medical care than white troops. (There were only eight black doctors, and white physicians rarely volunteered for black units.) As a result, their death rate from diseases was twice as high as that of white soldiers. They served in segregated regiments led by white officers. There were fewer than 100 black officers in the 166 black regiments, none higher than captain. They received far lower pay than white soldiers did. Black and abolitionist leaders complained about this inequality, and several regiments served months without pay in protest. One brigade refused to pick up their arms until they got equal pay. Their sergeant was convicted of mutiny and publicly executed by a firing squad. Eventually, Congress voted to equalize military salaries.

Those blacks that were used as combat soldiers quickly proved their toughness and effectiveness in a series of engagements. Untested and poorly trained black troops repelled a forceful Confederate onslaught at Miliken's Bend on the Mississippi after white Union defenders had fled. The most famous test was a deadly storming of entrenched Confederate positions at Fort Wagner at the entrance of Charleston harbor. The 54th Massachusetts, under the command of a well-known young abolitionist, Robert Gould Shaw, led the charge. Its ranks consisted of free black volunteers, including Frederick Douglass' two sons, and runaway slaves. The courageous and doomed assault cost the regiment more than 40 percent of its soldiers, including the young colonel. (There is a monument to the 54th in Boston and the movie *Glory* retells its story.) The attack took place two days after the New York draft riots. Many newspapers drew an obvious moral: black men who fought for their country deserved rights more than white men who rioted against it. After serving a month with black troops, one officer wrote his wife, "I *know* that many of them are vastly the *superiors* of those (many of those) who would condemn them all to a life of brutal degradation." An Illinois private wrote his mother, "When you hear eney one say that the negro soldiers wont fight just tell them they ly for me...I have seen a great many fighting for our country. Then why should they not be free." In 1864, Lincoln commented, "So far as tested, it is difficult to say they are not as good soldiers as any."

The Confederate government was so worried at the prospect of their slaves being armed against them, that they threatened captured black regiments with death or enslavement. Lincoln largely forestalled this by promising to retaliate against Confederate prisoners on a one-to-one basis. There were, however, some instances of southern brutality against black soldiers. The most notorious was the massacre of surrendering black troops at Fort Pillow, Tennessee by the soldiers under the command of the "gallant cavalry genius," Nathan Bedford Forrest.

As manpower shortages worsened in the South, some leaders argued that the Confederate army should also recruit blacks, guaranteeing freedom "to every slave in the South who shall remain true to the Confederacy in this war." This amazing revolutionary idea naturally encountered powerful resistance. One general argued that slaves could never be soldiers: "The day you make a soldier of them is the beginning of the end of the revolution. And if slaves seem good soldiers, *then our whole theory of slavery is wrong.*" General Lee endorsed the recruitment of blacks. They could make "efficient soldiers," he argued. "I think we could at least do as well with them as the enemy, and he attaches great importance to their assistance." At the very end of the war, with the authorization of the Confederate Congress, black companies were actually raised in the South. The war ended before they could be used.

More than a third of the black troops died in Union service. Their sacrifice helped bolster their claim to equal citizenship after the war. They took great pride in their new status. One black soldier, finding himself face-to-face with his former master, a prisoner of war, said, "Hello Massa, bottom rail on top this time."

Prisoners of War

The Confederates refused to exchange black prisoners, bringing an existing prisoner exchange program to a halt. This worsened the tragic overcrowding and high death rate in prison camps. Conditions in both northern and southern prisons were poor. Prisoners suffered from bad sanitary conditions, diseased water supplies, as well as boredom and depression. The death rates were higher in southern prisons, largely due to the shortages of food and medicine that came with the collapse of the southern economy in the last year of the war. The most notorious Confederate prison was Andersonville in Georgia. In a stockade built for fifteen thousand prisoners, there were thirty-three thousand closely-packed men. Despite abundant pine forests around the prison, the men were not allowed to build huts to shelter them. A shocked local woman commented, "My heart aches for the poor wretches, Yankees though they are, and I am afraid that God will suffer some terrible retribution to fall upon us for letting such things happen." At least thirteen thousand prisoners died at Andersonville. After the war, the prison commandant was the only Confederate convicted of war crimes and executed. Once the Confederacy decided to enroll slaves in its own army, it dropped its refusal to exchange black prisoners, and a thousand prisoners a day were exchanged in the last few months of the war.

Thirteen thousand prisoners died at Andersonville.

Medical Care

As in the prison camps, disease was the main killer of soldiers in the Civil War. For every soldier killed in battle, two died of disease. The crowding together of thousands of men, particularly those from rural areas, made them susceptible to epidemics of childhood diseases like measles and mumps. (City boys who had already been exposed to these viruses were less vulnerable.) Other, more fatal, waves of illnesses resulted from bad food, contaminated water, and mosquitoes. These included typhoid, malaria, diarrhea, and dysentery. In one year 995 of every 1000 Union soldiers were afflicted with the latter two. One Union soldier recalled that the sound of thousands of men coughing "would drown out that of the beating drums." Although the ratio of diseases to battle deaths seems high by modern standards, it was actually far better than that of any other war before the twentieth century. (By contrast, the ratio in the 1898 Spanish-American War was 6 to 1.) The energetic young Surgeon General was correct when he proudly declared that the Union army's mortality rate from disease and battle wounds was "lower than had been observed in the experience of any army since the world began." This improvement was the result of vigorous efforts by the volunteer United States Sanitary Commission.

Still, by modern standards, "the Civil War was fought at the end of the medical Middle Ages." Research by Europeans like Louis Pasteur and Joseph Lister in the germ theory and antiseptic surgery was just beginning. Few understood the need to sterilize such surgical instruments as the horrific bone saw. Conditions were particularly bad in southern wards. A former Charleston socialite, turned nurse, complained about rats who "ate all the poultices applied during the night to the sick, and dragged away the pads stuffed with bran from under the arms and legs of the wounded." The large caliber soft lead bullets that came in at a low muzzle velocity tended to remain in arm or leg wounds, often after shattering the bone. The only way to prevent gangrene and other complications was to amputate the limb. The typical field hospital after a major battle had grisly piles of severed arms and legs. Other ills were countered by large doses of medications containing mercury or opium. Nevertheless, advances included the establishment of field hospitals and the creation of a trained ambulance corps.

Women on the Battlefield

Not only did women do most of the work in volunteer civilian agencies like the Sanitary Commission, but thousands also worked as nurses in army hospitals. Florence Nightingale in the 1854 Crimean War had elevated the nursing profession, previously defamed as menial or morally dubious. Many still worried that the rough and bloody atmosphere of a military hospital was no place for a gentle, respectable young woman. The Union appointed the famed reformer Dorothea Dix as superintendent of nurses. She insisted that her nurses be over thirty years old, "plain in appearance," and unadorned by jewelry. Eventually, 3,200 women met these requirements and served as northern army nurses, the first professional nurses in American military history. Perhaps the most famous of them, "Mother Bickerdyke," crusaded tirelessly to improve the health of the soldiers and won the admiration and respect of the normally ornery General Sherman.

Others were volunteers on the battlefield. A small, pretty woman in a bonnet and a bright red bow named Clara Barton arrived at Antietam with a wagonload of bandages and medicine. She worked tirelessly through the battle comforting the wounded and aiding the surgeons. One of the latter called her "the true heroine of the age, the angel of the battlefield." She continued her efforts through most of the war. Later, she worked to identify the remains of the POWs at Andersonville and, eventually, founded the American Red Cross. "Michigan Bridget" Divers who attached herself to her husband's cavalry regiment became famous for her courage and coolness under fire in removing wounded men from the battlefield. She also picked up a fallen soldier's weapon and fought alongside the men.

The U. S. Sanitary Commission distributed food, clothing, and medicine to the army and sent inspectors to the army camps to teach soldiers sanitary methods.

At least one woman, Mary Walker, served as a surgeon in the Union army. When the Confederates captured the pants-wearing Walker, they expressed astonishment "at the sight of a *thing* that nothing but the debased and depraved Yankee nation could produce." Walker was awarded the Medal of Honor for her battlefield and prison camp medical services. (It was rescinded by Congress two years before her death in 1917 and restored in 1977.)

The Confederate army was slower to allow "decent" white women to serve as nurses. At first, only slave women performed this task in army hospitals. Eventually, however, white women from "good families" volunteered and were authorized to work as nurses. One of the southern surgeons admitted he preferred the women to the "rough country crackers" who had been performing that duty and who did not "know caster oil from a gun rod."

Black women helped the Union army by working as laundresses and unofficial nurses. Hundreds of others hid Union soldiers and helped them to escape. Some were punished for bringing food to Union prisoners. Susie King Taylor, who had learned how to read and write, was recruited by Union officers when she was 14 years old to teach freed slaves. She married a black sergeant and served alongside him as a nurse and laundress. She also confided, "I learned to handle a musket very well while in the regiment, and could shoot straight and often hit the target." Harriet Tubman not only worked as a nurse and cook for the Union army, she also served as a spy, utilizing her "invisibility" as a black woman to learn important information about troop movements.

Several other women operated as spies for both sides, including society hostess, Rose O'Neal Greenhow, a close friend of former President James Buchanan.

She was arrested and deported to England, only to drown in a shipwreck trying to smuggle gold to the Confederacy. Belle Boyd carried messages and spied for Stonewall Jackson. She later made quite a career for herself on stage, recounting her dramatic adventures.

Both in the North and the South (although more in the former), there were a number of women who dressed as men and fought in the war. The best research has uncovered 150 women soldiers. Several of these were promoted to sergeant, a few to lieutenant, and one even became a captain. Albert D.J. Cashier, whose real name was Jennie Hodgers, fought in numerous battles from 1862 to 1865. After the war, she collected a pension for disabled soldiers and was active in the Grand Army of the Republic, the Union veterans' organization. Her sex was not discovered until 1911 when she broke her leg and had to be treated by a physician.

While the efforts of these soldiers are interesting, the work of the women nurses had greater significance in advancing the professional status of nursing in America. After the war, nursing veterans started training programs, wrote textbooks, and even administered hospitals. Nursing became an important profession for women although the job description continued to include such menial activities as cleaning, doing laundry, and cooking for patients.

Women played a vital role in the Civil War. They maintained the homes and carried on the fieldwork that their men had left behind. They nursed patients in military hospitals and raised funds to support the war. Clara Barton, "Angel of the Battlefield," worked feeding, bandaging, and consoling the wounded. After the war was over, she founded the American Red Cross.

DOCUMENTS

THE EMANCIPATION PROCLAMATION (1863)

As the war continued, northern public opinion gradually moved to an acceptance of emancipation. European public opinion strongly supported freedom for the slaves, and it seemed as though measures taken to free them would positively impact Union foreign policy efforts. The slaves' own actions in fleeing their plantations to follow northern armies made the end of slavery seem more inevitable. Lincoln, in his cautious way, had come to the conclusion that it was time to take action. He was convinced to wait until after a Union victory, so a proclamation of emancipation would not seem like an act of desperation. After the Union "victory" at Antietam in September 1862, Lincoln issued his proclamation, which applied only to areas still in rebellion. It was not until the passage of the Thirteenth Amendment in 1865 that slavery was ended throughout the United States.

ABRAHAM LINCOLN

Whereas on the 22d day of September, A.D. 1862, a proclamation was issued by the President of the United States, containing among other things, the following, to wit:

That on the 1st day of January, A.D. 1863, all persons held as slaves within any State or designated part of a State the people whereof shall then be in rebellion against the United States shall be then, thenceforward, and forever free; and the executive government of the United States, including the military and naval authority thereof, will recognize and maintain the freedom of such persons and will do no act or acts to repress such persons, or any of them, in any efforts they may make for their actual freedom.

That the executive will on the 1st day of January aforesaid, by proclamation, designate the States and parts of States, if any, in which the people thereof, respectively, shall then be in rebellion against the United States; and the fact that any State or the people thereof shall on that day be in good faith represented in the Congress of the United States by members chosen thereto at elections wherein a majority of the qualified voters of such States shall have participated shall, in the absence of strong countervailing testimony, be deemed conclusive evidence that such State and the people thereof are not then in rebellion against the United States.

Now, therefore, I, Abraham Lincoln, President of the United States, by virtue of the power in me vested as Commander-in-Chief of the Army and Navy of the United States in time of actual armed rebellion against the authority and government of the United States, and as a fit and necessary war measure for suppressing said rebellion, do, on this 1st day of January, A.D. 1863, and in accordance with my purpose so to do, publicly proclaimed for the full period of one hundred days from the first day above mentioned, order and designate as the States and parts of States wherein the people thereof, respectively, are this day in rebellion against the United States .... (Here he lists the states – ed.)

And by virtue of the power and for the purpose aforesaid, I do order and declare that all persons held as slaves within said designated States and parts of States are, and henceforward shall be, free; and that the Executive Government of the United States, including the military and naval authorities thereof, will recognize and maintain the freedom of said persons.

And I hereby enjoin upon the people so declared to be free to abstain from all violence, unless in necessary self-defense; and I recommend to them that, in all cases when allowed, they labor faithfully for reasonable wages.

And I further declare and make known that such persons of suitable condition will be received into the armed service of the United States to garrison forts, positions, stations, and other places, and to man vessels of all sorts in said service. And upon this act, sincerely believed to be an act of justice, warranted by the Constitution upon military necessity, I invoke the considerate judgment of mankind and the gracious favor of Almighty God.

Source: John Nicolay and John Hay, eds., *Complete Works of Abraham Lincoln* (Lincoln Memorial University, 1894), VIII: 161-164.

1. The Emancipation Proclamation has been characterized as about as exciting as a cargo bill. Do you think that is true? Why do you think Lincoln, a master of wonderful language, made the language of the proclamation so ordinary?
2. Upon what presidential power does the president base his action?
3. Why would some observers criticize the principle of the proclamation as declaring that one human being cannot own another "unless he is loyal to the United States"?
4. In that case, why did so many abolitionists and blacks celebrate the issuance of the Proclamation?
5. Which view do you think has more validity?

BLACK TROOPS IN COMBAT

The Emancipation Proclamation provided for the use of black troops by the Union army. Many Union soldiers remained resentful. Most, however, came to understand that blacks could help fill the Union's manpower needs. By the war's end, there were 180,000 blacks in the Union army. Many northern districts filled their troop quota with blacks. Despite this, they were treated unequally, receiving far lower pay. After protests, Congress eventually voted to equalize military salaries. Those blacks used as combat soldiers quickly proved their toughness and effectiveness in a series of engagements.

Reminiscence of a Former Black Soldier in the Union Army

At first the faintest intimation that Negroes should be employed as soldiers in the Union Army was met with derision. By many it was regarded as a joke. The idea of arming the ex-slaves seemed ridiculous to most civil and military officers.... Most observing and thoughtful people concluded that centuries of servitude had rendered the Negro slave incapable of any civil or military service.... Some officers talked of resigning if Negroes were to be called upon to fight the battles of a free republic. The privates in regiments from large cities and border States were bitter and demonstrative in their opposition. The Negro volunteers themselves were subjected to indignities from rebel civilians within the Union lines, and obtained no protection from the white troops.

Source: George Washington Williams, *A History of the Negro Troops in the War of the Rebellion, 1861-65* (New York, 1888), pp. 66-67, 90-91.

Letter written by an Unnamed Soldier in the Massachusetts Fifty-fifth Infantry

Why are we not worth as much as white soldiers? We do the same work they do, and do what they cannot... just let them think of the charge at Fort Wagner, where the colored soldiers were cruelly murdered by the notorious rebels. Why is it that they do not want to give us our (just] pay when they have already witnessed our deeds of courage and bravery.... If we had staid at home with our fathers and mothers, wives and sisters, and dear ones at home, we could have received from $1 00 to $1-50 per day.
[African-American troops received $7 a month – ed.]

Source: The *Christian Recorder*, March 5,1864.

Black Soldiers Triumph at Battle of Petersburg, July 1864

...The rebel cannon opened. The sons of Africa did not flinch, but took their positions with deliberation. They had been slaves; they stood face to face with their former master....The [Confederate] flag in front of them waving in the morning breeze was the emblem of oppression; the banner above them was the flag of the free....

The Rebels were on a knoll in the field, and had a clear sweep of all the approaches. The advancing troop must come out of the woods, rush up the slope, and carry it at the point of bayonet, receiving the tempest of musketry and canister.

[General] Hinks deployed his line. At the word of the command the colored men stepped out from the woods, and stood before the enemy. They gave a volley, and received one in return. Shells crashed through them, but unheeding the storm with a yell they started up the slope upon the run. They received one charge of canister, one scathing volley of musketry. Seventy of their number went down, but the living hundreds rushed on. The Rebels did not wait their coming, but fled towards Petersburg, leaving one of the pieces of artillery in the hands of assailants, who leaped over the works, turned it in a twinkling, but were not able to fire upon the retreating foe, fleeing in consternation towards the main line of entrenchments two miles east of the city.

The colored troops were wild with joy. They embraced the captured cannon with affectionate enthusiasm, patting it as if it were animate, and could appreciate the endearment.

"Every soldier of the colored division was two inches taller for that achievement," said an officer describing it.

Source: Charles Carleton Coffin, *Four Years of Fighting*, 1866

1. According to the first memoir, what was the initial reaction of Union soldiers to the enlistment of black troops?
2. What injustice(s) did black troops protest against?
3. How did the black troops perform in combat, according to the last writer?
4. What long-term results do you think would flow from the performance of black troops in the war?

THE HOME FRONT

The seemingly endless slaughter and inconclusive engagements hurt civilian morale on both sides. In the North, the conscription law with its obvious class bias in its exemption and substitution clauses led to popular indignation. The worst explosion occurred in New York City on July 13, 1863—one of the bloodiest riots of American history. The ***New York Times****, like most opinion leaders, was vehement in its condemnation of the riots.*

The New York City Draft Riots

The mob in our city is still rampant.... The monster grows more dangerous as he grows desperate....

It is too true that there are public journals who try to dignify the mob by some respectable appellation. The Herald characterizes it as the people and the World as the laboring men of the City....The people of New-York and the laboring men of New-York are not incendiaries, nor robbers, nor assassins. They do not hunt down men whose only offense is the color God gave them: they do not chase and insult and beat women; they do not pillage an asylum for orphan children, and burn the very roof over those orphans' heads. They are civilized beings, valuing law and respecting decency: and they regard with unqualified abhorrence the doings of the tribe of savages...in their midst.

...You may as well reason with the wolves in the forest as with these men in their present mood ....-*Give them grape and plenty of it.*

OBJECT OF THE MOB. If this mob was originated in a passionate spirit of resistance to the Conscription law, it very soon changed its purpose, and assumed the character of merely a mob for robbery, plunder and arson. This is shown in the rifling of houses, hotels and stores, and the assaults and felonies upon the persons of unoffending citizens. Some of the ringleaders are noted thieves, who have served out several terms in Sing Sing and other penitentiaries and prisons. Hundreds of the workmen who joined with the crowd on Monday, were, of course, as honest as the average of us, but they were at once joined by all the knaves of the City who saw...an opportunity for plunder....

LAW AND LIBERTY. ....A mob is un-American, antiAmerican. Every grievance can here be remedied, every wrong can here be righted by law, which has its power in the will of the people and "its fountain in the bosom of God." It will be a dark day for the liberties of America, for its honor, its greatness, its power, its glory, when this excrescence of European despotism fastens itself upon our free institutions and society. Every man who prides himself in the name of an American must use his determined efforts to drive back this black and deadly tide of human depravity.

Source: Editorial in the *New York Times*, Wednesday, July 15, 1863

Response of a Rioter

You will no doubt be hard on us rioters tomorrow morning,, but that 300-dollar law has made us nobodies, vagabonds and cast-outs of society, for whom nobody cares when we must go to war and be shot down. We are the poor rabble, and the rich rabble is our enemy by this law. Therefore we will give our enemy battle right here, and ask no quarter. Although we got hard fists, and are dirty without, we have soft hearts and have clean consciences within, and that's the reason we love our wives and children more than the rich, because we got not much besides them, and we will not go and leave them at home for to starve.... Why don't they let the nigger kill the slave-driving race and take possession of the South, as it belongs to them.

Source: Letter to the editor of the *New York Times*, by "A POOR MAN, BUT A MAN FOR ALL THAT," July 15, 1863

1. How does the *New York Times* characterize the actions of the New York draft rioters?
2. What are the explanations of the rioter/letter-writer for the actions of the rioters?
3. What do you think was the real reason for the riots?

ROBERT E. LEE

Chapter Eight

THE TIDE OF WAR TURNS

LEE'S GREATEST VICTORY

Chancellorsville

Despite the long-term positive consequences of the Emancipation Proclamation, after the miserable failure of Fredericksburg, Lincoln desperately needed a Union victory to boost northern resolve in 1863. General "Fighting Joe" Hooker replaced the demoralized Burnside. Known for his courage in earlier battles and his willingness to act bravely (some would say rashly), Hooker was immensely popular with his men who appreciated his hard drinking reputation. "Our leader is Joe Hooker, he takes his whiskey strong," they sang.

Lincoln chose him despite public statements suggesting that the president was an imbecile and that the nation needed a military dictator. In a remarkable letter Lincoln informed him, "Only those generals who gain successes can set up dictators. What I ask of you now is military success and I will risk the dictatorship." Hooker quickly moved to restructure the army, improve rations and sanitation, and insure prompt issuance of back pay. Morale recovered. Critics were skeptical noting that, under Hooker, army headquarters had become "a combination of barroom and brothel." (Hooker had attempted to better control the growing number of prostitutes by creating a red-light district in Washington that quickly was known as "Hooker's Division." Later, according to legend, the women came to be called "hookers.")

A seemingly confident Hooker moved his resurgent army to **Chancellorsville** where he outnumbered Lee's forces by 2 to 1. Hooker successfully completed a

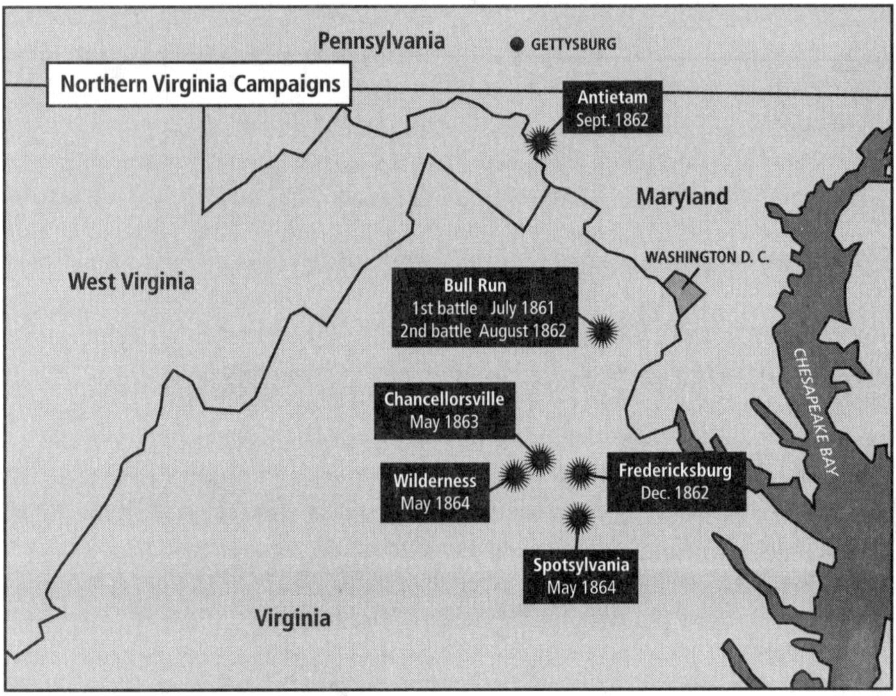

huge turning maneuver that put the center of his flank at the tiny country crossroads at the end of April 1863. "My plans are prefect," he boasted, "and when I carry them out, may God have mercy on Bobby Lee; for I shall have none." His bravado, however, was more an attempt to lift his own failing spirits. Hooker's main corps commander was Dan Sickles, a raunchy adventurer who, three years earlier, had been acquitted of murdering his wife's lover on the then odd plea of temporary insanity. (After the war, Sickles became an occasional lover of the Queen of Spain.)

Lee boldly divided his forces for an audacious strike at the Union army. Lee stood firm and acted aggressive with less than one-third of his army, creating the impression of real strength. Meanwhile, Stonewall Jackson took the other two-thirds of the men and pushed through the woods toward Hooker's rear. As a tactician, Jackson believed, "Always mystify, mislead, and surprise the enemy." With the Confederates out on a limb, any sort of attack by Hooker would have destroyed the Confederate army. Despite his favorable position, however, Hooker astonished his corps commanders by ordering disengagement. He later admitted that he had lost his nerve, "I just lost confidence in Joe Hooker." Lee was able to maneuver his outnumbered forces to keep Hooker in a state of stunned confusion. On May 2, Confederate troops, shrieking the ear-splitting Rebel yell, burst upon the surprised Union forces in a two-mile line from out of the woods. The following day, southern units plunged blindly into the deep Wilderness to engage equally desperate northern troops. After substantial casualties, Hooker retreated on May 5, 1863. Chancellorsville, a total defeat, seemed to be a shattering blow to northern morale.

Hooker lost 18,000 men to 12,000 Confederate casualties. But the Confederate victory was far more costly to the winners than seemed apparent. Southern losses represented a higher proportion of their effective strength. The drain on the officer corps was particularly damaging. Their code of honor impelled them to lead their men by exposing themselves almost recklessly to enemy fire. (Fifty-five percent of Confederate generals were killed or wounded in the war, a rate triple that of Union generals.) The loss of Lee's most daring associate, Stonewall Jackson, was only the most famous example. Despite this personal loss, Lee's Army of Northern Virginia still seemed unbeatable after two years of war. Lee thought he saw the way open to a final victory. "General Lee," one of his subordinates remarked, "believed that the Army of Northern Virginia, as it then existed, could accomplish anything." This overconfidence would eventually prove to be fatal. Lincoln believed that he had the manpower to crush the southern armies, but he had not yet found the general with the will to do it.

The Death of Stonewall Jackson

In the moonlight on May 2, in an area filled with smoke, General Stonewall Jackson was riding with a small contingent of his men. He was looking for a route in the Wilderness to be able to block any Union retreat. As he headed back to Confederate lines, the noise of his horses led a startled North Carolina brigade to fire wildly. "You are firing at your own men," one of Jackson's officers shouted. A major with the brigade responded, "It's a lie! Pour it into them boys!" The volley killed four of the men in the group. Three of the bullets hit Jackson, two shattering his left arm. Staff members tried to shield him with their bodies. As they carried him back, they fell, dropping him on his mutilated shoulder and recommencing the severe arterial bleeding. As was common with such injuries, the doctor was forced to amputate his arm.

Informed of the grim news, a dismayed General Lee declared, "He has lost his left arm, but I have lost my right." Still, Lee believed that Jackson would recover, "God will not take him from us now that we need him so much." At first, Lee appeared to be right, as Jackson seemed to be recovering at a country house where he had been taken by ambulance. On the morning of May 7, however, Jackson complained of a sharp pain in his side, and the doctors realized that pneumonia had set in. His wife arrived that day and warned him that he was dying. "My wish is fulfilled," he responded, "I have always desired to die on Sunday." On Sunday, May 10, after desperately gasping for breath Jackson died, murmuring, "Let us cross over the river and rest under the shade of the trees."

Gettysburg

Lee hoped to thwart any Union plan to launch a summer campaign in Virginia and pulverize federal troops occupying the northern Shenandoah Valley. He also wanted to give Virginians relief from war and their farmers a chance to replenish their crops and livestock by foraging in a rich untapped area in Pennsylvania, just north of Maryland. At the same time, bringing the war to the North might increase Union war weariness and relieve Virginia from the pressure of the Union campaign to capture Richmond by forcing the Union army to defend its own territory. As Lee's army headed toward Harrisburg, Pennsylvania on the strategic Susquehanna River in June 1863, the northeastern public panicked. Lincoln reasoned, correctly, that Lee might be vulnerable so far from his base. He sent reinforcements to Hooker, informing the general that this was "the best opportunity we have had since the war began." When the paralyzed general replied, "I don't know whether I am standing on my head or feet," he was relieved of his command. A surprised General George Meade replaced him; an unflappable, steady officer nicknamed "a damned old goggle-eyed snapping turtle." Meade quickly moved the Army of the Potomac to block Lee and put him in the bind of having to either attack or retreat.

On June 30, Confederate troops heard the rumor that there was a huge supply of shoes stored in the little town of Gettysburg, important for the footsore men. As they headed to the town, they clashed with advanced units of Union cavalry. All the Confederate and Union divisions in the region quickly converged on the area. Lee rejected the option of withdrawing and ordered assaults against the Union lines. Since they were closer to the action, the Confederates were able to concentrate their troops more rapidly. Although desperate Union defenders were able to forestall disaster on July 1, it seemed as if the Southerners were close to victory. By the next day, however, the remaining Union troops arrived and occupied a long north-south ridge. An open field lay between the two armies and, on July 2, waves of Confederate troops hurled themselves across the field against the right and left flanks of the Union forces. Federal forces held firm to their positions on the ridge and two dome-shaped hills known as Big Round Top and Little Round Top despite fierce attacks. The sun rose on July 3 over the two armies facing each other across a valley. The Army of Northern Virginia, the core of the Confederate Army under the command of Robert E. Lee, was on top of Seminary Ridge in a line that stretched for several miles. Opposite them, the Army of the Potomac under Meade occupied Cemetery Ridge.

Lee's "blood was up" and he wrongly believed that the Union forces were demoralized and that his own men were invincible. On July 3, he ordered a direct attack on the enemy's center, an almost unthinkable mistake. Under the command of the unfortunate General George Pickett, a Confederate force of thirteen

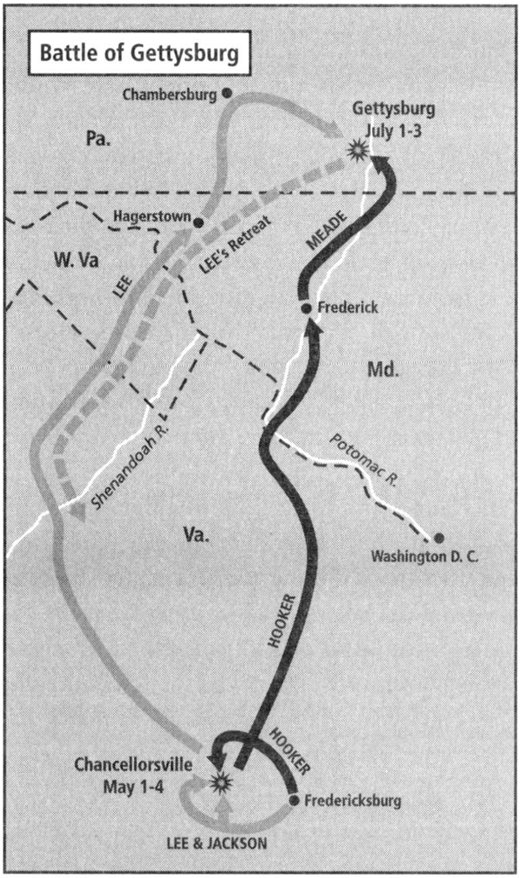

The bloody Gettysburg Battle included 23,000 Union and 28,000 Confederate casualties, which was one-third of Lee's effective force.

thousand men marched in perfect order over a mile across an open field and up a slope only to meet withering fire from the entrenched Union forces. Some thought it a glorious charge, but the cost was ghastly. More than half of Pickett's troops were killed or wounded, including all three of his brigade commanders and all thirteen of his colonels. Every one of the University Greys, a company of University of Mississippi students, was either killed or wounded. One brigade of the Ninth Virginia Infantry with 1,287 men and 140 officers suffered a loss of 942 killed, wounded, or missing. Its "cool and handsome" leader, General Richard B. Garnett, calmly rode around his men to rally them and keep them in close order. As one of his majors later reported, "He was shot from his horse while near the center of the brigade, within about 25 paces of the stone wall." As the decimated remnants of "Pickett's charge" retreated, the victorious Union soldiers shouted, "Fredericksburg! Fredericksburg!" A chastened General Lee rode among the survivors, telling them, "It's all my fault," as indeed it was. One historian has commented, "Gettysburg was the price the South paid for having R.E. Lee."

The staggering casualties in this bloodiest of battles of a bloody conflict included 23,000 Union men and 28,000 Confederates, an unbelievable one-third of Lee's effective force. A Union general wrote, "I tried to ride over the field, but could not, for the dead and wounded lay too thick to guide a horse through them." On July 4, through a driving summer rainstorm, Lee's dispirited men began their long retreat. Despite Lincoln's urging, the cautious Meade failed to pursue Lee's army, allowing it to slip back across the Potomac. "We had them within our grasp," a dejected Lincoln lamented. "We had only to stretch forth our hands and they were ours. And nothing I could say or do could make the Army move." Northern public opinion was more forgiving as news from the West added to the feeling of a great victory.

Vicksburg

Lincoln, who had once followed the Mississippi from Illinois to New Orleans as a young flatboatman, understood that Vicksburg was the key to control of the river and ultimate Union victory: "The war can never be brought to a close until the key is in our pocket." But Vicksburg, the "Gibraltar of the West," seemed impregnable on its high bluff on the river's eastern side, surrounded by bayous and swamps on its north and west. U.S. Grant, who had been given command of that area, launched a daring campaign to march his army down the river, cross below

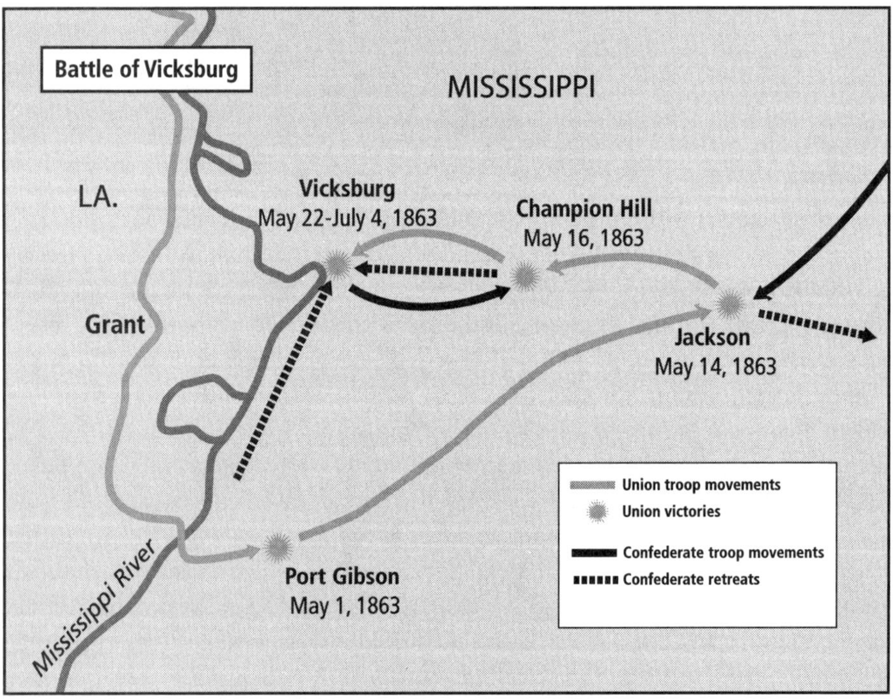

Vicksburg's defenses, and surprise the town by attacking it from the rear. This risky maneuver plunged Grant's forces into enemy territory cut off from their base of supplies. The divided and uncoordinated Confederate command was totally confused by Grant's actions. He easily seized Jackson, Mississippi and its rail communications and forced the Confederate army back into Vicksburg.

After two unsuccessful assaults on the city's defenses, the Union army settled in for a siege, while Union gunboats bombarded the hapless inhabitants. Hundreds of trapped civilians lived in caves dug in the yellow clay hillsides. Food ran out, and both soldiers and civilians were forced to eat mules and rats. One Confederate soldier wrote that fried rats had a flavor "fully equal to that of squirrels." When a soldier gave a little girl a songbird for a pet, her mother made it into soup. Even drinking water became scarce, and people were reduced to dipping from ditches and mud-holes. One less-than-noble Vicksburg lawyer had his own private supply of fresh water. While many suffered from thirst, his wife wrote, "every night in my subterranean dressing room a tub of cold water is the nerve-calmer that sends me to sleep." Houses were in ruins. The defiant local newspaper was being printed on the back of wallpaper.

At last, after a 47-day siege, the beleaguered defenders surrendered the city and a 30,000-man army on July 4, 1863, the day Lee withdrew from Gettysburg. The embittered citizens of Vicksburg refused to celebrate July 4th again until their patriotism was reawakened in World War II. The victory, "the single most successful Union campaign of the war," was exuberantly celebrated in the North. A few days later, **Port Hudson**, the last Confederate bastion on the Mississippi, also surrendered. The Mississippi had become a Union highway. "The Father of Waters," a thankful Lincoln proclaimed, "again goes unvexed to the sea." The Confederacy, as the "Anaconda plan" had envisioned, had been split in two.

The losses at Gettysburg and Vicksburg unnerved the people of the South. One Confederate soldier wrote to his sister, after his experiences at Gettysburg: "They are awhiping us...at every point... I hope that we that is alive yet would get home agane." "We are in the depths of gloom," Jefferson Davis conceded, "We are now in the darkest hour of our political existence."

Chattanooga

That fall, Grant capped his Vicksburg success with another great victory at Chattanooga. The front was almost lost in the costly **Battle of Chickamauga** in September. The Union commander, Rosecrans, made a nearly fatal mistake, pursuing retreating Confederate troops into a trap. He was only saved from a worse disaster by the efforts of the Virginian George "Old Pap" Thomas whose stubborn defense earned him the nickname, "the Rock of Chicamauga," and enabled the Yankees to retreat to Chattanooga. An amazed French battlefield correspondent compared the carnage to a catfight. "The two armies meet and fight and slaughter each other with the utmost fury. Then they fall back and reorganize for another general massacre. Positively, the war will end when the last man is killed." Grant, wryly responding, "our cat has the longer tail," rushed to the besieged city and quickly replaced the inept Rosecrans with Thomas. "When Grant arrived," one officer remembered, "we began to see things move."

On November 23, Grant attacked. The battle seesawed for three days until some of Thomas' men, inexplicably and illogically, charged the entrenched center of the Confederate army at Missionary Ridge. Led by the small, slight, but combative General Phil Sheridan, they fought their way to the summit, shouting, "Chickamauga! Chickamauga!" as Confederate resistance crumbled. The Tennessee River was now under Union control, the Confederacy split north and south as well as east and west, and the way was open to Atlanta. Perhaps most important, finally, Lincoln found a general. Early in 1864 he elevated Grant to general-in-chief of all Union armies.

The Gettysburg Address

When the armies had pulled out of Gettysburg, they left thousands of rotting bodies, horse and human. While the horses and mules could be, and were, burned, the eight thousand soldiers were barely covered by teams of Union soldiers, Confederate prisoners, and civilians who struggled against nausea and swarms of bluebottle flies. The disheartening sight of the putrid and steaming makeshift graveyard became a national scandal and led to a call for a national burial ground to honor those who died for their country. The cemetery was dedicated in November. After a lengthy oration by the famed public speaker Edward Everett, President Lincoln in his high-pitched, almost shrill, Kentucky-accented voice delivered his famed 272-word address. In it, he reminded Americans that their nation had been "conceived in Liberty and dedicated to the proposition that all men are created equal." He resolved that "these dead shall not have died in vain" and that "government of the people, by the people, for the people, shall not perish from the earth." In those relatively few words, Lincoln had been able to articulate the feelings of the northern public. The language of the address has resonated so much down through the years that the national memorial program for the one-year anniversary of the 9/11 attack in 2002 included a reading of the Gettysburg Address.

1864-5: THE FINAL STAGE

Grant certainly did not look heroic. He disliked uniforms and always seemed dust-covered and disheveled. Unlike all of his predecessors, however, Grant was able to effectively handle and coordinate the vast array of forces the Union had assembled. He was steady and clear-headed and absolutely focused on victory. "The art of war," he once said, "is simple enough. Find out where your enemy is. Get him as soon as you can and keep moving on." Grant was also unfazed by the supposed greatness of Lee. When he took command of the eastern campaign, he was annoyed by the staff's constant worries about "Bobby Lee." He finally admonished them, "I'm tired of hearing about Bobby Lee. You'd think he was going to do a double somersault and land in our rear. Quit thinking about what he's going to do and think about what you're going to do to him." Grant's stability also enabled his volatile colleague and friend, William Tecumseh Sherman, to become a great field commander. Sherman, a smarter more knowledgeable general, understood the importance of Grant's reassuring presence to his campaigns. "I knew wherever I was that you thought of me," he wrote Grant, "and if I got in a tight place you would come—if alive."

The worsening conditions in the South seemed likely to affect the Confederate troops. "What man is there that would stay in the army and no that his family is sufring at home?" one irate citizen wrote to the war department. With the support of their families and neighbors many men ran away from the army. The diarist Mary Chestnut watched military police dragging a man back to the army as his distraught wife shouted, "Desert agin, Jake! You desert agin, quick as you kin. Come back to your wife and children." One southern woman wrote to her army husband, "What do I care for patriotism? My husband is my country. What is country to me if he be killed?" By the end of 1863 one-third of the Confederate army was AWOL. Discontent within the Confederacy increased. Some newspapers even openly called for peace. The North Carolina *Raleigh Daily Progress* announced, "We are for peace because there has been enough of blood and carnage, enough of widows and orphans." By 1864, there were entire towns and counties, particularly in mountain districts, dominated by deserters.

Despite this, the Confederates were able to continue fierce resistance for another year. Unlike Union veterans whose three-year enlistments freed them to return home in the spring of 1864, Confederate enlistees served for the duration of the war. The two-thirds who did not desert were among the most rugged and hardy men ever to fight in any war. Religious revivals sweeping through the Confederate armies in 1863 led thousands to "profess their faith in Christ." Prayer groups multiplied in almost all regiments. The prospect of their deaths in battle seemed less alarming to those who believed in eternal salvation. As a result, they fought even more tenaciously. One Confederate soldier, who had been wounded three times, wrote, "i trust in god to Protect me in the Battle field if he sees Proper that i should get kild no living man can help it and if it is not his will that i should get kild i don't Care for the Balls."

By contrast, many of the new recruits, bounty men, substitutes, and conscripts, pouring into Union regiments in 1864, were unpromising military material. Fortunately for the Union, generous bounties and furloughs, as well as a sense of duty, led more than half of the federal three-year volunteers to reenlist in the spring of 1864. In fact, the ideals of honor and endurance seemed to grow, rather than decline, in the last dreadful year of the war. Still, the untrustworthiness of the new soldiers reduced the North's seemingly overwhelming numerical superiority and, together with the South's advantage of fighting a defensive war, helped even the odds for the Confederacy's survival.

Bioterrorism

The threat of bioterrorism did not originate in the twenty-first century. During the Civil War southern sympathizers concocted a plan to spread the dreaded disease of yellow fever in northern cities. At the time, there was no known treatment for yellow fever, which spread rapidly through cities causing swift death after the victims bled through their noses and mouths and threw up black dried blood.

In 1864 a mysterious doctor, Luke Blackburn, arrived in Bermuda where a yellow fever epidemic was decimating the population. For a month he devotedly cared for the sick and dying, declining to accept any money for his efforts. His real motive, however, was to obtain clothing, blankets, and sheets contaminated by victims of yellow fever. He filled three trunks with these items, many stained with black vomit, and tried to ship them to Canada. From there, he planned to bring them to New York where he expected to start an epidemic.

A spy, who informed the United States consul about Dr. Blackburn's nefarious schemes, thwarted the plot. Despite the efforts of a Confederate spy to warn the keeper of the clothing, a Mr. Swan, that the conspiracy had been uncovered, Mr. Swan was caught "preparing to burn the damaging articles" and sent to prison. The plot was revealed in the North on the same day that Lincoln was assassinated. Dr. Blackburn, called the "fever fiend" by northern newspapers, was charged with murder but was not prosecuted due to insufficient evidence. He later returned to his home state of Kentucky where he was elected governor in 1879. He resumed his medical practice there and became known for his courageous work in fighting yellow fever with disinfectants and quarantines.

Ironically, the plot (and another similar one) would never have worked. In 1901 it was discovered that infected mosquitoes, rather than people, spread yellow fever.

Battles in the East: 1864

Grant had promised Lincoln when he was given command of the armies, "what ever happens, there will be no turning back." Grant's goal in May 1864 was to coordinate the armies in the East and West to strike simultaneous blows against the Confederate lines. The Army of the Potomac was expected to so completely occupy Lee's forces that he would be unable to send reinforcements to the West where Sherman would be driving toward Atlanta. Lee hoped to demolish the Union determination to continue the conflict by compelling Grant to assault fortified positions and suffer unacceptable casualty levels. There would be a presidential election that fall and a continuing bloody stalemate might cost Lincoln the election and bring in a president willing to let the South go.

On May 4, a beautiful spring day, the Army of the Potomac marched forward, bands playing and banners waving. Lee's sixty thousand Confederates surprised them in a thickly tangled wooded area known as the Wilderness on the following day. For the next two days the two armies fired blindly at each other in woods so thick that, "No one could see the fight fifty feet from him." Brigades got lost in the forest and fired at their own men. Rifle flashes set the underbrush on fire, burning hundreds of wounded men alive. Skeletons poked out of graves dug the year before that had been washed away by rain. The Confederate attack was successful. The gruesome **Battle of the Wilderness** cost Grant 17,000 men (and the Confederates 11,000). The distressed general returned to his tent and wept. Weary veterans were certain that, as it always had in past defeats, the Army of the Potomac would retreat. Instead, Grant ordered the army to continue to march *south*. Although they had just come through hell and could expect more of the same, Union soldiers were exhilarated. "Our spirits rose," one remembered, "We marched free. The men began to sing."

Grant's army continued on, trying to reach Lee's communications and turn his flank at the strategically important crossroads of **Spotsylvania**. After furious assaults over several days, the Rebel lines held. But Grant continued his grim pursuit of Lee. "We have met a man this time," wrote one Southerner, "who either does not know when he is whipped, or cares not if he loses his whole Army." After a brief pause when heavy rains made the roads impassable, the two armies moved to a crossroads called **Cold Harbor**. Lee arrived first and his men entrenched themselves to await the inevitable attack. Union soldiers, understanding the perils that lay ahead, wrote their names and addresses on pieces of paper that they pinned to their coats, "so that their bodies might be recognized and their fate made known to their families." The resulting futile onslaught cost 12,000 Union casualties, almost 7,000 in the first few minutes. Grant later wrote, "I have always regretted that last assault at Cold Harbor was ever made...no advantage whatever was gained to compensate for the heavy loss we sustained." In the

This photograph of Grant at Cold Harbor was taken by the famous Civil War photographer Matthew Brady.

month since Grant first encountered Lee in the Wilderness, his army had suffered 50,000 casualties, half as many as in the previous three years of the war. "Grant is a butcher," said Mary Lincoln, reflecting the views of many, "He loses two men to the enemy's one…I could fight as well myself." Lincoln himself, however, stood by his general, "You will succeed," he wrote to Grant, "God bless you all."

Despite the slaughter, Grant kept going. Grant hoped to outmaneuver Lee and defeat the enemy in open battle. By this time, however, Lee realized that there was no offensive tactic or strategy left that would cause the South to "win" the war. If he and his men could hang on long enough to administer continuing severe losses to the Yankees, perhaps *they* would give up pushing to win. The result was a horrible "war of attrition." In an attempt to avoid this, Grant hurried his men to **Petersburg**, a communications center south of Richmond, to Lee's rear. Lee's army arrived just in time to save the city, helped by the reluctance of some Union generals to mount an attack. Once again, the two armies crippled each other, but Grant dug in for a siege that was to last almost ten months, gradually cutting off supply access routes to Petersburg and Richmond. At the front, the men lived in a maze of trenches, beset by flies, driving rains, enemy fire, and the merciless Virginia sun. A spectacular, though poorly organized, attempt to dig a mine shaft under Confederate defenses and blast an enormous hole in their trenches failed as Union troops were trapped in the giant pit without any way out. Enraged Rebel soldiers shouting, "Take the white man! Kill the nigger!" killed hundreds of surrendering black troops. The siege continued.

Northerners increasingly believed that the war was going nowhere. Peace Democrats (the "Copperheads") loudly declared that, unless the country elected one of them as president, the crazy war to free the slaves would continue until every white man was dead. Horace Greeley, generally a supporter of the war, wrote in his *Tribune*, "Our bleeding...almost dying country...shudders at the prospect of further wholesale devastation, of new rivers of human blood." Lincoln's chances of reelection that fall seemed dimmer than ever.

But there was bad news for the Confederacy in the beautiful, fertile **Shenandoah Valley**. Grant had sent feisty General Phil Sheridan to leave the valley "a barren waste." The purpose of Sheridan's actions was to force Southerners to stop aiding the Rebel war effort, particularly the widespread guerilla activities. Sheridan destroyed railroad lines, crops, livestock, mills, and barns and boasted that, in the future, a crow flying over the valley would have to carry its own supplies. Unlike modern "total war" campaigns, however, Sheridan never directed operations against innocent civilians. His men followed him loyally, marching hundreds of miles up and down the Valley, sometimes without shoes. One private assured his wife from his hospital bed that we would do it again: "I cannot believe Providence intends to destroy this Nation, this great asylum for the oppressed of all other nations and build a slave oligarchy on the ruins thereof." Following the little man on his great black horse, Sheridan's soldiers beat back a last effort of the Confederate army to reopen the Valley. A delighted Lincoln informed Sheridan, "When this particular war began, I thought a cavalryman should be at least six feet four inches high, but I have changed my mind. Five feet four will do in a pinch."

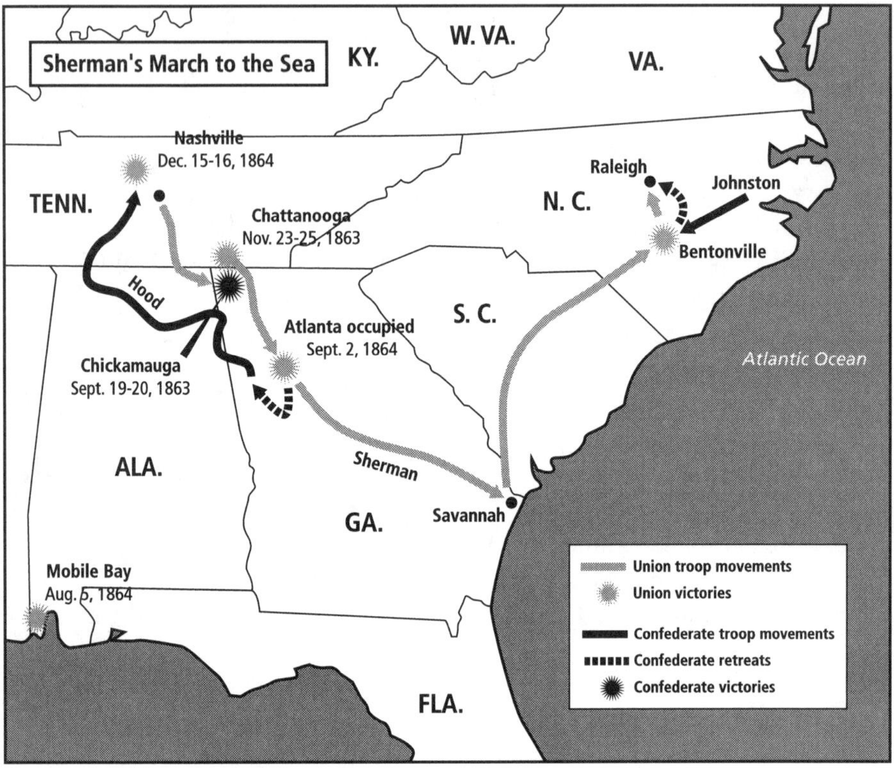

Beginning of the End: 1864

Meanwhile, events in the western part of the war were moving even more decisively in favor of the Union. **Mobile Bay** was the major port still open to southern shipping. The 63-year-old Admiral David Farragut, who had lashed himself to the rigging of his flagship, led a flotilla of fourteen wooden and four ironclad ships through the underwater mines and past the defending guns of the fort. "Damn the torpedoes, full speed ahead!" he supposedly shouted. The fort and the defending fleet surrendered, further limiting Confederate ability to obtain supplies.

General Sherman, who some historians have called "the first truly modern general," was at this time beginning his slow march through Georgia. Sherman was Grant's closest friend and lieutenant. He once explained, "Grant stood by me when I was crazy and I stood by him when he was drunk; and now we stand by each other always." Sherman was opposed by the sly Joseph Johnston who cautiously fell back, making the Union troops pay for every mile of their advance. But President Davis had never really trusted Johnston and, in July, removed him from command, convinced he lacked the determination to win. Davis replaced

Sherman left Atlanta in ruins, 1864

him with General John Hood, a brave but rash officer who had lost one leg and the use of an arm. Hood fell into Sherman's trap by attacking the superior Union forces. Sherman defeated Hood and occupied Atlanta on September 2, a deadly blow to southern morale. "Atlanta is ours, and fairly won," Sherman wired Washington. The victory made a mockery of the Democratic claims that the war was a "failure" and helped assure Lincoln's reelection.

Sherman then left Atlanta "smouldering and in ruins" to continue his famous "**March to the Sea**." He planned to live off the land, destroying resources as he moved. He swore he would, "make Georgia howl." Sherman felt that the best way to ultimately defeat the enemy army was to break the will of the civilians who nurtured it. "We cannot change the hearts of the people of the South," he declared with some sadness, "but we can make war so terrible...and make them so *sick* of war that generations will pass away before they again appeal to it." An army of seasoned veterans who had undergone "a rigorous weeding-out process," so that "only the best fighting material" remained carried out the march. The army focused on destroying the major east-west railroads, using special tools to twist the iron rails. The path they cut through Georgia, 60 miles wide and more than 200 miles long, had a devastating impact, both in actual destruction and in the fears it created in the hearts of the civilians. But one historian argues that the extent to which houses and towns were burned has been greatly exaggerated by popular myth. For the most part, he asserts, "Georgia whites suffered primarily the loss of crops and livestock." The chaos was increased by the thousands of exultant slaves who flocked to Sherman's army. On December 22, Sherman telegraphed a delighted Lincoln, "I beg to present you, as a Christmas gift, the city of Savannah, with 150 heavy guns and plenty of ammunition; also, about 25,000 bales of cotton." Southern morale was crumbling. Southern soldiers deserted in increasing numbers, responding to letters like the pitiful entreaty one Confederate soldier received from his wife: "We haven't got nothing in the house to eat...If you put off a-coming, 'twont be no use to come, for we'll all hands of us be out there in the grave yard with your ma and mine." By the second half of 1864, more than half of the army was gone. Grant and Sherman now began to think of a second thrust: northward through the Carolinas.

THE WAR FINALLY ENDS

As late as the summer of 1864, the conclusion of the conflict was not so easy to discern by observers at the time. The horrific casualties suffered by the Army of the Potomac in the period between the Battle of the Wilderness and Petersburg had caused deep despondency in the North. Democrats spread the notion that, if Lincoln would only drop his insistence on emancipation, the war would end. Despite some bending under this pressure, Lincoln responded, if he agreed "to return to slavery the black warriors" who fought for the Union, "I should be damned in time & in eternity." Lincoln understood the consequences. He informed a friend in August, "I am going to be beaten and unless some great change takes place, *badly* beaten."

The Election of 1864

Remarkably, in the midst of bitter conflict, the presidential election was held as scheduled. Confederate agents carefully cultivated the antiwar faction in the North. Southern military leaders even planned campaigns to hold out until the November election. One Confederate War Department official noted, "If we can only *subsist*...giving an opportunity for the Democrats to elect a President...we may have peace." Republicans, despite misgivings, renominated Lincoln at their June convention. To bolster his candidacy, they added a War Democrat, Andrew Johnson of Tennessee, to run for vice president on the new Union Party label.

When the Democratic convention met in Chicago at the end of August, they adopted a peace platform. "After four years of failure to restore the Union by the experiment of war," the platform demanded that hostilities cease and that the

"Federal Union" of the states restored. Then, they nominated General George McClellan for president. McClellan, a War Democrat, was seeking vindication after his removal by Lincoln two years earlier. McClellan, however, rejected the peace plank. He specified reunion (but not emancipation) as a precondition for peace. Despite this mixed message, Southerners were buoyed by the possibility of a Democratic victory that "must lead to peace and our independence" if "for the next two months *we hold our own and prevent military success by our foes*." Democrats published speculations about Lincoln's supposed black ancestry, cartoons depicting black men kissing white women, and semi-obscene verses about the racial mixing that Lincoln's election would bring about.

These racist appeals had minimal attraction for northern voters when the thrilling news of Sherman's capture of Atlanta reached the public three days after the Democratic convention. This was followed by word of Sheridan's spectacular campaign in the Shenandoah Valley. Republican newspapers gloated about these victories: "OLD ABE'S REPLY TO THE CHICAGO CONVENTION." In the end, Lincoln won a smashing victory, gaining 55 percent of the popular vote and an electoral college triumph of 212 to 21. The Republicans also increased their majorities in both houses of Congress to more than three-fourths.

In an extraordinary experiment in democracy, most states allowed soldiers to vote in an election that would determine whether they would continue to fight. Although 40 to 45 percent of them had been Democrats and McClellan had been a popular commander, an astounding 80 percent of the soldier vote went to Lincoln. The soldiers could not bear to support a party that declared the war a failure. One private wrote home that he gave "the rebelion another thump this fall by voting for old Abe. I cannot afford to give three years of my life to maintaining this nation and then giving them Rebles all they want." Everyone understood the meaning of Lincoln's reelection. It demonstrated, a perceptive British war correspondent noted, that the North was determined to fight to the end, "they will fight on…as long as they have men, muskets, powder…."

The Thirteenth Amendment

The dramatic change that had taken place in Union war aims was vividly demonstrated on January 31, 1865, by the congressional approval of the Thirteenth Amendment abolishing slavery. This amendment forever eliminated the likelihood that Lincoln's wartime emancipation measures could be overturned by the Supreme Court or rescinded by southern states after the war. The passage was assured by the votes of sixteen War Democrats in addition to the Republicans. The most uproarious demonstration in the history of Congress broke out. Black spectators in the galleries hugged each other and wept jubilant tears. The House took the rest of the day off "in honor of this immortal and sublime event." The following day John Rock of Massachusetts, a lawyer, dentist, physician, and orator who was fluent in French and German, was admitted to practice before the Supreme Court. Eight years earlier the Supreme Court, in the *Dred Scott* Decision, had ruled that blacks were never eligible to be U.S. citizens. John Rock was a black man. Within three months, every northern state legislature except New Jersey had ratified the Thirteenth Amendment.

Sherman's March Through the Carolinas

In February 1865 Sherman's army continued the second phase of its campaign, smashing through the Carolinas, destroying resources, and spreading demoralization among the civilians. He was advancing towards Lee's rear to put the main Confederate army in a vise between his forces and Grant's. It was an unusually wet winter, and the men were forced to cross swamps and rivers swollen by rain. A Confederate general believed that, "it was absolutely impossible for an army to march across lower portions of the State in winter." But the Yankees managed a steady advance of ten miles a day. The men, including Sherman himself, often

Southern General Robert E. Lee (right) and Northern General William Tecumseh Sherman (left)

slept in trees to avoid the soggy ground. As they continued through the Carolinas, thousands of slaves fled to their lines. At one point, Sherman measured the blacks who followed behind his forces in *miles*. His men had less frequent contact with southern whites, since rumors of Yankee abuses (whether true or not) led thousands to flee to "safer" places. It was true that South Carolina, particularly, was treated far more harshly than Georgia was. Many men believed that South Carolina deserved more punishment for causing the war. As one plundering soldier put it, "Here is where treason began, and, by God, here is where it shall end."

The burning of Columbia, the capital of South Carolina, helped feed the fears of southern whites. (Historians, generally, feel that the conflagration resulted from the combined activities of Confederate cavalrymen, vengeful liber-

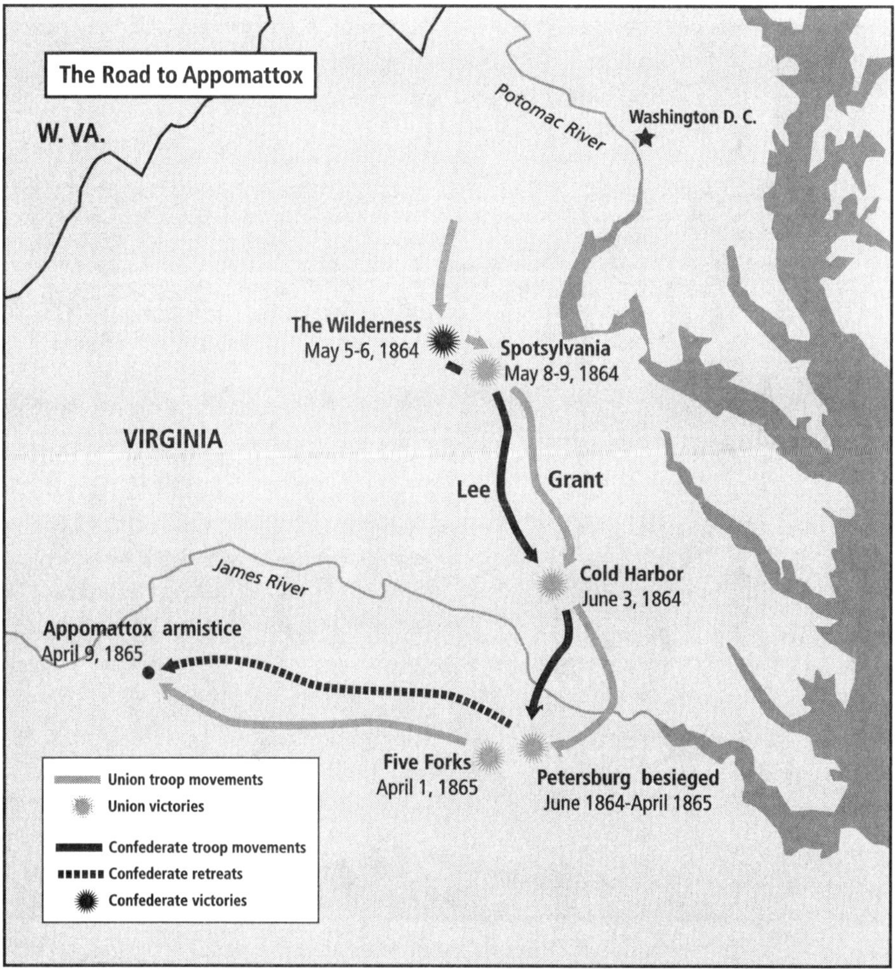

ated prisoners-of-war, drunken Union soldiers, and gale-force winds in an area of accumulated cotton stores.) When Charleston surrendered on February 18, the colonel of a black regiment received the formal capitulation. His men, some of whom had once been slaves in that city, marched in singing "John Brown's Body" to the joyful cheers of the city's blacks. Two months later, William Lloyd Garrison and other abolitionists took part in a ceremonial raising of the American flag over Fort Sumter, exactly four years after it had been taken down in surrender.

Meanwhile, Sherman's men continued north into North Carolina, effectively sealing off the path to Lee's army. At the same time, Sheridan's cavalry once again raided the Shenandoah Valley, successfully disrupting both canal and rail communications to Richmond. Another major raid resulted in the capture of Selma and Montgomery in Alabama and Columbus, Georgia. This disabled the last

Richmond, Virginia lay in ruins after the war.

area in the South that might have helped continue the war. Southern morale was completely demolished, and defeatism saturated the Confederacy.

Appomattox

When winter came, suffering grew worse in the Petersburg trenches. Large numbers of famished and desperate Confederate soldiers began to cross over to Union lines. Grant launched a massive attack against the crumbling Confederate defenses in Petersburg on April 2. By April 3, the Rebels were forced to evacuate Petersburg and Richmond, which they left ablaze. The following day, accompanied by an escort of black cavalry, President Lincoln visited the ravaged Confederate capital. As he walked, ecstatic blacks, shedding happy tears, surrounded him. "I know I am free," one man exclaimed, "for I have seen Father Abraham and felt him." White onlookers in Richmond, surveying the cheerful chaos, realized that their world was about to be turned upside down.

Lee hoped to slip away, but he was blocked by Union troops. By April 9, Lee realized that his situation was hopeless. He rejected suggestions by some of his officers that the army should scatter into the forests and pursue a campaign of guerilla warfare. He announced: "It would be useless and therefore cruel to provoke the further effusion of blood, and I have arranged to meet with General Grant with a view to surrender." In a spotless new uniform, he met the mud-splattered and somewhat bedraggled Grant at the McClean farmhouse in the little village of Appomattox Courthouse, west of Richmond. Lincoln had written Grant, "Give them the most liberal terms. Let them have their horses to plow with, and, if you like, their guns to shoot crows with. I want no one punished." Grant agreed, even offering Union rations to the hungry defeated Rebel forces. Grant was saddened by "the downfall of a foe who had fought so long and valiantly, and had suffered so much for a cause, though that cause was, I believe, one of the worst for which a people ever fought."

Within a few weeks, other Confederate forces laid down their arms. Jefferson Davis, who had fled westward in the hopes of rallying Southerners to continue the conflict, was captured in Georgia in May. He was imprisoned for two years and then released to a quiet retirement in which he wrote his memoirs. Edmund Ruffin, an old "fire-eater," who had fired one of the first shots at Fort Sumter, fatally shot himself in the head rather than live in a Union with "the perfidious, malignant and vile Yankee race." On April 14, President Lincoln and his wife prepared to relax after the stresses of a long and bloody war by viewing a comedy at Ford's Theater. The terrible tragedy of his assassination undoubtedly altered the history of America after the Civil War ended.

Lincoln's Assassination

April 14, 1865, was Good Friday. It was the fourth anniversary of the surrender of Fort Sumter. At a ceremony in the remains of the old fortress, Major Robert Anderson, its former commander, hoisted the weather-beaten, ragged old flag he had been forced to pull down in 1861. That evening, a weary President Lincoln and his wife relaxed at Ford's Theater, which was showing a popular comedy, ***Our American Cousin****, in a benefit performance for disabled Union veterans. The theater was packed, and the cast ad-libbed "many pleasant allusions" to the president, to the delight of Lincoln and the audience.*

The nation had come through the greatest threat ever to its existence and now faced further overwhelming challenges. But the leader whose burdens and trials had made him appear to be much older than his fifty-six years seemed to be equal to the task. "I am a tired man," Lincoln said at the end of the war, "Sometimes I think I am the tiredest man on earth." He had overcome his frequent bouts of depression and his personal grief over the death of his lively, inquisitive, and much-loved eleven-year-old son, Willie. (Mary, his wife, never completely regained her stability after a nervous breakdown brought on by her child's death.) Lincoln had also managed to surmount the despair he felt at the death of thousands of Americans in the war. His success in meeting national and personal crises underscored both his greatness and his compassion.

The president was haunted by his dreams. Some, like those about the dead Willie, gave him comfort. Others were alarming, particularly recurring images of assassination. In one such dream, the loud weeping of mourners surrounding a body lying in state awakened Lincoln. When he asked a soldier who the corpse was, he was told, "The President. He was killed by an assassin." His friend Ward Lamon, his self-appointed bodyguard, and Secretary of War Stanton were both alarmed enough about possible dangers to the president's safety to provide cavalry escorts for his carriage and a District of Columbia policeman to accompany him to the theater.

Amidst the joy of surrender celebrations and the merriment of the theater, however, the security precautions had disintegrated. The policeman, who had been charged with guarding the president, carelessly left his post at the door of the president's box to see the play. Right about the time of the Fort Sumter ceremony, John Wilkes Booth, a young actor, had gone to the theater to pick up his mail. There, he learned about the special performance that the president would attend. As the laughter rose in the theater, Booth made his way to the president's box, derringer pistol and dagger in hand. At the outer door, he was briefly stopped but showed his card and confidently claimed that the president, who was known to enjoy actors, had asked him to come.

Booth was a member of one of America's great acting families. Although overshadowed by his father and his brother, Edwin (who was believed by many to be

America's finest actor), John was a fairly successful actor in his own right, earning an impressive $20,000 a year. He was, however, unstable, egotistical, and a fanatical Confederate sympathizer. He obsessed about Lincoln whom he saw as a tyrant responsible for all the nation's problems. Booth had recruited a strange group of malcontents from Washington's underworld, including a Confederate deserter, a Rebel spy, and a mentally handicapped druggist's clerk. Lee's surrender thwarted his original plan to kidnap the president and bring him to Richmond, so he resolved instead to kill Lincoln, Vice President Johnson, and Secretary of State Seward. The conspirator assigned to kill Johnson lost his nerve. The other accomplice did stab and seriously wound Seward who eventually recovered.

Meanwhile, Booth, after downing two brandies for courage, stepped into the president's box, pointed his small 44-caliber single shot derringer at Lincoln's head and fired. After slashing the arm of a major who tried to detain him, Booth vaulted over the box and landed on stage, breaking a leg. He shouted something to the dazed audience. Some said it was "sic temper tyrannis" ("thus be it ever to tyrants"), Virginia's state motto. Then he hobbled off stage out into the alley where he mounted his waiting horse and clattered off into Washington's dark streets. Booth's bullet had torn through the president's brain. An army surgeon, who had been sitting in the audience, pronounced the wound to be mortal.

Soldiers carried the unconscious president across the street to a room in a boarding house. There he lingered for the night, surrounded by stricken members of his cabinet, with his wife sobbing uncontrollably in the next room. He died the next morning at 7:22. Tears cascading down his face, Edmund Stanton declared, "Now he belongs to the ages."

Within minutes, the telegraph carried the tragic news to a stunned nation. No American president had ever been killed before. People openly wept in the streets. Navy Secretary Gideon Welles noted that blacks were especially overwhelmed by Lincoln's death, just as victory over slavery occurred: "the hopeless grief (of those poor colored people) affected me more than almost anything else." For fourteen days, millions of Americans stood along the tracks and watched silently as a nine-car train carried Lincoln's body, and the small coffin of his son Willie, the 1,662 miles from Washington back home to Springfield Illinois. The president's murder on Good Friday had made him into a Christ-like figure. It gave new meaning to the final verse of the "Battle Hymn of the Republic": "As He died to make men holy, Let us die to make men free."

By April 26, Union troops had trapped John Wilkes Booth in a burning Virginia barn and shot him in the head. As he lay dying, he whispered, "Tell my mother I died for my country...I did what I thought was best." Four of his accomplices were hanged, and four others were sentenced to hard labor, including the hapless Dr. Samuel Mudd, whose sole crime seemed to be setting Booth's broken leg.

John Wilkes Booth assassinated President Abraham Lincoln.

Lincoln's assassination was a stunning blow to the nation. The *Richmond Whig* on April 17, 1865, declared that it was, "The heaviest blow which has ever fallen upon the people of the South." It lamented, "Just as everything was happily conspiring to a restoration of tranquility, under the benignant and magnanimous policy of Mr. Lincoln, comes this terrible blow. God grant that it may not rekindle excitement or inflame passion again." The mood of the northern public after the assassination did seem to be one of anger, bitterness, and cries for vengeance against Confederate leaders. Yet Lincoln, in his moving second inaugural address, had declared, "With malice toward none; with charity for all; with firmness in the right...let us strive...to bind up the nation's wounds." With the death of this great man, would it be possible to balance "charity" and "firmness" and create "a just and a lasting peace?"

The devastation to the South and its slave-based civilization was profound. In May of 1865, Whitelaw Reid, a correspondent for the Republican *Cincinnati Gazette,* traveled south to report on the impact of the war. South Carolina where Sherman's army had operated, "looked for many miles like a broad black streak of ruin and desolation." Columbia, its capital, was a wasteland where not one store remained standing in the business district. Other cities, like Atlanta, Richmond, and Selma, suffered similar damage. In all, over $1 billion of physical destruction had been suffered by the South.

Human losses were also enormous. More than 10 percent of the South's white male population had died. Many others were crippled, physically or emotionally. The economy was also in tatters. The banking system based on Confederate bonds was destroyed. Personal savings were gone as Confederate currency lost its value. The patrician plantation world seemed to be completely annihilated. Not only did Southerners lose their enormous investments in slaves, but the southern economy as a whole also suffered painful losses. The countryside in the war zones was impoverished. Two-thirds of the South's railroads were out of commission and had to be rebuilt. The section that had once been the nation's richest became its poorest for many years to come.

The most significant achievement of the war was the emancipation of four million black slaves. Lincoln had called for "a new birth of freedom." What would this mean for former slaves whose humanity had finally, if reluctantly, been recognized? Near the end of the war, an Ohio captain responded to a well-written letter from his ten-year-old son: "It tells me that while I am...fighting the battels of our country...and endeavoring to secure for each and every American citizen of every race, the rights garenteed to us in the Declaration of Independence...I have children growing up that will be worthy of the rights that I trust will be left for them." The war left unresolved the issue of whether equal rights for all would truly replace slavery. Perhaps Reconstruction would settle that issue.

DOCUMENTS

THE GETTYSBURG ADDRESS (1863)

In July 1863 the Confederate army, which had moved into Pennsylvania, was decisively defeated at Gettysburg. This was the last Confederate invasion of the North. The disheartening sight of thousands of rotting corpses became a national scandal. Four months later, a national cemetery was finally dedicated. After a lengthy oration by famed public speaker Edward Everett, Lincoln delivered a 272-word address that articulated the feelings of the northern public.

Fourscore and seven years ago our fathers brought forth on this continent a new nation, conceived in liberty, and dedicated to the proposition that all men are created equal.

Now we are engaged in a great civil war, testing whether that nation, or any nation so conceived and so dedicated, can long endure. We are met on a great battle-field of that war. We have come to dedicate a portion of that field as a final resting-place for those who here gave their lives that that nation might live. It is altogether fitting and proper that we should do this.

But, in a larger sense, we cannot dedicate—we cannot consecrate—we cannot hallow—this ground. The brave men, living and dead, who struggled here, have consecrated it far above our poor power to add or detract. The world will little note nor long remember what we say here, but it can never forget what they did here. It is for us, the living, rather, to be dedicated here to the unfinished work which they who fought here have thus far so nobly advanced. It is rather for us to be here dedicated to the great task remaining before us—that from these honored dead we take increased devotion to that cause for which they gave the last full measure of devotion; that we here highly resolve that these dead shall not have died in vain; that this nation, under God, shall have a new birth of freedom; and that government of the people, by the people, for the people, shall not perish from the earth.

Source: John Nicolay and John Hay, eds., *Complete Works of Abraham Lincoln* (Lincoln Memorial University, 1894), IX: 209-210.

1. Why do you think that Edward Everett, a famed orator who spoke for two hours at the dedication of the cemetery, told Lincoln that while his speech would be rapidly forgotten, Lincoln's would never be and he would "gladly exchange my hundred pages for your twenty lines"?
2. What does Lincoln suggest was the real underlying meaning of the Civil War?
3. Why do you believe that this brief speech has resonated through the years?

PROBLEMS IN THE SOUTH

Suffering was widespread in the South where the morale of soldiers was undermined by the misery of their loved ones at home. Those in the paths of invading armies struggled to exist from day to day. The destruction in the wake of Sherman's "March to the Sea" was described by the 24-year-old Eliza Andrews, the daughter of a Unionist slaveholder.

A Soldier's Letter (1864)

After an absence of ten months in the army, I obtained a furlough and what joy did I anticipate in once more pressing my wife and little ones to my bosom. But imagine my feelings when told by my wife that she could not get bread enough for my children. She said that she had been to five gentlemen and could get no corn, while some in her immediate neighborhood had been known to ship corn to Augusta that they might get extortionate prices. Most of the time of my absence I have been on the march through Mississippi, Alabama and upper Georgia, many times with nothing but wet clay for my bed. I have seen my comrades fall on my right and my left, I have heard the whistling of bullets and seen them strike within a few inches of me; but all those hardships and dangers only nerved my arm to strike one more blow for my country and her honor. But, sir, when I am told that my little ones are suffering for want through the avarice of those for whom I stand as a wall between the enemy and their property, I feel this the greatest hardship of all. Why, Mr. Editor, the Beast Butler [a Union general] with all his refinements of cruelty could not serve them worse.

Source: Letter to the *Savannah Republican*, February 23,1864

Diary of a Georgia Girl (1864)

ELIZA ANDREWS

December 24, 1864.—About three miles from Sparta we struck the "burnt country;" as it is well named by the natives, and then I could better understand the wrath and desperation of these poor people. I almost felt as if I should like to hang a Yankee myself. There was hardly a fence left standing all the way from Sparta to Gordon. The fields were trampled down and the road was lined with carcasses of horses, hogs, and cattle that the invaders, unable either to consume or to carry away with them, had wantonly shot down, to starve out the people and prevent them from making their crops. The stench in some places was unbearable; every few hundred yards we had to hold our noses or stop them with the cologne Mrs. Elzey had given us, and it proved a great boon. The dwellings that were standing all showed signs of pillage, and on every plantation we saw the charred remains of the ginhouse and packing screw, while here and there lone chimney stacks, "Sherman's sentinels," told of homes laid in ashes. The infamous wretches! I couldn't wonder now that these poor people should want to put a rope round the neck of every red-handed "devil of them" they could lay their hands on. Hayricks and fodder stacks were demolished, corncribs were empty, and every bale of cotton that could be found was burnt by the savages. I saw no grain of any sort except little patches they had spilled when feeding their horses and which there was not even a chicken left in the country to eat. A bag of oats might have lain anywhere along the road without danger from the beasts of the field, though I cannot say it would have been safe from the assaults of hungry man.

Crowds of soldiers were tramping over the road in both directions; it was like traveling through the streets of a populous town all day. They were mostly on foot, and I saw numbers seated on the roadside greedily eating raw turnips, meat skins, parched corn—anything they could find, even picking up the loose grains that Sherman's horses had left. I felt tempted to stop and empty the contents of our provision baskets into their laps, but the dreadful accounts that were given of the state of the country before us made prudence get the better of our generosity. Before crossing the Oconee at Milledgeville we ascended an immense hill, from which there was a fine view of the town, with Governor Brown's fortifications in the foreground and the river rolling at our feet. The Yankees had burnt the bridge; so we had to cross on a ferry. There was a long train of vehicles ahead of us, and it was nearly an hour before our turn came; so we had ample time to look about us. On our left was a field where thirty thousand Yankees had camped hardly three weeks before. It was strewn with the debris they had left behind, and the poor people of the neighborhood were wandering over it, seeking for anything they could find to eat, even picking up grains of corn that were scattered around where the Yankees had fed their horses. We were told that a great many valuables were found there at first, plunder that the invaders had left behind, but the place had been picked over so often by this time that little now remained except tufts of loose cotton, piles of half-rotted grain, and the carcasses of slaughtered animals, which raised a horrible stench. Some men were plowing in one part of the field, making ready for next year's crop.

Source: Eliza Andrews, *The War-Time Diary of a Georgia Girl* (Appleton, New York, 1908).

1. What problem did the southern soldier find when he came home on a furlough?

2. What conditions does the Georgian, Eliza Andrews, find in the wake of Sherman's march?
3. Unlike the North, there were no government sponsored wartime organizations that employed women in the South. How did they cope with conditions?
4. In which section, the North or the South, do you feel the home front problems were more severe? Why?

THE DISPUTE OVER USING BLACK TROOPS IN THE SOUTH

As manpower shortages worsened in the South, some leaders argued that the Confederate army should also recruit blacks, guaranteeing freedom "to every slave in the South who shall remain true to the Confederacy in this war." Naturally, this proposal was met with powerful resistance. At the very end of the war, however, the desperation was so great that the Confederate Congress authorized the recruiting of black companies. Although such companies were actually raised, the war ended before they could be used.

OPPOSITION TO THE IDEA

The proposition is so strange—so unconstitutional—so directly in conflict with all of our former' practices and teachings—so entirely subversive of our social and political institutions—and so completely destructive of our liberties, that we stand completely appalled [and] dumfounded at its promulgation.

They propose that Congress shall conscribe two hundred and fifty thousand slaves, arm, equip and fight them in the field. As an inducement of them to be faithful, it is proposed that, at the end of the war, they shall have their freedom and live amongst us. "The conscription of negroes," says the Enquirer, "should be accompanied with freedom and the privilege of remaining in the States." This is the monstrous proposition. The South went to war to defeat the designs of the abolitionists, and behold! in the midst of the war, we turn abolitionists ourselves! We went to war because the Federal Congress kept eternally meddling with our domestic institutions, with which we contended they had nothing to do, and now we propose to end the war by asking the Confederate Congress to do precisely what Lincoln proposes to do—free our negroes and make them the equals of the white man! We have always been taught to believe that slaves are property, and under the exclusive control of the States and the courts. This new doctrine teaches us that Congress has a right to free our negroes and make them the equals of their masters....

Source: *Lynchburg (Va.) Republican*, November 2, 1864.

A Woman Favors the Idea

Mr. Editor:
A lady's opinion may not be worth much in such an hour as this, but I cannot resist the temptation of expressing my approbation of "The crisis the Remedy," copied from the Mobile Register. Would to God our Government would act upon its suggestions at once. The women of the South are not so in love with their negro property, as to wish to see husbands, fathers, sons, brothers, slain to protect it; nor would they submit to Yankee rule, could it secure to them a thousand waiting maids, whence now they possess one....

Source: *Macon (Ga.) Telegraph and Confederate,* January 11, 1865.

Confederate Congress Approves Use of Black Troops

The Congress of the Confederate States of America do enact, That in order to provide additional forces to repel invasion, maintain the rightful Possession of the Confederate States, secure their independence, and preserve their institutions, the President be, and he is hereby, authorized to ask for and accept from the owners of slaves, the services of such number of able-bodied negro men as he may deem expedient, for and during the war, to perform military service in whatever capacity he may direct.

Source: Confederate Congress, "An Act to Increase the Military Force of the Confederate States," March 13, 1865.

1. What argument against the use of slaves as troops is advanced by the *Lynchburg Republican*?
2. Why does the woman letter-writer favor the idea of using such troops?
3. Why do you think the Confederate Congress ultimately approved of such an action?
4. Had the war lasted long enough for such troops to actually be used, what impact would this have had upon the South and upon the rest of the war?

RECOLLECTIONS OF THE WAR'S HORRORS: 1875

The great American poet, Walt Whitman, served as a nurse in Union Army hospitals. Ten years later, when he wrote these recollections, the horrors of the war still remained vivid to him.

Walt Whitman

The dead in this war—there they lie, strewing the fields and woods and valleys and battle-fields of the South-Virginia, the Peninsula—Malvern Hill and Fair Oaks—the banks of the Chickahominy—the terraces of Fredericksburg—Antietam bridge—the grisly ravines of Manassas—the bloody promenade of the Wilderness—the varieties of the strayed dead, (the estimate of the War Department is 25,000 national soldiers kill'd in battle and never buried at all, 5,000 15,000 inhumed by strangers, or on the march in haste, in hitherto unfound localities—2,000 graves cover'd by sand and mud by Mississippi freshets, 3,000 carried away by caving-in of banks, &c.,)—Gettysburg, the West, Southwest—Vicksburg—Chattanooga—the trenches of Petersburg—the numberless battles, camps, hospitals everywhere—the crop reap'd by the mighty reapers, typhoid, dysentery, inflammations—and blackest and loathsomest of all, the dead and living burial-pits, the prison-pens of Andersonville, Salisbury, Belle Isle, &c., (not Dante's pictured hell and all its woes, its degradations, filthy torments, excell'd those prisons)—the dead, the dead, the dead—our dead—or South or North, ours all, (all, all, all, finally dear to me)—or East or West—Atlantic coast or Mississippi valley—somewhere they crawl'd to die, alone, in bushes, low gullies, or on the sides of hills—(there, in secluded spots, their skeletons, bleach'd bones, tufts of hair, buttons, fragments of clothing, are occasionally found yet)—our young men once so handsome and so joyous, taken from us—the son from the mother, the husband from the wife, the dear friend from the dear friend—the clusters of camp graves, in Georgia, the Carolinas, and in Tennessee—the single graves left in the woods or by the roadside, (hundreds, thousands, obliterated)—the corpses floated down the rivers, and caught and lodged, (dozens, scores, floated down the upper Potomac, after the cavalry engagements, the pursuit of Lee, following Gettysburg)—some lie at the bottom of the sea—the general million, and the special cemeteries in almost all the States—the infinite dead—(the land entire saturated, perfumed with their impalpable ashes' exhalation in Nature's chemistry distill'd, and shall be so forever, in every future grain of wheat and ear of corn, and every flower that grows, and every breath we draw) not only Northern dead leavening Southern soil—thousands, aye tens of thousands, of Southerners, crumble to-day in Northern earth.

And everywhere among these countless graves—everywhere in the many soldier Cemeteries of the Nation, (there are now, I believe, over seventy of them)—as at the time in the vast trenches, the depositories of slain, Northern and Southern, after the great battles—not only where the scathing trail passed those years, but radiating since in all the peaceful quarters of the land—we see, and ages yet may see, on monuments and gravestones, singly or in masses, to thousands or tens of thousands, the significant word Unknown....

Source: *The Complete Works of Walt Whitman* (New York, 1902): 137-139.

1. What are the main images Walt Whitman retained of the war?
2. What impact do you think these images and similar ones by other observers would have had on public opinion in the years after the war?
3. Why do you think Walt Whitman served as a nurse during the war?

SECOND INAUGURAL ADDRESS (1865)

Although the depressing events on the military front convinced Lincoln that he would not be reelected in 1864, victories in Atlanta and Mobile Bay swung public opinion back to Lincoln. He won a substantial victory in the election. In his Second Inaugural Address on March 4, 1865, Lincoln looked forward to peace and the elimination of slavery. At an April 14 cabinet meeting, he implored these leaders to reject animosity and reprisals. He was assassinated that evening.

ABRAHAM LINCOLN

FELLOW-COUNTRYMEN:—At this second appearing to take the oath of the presidential office there is less occasion for an extended address than there was at the first. Then a statement somewhat in detail of a course to be pursued seemed fitting and proper. Now, at the expiration of four years, during which public declarations have been constantly called forth on every point and phase of the great contest which still absorbs the attention and engrosses the energies of the nation, little that is new could be presented. The progress of our arms, upon which all else chiefly depends, is as well known to the public as to myself, and it is, I trust, reasonably satisfactory and encouraging to all. With high hope for the future, no prediction in regard to it is ventured.

On the occasion corresponding to this four years ago all thoughts were anxiously directed to an impending civil war. All dreaded it, all sought to avert it. While the inaugural address was being delivered from this place, devoted altogether to saving the Union without war, insurgent agents were in the city seeking to destroy it without war—seeking to dissolve the Union and divide effects by negotiation. Both parties deprecated war, but one of them would make war rather than let the nation survive, and the other would accept war rather than let it perish, and the war came.

One eighth of the whole population was colored slaves, not distributed generally over the Union, but localized in the southern part of it. These slaves constituted a peculiar and powerful interest. All knew that this interest was somehow the cause of the war. To strengthen, perpetuate, and extend this interest was the object for which the insurgents would rend the Union even by war, while the Government claimed no right to do more than to restrict the territorial enlargement of it. Neither party expected for the war the magnitude nor the duration which it has already attained. Neither anticipated that the cause of the conflict might cease with or even before the conflict itself should cease. Each looked for an easier triumph, and a result less fundamental and astounding. Both read the same Bible and pray to the same God, and each invokes His aid against the other. It may seem strange that any men should dare to ask a just God's assistance in wringing their bread from the sweat of other men's faces, but let us judge not, that we be not judged. The prayers of both could not be answered. That of neither has been answered fully. The Almighty has His own purposes. "Woe unto the world because of offenses; for it must needs be that offenses come, but woe to that man by whom the offense cometh." If we shall suppose that American slavery is one of those offenses which, in the providence of God, must needs come, but which, having continued through His appointed time, He now wills to remove, and that He gives to both North and South this terrible war as the woe due to those by whom the offense came, shall we discern therein any departure from those divine attributes which the believers in a living God always ascribe to Him? Fondly do we hope, fervently do we pray, that this mighty scourge of war may speedily pass away. Yet, if God wills that it continue until all the wealth piled by the bondsman's two hundred and fifty years of unrequited toil shall be sunk, and until every drop of blood drawn with the lash shall be paid by another drawn with the sword, as was said three thousand years ago, so still it must be said, "The judgments of the Lord are true and righteous altogether."

With malice toward none, with charity for all, with firmness in the right as God gives us to see the right, let us strive on to finish the work we are in, to bind up the nation's wounds, to care for him who shall have borne the battle and for his widow and his orphan, to do all which may achieve and cherish a just and lasting peace among ourselves and with all nations.

Source: James D. Richardson, ed., *A Compilation of the Messages and Papers of the Presidents* (Government Printing Office, Washington, D.C., 1897-1907), VIII: 3477-3478.

1. What does Lincoln seem to suggest was the basic cause of the Civil War?
2. How does this differ from what he had originally suggested caused the war?
3. Why, do you think, this Second Inaugural Address is consider one of the greatest American speeches?
4. What future does Lincoln want to create after the war ends?
5. How might his assassination have changed the history of America after the war?

PART IV

RECONSTRUCTION: the Turning Point that Never Turned

Chapter Nine

RADICAL RECONSTRUCTION

WARTIME RECONSTRUCTION

The questions that formed the core of Reconstruction surfaced during the war. After the Emancipation Proclamation, Northerners of every political stripe assumed that the South would emerge from the war as a society without slavery. But what system of labor would replace the institution of slavery? Would four million newly freed slaves become citizens? If they did, what rights would they enjoy and what role would they play in the social and political life of the South? Could the states of the Confederacy rejoin the union? If so, under what terms? Should the president or Congress set these terms?

Military officers, during the war, often had to make decisions about what to do with thousands of ragged freed slaves who flocked to Union armies when they learned about emancipation. Despite his openly expressed contempt for both radical ideas and freedmen, General Sherman issued a special order reserving confiscated land for the resettlement of freed people on plots of forty acres per family. He also sanctioned lending army mules to the new farmers (leading, perhaps, to the later poignant demand for "forty acres and a mule.") By the end of the war, more than forty thousand people had been resettled in that area of coastal South Carolina and Georgia. By 1865, 20 percent of the farmland under Union control was being worked by independent black farmers. In 1863 General Grant declared that Davis Bend, the estate of Jefferson Davis and his brother, should become a "negro paradise." Davis' former slaves and other black farmers leased its thousands of acres. By 1865 they were raising successful cotton and food crops and earning a profit of nearly $160,000. They formed their own government, including elected judges and sheriffs. Black people desired, above all, to become independent farmers, and some radical Republicans hoped that the future would see a South of black yeoman farmers working their own land.

Events in Louisiana, however, were more indicative of the labor system that would develop in the South. There, the military commander believed that restoring the plantation system could end the army's burden of caring for black refugees. Former slaves would be coerced into signing yearly contracts with loyal planters and forbidden to leave without permission of the owners. Despite the program's limited success in reviving the state's agricultural system, most army officials operated under the assumption that freed slaves should continue to be plantation laborers.

Northern freedmen's aid societies, founded by abolitionists, attempted to accomplish another radical vision of the future, that of an educated black population, able to fulfill the demands of citizenship. During the war, they sent more than a thousand teachers to the occupied South, precursors of two thousand more who arrived in the early postwar period. Most came from New England, and three-quarters were women. Most were white (although 20 percent were blacks, many of whom were themselves only minimally educated). They strove to instill the Protestant work ethic and the values of self-discipline in the 200,000 or so students they reached. After the war, the freedmen's education program was greatly

The Freedmen's Bureau established schools attended by ex-slaves. Many of the teachers were white women from the North.

expanded in a concentrated effort to erase illiteracy. The black scholar and leader, W.E.B. Du Bois, later commented that these missionary teachers were the unsung heroes of the Civil War who "came not to keep the Negroes in their place, but to raise them out of the defilement of the places where slavery had wallowed them....This was the gift of New England to the freed Negro."

Lincoln attempted to deal with the issue of restoration of the southern states to the Union in December 1863, a year after the Emancipation Proclamation. He issued the Proclamation of Amnesty and Reconstruction, his first extensive program for reconstruction. In it, Lincoln offered the re-establishment of all rights "except as to slaves" to those in conquered areas who took a loyalty oath to the federal constitution. Only high-ranking confederate military and civil officials would be excluded. When 10 percent of the 1860 voting population had taken the oath, a new state government would be established, abolishing slavery. Lincoln based his policy on the theory of the "indissoluble Union." Since states could not legally secede, they were still a part of the Union. The purpose of reconstruction was to enable loyal citizens to regain control of their governments. Lincoln never saw this policy, issued in the midst of war, as an unchangeable blueprint for postwar reconstruction. He hoped to use his "Ten Percent Plan" to weaken the Confederacy by gaining the support of former southern Whigs, at best hesitant secessionists. He also wanted to get emancipation into as many southern state constitutions as possible.

Radical Republicans, led by Charles Sumner and Benjamin Wade in the Senate and Thaddeus Stevens in the House, objected to allowing former rebels back into the Union so easily. They wanted to ensure that committed Unionists controlled southern governments and that the freedom and civil rights of blacks would be protected. They argued that, by seceding, southern states had committed "state suicide," reverting to territories that had to apply to Congress for readmission to the Union. When representatives of a Louisiana government that followed Lincoln's plan showed up in 1864, Congress refused to seat them. That same year, Republicans in Congress produced their own view of reconstruction in the Wade-Davis Bill. This law would have required an oath of allegiance from 50 percent of the voters, rather than 10. Then elections would be held for delegates to a state constitutional convention, with the vote restricted to those who could take an "iron clad oath" that they had never voluntarily aided the Confederacy. This measure would have postponed Reconstruction for a very long period. Lincoln, fearing its consequences for the war effort, pocket-vetoed it.

Although some historians later saw this as evidence of the irreconcilable differences between the moderate, charitable views of the president and the harsh unyielding attitudes of Radicals in Congress, Lincoln himself insisted that he was not "inflexibly committed to any single plan of restoration." Lincoln tended to be flexible and pragmatic, adjusting his ideas to the political circumstances. He

Congressman Thaddeus Stevens of Pennsylvania, the leader of Radical Republicans in the House, pushed for a stricter Reconstruction policy and for equality of African Americans.

worked with his radical opponents in January 1865 to gain passage of the Thirteenth Amendment, abolishing slavery throughout the nation and ensuring that wartime emancipation measures could never be overturned. He also signed a bill creating the Freedmen's Bureau as a relief agency in the South for refugees of both races. It was empowered to draft and enforce labor contracts, aid blacks to become independent farmers, and assist in the operation of freedmen's schools.

Lincoln moved closer to compromise with Congress. He confided to a friend that he "had no plan for reorganization, but must be guided by events." He tried to partially meet the demands of radical critics and free blacks for black suffrage in the South. He suggested, in his last public speech (April 11, 1865), that the vote be extended to literate blacks and the larger group of those who had served in the Union armies. The *New York Times* noted that Lincoln did not seem to feel the time had yet come for "the statement of a settled reconstruction policy." At a cabinet meeting on the morning of his assassination, Lincoln endorsed a plan to substitute military occupation for civilian government in the Confederate states to ensure the enforcement of black civil rights. The bullets from Booth's gun prevent us from ever knowing whether this gifted and practical politician could have successfully negotiated the contradictions between the competing goals of "charity," "firmness," and "justice."

PRESIDENTIAL RECONSTRUCTION

Andrew Johnson, the man who succeeded Lincoln, seemed to many to have a remarkably similar background to his predecessor. Both rose from rural poverty and little or no formal education to realize their ambitions and achieve success in the public arena. Johnson had been an illiterate tailor whose school teacher wife taught him to write. He acquired a farm and slaves and climbed the political ladder in Tennessee, eventually becoming governor and senator. Johnson resented the snobbery he felt from the old-time plantation southern leadership. "Some day I will show the stuck-up aristocrats who is running the country," he once vowed. When the Civil War broke out, Johnson was an ardent Unionist, the only senator from a Confederate state who spoke out against secession. As wartime governor of occupied Tennessee, he sternly declared, "Treason must be made odious, and traitors must be punished and impoverished." He promised anxious blacks that he would "be your Moses, and lead you through the Red Sea of war and bondage to a fairer future of liberty and peace." Such comments, coupled with the need to build bisectional support, particularly in the border states, led Lincoln to pick Johnson for vice president in 1864. His thunderous speeches against the "slaveocracy" also led many Radical Republicans to believe that the new president would be more sympathetic to their point of view than Lincoln had been.

Lincoln and the radicals had misread Johnson, however. The struggle to overcome poverty seemed to have given Lincoln an empathy for others, wit, and the political skills of tact and flexibility. The same struggle embittered Johnson and made him into a suspicious man who, despite personal courage, was intolerant of other views, stubborn, and unable to compromise. Unlike Lincoln, Johnson never viewed slavery as a great moral evil. "Damn the Negroes," he once declared, "I am fighting these traitorous aristocrats, their masters." He believed that nonslaveholding whites were the main victims of slavery, oppressed by the combination of slaves and their masters. He saw no role for the freedmen in a reconstructed South and hoped that they would leave the country. "White men alone must manage the South," he announced. He insisted to Congress that blacks had "less capacity for government than any other race of people...Wherever they have been left to their own devices they have shown a constant tendency to relapse into barbarism." He was a committed Jacksonian in that he favored states' rights and was as suspicious of the "bloated, corrupt aristocracy" of the banks and corporations emerging in the North as he had been of the southern patricians.

With Congress not due to meet again until December 1865, Johnson was free to implement his own reconstruction policy. Lincoln's tentative reconstruction initiatives based on the wartime theory of indestructible states had become set in stone in Johnson's limited imagination. This was coupled with a rigid view of states' rights that would not allow any real role for the federal government in Reconstruction. Johnson's restoration policy (as he insisted on calling it) became clear in two proclamations he issued in May 1865. One offered amnesty and return of all property, except slaves, to every white man who swore to an oath of future loyalty. Political and military leaders of the Confederacy and those with property valued at more than $20,000 were excluded but given the opportunity to apply to the president for individual pardons. Under the second proclamation, the newly loyal electorate would choose members to a constitutional convention in each state. Despite his stated support for states' rights, Johnson made it clear that he expected each convention to nullify secession, accept the abolition of slavery, and repudiate all Confederate debts. After that, elections would be held for state and federal officials, and reconstruction would be complete. Under these terms, Presidential Reconstruction moved along rapidly. Southern congressmen arrived to claim their seats by the time Congress reconvened in December. But Johnson had misinterpreted northern and congressional opinion as completely as the radicals had misunderstood Johnson's true nature earlier. As a result of the actions of these reconstructed governments, Congress refused to seat the southern congressmen.

The same president who had spoken sternly about "treason" in April was speaking eloquently of the need to be "forbearing and forgiving" about the past sins of the South by the fall. Despite his often-expressed hatred of the old aristocrats, the ego of the former illiterate tailor's apprentice was gratified when members of the proud southern ruling class came to him to humbly beg for pardons. "I remember the taunts, the jeers, the scowls with which I was treated," the president noted. He was gratified by their confessions of error and their expressions of "sincere respect" for his "desire and intention to sustain southern rights in the Union." He quickly granted 13,500 pardons to ex-Confederates who were now free to return to power in their states.

Southern Defiance and the Black Codes

When the Confederate armies surrendered, Southerners, as an observer remarked at the time, were "so despondent that if readmission at some future time under whatever conditions had been promised, it would have been looked upon as a favor." But presidential generosity and support led to obstinate overconfidence by southern leaders. Johnson, now the captive of southern interests, could not respond to their open defiance. As a result, several states repealed secession instead of repudiating it. Mississippi refused to ratify the Thirteenth Amendment, and Arkansas even appropriated funds for Confederate veterans' pensions. Northerners, who expected some acknowledgment of defeat by the South, were astounded when some states elected the newly pardoned ex-Confederates to local, state, and even national office. In the most publicized example, Georgia chose Alexander Stephens, the former vice president of the Confederacy, as one of its senators.

The inability of southern whites to accept the free labor ideology of the North was even more disturbing to many Northerners. Southern state legislatures in 1865 and 1866 passed a series of Black Codes, ostensibly to define the legal rights of the newly freed blacks. Most southern whites were unable or unwilling to accept even minimal notions of legal equality between the races. The codes did concede blacks the rights to have legal marriages, sign contracts, sue and be sued, and obtain property. Southerners claimed that these were substantial advances. However, the codes denied the freed people such basic rights as that of free assembly, bearing arms, serving on juries, testifying against whites in court, voting, or holding office. Although many of these prohibitions existed in the still white supremacist North as well, these open attempts to restrict the Union's most loyal followers in the South irritated many Northerners.

The provisions of the codes that related to labor and vagrancy angered Northerners the most, as they seemed to foreshadow an attempt to bring back plantation slavery. The laws defined vagrancy so broadly that any black who did not have an annual contract to work on a plantation could be arrested, fined, and hired out as an unpaid laborer to any planter who paid the fine. Blacks, who wanted to enter any other occupation but agriculture, needed special licenses from the state. Children, in homes not deemed to be "adequate," could be sent as "apprentices" to white "guardians," their former owners. Although the army and Freedmen's Bureau suspended enforcement of the worst provisions of the Black Codes, their implications had a deep impact on northern public opinion. Stories in northern newspapers bolstered the image of unrepentant, arrogant Confederates. One influential Republican commentator reported, "It is a stubborn fact that our truest friends are threatened and persecuted and that the negro is denied his freedom whenever the population has a chance to act upon its own impulses without immediately being checked."

The Split Between President and Congress

When the representatives of the Johnson governments arrived to take their seats in December 1865, the stage was set for a direct conflict between the president and Congress. Johnson had hoped to create a new centrist Union coalition of Democrats, southern whites, and moderate Republicans. To do so, however, he would have to compromise on the issue of freedmen's rights. Johnson's friends knew that he would never compromise, preferring a messy struggle. "A fight between the Radicals and the Executive is inevitable," said one, "Let it come. The sooner the better for the whole country."

Many Republicans believed that the future of their party was at stake. An ironic result of the Thirteenth Amendment came out of the elimination of the three-fifths clause in the Constitution. The South would increase its political power by adding 15 to 20 seats, as the entire black population would now count in allotting seats in the House. This hardly seemed fair to Republicans, since these Johnsonian governments were denying the most basic rights to blacks. In addition, Rebels whose treason had been ignored by presidential pardons were running those governments. (Ten Confederate generals and nine former Confederate congressmen were in the group of southern representatives asking to be seated.) It was not surprising that Congress refused to seat the eighty southern representatives. Congressional Republicans also rejected Johnson's "restoration" plans. Instead, Congress appointed a Joint Committee of Fifteen on Reconstruction.

Moderates, however, dominated the Joint Committee. Compromise still seemed possible. These moderate Republicans conferred with Johnson and believed they had his support for two bills to protect the rights of freed people. The first extended the life of the Freedmen's Bureau, enlarged its legal powers in civil rights cases, and authorized it to build and maintain schools. Johnson dismayed the moderates in February 1866 by vetoing the bill. Democrats organized a mass rally to support the veto. Johnson delivered an extraordinarily unrestrained speech attacking the radicals as traitors and Judases. He portrayed himself as Christ who would willingly shed his blood to "vindicate the Union and the preservation of this government in its original purity and character." The speech was so intemperate that many Americans wondered if the president was drunk.

Despite their disillusionment over the president's behavior, most moderate Republicans still hoped to avert a complete break. They modified the Freedmen's Bureau bill to meet some of the presidential objections and passed a relatively modest Civil Rights bill. The bill sought to overturn the *Dred Scott* decision and the Black Codes. It defined blacks as citizens, entitled to protection to property, contracts, and equality under the law. To appease Johnson, the bill did not give blacks the vote or the right to desegregated public facilities. Despite this attempt at compromise, the president shocked the moderates again by vetoing the Civil Rights bill and the second Freedmen's Bureau bill. He made any future reconciliation with Congress virtually impossible by arguing that Reconstruction was already complete under his policies, and only the individual states could deal with the freedmen. Democrats applauded his stand. If Congress had its way, one Democratic paper declared, "how long will it be...before it will say the negro shall vote, sit in a jury box, and intermarry with your families? Such are the questions put by the President." But the veto turned potential allies among moderate Republicans into unyielding enemies. "He has broken the faith, betrayed his trust, and must sink from detestation to contempt," declared one disillusioned senator who had tried to work with Johnson. Rather than isolating the radicals, Johnson's actions pushed the moderates closer to the radical position. Congress was able to override both presidential vetoes.

The Fourteenth Amendment

The Joint Committee on Reconstruction, faced with the break with the president, sought to develop a constitutional amendment that would unify Republicans. It would do so by placing the rights of freedmen under national protection where they could not be touched by presidential actions or shifting political currents. Republicans also hoped that the Fourteenth Amendment would provide the terms under which the defeated South could return to the Union. This amendment, which quickly gained the necessary two-thirds vote in Congress, may well be the most important single amendment in the United States Constitution. Much of its significance came from later interpretations. But even at the time, it provided a national guarantee of equality before the law.

The first section of the amendment defined citizenship in the nation as belonging to "all persons born or naturalized in the United States." Thus, any blacks born in America were now automatically citizens, nullifying the *Dred Scott* decision. No state could abridge "the privileges and immunities" of a citizen of the United States, "deprive any person of life, liberty, or property without due process of law," or deny "equal protection of the laws." In later years this section, the heart of the amendment, was subject to a variety of interpretations. Conservative courts at the end of the century ruled that corporations were "legal persons," and state attempts to regulate them were unconstitutional. In the mid-twentieth century, the "equal protection" provision became the foundation for overturning state mandated segregation of the races.

The second section was a compromise on the issue of black suffrage. It did not grant blacks the right to vote, but it did provide for a reduction in a state's representation, proportional to the number of male citizens denied the vote. If southern states declined to extend the votes to blacks, at least they would not benefit from the increased representation that derived from the end of the three-fifths clause. The third section was the most controversial at the time, since it barred from national or state office all men who had aided the rebellion after swearing allegiance to the Constitution. This was designed to exclude the pre-war ruling class from power. The fourth section guaranteed the Union debt and repudiated the Confederate debt.

As a whole, the Fourteenth Amendment presented the minimum terms northern public opinion expected from the defeated South. After all, it did not confiscate land from Confederate supporters or leaders, did not deny them the vote, or even force them to accept black suffrage. It seems likely that Reconstruction would have been over if the South accepted the amendment. Tennessee, controlled by political enemies of Johnson, quickly ratified the amendment in 1866 and was promptly admitted back into the Union. Johnson, however, still totally misunderstanding northern public opinion, urged the excluded states to reject the amendment. He argued that the amendment was illegal because it kept the southern states out of the Congress that passed it. The ex-Confederate states unwisely followed his advice.

Johnson convinced his southern admirers that he could rally popular support in the North for his Reconstruction plans and administer a well-deserved whipping to the Radicals in the congressional elections of 1866. The president attempted to launch a National Union movement to support his objectives. This movement, however, failed to get off the ground as a result of basic problems that undermined it in the eyes of the northern public. Growing violence in the South alarmed Northerners. In May 1866, a quarrel in Memphis between recently discharged black veterans and local whites, led by Irish policemen, erupted into a three-day riot. The white mobs killed forty-six blacks, raped five black women, and burnt or looted hundreds of black homes, schools, and churches. The Memphis riot proved, the *New York Tribune* observed cynically, "that the Freedmen's Bureau ought to be abolished forthwith, and the blacks remitted to the paternal care of their old masters, who 'understand the nigger...a great deal better than the Yankees can.'" Three months later, a similar riot rocked New Orleans when a mob attacked delegates to a black suffrage convention, killing thirty-four blacks and three of their white allies, and injuring over one hundred more. Many Northerners agreed with the assessment of one observer that Johnson's lenient policies had caused this "barbarism of the rebellion in its renaissance." The president certainly did not ease these concerns when he delivered a speech in which he blamed the Republicans for inciting the mob and offered no sympathy for the victims.

In fact, the greatest problem faced by the National Union movement may well have been the president himself. Johnson had been an effective speaker in Tennessee, so he decided to take his case to the northern public. He launched his August-September 1866 "swing around the circle," a campaign tour to influence northern voters in the up-coming congressional elections. (He was the first president ever to do this.) The trip was an unmitigated disaster. His rough country style, which played so well in Tennessee, turned off northern voters. He allowed hecklers, planted by Radicals, to draw him into shouted exchanges of insults. "Why not hang Thad Stevens and Wendell Phillips," he exclaimed at one stop. The president had lost all control of himself and, in doing so, he lost command of the country.

Finally, the Republicans were able to brush the Democrats, by now Johnson's main supporters, with the tar of treason against the Union. This was a tactic later known as, "waving the bloody shirt." One Republican speaker declared, "Every unregenerate rebel calls himself a Democrat.... Every man who labored for rebellion in the field, who murdered Union prisoners...who conspired to bring about civil war in the loyal states...calls himself a Democrat." The election had also become a referendum on the Fourteenth Amendment, overwhelmingly favored by northern public opinion.

All these factors help explain a victory so lop-sided that it surprised even the most committed Radical Republican. The Radicals now had a veto-proof majority of more than two-thirds in both houses of Congress. The northern electorate had clearly decided that the victory in the war must lead to a fundamental transformation of the South. Republicans even swept Johnson's own state of Tennessee. Its new Republican governor gleefully said, "Give my respects to the dead dog in the White House."

The New Orleans Riots and the Growth of Violence in the Reconstruction South

In 1866 the Reconstruction Governor of Louisiana, James Wells, disgusted with the recalcitrance of his "rebel" legislature, decided to reconvene a constitutional convention that had been adjourned in 1864. New Orleans conservatives viewed this as a radical assault on the liberty of the people of Louisiana by forcing black suffrage upon them. Many whites believed this would lead to the "Africanization of the South," with its resulting humiliation of whites, anarchy, and miscegenation (racial mixing). They predicted bloodshed and racial conflict if such a measure was ever introduced. As is often the case, oratorical excesses lead to mob brutality.

On a blistering, humid Monday, July 30, a procession of a hundred or so blacks marched to support the convention, carrying an American flag. As they paraded, they were challenged by a young white man who either insulted them or blocked the street (witness accounts differed). He was knocked to the ground by a black in the procession. Shots were fired, and the police tried to arrest one of the marchers. Mobs of whites and police lining the streets began to throw rocks and to fire at the blacks. The marchers, mostly unarmed and certainly unprepared for street combat, tried to flee to the convention hall.

The police rushed to the scene and, rather than restoring order, joined the mob in attacking the blacks. While conservative leaders watched in approval, the mob was made up largely of poorer whites, particularly young boys and Confederate veterans.

Police rushed to the entrance of the convention hall, firing wildly into the terrified crowd of delegates and blacks. A Confederate veteran, who had lost both of his arms in the war, urged the mob to "kill every son of a bitch in the building and not let any escape." The enraged mob, accompanied by police and firemen, rushed into the building smashing windows and furniture and attacking its frightened occupants. Some blacks, who fell to their knees and begged for their lives, were murdered. Others ran to the second floor and jumped out of the windows to the street below where the mob beat and shot them. Wounded men were dragged from the building and savagely beaten and killed. The police rounded up prisoners and allowed the mob to attack them as they were dragged through the streets. A former governor who was leading the convention was pulled through the streets, his body covered with blood and his clothes torn off, as the crowd entreated the police to kill him. A radical leader was beaten and shot at while in police custody, and his almost lifeless body was tossed into a filthy cart. He died shortly thereafter. After a few hours, federal troops arrived to place New Orleans under martial law and restore order.

The casualty figures reveal the severity of the riot. In a relatively brief period, 34 blacks and 3 white Unionists were killed, and 119 blacks and 17 of their white allies were wounded. Only one "rebel" died in the conflict. The Republican Congress established a committee to investigate the incident. Its report accused city authorities of inciting the riot and President Johnson of encouraging such violence. The Democratic minority report denied the legitimacy of the convention and condemned the radicals and blacks for aggravating the white mob and the police.

In the 1866 congressional elections Republicans denounced President Johnson for encouraging such brutality. The **Chicago Tribune** *reflected the views of many Northerners when it editorialized: "Blood is upon his hands, the blood of innocent, loyal citizens, who had committed no crime but that of seeking to protect themselves against rebel misrule, which he, Andrew Johnson, had foisted upon them." The battle was joined. Radical politicians used the lessons of New Orleans to justify their sterner reconstruction policies, and southern white conservatives drew their own lessons about the effectiveness of intimidation.*

Reconstruction Acts

Led by Thaddeus Stevens, Speaker of the House, and Ben Wade, President Pro Tem of the Senate, Radicals believed that they had won a mandate from the public to substitute a congressional reconstruction plan for the president's failing program. Egged on by the president, the southern states continued to reject the Fourteenth Amendment, the easiest terms they could have reasonably expected. Exasperated moderates then reached a compromise with Radicals on a Reconstruction Act.

The Reconstruction Act of 1867 rejected Johnson's views that the southern states should be immediately admitted to the Union without qualifications. It also rebuffed Radical demands for an indefinite military occupation, coupled with confiscation and redistribution of plantation lands to provide a foundation for the economic independence of the freedmen. Instead, the act temporarily divided the old Confederacy (except Tennessee) into five military districts. An army general who could use the army and the Freedmen's Bureau to register voters and protect lives and property would supervise each. The act then laid out the steps to create new state governments and admit them to the Union. First, each state would hold a constitutional convention with delegates chosen by all adult males regardless of "race, color, or previous condition." (But not ex-Confederates barred by the Fourteenth Amendment.) The new governments had to allow the same "impartial" suffrage and ratify the Fourteenth Amendment. When these conditions were met, states could send representatives to Congress. The president vetoed the act, protesting that "the people of the South...were to be trodden under foot to protect niggers."

Congress rapidly and overwhelmingly overrode the veto. All but three states—Mississippi, Texas, and Virginia–agreed to these requirements by June 1868. The Fourteenth Amendment became part of the Constitution in July. (Those last three states were readmitted in 1870.) The Reconstruction Act, in insisting on black suffrage in the South, combined the idealism of the Radicals with political realism. The black vote might make it possible to establish the Republican Party

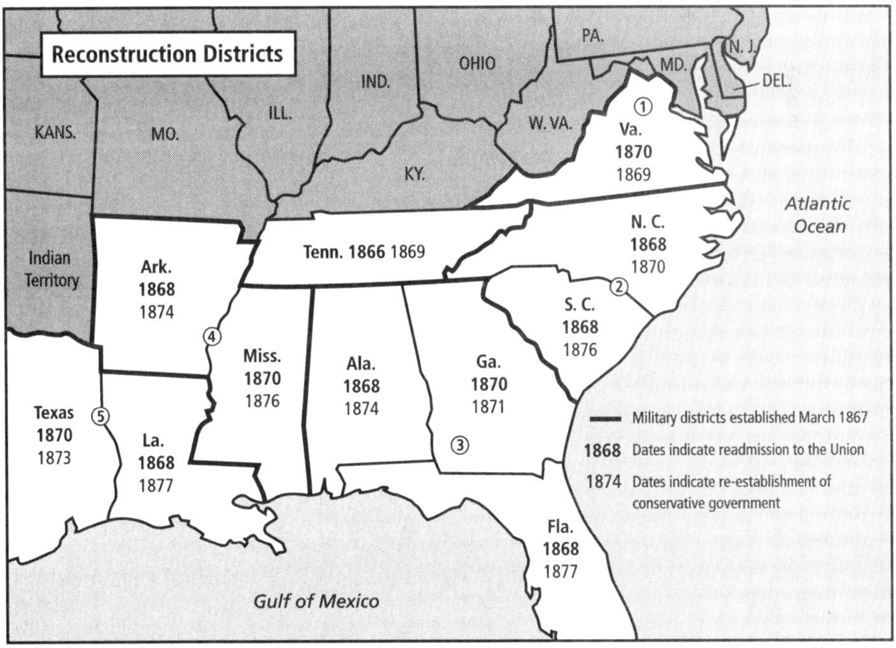

in the South. Some people felt that it would allow blacks to defend themselves and free the nation of the need for continued federal occupation and intervention.

President Johnson, firm in his belief that reconstruction was a dangerous revolution, sought to thwart the will of Congress through the use of his appointment powers. Congress, in turn, tried to limit Johnson's ability to do mischief by passing the Tenure of Office Act. This act prevented the president from dismissing any federal official whose appointment had required Senate confirmation, until the Senate approved his successor. This was designed to prevent Johnson from removing Republican officials who supported congressional reconstruction, particularly Secretary of War Edwin Stanton. Stanton not only supported Radical Reconstruction, but he was in a key position to aid in its enforcement and act as an internal cabinet spy for his friends in Congress.

Radical Republicans turned their attention to reforms at the state level in the North, designed to eliminate obstacles to individual advancement. This was in accord with the party's free-labor ideology that had been at the heart of its opposition to slavery. Michigan expanded state institutions for orphans and the disabled, outlawed racial segregation, and instituted free compulsory public education. Massachusetts' Republicans succeeded in banning racial discrimination in public accommodations and limiting child labor. An ambitious program of reform in New York included a Tenement House Act, Free School Law, Metropolitan Health Act, a Normal School Act that set up eight state teachers' colleges, and the establishment of a State Board of Charities. Despite these undoubted advances, however, most northern blacks remained in unskilled, low-wage jobs and substandard housing. The arrival of increasing numbers of European immigrants caused many to lose such jobs as barbers and construction workers where they had long predominated. Nevertheless, public life and political rights were now open to them in ways unheard of before the war. The overwhelming majority of blacks, however, continued to live in the South.

The most important effort for radical reform in the North was the push to extend the vote to blacks. But northern voters, frightened by the vicious, racist rhetoric of the Democrats and their conservative allies, rejected black suffrage amendments. A French newspaperman noted wryly, "Any Democrat who did not manage to hint in his speech that the negro is a degenerate gorilla, would be considered lacking in enthusiasm." As a result, the Democrats made major gains in the local and state elections of 1867. This emboldened Johnson and his allies. The president treated serenaders at the White House to a "victory speech." One of his aides crowed, "Any party with an abolition head and a nigger tail will soon find itself with nothing left but the head and the tail."

Presidential Impeachment

Johnson, in the mistaken belief that northern public opinion was now behind him, renewed his efforts to obstruct congressional reconstruction. Ignoring the advice of General Grant, he removed military commanders who seemed too enthusiastic in their enforcement of Radical reconstruction policies and replaced them with officers more sympathetic to southern whites. Finally, Johnson decided to directly challenge Congress by removing Secretary of War Stanton, in violation of the Tenure of Office Act. (Congress had refused to confirm Stanton's suspension.) At the advice of Republican senators, Stanton barricaded himself in his office and refused to turn over the keys to his supposed replacement. The latter arrived complete with a major hangover from a premature celebration of his new position.

After this debacle, the House voted to impeach (indict) Johnson by a strictly party-line vote of 126 to 47 even before the actual charges had been listed. Nine of the eventual charges referred to violations of the Tenure of Office Act. The tenth accusation was that Johnson had been "unmindful of the high duties of his office" and had tried to bring Congress into "disgrace, ridicule, hatred, contempt, and reproach."

As the Constitution provides, the Senate acts as jury in cases of impeachment, with the Chief Justice of the Supreme Court serving as presiding judge. A two-thirds vote is required to remove a president. Despite the elaborate legal language, it was clear that the president was really being tried for his unyielding opposition and attempts to sabotage Republican reconstruction, as well as his general incompetence. An influential group of moderate Senate Republicans worried about establishing a precedent by which two-thirds of Congress could remove any president who disagreed with them. This might destroy the constitutional system of checks and balances by creating an all-powerful legislative branch like that of Great Britain. In addition, these same moderates distrusted the Radical views and temperament of Benjamin Wade, the president pro tem of the Senate, who would succeed Johnson. (The vice presidency was vacant.) The president's lawyers quietly let these moderates know that, in the future, he would stop denouncing Congress and would enforce the Reconstruction Acts. As a result, thirty-five senators voted for conviction, one short of the necessary two-thirds. Seven Republicans voted with the twelve Democrats to provide the margin of Johnson's "victory." Several others were ready to support the president if their votes were needed. Contrary to later myths, the seven were not "martyrs" who were read out of the party. The crisis that had the potential to shake up the entire constitutional system ended without changing it in any fundamental way.

As a result of controversy over his reconstruction policies, President Andrew Johnson was impeached by the House of Representatives. He escaped conviction by a single vote in the Senate.

The Election of 1868

Although Johnson had been humbled by his narrow escape, the acquittal also weakened the position of the Radicals within the Republican Party. General Ulysses S. Grant had emerged from the Civil War as the Union's leading military hero. Although he had supported congressional actions in a bitter split with Johnson, Grant was not known to have any particular ideological convictions. Conservative northern businessmen, although unenthusiastic about Radical reconstruction, felt that any attempt to reopen the now settled issue would cause political and economic chaos. They believed a Grant presidency would bring stability and conditions conducive to investment in the South. Grant easily won the Republican nomination on a platform that bragged about "the assured success of the reconstruction policy of congress."

The Democrats rejected Johnson and his many liabilities and drafted the colorless Governor of New York, Horatio Seymour. Since Seymour had denounced Lincoln during the war as a military despot and had referred to the draft rioters as "my friends," he handed the issue of loyalty and patriotism to the Republicans. As a result, Democrats ran on a platform denouncing Reconstruction as "unconstitutional, revolutionary, and void." Frank Blair of Missouri, the party's vice presidential candidate, had an outstanding record as a Union general during the war. But he frightened many northern voters by suggesting that the army should be used to break up the unconstitutional Republican governments in the South. He also condemned Republicans for putting the South under the heels of "a semi-barbarous race of blacks who are worshippers of fetishes and polygamists" and want only to "subject white women to their unbridled lust." Racist comments like these made this the last presidential campaign to openly bring up the issue of white supremacy.

Republicans replied by "waving the bloody shirt" even more vigorously. The same Democrats who had betrayed their country during the war, Republicans charged were now proposing "government by assassination and violence, instead of government by law." Events in the South seemed to confirm Republican warnings. Extra-legal terrorist groups began to wreak havoc on law and order in the South. The Ku Klux Klan was founded as a social club in 1866 in Tennessee. Its members came from all classes within southern white society. Its leaders included Confederate generals and other officers, headed by the renowned cavalry leader, General Nathan Bedford Forrest. By 1868 it had become an organization of hooded vigilantes, dedicated to preserving white supremacy. In the 1868 election the Klan engaged in an organized reign of terror directed at blacks and white

The Ku Klux Klan was dedicated to preserving white supremacy by terrorizing blacks and white Republicans.

Republican leaders. Assassins murdered a Republican congressman from Arkansas and three members of the South Carolina legislature. In Georgia, threats and beatings kept blacks from the polls. Eleven Georgia counties with black majorities did not tabulate a single Republican vote. In Louisiana rampaging Klansmen killed more than a thousand people, mostly blacks. In one parish (county) alone, the estimated death toll was two hundred blacks, leading a local Democratic leader to declare that this taught blacks a "wholesome lesson." On election day, there wasn't even one Republican vote in an area that had cast over 4,700 Republican votes seven months earlier.

These methods enabled the Democrats to carry Georgia and Louisiana and reduce Republican margins elsewhere in the South. By lending credence to Republican charges that the Rebels were trying to regain power through terror, however, the lawlessness in the South probably helped Republicans in the North. Grant won just about the same percentage of the northern vote (55 percent) as Lincoln had in 1864 and carried all but three of the northern states. Grant won an overwhelming electoral majority of 214 to 80. The Republicans retained a substantial margin in the House and Senate. Nevertheless, the great Civil War hero had actually received only about 53 percent of the popular vote against a weak and discredited opponent.

The Fifteenth Amendment

Grant's election assured the continuation of Reconstruction, but it also meant that a new Republican leadership would direct it. House Speaker Thaddeus Stevens, the leading exponent of protecting the rights of freed people and guaranteeing their economic independence, died in August 1868. The mass of mourners that filed past his body as it lay in state in the Capital was eclipsed only by Lincoln. True to his principles, he was buried in a black cemetery so that "I might illustrate in death the principles which I advocated through a long life, Equality of Man before his Creator." His death, followed the next year by that of Edwin Stanton and the loss of his Senate seat by Benjamin Wade, signaled the passing of the old generation of Radicals. The new leadership was more practical than idealistic, and driven more by economic concerns.

These Republican leaders worried that a resurgent Democratic Party, bolstered by "rebel" votes, might evict them from power. It seemed to many that it was now crucial to ensure their electoral base by extending black suffrage throughout the country. Blacks still could not vote in 11 of the 21 northern states or the 5 border states. In addition, the vote in the 10 former Confederate states depended on the Reconstruction Acts that could easily be repealed once reconstruction was over. Many Republicans felt a moral obligation to secure the vote for blacks. Naturally, blacks who could vote overwhelmingly favored the party of emancipation, the Republicans. Thus, as one Republican congressman noted, "Party expediency and exact justice coincide for once."

When Congress assembled in December 1868, it moved quickly to pass the Fifteenth Amendment to secure black suffrage. It rejected a Radical proposal to guarantee the right to vote to all male citizens over 21. Such an amendment might be rejected by northern and western states who imposed their own limits on voting directed against the foreign born and the Chinese in the Far West. As approved, the amendment prohibited the states from denying the right to vote only "on account of race, color or previous condition of servitude." The warnings of one Radical congressman: "Let it remain possible to still disfranchise the body of the colored race in the late Rebel states and I tell you it will be done," proved to be prophetic. Southern whites were ultimately able to use loopholes that seemed to permit denial of the right to vote on supposedly nonracial grounds. These included literacy and property qualifications. Within thirty years, few southern blacks were able to vote.

The Fifteenth Amendment was ratified by March 1870. Many relieved Republicans agreed that the passage of the amendment was "the last great point that remained to be settled of the issues of the war." Blacks were already playing a significant role in the newly established southern governments.

RADICAL RECONSTRUCTION: MYTH AND REALITY

A remarkable period began in southern history after the passage of the Reconstruction Acts. For the first time ever, governments rested on universal manhood suffrage, without regard to race. All citizens were entitled to "equal protection of the laws." Blacks could now vote, serve on juries, and even hold office. For whites, this was a profoundly disquieting experience, a world "suddenly turned bottom-side up."

The confusion and agitation of the whites led them to characterize Reconstruction as the "tragic era" of an occupied South. Bolstered by later books and films, like *Birth of a Nation* and *Gone With the Wind*, they painted a picture of a society gone mad. In this legend ignorant blacks dominated the governments and ran wild: "It is barbarism overwhelming civilization by physical force. It is the slave rioting in the halls of his master," said one observer. These power mad slaves were aided by villainous northern "carpetbaggers" who came South "like buzzards" to strip the helpless South of its few pitiful possessions. The even more treacherous "scalawags," Southerners who sold out their own people for profit, in turn, abetted them.

This myth, which remained embedded in the American psyche for over a century, bore little resemblance to reality. Blacks did not dominate any of the new governments. (Only South Carolina had a black majority in its legislature.) Military occupation was never widespread and lasted as long as eight years in only three states (South Carolina, Florida, and Louisiana). A small minority of carpetbaggers were the unscrupulous adventurers of the legend. The majority were middle-class Union veterans who decided to make their homes in the South. Some of these were entrepreneurs who came for business opportunities. Many were teachers, missionaries, and Freedmen's Bureau agents. Some were idealists like Adelbert Ames, the future Governor of Mississippi, convinced that he "had a Mission with a large M" to help the freed people. Southern supporters of Reconstruction, the so-called "scalawags," also had varied motives. Most had been wartime Unionists in upland counties or pre-war Whigs who had been reluctant secessionists. Some were formerly ardent secessionists who concluded that accommodation would bring economic development to the South. These included General Longstreet, Lee's old lieutenant, who accepted a federal post and campaigned for Grant.

Blacks and Reconstruction

Blacks saw Reconstruction as an opportunity to gain independence and equality. They long remembered the time when "de freedom sun shine out" as the great turning point of their lives. One man recalled, "I felt like a bird out of a cage. Amen. Amen. Amen. I could hardly ask to feel any better...." Now they sought to achieve personal independence and a black community apart from white authority.

Right at the beginning of Reconstruction, blacks tested their new freedom by holding meetings and unsupervised religious services, previously forbidden under slavery. They purchased prohibited items like guns and liquor, flaunted outrageous finery, and even refused to move aside for whites on the sidewalks. Anxious whites complained bitterly about this "insolence" and "insubordination." Many, now free from slavery's restrictions on travel, took to the roads. Between 1865 and 1870 the black population of the ten largest cities in the South doubled. Unfortunately, jobs were scarce, and new segregated neighborhoods arose, consisting largely of broken-down shanties.

The most poignant reason for movement was the attempt to reunite family, the central institution of the black community. One freedman, for example, requested the assistance of the Freedman's Bureau in locating "my own dearest relatives," whom he had not seen in 24 years. Slave marriages had not been recognized under southern law, so couples rushed to make their relationships legal. By 1870, the overwhelming majority of African Americans lived in two-parent households.

Relationships within the family also changed. Under slavery, black men and women had experienced "the rough equality of powerlessness." Now, many hoped to create the kind of patriarchal family that was typical in white American households. In the early years of reconstruction many black women withdrew from field labor, hoping to devote themselves to more domestic responsibilities. Black men were able to play a role in political and public life, while black women, like white women, were not. The Freedman's Bureau reinforced these separate roles by appointing men as heads of household who could sign labor contracts for their families. Black ministers preached that the woman's role was to make the house "a place of peace and comfort" for her husband. The shift from field to home, however, was only temporary. The rise of sharecropping made families responsible for their plots of land. All members had to work this land. In addition, the extreme poverty of most black families, which worsened in the depression of the 1870s, made women's labor a necessity. Thus, a much higher percentage of married black women than white woman had to work outside of the home. Still, both black men and women struggled to maintain family stability as the cornerstone of the African-American community.

The other key community institution was the black church. Freedmen quickly withdrew from biracial congregations in which they had been required to sit in the back or in the gallery. They pooled their limited resources and built separate black churches. The church was "the first social institution fully controlled by black men in America." Churches became the centers of community life. Ministers were the most respected members of the community, active in political as well as religious life. They fostered a spirit of community self-help that led to the formation of fraternal, charitable, mutual aid, and burial societies.

The freed people's thirst for self-improvement was evident in the push to establish schools, another key institution. In 1860, over 90 percent of the black population in the South was illiterate. Observers have noted, "the almost sacred nature to the Negroes' attitude towards education." Despite all obstacles put in their way, most agreed with Frederick Douglass that, "the pathway from slavery to freedom was literacy." The freed people, themselves, took the initiative to raise money for schools and teachers' salaries. Many of the schools were supported, at least in part, by tuition, generally \$1 to \$1.50 a month per child. This was a substantial burden to a man who may have earned \$10 a month for his labors. The Freedman's Bureau generally came into the picture after schools had been started, offering some modest financial support and supplies of books. This drive for education continued long after the Freedmen's Bureau ended.

The records of the Bureau contained poignant requests for aid: "You must kno that our people are very poor and if we are not helpt we will remain in ignorants a long time." Many of the schools faced active, even violent, hostility from local whites. Particularly in the smaller towns, most of the teachers were freed people, often only semi-literate themselves. One apologized, "I never had the chance of goen to school for I was a slave until freedom....I am the only teacher because we cannot doe better now." Most of these black teachers earned a modest living, often hardly more than that of a field hand. Some became leaders of the community, even gaining political office.

Surprisingly, many southern whites taught in the small town and rural schools for blacks. Most were people of limited means who hoped to earn a modest livelihood. One wrote, "I consider myself a pioneer in this laudable cause and being a widow with three children to support, I have undertaken this at the sacrifice of my friends." Northern philanthropic and religious groups also played a part by opening schools in the cities and sending New England "schoolmarms" to inculcate accepted middle-class standards of behavior. Eventually, reconstructed state governments began using tax dollars to support separate public schools for children of both races. By 1900, the black illiteracy rate had been cut in half. Even more might have been accomplished had the early valiant efforts been sustained by later white governments. Despite the limitations, W.E.B. Du Bois (a noted African-American scholar and writer) believed that the establishment of a public school system enabled blacks to avoid re-enslavement. It helped them to build an inner culture that withstood the shocks of the outer world.

Blacks, rebuilding their lives and creating their own institutions, realized that true freedom would be achieved solely through economic independence. That, they believed, could only be attained by ownership of land. "What's de use of being free if you don't own land enough to be buried in?" one freedman asked. African Americans also felt that they were entitled to land that had been developed through the sweat of their own and their ancestors' labor over many generations. Some Radicals, like Thaddeus Stevens, favored confiscation of Confederate plantations and their redistribution in 40-acre plots to freedmen. Radicals warned that "to give the slaves only freedom without the land, is to give them only the mockery of freedom which the English or Irish peasant had." But the idea was too extreme for most Republicans. As a result, only a few freedmen gained the economic autonomy for which they had dreamed. Most had to work for white landowners.

Nevertheless, blacks did manage to force basic changes in plantation agriculture. While many worked for wages, more settled for an arrangement under which they would get a share of the crop. Planters divided their estates into small plots that they rented to the freedmen. The sharecropper generally could keep one-third of the year's crop after paying for use of the land and necessary supplies, seed, and work animals. Blacks preferred a system that freed them from gang labor and daily white supervision. Poor whites, as well as blacks, became sharecroppers. Planters gained greater stability, as all members of the sharecropping family worked to produce a crop. Eventually, many families were caught up in a web of debt. Even had they been given the small plots of land that they expected, black families, lacking credit or power, would undoubtedly still have suffered eco-

The schools built by the Freedman's Bureau were segregated but allowed the children in the South to get a formal education.

nomically. But land redistribution would certainly have shaken the foundations of southern society by creating a group of middle-class black farmers.

Despite setbacks, southern blacks had taken important steps in organizing their own lives. They sponsored newspapers that became a powerful resistance force. They sought to protect these gains by mobilizing and voting in large numbers. At the beginning of Reconstruction, about half of the men qualified to vote were black. Freedmen were the majority of voters in Alabama, Florida, Louisiana, Mississippi, and South Carolina. Despite this, they held only 15 to 20 percent of the government positions. Blacks served as lieutenant governors, secretaries of states, treasurers, and superintendents of education. Sixteen blacks sat in Congress during Reconstruction, including two senators (Hiram Revels and Blanche Bruce of Mississippi). Over six hundred were state legislators and countless more held local positions like sheriff, justice of the peace, and even mayor. Most of these black politicians were young men. Those at the upper levels tended to come from the free black community, largely from the North, and were often college-educated. Many of those at the state and local levels were far less-educated ex-slaves who had held positions of trust within the slave community, particularly drivers and artisans.

Freedmen eagerly joined Union Leagues that mobilized their votes for the Republicans. Black voters were not the ignorant, easily-led dupes described by disgruntled whites. The political agenda of freed people included protection of their wages or shares of crops, a tax-supported public school system, assurance of equality before the law, and defense against the violence of white vigilantes. They were, perhaps surprisingly, uninterested in vengeance against their former masters or in any real push for genuine social integration. The Reconstruction governments, established with their support, now faced the substantial challenge of fulfilling the aspirations of these constituents for a better, more just South. At the same time, they confronted the daunting task of rebuilding a war-torn land in which the average wealth of whites had fallen by one-half.

Most blacks worked as sharecroppers on land owned by whites. In this photograph, black sharecroppers pick cotton. Because the price remained low, sharecroppers often fell into debt and were tied to the land.

Republican Rule in the South

Under the rule of the Radical Republicans, both races were able to make considerable social and political progress. The new constitutions ended property qualifications for voting for whites, as well as blacks. They abolished imprisonment for debt and, for the first time, recognized the property rights of married women. Above all, these constitutions established the rights of blacks and whites to public schools.

Still, many white Southerners were deeply disturbed by the support of black schools at public expense. They believed that education would "spoil" blacks, making them discontented and difficult to handle. Despite this, Reconstruction governments increased support for schools, including night schools for adults. Poor white children also, for the first time, were able to take advantage of the new educational system. The Freedman's Bureau and northern philanthropic agencies helped establish black colleges such as Fisk, Hampton, and Tougaloo, initially to train black teachers. Republican governments, for the first time ever in the South, accepted the principle that the state should be responsible for public education.

Also for the first time, Republican state governments built hospitals, orphan asylums, and institutions for the blind, deaf, and mentally ill. Some local governments even provided food, firewood, and free medical care for the poor. State governments attempted to rebuild bridges, public buildings, roads, and other facilities demolished by the war. They provided state aid to railroads destroyed by the war. Most of the investment and construction had to go to rebuilding the railroads. This was accomplished by 1872, and 3300 additional miles were added.

Senator Blanche Bruce of Mississippi was one of a small number of blacks who reached high public office during Reconstruction. There were two African-American senators and sixteen congressmen.

Southern Republicans also set up industrial commissions to attract investors to the South, with rather limited success.

Though the achievements of these Reconstruction governments were substantial, they were costly. An entire public school system had to be built. Railroads and rebuilding a war-torn land required substantial funds. As a result, taxes and debts ballooned during Republican rule. Economic problems brought many of the railroads to the verge of bankruptcy. Although no higher than the taxes in the rural Midwest at the time, southern taxes in 1870 were four times as high as they had been in 1860. Small white landowners had to pay a larger share of taxes than ever before. Their anger at their increased financial burden turned many of these early supporters against the Republicans. In addition, many refused or were unable to pay their taxes. This diminished the services Republican state governments tried to provide, led to economic turmoil, and discredited those governments in northern, as well as southern, eyes.

Corruption in the Reconstruction South further tarnished the image of these governments. One contemporary observer exclaimed, "Such a Saturnalia of robbery and jobbery has seldom been seen in a civilized country....greed was unchecked and roguery unabashed." This view became accepted as the key historical truth about Reconstruction. Certainly, profiteering was widespread. The unprecedented sums of money that these new governments were handling led to bribery, kickbacks, and skimming of public funds. Many officials, in fact, saw nothing wrong with helping themselves to a share of the expanding state budgets. This was, however, only a reflection of what was happening throughout the nation. The Tweed Ring (a Democratic machine in New York) probably stole more from the people than all the southern governments combined. Southern railroad "rings" were only pale imitations of Wall Street "robber barons." Although it may have been unfair, the dishonesty in the southern governments further damaged Reconstruction in the view of northern public opinion.

Despite its achievements, Republican Reconstruction government never met its original exalted goals of remaking southern society in a more egalitarian mold. For example, it was one thing to build schools and quite another to integrate them. White parents did not want their children to share classrooms with blacks. Although New Orleans successfully integrated several thousand students, this bold experiment was not repeated elsewhere. Even black legislators did not seem to believe that interracial schooling was practical and preferred to stress fair division of school funds. Although the system of legalized segregation in public accommodations did not yet exist, discrimination was widespread. Black demands led to laws establishing the right to equal access to public places and transportation. These laws, however, were rarely enforced.

Land ownership presented another fundamental issue that Republican governments failed to confront. Only South Carolina set up a land commission to purchase acreage and resell it to freed people on easy credit terms. After a shaky start, the commission did succeed in establishing fourteen thousand black families on homesteads. One such community, Promised Land, is still in existence. Outside of South Carolina, the hopes of the freed people were disappointed. Most white Republicans, although committed to equality of citizenship, opposed any state attempts to redistribute property. As one paper pointed out at the time, the lack of any land of their own, coupled with the antagonism of the white elite, meant that freedmen "cannot rise.... They must be servants to others, with no hope of bettering their condition." In the long run, this proved to be only too true and was, perhaps, the greatest failure of Reconstruction.

THE GRANT ADMINISTRATION AND NORTHERN POLITICS

When they elected Grant president in 1868, most Americans assumed that he would bring the same superb leadership skills to the job that he had demonstrated as a victorious general. But Grant's experiences on the battlefield did not adequately prepare him for the complexities of the presidential office. His lack of any deep ideological convictions, as demonstrated by his slogan, "Let Us Have Peace," further limited his forcefulness in office. Although he had shrewder political instincts than he is generally given credit for, Grant was often naive in choosing his associates. As someone who had consistently failed in business, he particularly admired successful businessmen and turned to them for advice.

Government Corruption

During the Grant years, it seemed as though corruption infected officials in every region and at every level of government. As the economy soared in the North (by 1873 industrial production was 75 percent greater than its 1865 level), opportunities for profiteering also grew. Influence-peddlers crowded state legislatures, seeking advantages for their railroad, mining, or lumber companies. Even relatively honest officials saw nothing wrong in accepting money or favors from businessmen in return for preferential laws or contracts. Local, state, and even federal governments were not well equipped to deal with the demands created by economic growth and increased government services and benefits. This led to alliances between businessmen and politicians that produced the ever-expanding corruption of the era.

Although he himself was honest, Grant surrounded himself with people who saw public office as a road to personal profit. During his two terms, his secretary of war, his vice president, many treasury and naval officials, and even his private secretary were involved in public scandals. Government promotion of railroad development offered one prime opportunity. By 1872, the federal government had distributed well over 100 million acres of public land and millions of dollars for railroad construction, particularly to the new transcontinental lines, the Central Pacific and the Union Pacific. This led to the era's most famous scandal, that of the Credit Mobilier. This was a "dummy" corporation created to receive construction contracts from the Union Pacific. An inner circle of Union Pacific stockholders formed it. These men made exorbitant profits by awarding themselves contracts at greatly inflated costs. To forestall congressional inquiry, the company distributed stock to important members of Congress and federal government officials. The resulting scandal that broke in 1872 implicated several important Republican leaders, including the vice president.

Other scandals hit the Grant administration even harder. The Secretary of War had to resign or face impeachment when it was revealed that he had taken kickbacks from government-appointed traders in Indian Territory. Another investigation uncovered the widespread Whiskey Rings that looted millions of dollars from federal excise taxes. Investigations revealed that the president's secretary was at the center of the rings. Only Grant's intervention saved him from prison. One observer has noted, "It was the age of the audacious confidence man, and Grant was the incurable sucker. He easily fell victim to their trickery...because he could not believe that such people existed."

Foreign Policy in the Grant Years

Grant's best cabinet appointment was, undoubtedly, his Secretary of State, Hamilton Fish, an aristocratic New Yorker. His greatest success resulted from quiet and persistent diplomacy to settle damage claims against the British. These were based on the wartime destruction caused by the *Alabama* and other British-built vessels that had preyed on Union shipping. Eager to maintain American friendship, the British agreed to the 1871 Treaty of Washington, which set up an international arbitration tribunal to settle claims. The tribunal awarded the United States $15.5 million for damages done by the British-made ships. This was not only a victory for American diplomacy, it also established an important precedent for settling international disputes and helped improve relations with Britain.

The biggest foreign policy disaster during the Grant years was the attempt to take over Santo Domingo (the Dominican Republic today). After the victory of nationalism in the Civil War, many Americans once again embraced the ideas of Manifest Destiny. In 1867, Secretary of State Seward had negotiated a treaty with Russia to purchase Alaska for $7.2 million. Despite derisive comments about "Seward's Folly," this set a precedent for annexing territory not connected to the continental United States. Various promoters and speculators used their influence with Grant's private secretary to lobby for annexation of Santo Domingo. Although they succeeded in getting Grant to agree to a treaty, the Senate refused to ratify it, leading to further splits within the Republican Party.

"Liberal" Republicans

Many reformers came to detest what they saw as the unbridled materialism and corruption in American life. They blamed the Grant administration and its southern allies for this state of affairs. Reformers formed their own "Liberal Republican" Party to attempt to establish a government "which the best people of this country will be proud of." They came to believe that, in the South, the best people were former Confederates kept from power by Republican governments. It seemed to them that "Carpetbag-Negro government" and "bayonet rule" afflicted the South, just like "Grantism" harmed the national body politic.

DOCUMENTS

TO MY OLD MASTER, COLONEL P.H. ANDERSON, BIG SPRING, TENNESSEE

The newly freed slaves had struggled for their freedom. They aided the Union cause during the Civil War. At the war's end, they were overjoyed by their hard-won liberty. In this letter, Jourdon Anderson lets his former master know exactly how he really felt about being a slave and what he thinks about his new life.

Sir: I got your letter, and was glad to find that you had not forgotten Jourdon, and that you wanted me to come back and live with you again, promising to do better for me than anybody else can. I have often felt uneasy about you. I thought the Yankees would have hung you long before this, for harboring Rebs they found at your house. I suppose they never heard about your going to Colonel Martin's to kill the Union soldier that was left by his company in their stable. Although you shot at me twice before I left you, I did not want to hear of your being hurt, and am glad you are still living. It would do me good to go back to the dear old home again, and see Miss Mary and Miss Martha and Allen, Esther, Green, and Lee. Give my love to them all, and tell them I hope we will meet in the better world, if not in this. I would have gone back to see you all when I was working in the Nashville Hospital, but one of the neighbors told me that Henry intended to shoot me if he ever got a chance.

I want to know particularly what the good chance is you propose to give me. I am doing tolerably well here. I get twenty-five dollars a month, with victuals and clothing; have a comfortable home for Mandy—the folks call her Mrs. Anderson—and the children—Milly, Jane, and Grundy—go to school and are learning well. The teacher says Grundy has a head for a preacher. They go to Sunday school, and Mandy and me attend church regularly. We are kindly treated. Sometimes we overhear others saying, "Them colored people were slaves" down in Tennessee. The children feel hurt when they hear such remarks; but I tell them it was no disgrace in Tennessee to belong to Colonel Anderson. Many darkeys would have been proud, as I used to be, to call you master. Now if you will write and say what wages you will give me, I will be better able to decide whether it would be to my advantage to move back again.

As to my freedom, which you say I can have, there is nothing to be gained on that score, as I got my free papers in 1864 from the Provost-Marshal General of the Department of Nashville. Mandy says she would be afraid to go back without some proof that you were disposed to treat us justly and kindly; and we have concluded to test your sincerity by asking you to send us our wages for the time we served you. This will make us forget and forgive old scores, and rely on your justice and friendship in the future. I served you faithfully for thirty-two years, and Mandy twenty years. At twenty-five dollars a month for me, and two dollars a week for Mandy, our earnings would amount to eleven thousand six hundred and eighty dollars. Add to this the interest for the time our wages have been kept back, and deduct what you paid for our clothing, and three doctor's visits to me, and pulling a tooth for Mandy, and the balance will show what we are in justice entitled to. Please send the money by Adam's Express, in care of V. Winters, Esq., Dayton, Ohio. If you fail to pay us for faithful labors in the past, we can have little faith in your promises in the future. We trust the good Maker has opened your eyes to the wrongs which you and your fathers have done to me and my fathers, in making us toil for you for generations without recompense. Here I draw my wages every Saturday night; but in Tennessee there was never any pay-day for the Negroes any more than for the horses and cows. Surely there will be a day of reckoning for those who defraud the laborer of his hire.

In answering this letter, please state if there would be any safety for my Milly and Jane, who are now grown up, and both good-looking girls. You know how it was with poor Matilda and Catherine. I would rather stay here and starve—and die, if it come to that—than have my girls brought to shame by the violence and wickedness of their young masters. You will also please state if there has been any schools opened for the colored children in your neighborhood. The great desire of my life now is to give my children an education, and have them form virtuous habits.

Say howdy to George Carter, and thank him for taking the pistol from you when you were shooting at me.

FROM YOUR OLD SERVANT,
JOURDON ANDERSON

1. What point do you think Jourdon Anderson was trying to make to his old master?
2. Do you think he ever intended to go back? Why or why not?
3. What does this letter tell you about freed people and their aspirations?

THE BLACK CODES

At the end of the war, in 1865 and 1866, southern state legislatures passed a series of "Black Codes," supposedly to codify legal rights for newly freed blacks. In reality, most of the codes denied blacks many basic rights. Many Northerners believed that the provisions of the codes foreshadowed an attempt to reinstitute plantation slavery.

The Black Code of St. Landry's Parish, 1865

Whereas it was formerly made the duty of the police jury to make suitable regulations for the police of slaves within the limits of the parish; and whereas slaves have become emancipated by the action of the ruling powers; and whereas it is necessary for public order, as well as for the comfort and correct deportment of said freedmen, that suitable regulations should be established by their government in their changed condition, the following ordinances are adopted, with the approval of the United States military authorities commanding in said parish, viz:

SECTION *1. Be it ordained by the police jury of the parish of St. Landry,* That no negro shall be allowed to pass within the limits of said parish without a special permit in writing from his employer. Whoever shall violate this provision shall pay a fine of two dollars and fifty cents, or in default thereof shall be forced to work four days on the public road, or suffer corporeal punishment as provided hereinafter.

SECTION *2. Be it further ordained,* That every negro who shall be found absent from the residence of his employer after 10 o'clock at night, without a written permit from his employer, shall pay a fine of five dollars, or in default thereof, shall be compelled to work five days on the public road, or suffer corporeal punishment as hereinafter provided.

SECTION *3. Be it further ordained,* That no negro shall be permitted to rent or keep a house within said parish. Any negro violating this provision shall be immediately ejected and compelled to find an employer; and any person who shall rent, or give the use of any house to any negro, in violation of this section, shall pay a fine of five dollars for each offence.

SECTION *4. Be it further ordained,* That every negro is required to be in the regular service of some white person, or former owner, who shall be held responsible for the conduct of said negro. But said employer or former owner may permit said negro to hire his own time by special permission in writing, which permission shall not extend over seven days at any one time. Any negro violating the provisions of this section shall be fined five dollars for each offence, or in default of the payment thereof shall be forced to work five days on the public road, or suffer corporeal punishment as hereinafter provided.

SECTION *5. Be it further ordained,* That no public meetings or congregations of negroes shall be allowed within said parish after sunset; but such public meetings and congregations may be held between the hours of sunrise and sunset, by the special permission of writing of the captain of patrol, within whose beat such meetings shall take place. This prohibition, however, is not intended to prevent negroes from attending the usual church services, conducted by white ministers and priests. Every negro violating the provisions of this section shall pay a fine of five dollars, or in default thereof shall be compelled to work five days on the public road, or suffer corporeal punishment as hereinafter provided.

SECTION *6. Be it further ordained,* That no negro shall be permitted to preach, exhort, or otherwise declaim to congregations of colored people, without a special permission in writing from the president of the police jury. Any negro violating the provisions of this section shall pay a fine of ten dollars, or in default thereof shall be forced to work ten days on the public road, or suffer corporeal punishment as hereinafter provided.

SECTION *7. Be it further ordained,* That no negro who is not in the military service shall be allowed to carry fire-arms, or any kind of weapons, within the parish, without the special written permission of his employers, approved and indorsed by the nearest or most convenient chief of patrol. Any one violating the provisions of this section shall forfeit his weapons and pay a fine of five dollars, or in default of the payment of said fine, shall be forced to work five days on the public road, or suffer corporeal punishment as hereinafter provided.

SECTION *8. Be it further ordained,* That no negro shall sell, barter, or exchange any articles of merchandise or traffic within said parish without the special written permission of his employer, specifying the articles of sale, barter or traffic. Any one thus offending shall pay a fine of one dollar for each offence, and suffer the forfeiture of said articles' or in default of the payment of said fine shall work one day on the public road, or suffer corporeal punishment as hereinafter provided.

SECTION *9. Be it further ordained,* That any negro found drunk within the said parish shall pay a fine of five dollars, or in default thereof shall work five days on the public road, or suffer corporeal punishment as hereinafter provided.

SECTION *10. Be it further ordained,* That all the foregoing provisions shall apply to negroes of both sexes.

SECTION *11. Be it further ordained,* That it shall be the duty of every citizen to act as a police officer for the detection of offences and the apprehension of offenders, who shall be immediately handed over to the proper captain or chief of patrol.

SECTION *12. Be it further ordained,* That the aforesaid penalties shall be summarily enforced, and that it shall be the duty of the captains and chiefs of patrol to see that the aforesaid ordinances are promptly executed.

SECTION *13. Be it further ordained,* That all sums collected from the aforesaid fines shall be immediately handed over to the parish treasurer.

SECTION *14. Be it further ordained,* That the corporeal punishment provided for in the foregoing sections shall consist in confining the body of the offender within a barrel placed over his or her shoulders, in the manner practiced in the army, such confinement not to continue longer than twelve hours, and for such time within the aforesaid limit as shall be fixed by the captain or chief of patrol who inflicts the penalty.

1. What do you think was the real purpose of this Black Code?
2. Which provisions would be most troubling to freedmen? To northern public opinion?

THE ISSUE OF LAND FOR THE FREED SLAVES

It was clear to some Radical Republicans that the only way freed people could expect to achieve real independence was if they could have their own land to farm. This land would have to be taken from plantation owners and Confederate leaders. Most Americans believed that such a policy was contrary to deeply-held ideas about economic rights. Radical Republican Congressman Thaddeus Stevens argued in favor of confiscation and redistribution of southern land. The **New York Times** *opposed such redistribution, while the former slaves expressed their deep desire to own their own land.*

From a speech by THADDEUS STEVENS, 1865

We especially insist that the property of the chief rebels should be seized and appropriated to the payment of the national debt, caused by the unjust and wicked war they instigated.... There are about 6,000,000 of freedmen in the South. The number of acres of land is 465,000,000. Of this those who own above 200 acres each number about 70,000 persons, holding in the aggregate—together with the states—about 394,000,000 acres. By forfeiting the estates of the leading rebels the government would have 394,000,000 of acres besides their town property, and yet nine-tenths of the people would remain untouched. Divide the land into convenient farms. Give, if you please, forty acres to each adult male freedman. Suppose there are 1,000,000 of them. That would require 40,000,000 acres, which deducted from 394,000,000 leaves 354,000,000 acres for sale. Divide it into suitable farms, and sell it to the highest bidders. I think it, including town property, would average at least $10 per acre. That would produce $3,540,000.

The whole fabric of southern society must be changed and never can it be done if this opportunity is lost. Without this, this government can never be, as it has never been, a true republic.... How can republican institutions, free schools, free churches, free social intercourse exist in a mingled community of nabobs and serfs? If the South is ever made a safe republic let her lands be cultivated by the toil of... free labor....

Nothing is so likely to make a man a good citizen as to make him a freeholder. Nothing will so multiply the production of the South as to divide it into small farms. Nothing will make men so industrious and moral as to let them feel that they are above want and are the owners of the soil which they till.... No people will ever be republican in spirit and practice where a few own immense manors and the masses are landless. Small and independent landholders are the support and guardians of republican liberty.

NEW YORK TIMES, July 9, 1867:

[Land confiscation] is a question not of humanity, not of loyalty, but of fundamental relation of industry to capital; and sooner or later, if begun at the South, it will find its way into the cities of the North.... An attempt to justify the confiscation of southern land under the pretense of doing justice to the freedmen, strikes at the root of property rights in both sections. It concerns Massachusetts as much as Mississippi.

Conversation between a Freedman and a General at Fort Smith Arkansas
Reported by the Joint Congressional Committee on Reconstruction, 1867:

FREEDMAN: Sir, I want you to help me in a personal matter.
GENERAL: Where is your family?
FREEDMAN: On the Red River.
GENERAL: Have you not everything you want?
FREEDMAN: No sir.
GENERAL: You are free!
FREEDMAN: Yes sir, you set me free, but you left me there.
GENERAL: What do you want?
FREEDMAN: I want some land; I am helpless; you do nothing for me but give me freedom.
GENERAL: Is not that enough?
FREEDMAN: It is enough for the present; but I cannot help myself unless I get some land; then I can take care of myself and my family; otherwise I cannot do it.

1. What was Thaddeus Steven's plan? To whom do you think the plan would appeal?
2. What are the grounds for his argument that his plan would strengthen democracy and agricultural production? Do you agree?
3. What is the basis for the *New York Times*' opposition to confiscation and redistribution of southern lands? Who would find its argument convincing? Why?
4. How does the freedman look at this issue?

EDUCATING THE FREED PEOPLE

Most Americans believed in a close connection between education and democracy. Under slavery laws, masters had been prohibited from teaching reading and writing to slaves. Now that they were free, blacks thirsted for the knowledge that had once been denied to them.

Dedicated Teachers and Determined Students, 1869

RALEIGH, N.C., FEB 22, 1869

It is surprising to me to see the amount of suffering which many of the people endure for the sake of sending their children to school. Men get very low wages here—from $2.50 to $8 per month usually, while a first-rate hand may get $10, and a peck or two of meal per week for rations—and a great many men cannot get work at all. The women take in sewing and washing, go out by day to scour, etc. There is one woman who supports three children and keeps them at school; she says, "I don't care how hard I has to work, if I can only send Sallie and the boys to school looking respectable." Many of the girls have but one decent dress; it gets washed and ironed on Saturday, and then is worn until the next Saturday, provided they do not tear it or fall in the mud; when such an accident happens there is an absent mark on the register.... One may go into their cabins on cold, windy days, and see daylight between every two boards, or feel the rain dropping through the roof; but a word of complaint is rarely heard. They are anxious to have the children "get on" in their books, and do not seem to feel impatient if they lack comforts themselves. A pile of books is seen in almost every cabin, though there be no furniture except a poor bed, a table and two or three broken chairs.

MISS M. A. PARKER
In *American Freedman, April 1869*

SYDNEY ANDREWS *quoted in the Joint Report* on Reconstruction, 39th (U.S.) *Congress, 1st Session, 1866:*

Many of the negroes...common plantation negroes, and day laborers in the towns and villages, were supporting little schools themselves. Everywhere I found among them a disposition to get their children into schools, if possible. I had occasion very frequently to notice that porters in stores and laboring men in warehouses, and cart drivers on the streets, had spelling books with them, and were studying them during the time they were not occupied with their work. Go into the outskirts of any large town and walk among the negro inhabitants, and you will see children and in many instances grown negroes, sitting in the sun alongside their cabins studying.

CAPTAIN C. M. HAMILTON *in a letter to the Office* of the Adjutant General in Washington, D.C., 1866:

The night school has been frequently disturbed. One evening a mob called out of the school house, the teacher, who upon presenting himself was confronted with four revolvers, and menacing expressions of shooting him, if he did not promise to quit the place, and close the school. The freedmen promptly came to his aid and the mob dispersed.

About the 18th or 19th of the month, I was absent...when a formidable disturbance took place at the school. The same mob threatened to destroy the school that night, and the freedmen, learning this, assembled...at their place of instruction in a condition of self-defense.

I understand that not less than forty colored men armed to protect themselves, but the preparation becoming known to the *respectable, rowdies,* they only maneuvered about in small squads, and were wise enough to avoid a collision.

1. What evidence do the documents in this section show about the significance of education for freed people?
2. What barriers did these blacks have to overcome to get some education?
3. What is meant by "respectable rowdies"? Why would they assault a school?

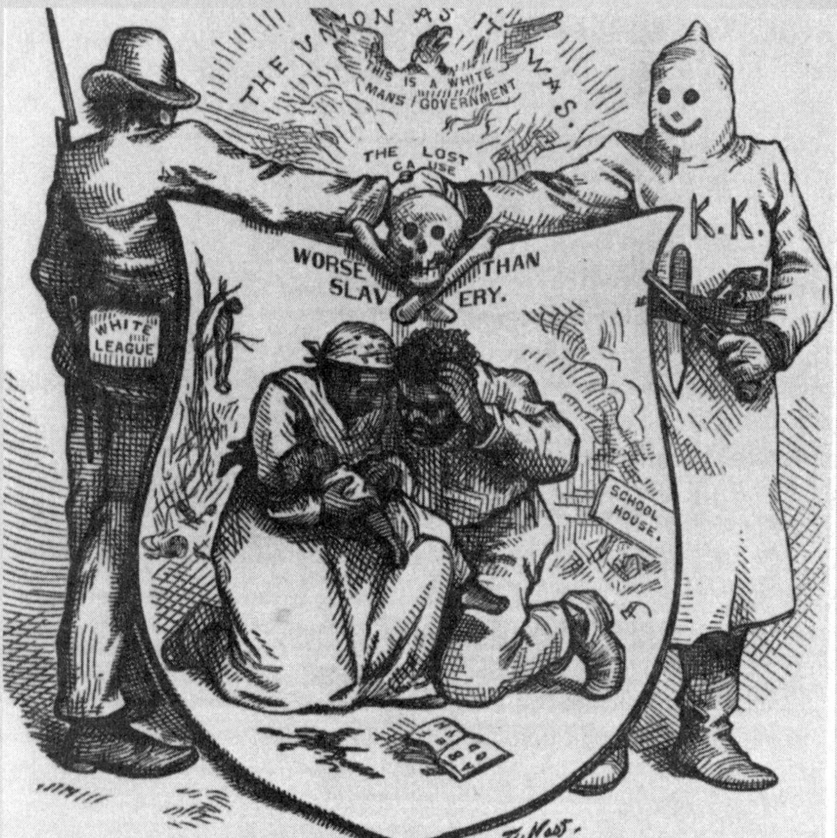
THE UNION AS IT WAS.
THIS IS A WHITE MANS GOVERNMENT
THE LOST CAUSE
WORSE THAN SLAVERY.
WHITE LEAGUE
K.K.
SCHOOL HOUSE.
Th. Nast.

Chapter Ten

RETREAT FROM RECONSTRUCTION

WOMEN AND RECONSTRUCTION

When blacks achieved political rights, women continued to be "the only class of citizens wholly unrepresented in the government." Abolitionists and feminists had long been allied in the American reform movement. When the issues of black male citizenship and suffrage arose in the debates over the Fourteenth and Fifteenth Amendments, women's rights advocates hoped that woman suffrage would be next. They were disappointed when many of their old abolitionist allies deserted them, declaring, "It is the Negro's hour, not the woman's."

The Fourteenth Amendment added the word "male" to the Constitution for the first time (in its description of inhabitants entitled to vote). Militant feminists, led by Elizabeth Cady Stanton and Susan B. Anthony, opposed the Fifteenth Amendment for prohibiting racial but not sexual discrimination in voting. Stanton believed that an extension of the vote that led to universal manhood suffrage only underscored the powerlessness of women and their declining status. Educated and informed women, like the reformers, Stanton argued, were far more qualified to make political decisions than immigrants and freedmen "who do not know the difference between the monarchy and the republic." The already small feminist movement split into a radical wing, headed by Stanton and Anthony, and a more moderate group that accepted the Reconstruction amendments. Susan B. Anthony actually faced trial for voting in the election of 1872. Both groups

Susan B. Anthony (left) and Lucy Stone (right) were feminist leaders whose followers split over support for the Fifteenth Amendment. Anthony headed the more radical wing while the moderate group accepted the Reconstruction amendments.

continued to fight for women's suffrage, although they were unable to achieve their goals in this era. They were more successful in obtaining property rights for married women. The abolitionist-feminist alliance had totally disintegrated, further weakening supporters of Reconstruction.

The Election of 1872

As Grant's renomination became a certainty by 1872, a group of members of his own party, who disagreed with his appointments and policies, launched the Liberal Republican movement. They stressed civil service reform to end the abuses of political corruption and urged amnesty in the South. They hoped to attract candidates of "superior intelligence and superior virtue." As a compromise candidate for the presidency, they nominated Horace Greeley, editor of the *New York Tribune,* the most prominent newspaperman in the country. In his 40 years as a journalist, Greeley had supported a wide variety of contradictory positions. Before the Civil War, he had been a staunch abolitionist. After, he moved from advocating tough postwar reconstruction to becoming the leading spokesman for self-government and amnesty in the South. Despite his years of attacks directed at Democrats, the Democratic Party decided to endorse Greeley under the slogan, "Anything to beat Grant."

Greeley's eccentricities, however, made him vulnerable to ridicule. In addition, Greeley's stress on southern self-government proved to be counter-productive, as many northern voters still distrusted the white South. Thomas Nast, the *Harper's Weekly* cartoonist who had helped destroy the Tweed Ring, had a similar field day with Greeley. His best-known campaign cartoon showed pirate captain Greeley bringing his boat next to the ship of state while armed Confederates waited below to board and demolish it. Another portrayed Greeley stretching a hand over Lincoln's grave to clasp the hand of John Wilkes Booth!

Despite vigorous campaigning, Greeley's candidacy began to lose steam. Grant won 56 percent of the popular vote, the largest margin for any candidate from 1828 to 1904. He carried every northern state and 10 of the 16 southern or border states. The Republicans were also able to regain their two-thirds margin in both houses of Congress. Weary from campaigning, depressed by the results, and mourning the death of his wife, Greeley died three weeks later. The Liberal Republican movement also collapsed. But, when the nation's prosperity dissolved into depression in 1873, Republicans grew more vulnerable to the issues of reform and reconciliation that had been raised unsuccessfully in the election.

Grant's landslide reelection victory seemed, at least on the surface, to reaffirm the nation's support for continued reconstruction. Many Northerners, however, were becoming increasingly disillusioned with southern Republicans. Except for the Radical Republicans, few Northerners had ever been deeply committed to racial equality. New issues arising from depression and unemployment led northern voters, who had never had much real sympathy for the difficulties of southern blacks, to lose any remaining interest in their plight.

RETREAT FROM RECONSTRUCTION

Increase in Terrorism

The waves of terror instituted by the Klan and Klan-like organizations in the South directed against blacks and Republicans continued to grow during the 1870s. The death toll was in the hundreds. Northerners expressed their amazement at the inability of southern Republicans to maintain order. Attempts by Republican officials to use militia to contain the violence proved to be ineffective. White troops were unreliable because the Klan often infiltrated their ranks. Black militia units increased white anger and led to fears of race warfare. Even when Klansmen were arrested, it was difficult to protect witnesses and find a jury that would convict. One case in Mississippi was dismissed when five key witnesses were murdered. When the governor of North Carolina sought to crush the Klan by declaring marital law, the Democratic-controlled legislature impeached him and discharged him from office in 1871. (He was the first American governor ever to be so removed.)

Congress finally responded to the increasing violence by passing a series of Enforcement Acts, the most extensive of which was the Ku Klux Klan Act of 1871. For the first time, conspiracies to deny citizens equal protection of the law could be prosecuted in federal courts. The president could declare martial law in any community victimized by terror and could even suspend

Hooded and robed Ku Klux Klan members often attacked blacks or threatened them with violence.

habeas corpus. Led by a new, crusading attorney general, the federal government did intervene in South Carolina and successfully prosecuted several hundred Klansmen elsewhere in the South. By 1872, federal power had broken the back of the Klan and appeared to have returned the rule of law to the South.

Unfortunately, the return to some semblance of order was short-lived. Congressional Republicans began to retreat from their commitment to "carpet-bag governments" in the South. One politician bluntly announced, "The truth is our people are tired out with this worn out cry of 'Southern outrages'!!!" By 1872, Congress had extended amnesty to all but a handful of Confederate leaders and the Freedman's Bureau was allowed to expire. "White Leaguers" in Louisiana killed over one hundred blacks in the town of Colfax. But the entrance of federal troops into the state to end the increasingly bitter conflict provoked cynical complaints in Congress about "federal despotism."

In 1873, the great postwar economic growth suddenly collapsed in a financial panic. Disastrous unemployment and wage cuts led to bitter strikes and protests. Class divisions threatened social harmony. Frightened Republican businessmen became more sympathetic to southern whites who seemed to be facing the same problems of disorder with lower class blacks. Conservative doctrines, stressing business interests, replaced equal rights for blacks as the Republican Party's central ideology.

As always in hard economic times, the voters turned against the party in power. In the greatest turnaround in the nineteenth century, the huge Republican majority in the House of Representatives became a 60-seat Democratic majority. In New York, where Democrat Samuel Tilden piled up an amazing 50,000-vote majority for governor, a paper declared, "The election is not merely a victory but a revolution." For the first time in a generation, even Massachusetts elected a Democratic governor. Although the depression was the main reason for the Republican defeat, many leaders blamed the party's southern reconstruction policies for the debacle. *The Prostrate State*, an influential and widely read book by James Pike, a northern journalist, indicted supposed "Negro rule" in South Carolina. It reinforced the idea that governmental corruption and extravagance were the results of power given to "a mass of black barbarism...the most ignorant democracy that mankind ever saw." Some Republican leaders openly spoke of "unloading" the weight of southern reconstruction governments.

The Civil Rights Act of 1875

The second Grant administration witnessed a general retreat from Reconstruction. The Supreme Court issued a series of decisions in the 1870s that seriously undercut the protections for blacks, seemingly guaranteed by the Fourteenth Amendment. In one particularly devastating decision, the Court overturned convictions obtained against violent terrorists under the Enforcement Act. The Court ruled that the amendment allowed the federal government to act only against violations of rights by *states*, rather than individuals. Only local or state authorities could punish individual crimes. This made it almost impossible to prosecute criminals whose violence against blacks was ignored by local officials.

The last of the old radical "lions," Charles Sumner, Senator from Massachusetts, tirelessly labored to secure the passage of the Civil Rights Act to safeguard the fast-fading dream of equality. This measure prohibited racial discrimination in public accommodations, jury selection, cemeteries, and transportation. On his death bed Sumner entreated a visitor, "You must take care of the civil-rights bill,...don't let it fail." Its passage was the final tribute of his colleagues to a man whose entire public life had been devoted to ending slavery and achieving civil rights for African Americans. Although the law seemed to call for an unparalleled demonstration of federal powers, in practice it was rarely enforced. It remained a statement of principles, rather than action, until it was declared unconstitutional by the Supreme Court in 1883.

The "Redeemers" Regain Power

The nationwide depression had hit rural white Southerners with particular force. High taxes and a precipitous drop in crop prices combined to undermine the economic position of independent white small farmers. Many joined black farmers in the ranks of the landless. Democrats were able to use racism to rally backcountry whites whose economic frustrations turned them against southern Republican governments.

The "Mississippi Plan," which enabled Democrats to regain power in that state in 1875, became the model for "redeemers" throughout the South. The Democrats were trying to "redeem" their states from Republican and carpetbagger control. The first step of the plan was to force the 15 percent of the state's whites who considered themselves Republicans to switch sides through threats and ostracism. The next step was to use violence to intimidate black voters and break up Republican rallies. In broad daylight "Rifle Clubs" marched undisguised and shot down blacks "just the same as birds." In one such incident, mobs murdered thirty-five blacks and two whites in Vicksburg. Democratic newspapers in the state proclaimed the slogan, "Carry the election peacefully if we can, forcibly if we must." The governor of Mississippi, a Civil War Medal of Honor winner and one of the best carpetbag governors, appealed to President Grant for federal troops to control the violence. Northern party leaders, worried that military intervention would cost the Republicans a closely fought contest in Ohio, persuaded the president not to act. In a sentence that summarized the northern retreat from Reconstruction, the attorney general informed the governor, "The whole public are tired out with these annual autumnal outbreaks in the South, and the great majority are now ready to condemn any interference on the part of the Government." As a result, armed men threatened to kill freedmen who voted and openly destroyed ballot boxes with Republican votes. They shot one black state senator in the back. This contempt for federal law and the Constitution of the United States resulted in an overwhelming Democratic victory in Mississippi. It seemed apparent that whatever the results of the presidential election of 1876, Reconstruction itself would not survive.

The Disputed Centennial Election

Millions of American flocked to Philadelphia in 1876 to celebrate America's centennial at an enormous exposition dedicated to the "Progress of the Age." Despite the continuing economic depression and rampant labor conflict, the exhibits extolled new inventions and the possibilities of technological progress. Many groups were left out of the displays. Native Americans were seen only as quaint contrasts to an advanced civilization. A Woman's Pavilion featured women weavers but failed to mention the struggle for women's rights. Susan B. Anthony disrupted the July 4th program at the exposition to read a "Woman's Declaration of Independence." Blacks were not only invisible in the exhibits, they had even been barred from the construction crews that built the display halls.

American politics were nothing to celebrate about either in 1876. Successful intimidation of black voters and the declining courage of white Republicans resulted in Democratic "Redemption" of all southern states except South Carolina, Louisiana, and Florida. On the national level, the scandals that had overwhelmed the Grant administration burst into public view. This forced the Republicans to find a candidate of unquestioned honesty. They chose a former Civil War general, Governor Rutherford B. Hayes of Ohio, a drab "third-rate nonentity." The Democrats tried to seize the issue of reform by nominating Governor Samuel Tilden of New York, a millionaire corporate lawyer. Tilden had won a national reputation as a reformer when he broke up the infamous Tweed Ring in New York City. Both candidates were conservative men who favored sound money, reform, and limited government. The Democrats hoped to gain northern swing states by downplaying the "bloody shirt" issues of Civil War and Reconstruction.

Reports of a massacre in Hamburg, South Carolina hampered this Democratic strategy. There, whites murdered five captured black militiamen in cold blood, and looted and demolished black shops and homes. This atrocity enabled Republicans to revive northern fears of Democrats as unreconstructed rebels. Although Hayes did not do as well as Grant had in 1872, he was able to win all but four of the northern states, giving him 165 electoral votes. Tilden won a 250,000 popular vote plurality. (Although it has been estimated that at least 250,000 southern Republicans had been terrorized to prevent them from voting, neutralizing that margin of victory.) He carried New York, New Jersey, Connecticut, Indiana, and all the southern states under Democratic control, a total of 184 electoral votes. With only 185 electoral votes needed for victory, Tilden's triumph seemed evident. Two sets of conflicting returns, however, had arrived from South Carolina, Louisiana, and Florida. On the face of the returns, it appeared that Tilden had carried at least two of the states, but the Republican-controlled election boards certified Hayes as the winner in each state. While this might seem to have been a subversion of honest returns, it was actually impossible to tell what the results of an accurate count of the votes would have been. The Democrats had used fraud and force to keep blacks and Republicans from voting in the first place. For example, one Louisiana parish that had 1688 Republican voters in 1874 recorded only one in 1876.

Congress, lacking any clear guidance in the Constitution, faced an extraordinary predicament in determining who had really won. With a Republican Senate and a Democratic House, Congress decided to turn the problem over to an Electoral Commission consisting of five senators, five representatives, and five Supreme Court justices. The commission was balanced with seven Republicans and seven Democrats. The fifteenth member was to be an impartial Supreme Court justice. But, after some political maneuvering, this final member turned out to be Justice Joseph Bradley, a Republican, who cast the swing vote with the Republicans. By an eight to seven margin, the commission voted to award all twenty disputed electoral votes to Hayes, giving him the 185 electoral votes needed for victory. Many infuriated Democrats felt that they had been robbed and threatened action in the House.

While these proceedings were going on in public, negotiations continued behind the scenes between Republican leaders and "moderate" southern Democrats. Under this "Compromise of 1877," Southerners agreed to withdraw their opposition to Hayes' inauguration in return for Hayes' assurance that he would remove the remaining federal troops from the South and would appoint at least one Southerner to the cabinet. Hayes also agreed to support the Texas and Pacific bill to help subsidize the building of a southern transcontinental railroad. The Democratic Chairman later wrote, "Personally, I was satisfied that it would be better for the country to have four years of Republican Administration based upon fraudulent returns, than to have four years of civil war."

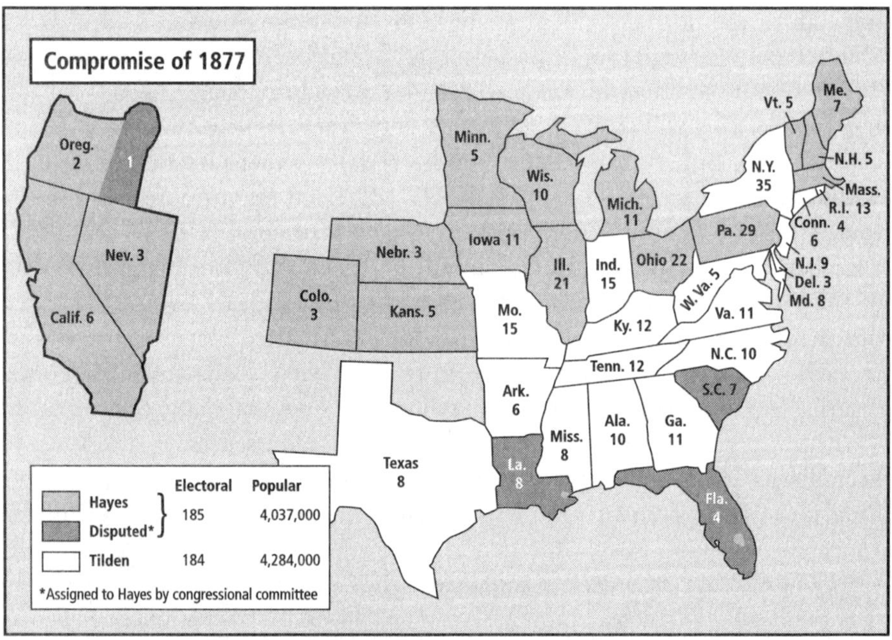

This was merely the final step in the abandonment of Reconstruction. As he had promised, Hayes did appoint a Southerner to the cabinet. David M. Key of Tennessee became Postmaster General, the position with the most patronage jobs. He promptly filled post offices and higher positions with ex-Confederates and other Democrats. A month after his inauguration, in April 1877, Hayes ordered the withdrawal of federal troops from Louisiana and South Carolina, causing the collapse of the last two Republican governments in the South. The Republican governor of South Carolina sorrowfully informed his distressed black supporters, "Today, by order of the President whom your votes alone rescued from overwhelming defeat, the Government of the United States abandons you...." Thus, the real losers of the 1876 election were not the Democrats but southern blacks whose last hopes for equality were crushed.

A triumphant Hayes made a speaking tour of the South. In Atlanta he assured blacks that their "rights and interests would be safer" in the hands of southern white men than in the guardianship of the federal government. A black newspaper, *The Colored Citizen*, described the dismal prospects for blacks in the optimistic year of America's Centennial: "For colored men to expect protection from the government is mere nonsense while Hayes is President, and for them to look for protection from the rebel State governments is foolishness; and for them to protect themselves by openly resisting or fighting is out of the question."

The Great Centennial Exhibition of 1876

On May 10, 1876, President Grant opened the Centennial Exhibition in Philadelphia. In the latter part of the twentieth and beginning of the twenty-first centuries, exhibitions and trade fairs no longer stir up any great excitement. But in 1876, the event seemed amazing to observers. ***Harper's Weekly*** *crowed: "The Centennial Exhibition will be a grand event in our national history, and, in every way worthy of the people whose progress in the arts and industries will be shown in the various departments."*

The public responded enthusiastically. In October alone more than two and a half million people attended the Exhibition. By November 10, the day it finally closed, over eight million visitors had paid the fifty cents entrance fee and another two million had gained free admission. One correspondent reported, "It is impossible to describe. Nothing but seeing it with your own eyes can give you any conception of its magnitude." The Main Building was an astonishing twenty-one and a half acres in area, larger than the entire famed

1851 Crystal Palace Exhibition in London. Thirty foreign countries sent exhibits, and foreign leaders attended including the Emperor of Brazil.

The main purpose, however, was to trumpet American progress. President Grant noted that after a hundred years of struggle to build a new nation, "we have yet done what this exhibition will show in rivaling older and more advanced nations in law, medicine and theology, in science, literature and the fine arts." The most popular exhibit, however, was Machinery Hall and the giant, 1,500 horsepower Corliss engine that provided the power for all the machines in the hall. The renowned writer, William Dean Howells, waxed eloquent about the mighty engine. It rose "loftily in the center of the huge structure, an athlete of steel and iron with not a superfluous ounce of metal on it; the mighty walking-beams plunge their pistons downward, the enormous fly-wheel revolves with a hoarded power that makes all tremble, the hundred life-like details do their office with unerring intelligence." Another impressive display in the Machinery Hall was the wallpaper printing press, which lowered production costs and enabled ordinary Americans to afford fancy wallpaper. It was one of many devices that were changing the lives of Americans of that era.

There were many other exhibits, as well. The Art Building, designed "in the modern Renaissance style," included art from throughout the world. It was intended to become a permanent art museum and is today the Philadelphia Museum of Fine Arts. The Agriculture Hall demonstrated impressive advances in farming. A grapevine, covering 12,000 square feet, had been moved from Santa Barbara, California to the Exhibition. American women contributed $30,000 to build their own pavilion that included displays of such laborsaving devices as a dishwashing machine and a machine for washing blankets. Close to the Women's Pavilion there was a little cottage demonstrating, "actual methods of education in use in the infant school system of Froebel, termed the 'Kindergarten,'" an idea he had developed in Germany. A hundred different carriages for public transportation were on display. A railroad took awed spectators for a tour of the grounds for a five-cent fare.

At a time of economic depression and political division, the Exhibition was a definite shot in the arm to the American people. Dark shadows or controversial issues were never mentioned. Americans could feel good about the nation's progress and potential. The Chicago **Tribune** *enthusiastically summed up its importance to people in 1876, "Come at all events, if you have to live six months on bread and water to make up for the expense."*

The Corliss engine was the most popular exhibit at the Great Centennial Exhibition of 1876. The engine provided the power to operate all of the machinery in Machinery Hall.

THE NEW SOUTH

The nation recovered from the depression after 1878. In the 1880s the American economy leaped forward at an astonishing pace. The South shared the buoyant mood that swept the country in the 1880s. The collapse of the last few Radical governments led to the domination of southern politics by a new class of men. These included merchants, bankers, railroad promoters, and even some industrialists. They allied with the old planter class, which, despite a decline of its prewar power, retained considerable influence in rural areas. They called themselves Redeemers, claiming that they had "redeemed" the South from corrupt and extravagant carpetbag rule. They proclaimed the beginning of a "New South" devoted to economic modernization and frugal government. They promised to relieve the North of a burden most Northerners did not want: the burden of Reconstruction and the establishment of equal rights for blacks.

Henry Grady, editor of the *Atlanta Constitution*, was the foremost exponent of the expansive New South ideology. He announced that there would be a new stress on the "gospel of work as the South's great need." He assured Northerners that the South had learned its lesson in its defeat and was now willing to embrace northern economic and social standards. In his famous 1886 speech, he promised that the New South understood "that her emancipation came because through the inscrutable wisdom of God her honest purpose was crossed, and her brave armies beaten." Southerners, he declared, were now glad that, "the American Union was saved from the wreck of war."

Booker T. Washington emerged as an African-American exponent of the New South. Washington, who had been born a slave, had worked his way up from poverty after being educated at Virginia's Hampton Institute. He hoped that other blacks would follow in his footsteps in seeking self-improvement. A young man during Reconstruction, he believed its policies had been mistaken. They were based on using the "ignorance of my race" to "punish the Southern white man by forcing the Negro into positions over the heads of the Southern whites." This "agitation" distracted the attention of black people "away from the more fundamental matters of perfecting themselves in the industries at their doors and in securing property."

In a famous 1895 speech at the Cotton States Exposition, Washington outlined his "Atlanta Compromise." Blacks would give up agitation for their rights and would concentrate on hard work to make them economically indispensable to whites. This economic importance would eventually lead to white acceptance. His New South institution, Tuskegee in Alabama, emphasized industrial education and improved agricultural methods as the path for black students. George Washington Carver did his pioneer research on the uses of the peanut at Tuskegee. By 1896, however, Washington's views were starting to be challenged by W. E. B.

Du Bois, who was a child of eight at the end of Reconstruction. DuBois contended that blacks should fight for complete social and political equality, an ideal that had been abandoned with the end of Reconstruction in 1876.

Despite the widespread publicity given to the ideas of New Southerners, the problem with the image they sought to build was that much of it was not accurate. Far from admitting that the Confederate cause had been wrong, most Southerners believed it had always been right. They were defenders of the "Lost Cause," including even slavery. Every Confederate Memorial Day, they paraded the red Confederate battle flag down the streets of small and large towns. (Even today, that flag remains a source of confrontation between white and black Southerners.)

A more important difficulty with the New South conception was the continuing backwardness of the southern economic and social system. The new state governments set out to reduce government spending and property taxes. In doing so, they retreated from Reconstruction commitments to a state that had responsibilities for the welfare of its citizens. Florida abandoned a nearly completed college, leaving the state without any institution of higher learning. Alabama closed public hospitals. Public schools were the principal victims of the cutbacks. Louisiana spent so little on its system that the percentage of literate whites actually declined between 1880 and 1900. Above all, black schools, so laboriously built and maintained, were hit the hardest as the gap between spending for black and white schools invariably widened.

Agriculture in the New South

This backwardness was nowhere more apparent than in agriculture. Broad new vagrancy laws reinforced planters' control over their labor force. These permitted the arrest of any unemployed person and made it a crime to leave a job before the expiration of a contract. Criminal laws increased the penalty for even the pettiest offense. The convict lease system expanded to permit the hiring out of most prisoners. Mines, railroads, lumber companies, and planters vied for these new forced laborers, most of whom were blacks convicted of minor transgressions.

Other laws gave planters control of property and credit, including precedence to their claims for their share of the crops. Even during Reconstruction, sharecropping had perpetuated black economic dependence upon whites. As the system evolved, the sharecropper had to borrow against future crops to pay his debts to the landowner and supply merchant. Inevitably, he became enmeshed in a web of debt from which escape was virtually impossible. The continued reliance on cotton led inescapably to over-production and declining prices, compounding the misery. The sharecropping system and its labor control worked against any efforts to mechanize southern agriculture. Most small white farmers succumbed

A white farm manager weighs the cotton picked by the black sharecroppers. The profits were split by the landowner and the sharecroppers with the landowner getting the lion's share.

to the same economic forces. In the Deep South, per capita income remained unchanged even in the great era of economic growth in America, 1880 to 1900.

Industry in the New South

Many New South crusaders concentrated on a campaign to develop industry. They achieved some success in the expansion of southern textile mills. The new fad of cigarette smoking led to the growth of the tobacco industry. Railroad construction continued at a rapid pace. Southern lines were integrated into the national railroad network under the control of northern capitalists. Despite these advances in industrialization, fueled by promises of low taxes, special concessions, and a docile labor force, the South remained overwhelmingly agricultural. In fact, even by 1900, the New South accounted for a smaller percentage of the nation's industry than the Old South had in 1860. (Industrialization had proceeded at a far more rapid pace in the North.)

While the new upper class continued to prosper, most Southerners, white and black, fell into even deeper poverty. Publicists touted the cotton mills as the salvation of poor whites. But when the poor white farmers gave up their struggle with the land and went to work in the mills, they replaced one life of destitution with another. Men earned wages of about 50 cents a day, and women and children supplemented family income at even lower wages. Companies controlled all aspects of life in company towns and the poor white worker found that, "I owe my soul to the company store." These mill villages did remain all-white and consciousness of racial superiority grew in importance as the century ended.

The Rise of Jim Crow

Illiteracy, lack of adequate nutrition and housing, and a system of social, economic, and political injustice trapped blacks in the "brave" New South. The disillusionment with the end of Reconstruction led more than fifty thousand blacks to seek opportunities in Kansas. These "Exodusters" represented only a small percentage of those who would have migrated if opportunities in the North were not still closed to them. Over 90 percent of black Americans in 1900 continued to live in the South.

Despite the end of Reconstruction in 1877 and the continuing intimidation and violence, black voting had not been entirely eliminated in the South. With their economic clout, the conservative upper classes felt that they could effectively manage the black vote. In the late 1880s and early 1890s, however, the growing agricultural unrest led to the formation of the Populist movement. For a while, it seemed that oppressed white and black farmers might get together and challenge conservative rule in the South. The Democratic leadership responded by reviving racist propaganda and returning to warnings about "Negro domination" and "revival of black Reconstruction" to discredit the Populists. The Democrats were successful in maintaining their power and reinforcing a one-party South. A major component of their efforts was the disfranchisement of black voters. Between 1890 and 1910 every southern state imposed poll taxes, literacy requirements, and property qualifications for voting. Four states even instituted a "grandfather" clause that allowed men to vote only if their ancestors had voted before 1867 (before blacks had been granted the vote). The Supreme Court eventually overturned this obvious violation of the Fifteenth Amendment, but not until 1915. These measures succeeded in an almost total elimination of black voting in the South. As late as 1896, 130,000 blacks continued to vote in Louisiana. By 1904, only 1,342 were still able to do so. Although there were loopholes to permit whites to vote, poll taxes and property qualifications did reduce the number of poor illiterate white voters as well.

Southern customs had long separated the races, but in the 1890s a series of Jim Crow laws made segregation into a rigid system. The term *Jim Crow* came from old blackface minstrel shows. It had come to mean a code for racial segregation in schools, industry, transportation, and all areas of public accommodation.

Under the leadership of Booker T. Washington, Tuskegee Institute became one of the country's leading black educational institutions. Ida B. Wells is perhaps best remembered for her antilynching crusade.

In 1896, the Supreme Court in *Plessy v. Ferguson* ruled that state-mandated separate railroad cars for blacks did not violate equal protection guaranteed by the Fourteenth Amendment if the separate facilities were equal. In an impassioned dissent, Justice John Harlan, a Southerner himself, declared, "The Constitution is colorblind." Later decisions, however, extended this "separate but equal" doctrine to other public facilities, particularly schools. Of course, accommodations were never really equal, and Jim Crow became central to the southern way of life.

There was also a dramatic increase in white violence in the 1890s, designed to keep blacks more firmly "in their place." The decade averaged 187 lynchings each year. The overwhelming majority of the victims were black. Some were well-planned public events, attracting large audiences and family outings. Some victims were accused of crimes, but the "crime" of many of the victims was "uppityness." Others supposedly made sexual advances to white women. The fear that white women might be attracted to black sexuality, encouraged as a strategy to terrify whites, was one of the underpinnings of rigid segregation. The lack of protection for African Americans in the South made Booker T. Washington's ideas of racial cooperation more popular. Other blacks, however, favored a more militant approach. In 1892, Ida B. Wells, a crusading black journalist in Memphis, launched an international antilynching movement. When she investigated the charges of "rape," she found virtually all of them untrue.

Segregation, combined with sharecropping and debt tenancy, stifled the ingenuity and economic potential of a large percentage of the southern population.

The South succeeded in marginalizing itself in the name of white domination. The New South, thus, had very little meaning for most Southerners—white or black. For African Americans, it meant the end of the dream that Reconstruction had encouraged. A black politician, ending his nine-year congressional career, conceded the extravagance of the earlier Reconstruction governments. But, he asked, "can the saving of a few thousand or a few hundred thousands of dollars compensate for the loss of the political heritage of American citizens?"

Albion Tourgee, a Union army veteran, went South after the Civil War, determined to be of service to the newly emancipated slave, as well as fulfilling his own ambitions. By 1876 he had been a Superior Court judge in North Carolina, fought the Ku Klux Klan, and overcame numerous threats on his life. Bitterly disillusioned with the abandonment of Reconstruction, he returned North and wrote the novel, *A Fool's Errand,* published in 1879. It became an enormous best seller. In the novel, Tourgee portrayed himself as the Fool who had believed the promises of Reconstruction and mocked the vanity of his own liberal expectations. By 1876, he believed that Americans were so preoccupied with economic progress that they abandoned all pretext of morality. Once blacks had been given the right to vote, "The conscience of the nation was satisfied, and it highly resolved that thereafter it would have peace, that the Negro *could* have no further ground of complaint....So it stopped its ears, and, when the south wind brought the burden of woe, it shook its head blankly, and said, 'I hear nothing, nothing! All is peace.'"

DOCUMENTS

THE SPLIT BETWEEN ADVOCATES OF WOMEN'S RIGHTS AND BLACK RIGHTS

The close alliance between women reformers and abolitionists was seriously tested by the dispute over universal suffrage. The women expected to see the right to vote extended to women, as well as blacks. Many advocates of rights for the freed people, however, argued that it was "the Negro's hour, not the woman's."

A petition drafted after the Civil War by ELIZABETH CADY STANTON and SUSAN B. ANTHONY, leaders of the women's movement and also abolitionists:

To the Senate and House of Representatives in Congress Assembled:
The undersigned citizens of the State of ______ earnestly but respectfully request that in any change or amendment of the Constitution you may propose to extend or regulate Suffrage, there shall be no distinction made between men and women.

Letter to Susan B. Anthony from abolitionist and advocate of suffrage for ex-slaves GERRITT SMITH, December 30, 1868

My Dear Susan B. Anthony: I this evening received your earnest letter. It pains me to be obliged to disappoint you. But I cannot sign the petition you sent me. Cheerfully, gladly can I sign a petition for the enfranchisement of women. But I cannot sign a paper against the enfranchisement of the Negro man, unless at the same time woman shall be enfranchised. The removal of the political disabilities of race is my first desire, of sex my second. If put on the same level and urged in the same connection, neither will be soon accomplished. The former will very soon be, if untrammeled by the other, and its success will prepare the way for the other.

A Response by Elizabeth Cady Stanton

[Gerritt Smith] does not clearly read the sign of the times, or he would see that there is to be no reconstruction of this nation, except on the basis of Universal Suffrage, as the natural, inalienable right of every citizen to its exercise....

As the aristocracy of this country is the "male sex" and as Mr. Smith belongs to the privileged order, he naturally considers it important, for the best interests of the nation, that every type and shade of degraded, ignorant manhood should be enfranchised, before even the higher classes of womanhood should be admitted to the polls.

This does not surprise us. Men always judge more wisely of objective wrongs and oppressions, than of those in which they themselves are involved. Tyranny on a southern plantation is far more easily seen by white men... [in] the north than the wrongs of the women of their own households....

Again, Mr. Smith refuses to sign the petition because he thinks that to press the broader question of "Universal Suffrage" would defeat the partial one of "Manhood Suffrage"; in other words to demand protection for women against her oppressors would jeopardize the black man's chances for securing protection against his oppressors. If it is a question of precedence merely, on what principle of justice or courtesy should woman yield her right of enfranchisement to the Negro? If men cannot be trusted to legislate for their own sex, how can they legislate for the opposite sex, of whose wants and needs they know nothing! It has always been considered good philosophy in pressing any measure to claim the uttermost in order to get something.... Henry Ward Beecher advised abolitionists, right after the war, to demand "Universal Suffrage" if they wished to secure the ballot for the new made freedmen. "Bait your hooks," said he, "with a woman and perhaps you will catch a Negro." But their intense interest in the Negro blinded them, and they forsook principle for policy. In giving woman the cold shoulder they raised a more deadly opposition to the Negro than any we had encountered, creating an antagonism between him and the very element most needed, especially in the South, to be propitiated in his behalf...

...There is no other ground on which to debate the question. Every argument for the Negro is an argument for woman and no logician can escape it....

Although those who demand "Women's Suffrage" on principle are few, those who would oppose "Negro suffrage" from prejudice are many, hence the only way to secure the latter is to end all this talk of class legislation, bury the Negro in the citizen, and claim suffrage for all men and women as a natural, inalienable right.

- ELIZABETH CADY STANTON, January 14, 1869

"Being Persons, Then, Women are Citizens"

Though the words persons, people, inhabitants, electors, citizens, are all used indiscriminately in the national and State constitutions, there was always a conflict of opinion, prior to the war, as to whether they were synonymous terms, but whatever room there was for doubts, under the old regime, the adoption of the Fourteenth Amendment settled that question forever in its first sentence:

All persons born or naturalized in the United States, and subject to the jurisdiction thereof, are citizens of the United States wherein they reside.

The second settles the equal status of all citizens:

No state shall make or enforce any law which shall abridge the privileges or immunities of citizens of the United States; nor shall any State deprive any person of life, liberty, or property without due process of law; nor deny to any person within its jurisdiction the equal protection of the laws.

The only question left to be settled now is: Are women persons? I scarcely believe that any of our opponents will have the hardihood to say that they are not. Being persons, then, women are citizens and no State has a right to make any new law, or to enforce any old law, which shall abridge their privileges and immunities. Hence, every discrimination against women in the constitutions and laws of the several States is today null and void, precisely as is every one against Negroes.

- SUSAN B. ANTHONY, November 1872

1. Why wouldn't Gerritt Smith sign the petition? Why did he want to separate the issues of women and blacks getting the vote?
2. How does Elizabeth Cady Stanton respond to his argument? What aspect of her response do you find most troubling?
3. What is the basis of Susan B. Anthony's claim that the Fourteenth Amendment also guaranteed women's rights?
4. Why did the women's movement split with their former abolitionist allies?

DIFFERING VIEWS ABOUT BLACKS IN RECONSTRUCTION IN THE SOUTH

Most white Southerners saw the Reconstruction era as a time period in which blacks, drunk with new-found power, lorded it over the oppressed white population. The reality, of course, was far different. Blacks never had real power in any state and were very moderate in their demands and votes. Albion Tourgee was a Northerner who served as a judge in the South, propelled by idealism. He was eventually disillusioned by the level of resistance to rights for freed people he found among southern whites. Thomas Dixon's best-selling novel, ***The Clansman****, reflected the attitudes of southern whites. (It later became the basis for the popular movie,* ***Birth of a Nation****, which was instrumental in disseminating negative images of blacks). The final document in this segment relates the experiences of a black man who gained some measure of authority during Reconstruction.*

From the Novel, *A Fool's Errand*
By the "carpetbagger," Albion Tourgee (1879)

When the second Christmas come, Metta wrote again to her sister:

"The feeling is terribly bitter against Comfort on account of his course towards the colored people. There is quite a village of them on the lower end of the plantation. They have a church, a sabbath school, and are to have next year a school. You can not imagine how kind they have been to us, and how much they are attached to Comfort.... I got Comfort to go with me to one of their prayer meetings a few nights ago. I had heard a great deal about them, but had never attended one before. It was strangely weird. There were, perhaps, fifty present, mostly middle-aged men and women. They were singing in a soft, low monotone, interspersed with prolonged exclamatory notes, a sort of rude hymn, which I was surprised to know was one of their old songs in slave times. How the chorus came to be endured in those days I can not imagine. It was—

'Free! free! free, my Lord, free!
An' we walks de hebben-ly way!'

"A few looked around as we came in and seated ourselves; and Uncle Jerry, the saint of the settlement, came forward on his staves, and said, in his soft voice, "'Ev'nin', Kunnel! Sarvant, Missus! Will you walk up, an' hev seats in front?'

'We told him we had just looked in, and might go in a short time; so we would stay in the back part of the audience.

"Uncle Jerry can not read nor write; but he is a man of strange intelligence and power. Unable to do work of any account, he is the faithful friend, monitor, and director of others. He has a house and piece of land, all paid for, a good horse and cow, and, with the aid of his wife and two boys, made a fine crop this season. He is one of the most promising colored men in the settlement: so Comfort says, at least. Everybody seems to have great respect for his character. I don't know how many people I have heard speak of his religion. Mr. Savage used to say he had rather hear him pray than any other man on earth. He was much prized by his master, even after he was disabled, on account of his faithfulness and character."

From the Novel, *The Clansman*
By Thomas Dixon Jr. (1905)

At noon Ben and Phil strolled to the polling-place to watch the progress of the first election under Negro rule. The Square was jammed with shouting, jostling, perspiring negroes, men, women, and children. The day was warm, and the African odour was supreme even in the open air....

The negroes, under the drill of the League and the Freedman's Bureau, protected by the bayonet, were voting to enfranchise themselves, disfranchise their former masters, ratify a new constitution, and elect a legislature to do their will. Old Aleck was a candidate for the House, chief poll-holder, and seemed to be in charge of the movements of the voters outside the booth as well as inside. He appeared to be omnipresent, and his self-importance was a sight Phil had never dreamed. He could not keep his eyes off him....

[Aleck] was a born African orator, undoubtedly descended from a long line of savage spell-binders, whose eloquence in the palaver houses of the jungle had made them native leaders. His thin spindle-shanks supported an oblong, protruding stomach, resembling an elderly monkey's, which seemed so heavy it swayed his back to carry it.

The animal vivacity of his small eyes and the flexibility of his eye-brows, which he worked up and down rapidly with every change of countenance, expressed his eager desires.

He had laid aside his new shoes, which hurt him, and went barefooted to facilitate his movements on the great occasion. His heels projected and his foot was so flat that what should have been the hollow of it made a hole in the dirt where he left his track.

He was already mellow with liquor, and was dressed in an old army uniform and cap, with two horse-pistols buckled around his waist. On a strap hanging from his shoulder were strung a half-dozen tin canteens filled with whiskey.

From—*The Autobiography of JOHN ROY LYNCH,* an ex-slave appointed justice-of-the peace in Natchez, Mississippi at age 22 (he later was elected a three-term congressman).

[A] case of some significance that came before me was that of a white man that I knew unfavorably and well. He had cursed, abused, and threatened the life of an inoffensive old colored man on account of a misunderstanding over a small business transaction. Upon the complaint of the colored man, a warrant was issued for the arrest of the party against whom the complaint was made. When he was brought before the court and the charges had been read to him and he was asked whether or not he was guilty as charged, he seemed to be somewhat surprised. "Why," he remarked, "do you mean to tell me that it is a crime for a white man to curse a nigger?" "Yes," the court replied. "It is a crime for a white man to curse a Negro as it is for a Negro to curse a white man." "Well," he exclaimed, "that's news to me. You certainly must be mistaken. If there is such a law, I never heard of it." The court then handed him the code and told him where he could find the section bearing upon the point at issue and requested him to read it for himself, which he did.

When he had finished, he exclaimed in a somewhat subdued tone: "Well, I'll be damned." The court then admonished him that if that remark should be repeated, he would be committed to the county jail for contempt of court. He quickly apologized and assured the court that no disrespect was intended. He said that he could not deny having used the language set forth in the affidavit, but he hoped the court would not be severe because he did not know and did not believe that in using that language he was violating any law. Since it was his first offense, he was let off with a fine of five dollars and costs which he promptly paid. It was the first and only time he was brought before me.

1. What are the differences in the ways Tourgee and Dixon see freed people and their conduct? Why do you think there are such great differences in their points of view?
2. Whose description do you feel is most accurate? Why?
3. Why do you think John Lynch considers his case to be "of some significance"? Do you agree or disagree?
4. What does his experience tell you about changes in the South during the era of Reconstruction?

RETREAT FROM RECONSTRUCTION

Eventually, Americans grew weary with the struggle to maintain the rights of black people. The Civil Rights Act of 1875 was the last attempt to guarantee such rights. Northern white commitment faded as other issues, such as economic depression and political scandals, drew their attention. Southern white violence, directed at white and black Republicans and any blacks asserting their rights, was carried out by groups such as the Ku Klux Klan. Democratic opponents of Reconstruction returned to political control of the South.

An excerpt from the speech of black Congressman Richard Harvey Cain of South Carolina on the floor of the House in support of the Civil Rights Act of 1875.

All we ask is that you, the legislators of this nation, shall pass a law so strong and so powerful that no one shall be able to elude it and destroy our rights under the Constitution and laws of our country. That is all we ask....

We do not want any discriminations to be made. If discriminations arc made in regard to schools, then there will be accomplished just what we are fighting against. If you say that the schools in the State of Georgia, for instance, shall be allowed to discriminate against colored people, then you will have discriminations made against us. We do not want any discriminations. I do not ask any legislation for the colored people of this country that is not applied to the white people. All that we ask is equal laws, equal legislation, and equal rights throughout the length and the breadth of this land.

[Another congressman] says that the colored men should not come here begging at the doors of Congress for their rights. I agree with him. I want to say that we do not come here begging for our rights. We come here clothed in the garb of American citizenship. We come demanding our rights in the name of justice. We come, with no arrogance on our part, asking that this great nation, which laid the foundations of civilization and progress more deeply and more securely than any other nation on the face of the earth, guarantee us protection from outrage. We come here, five millions of people—more than composed this entire nation when it had its great tea-party in Boston Harbor, and demanded its rights at the point of a bayonet—asking that unjust discriminations against us be forbidden. We come here in the name of justice, equity, and law, in the name of our children, in the name of our country, petitioning for our rights.

Congressional Record, 43rd Cong., 1st session, Vol.II, pt. 1

POLITICAL TERRORISM BY THE KU KLUX KLAN

Testimony by Harriet Hernandez

The following account by Harriet Hernandez, a former slave of Spartanburg, South Carolina, describes how the Klan used threats and violence to intimidate black Republican voters in the region. It is excerpted from her testimony in December 1871 before a congressional committee appointed to investigate Klan activities.

Question: Did the Ku-Klux: ever come to your house at any time?
Answer: Yes, Sir; twice.
Q.: Go on to the second time....
A.: They came in; I was lying in bed. Says he, "Come out here, Sir; Come out here, Sir!" They took me out of bed; they would not let me get out, but they took me up in their arms and toted me out—me and my daughter Lucy. He struck me on the forehead with a pistol, and here is the scar above my eye now. Says he, "Damn you, fall!" I fell. Says he, "Damn you, get up!" I got up. Says he, "Damn you, get over this fence!" And he kicked me over when I went to get over; and then he went to a brush pile, and they laid us right down there, both together. They laid us down twenty yards apart, I reckon. They had dragged and beat us

along. They struck me right on the top of my head, and I thought they had killed me; and I said, "Lord o' mercy, don't, don't kill my child!" He gave me a lick on the head, and it liked to have killed me; I saw stars. He threw my arm over my head so I could not do anything with it for three weeks, and there are great knots on my wrist now.

Q: What did they say this was for?

A: They said, "You can tell your husband that when we see him we are going to kill him."

Q: Did they say why they wanted to kill him?

A: They said, "He voted the radical ticket, didn't he?" I said, "Yes, that very way."

Q: When did your husband get back after this whipping? He was not at home, was he?

A: He was lying out; he couldn't stay at home, bless your soul.

Q: Has he been afraid for any length of time?

A: He has been afraid ever since last October. He has been lying out. He has not laid in the house ten nights since October.

Q: Is that the situation of the colored people down there to any extent?

A: That is the way they all have to do—men and women both.

Q: What are they afraid of?

A: Of being killed or whipped to death.

Q: What has made them afraid?

A: Because men that voted radical tickets they took the spite out on the women when they could get at them.

Q: How many colored people have been whipped in that neighborhood?

A: It is all of them, mighty near.

Report of the Joint Select Committee to Inquire into the Condition of Affairs in the Late Insurrectionary States (1872).

Excerpts from the original draft of the South Carolina 1876 Democratic Party campaign plan formulated by ex-Confederate general MARTIN W. GARY

[It is decreed] That the Democratic Military Clubs are to be armed with rifles and pistols and such other arms as they may command. They are to be divided into two companies, one of the old men, the other of the young; an experienced captain or commander to be placed over each of them. That each company is to have a first and second lieutenant. That the number of ten privates is to be the unit of organization. That each captain is to see that his men are well armed and provided with at least thirty rounds of ammunition. That the Captain of the young men is to provide a Baggage wagon in which three days rations for the horses and three days rations for the men are to be stored on the day before the election in order that they may be prepared at a moment's notice to move to any point in the County when ordered by the Chairman of the Executive Committee....

Every Democrat must feel honor bound to control the vote of at least one Negro, by intimidation, purchase, keeping him away or as each individual may determine, how he may best accomplish it....

Never threaten a man individually. If he deserves to be threatened, the necessities of the times require that he should die. A dead Radical is very harmless—a threatened Radical or one driven off by threats from the scene of his operations is often very troublesome, sometimes dangerous, always vindictive....

In the month of September, we ought to begin to organize Negro [Democratic] clubs, or pretend that we have organized them.... Those who join are to be taken on probation and are not to be taken into full fellowship until they have proven their sincerity by voting our ticket.

1. What is the basis for Congressman Cain's pleas for the passage of the Civil Rights Act of 1875?
2. What was the purpose of Klan threats and violence as shown by Harriet Hernandez's testimony? What do you think would be the result of such tactics?
3. What were the key elements of South Carolina Democratic Party's 1876 election plan? In what way did it intend to "control the vote" of freedmen? Why do you think the plan included an organization of "Negro Democratic" clubs?

CONCLUSION

THE IMPACT OF THE CIVIL WAR AND RECONSTRUCTION

Long after the Civil War was over, survivors were still haunted by the terrible and bloody conflict. "The generation that carried on the war has been set apart by its experience," Oliver Wendell Holmes, future Supreme Court justice and wounded war veteran, remarked in 1884. "It was given to us to learn at the outset that life is a profound and passionate thing." It had, indeed, been a war that divided families, as well as states. During the war, both sides sang "Battle Cry of Freedom" to the same music with very different words, since the South believed its own freedom rested on enslaving blacks. Both sides concluded that waging a remorseless war was the only way to achieve a just peace.

The impact of the war could be seen in the flood of memoirs, popular works, and scholarly histories that have continued to pour forth to the present. One hundred years later "The Battle Hymn of the Republic" inspired the civil rights movement, while "Dixie" and the Confederate flag remained potent symbols of southern opposition. (Even today, the Confederate flag retains its power as an emblem to many white and black Southerners.) The human cost was one reason for the war's strong impression on Americans. Almost 620,000 soldiers lost their lives (360,000 Union and 260,000 Confederate), more than in all other American wars combined until Vietnam. Another half million were wounded, many losing arms or legs. But the fascination with the Civil War stems even more from the pathos of inner conflict: a war, in the words of one historian "not only within the society or polity but often within the human heart."

There were also enormous financial and economic costs. It has been estimated that the total cost of the war was greater than $20 billion, a figure five times the total expenditures of the federal government from its beginning to 1861. As late as the 1880s, interest on the war debt took up 40 percent of the federal budget and Union soldiers' pensions accounted for another 20 percent. The destruction of the infrastructure of the South and its plantation and slave-based economy had a permanent impact upon the economic future of the South until well into the twentieth century.

The war also had a significant impact on the lives of women. Upper-class women, who had been active as volunteers during the conflict, responded to appeals to broaden "the women's sphere." Many became leaders of postwar charity and reform organizations. The war's casualties, over a million dead or wounded, created a generation of widows, spinsters, and wives whose husbands were disabled, all of whom desperately needed a source of income beyond an insubstantial widow's pension. So many attempted to support themselves as seamstresses that wages suffered a precipitous decline. The situation was even worse in the South where a larger proportion of men had died. Middle-class women found jobs as teachers, despite minimal qualifications, as the public school systems expanded. Factories employed large numbers of working-class women. Many of the 1.9 million newly freed slave women also poured into the labor force. The push for human equality in the aftermath of the war helped to inspire some female leaders to also push for the equality of women.

The Civil War was decisive in determining the nature of American nationality. Before the war, people said, "the United States are..." After, and in the future, they said, "the United States is..." The federal government was strengthened at the expense of the states. Before the war, the only federal agency that touched the lives of ordinary Americans was the post office. During the war, the federal government levied direct taxes and created a national banking system that issued standardized and reliable paper money. It provided free land to encourage settlement of the West, built a transcontinental railroad, and established large state universities. The United States government not only confiscated property and freed the slaves of southern citizens, it even set up the Freedmen's Bureau, a social welfare agency to take care of the freed people. Early amendments to the Constitution had limited the federal government's powers, but the Thirteenth Amendment began a precedent for amendments that expanded national powers and restricted those of the states. The victory of the "modernizing" North also meant that the nation as a whole would now accept the northern ideology of inevitable and continuous progress.

The Confederate Flag in the Year 2000

The continuing potency of the symbols of the Civil War can be seen in the conflict over the flying of the Confederate flag over the statehouse in Charleston, South Carolina. At the height of the civil rights struggles of the 1960s, many Southerners expressed their undying opposition to rights for blacks by defiantly flying the Confederate flag. Some states eventually lowered the flag, but it continued to flutter over South Carolina's capital. The issue arose again in the 1990s and 2000. Blacks and white supporters charged that the flag was the symbol of oppression, treason, slavery, and racism. Many white South Carolinians responded that the flag was an emblem of southern heritage, honor, and military courage. Led by the NAACP, many organizations agreed to boycott Charleston, refusing to hold meetings or conferences in that tourist-oriented city. The mayor of Charleston implored the state to take down the flag. The governor supported a compromise: the flag would be removed from atop the statehouse and placed over a Confederate memorial on the grounds of the capital. Defiant whites felt betrayed. Blacks maintained that the continuing presence of the flag on any official site in Charleston was a constant reminder that the South had failed to come to terms with the evils of slavery.

As the Civil War and Reconstruction faded from view, a romantic haze suffused the era. People clung to their haunting memories. In small towns throughout the North the Decoration Day (now Memorial Day) parade became an established ritual. The men, steadily growing older, marched down main streets with flags flying and bands playing. Orators rambled on about deeds of valor and loyalty to American ideals. The same ceremonies took place in the South, although on a different date. Organizations staged grand reunions of the "Blue and the Gray." Popular books and plays were devoted to reconciliation (particularly through romances between southern women and northern men). Black abolitionist Frederick Douglass struggled unsuccessfully to oppose remembering "with equal admiration...those who fought for slavery and those who fought for liberty and justice." Racism even reached the Grand Army of the Republic, which segregated its posts and forced black veterans to march behind whites in Memorial Day parades.

In the early twentieth century, historians, led by William Dunning of Columbia University, rewrote the history of Reconstruction. They believed that blacks were "children," incapable of understanding the freedom that Northerners unwisely thrust upon them. One bestseller even argued that, under Reconstruction, southern whites "literally were put to the torture" by "emissaries of hate" who inspired "lustful assaults" by blacks against white women. The black community understood a different version of Reconstruction. As one 88-year old former slave told an interviewer in the 1930s, "I know folks think books tell the truth, but they shore don't."

Reconstruction certainly succeeded in bringing the nation along a relatively peaceful path after the ending of the worst war in American history. The victorious and outraged North did not turn on the helpless South in an orgy of revenge through executions or confiscation of property. Except in songs and books, the defeated South did not inaugurate a period of guerrilla warfare. Perhaps most surprisingly, newly freed blacks did not seek revenge against their former masters. They never even attempted to seize the plantations.

In view of the pervasive racism of America of this era, it is less surprising that the constitutional amendments, the Freedmen's Bureau and the civil rights laws did not bring about permanent change, than that they were passed in the first place. In view of deeply held ideas about property rights, limited government, and black inferiority, the failure of Reconstruction seems almost inevitable. W.E.B. Du Bois commented, "The slave went free; stood a brief moment in the sun; then moved back again toward slavery."

Race in America 2000

*A poll, taken by the **New York Times** in July 2000, revealed the enduring racial divide in America. Although the majority of Americans, white and black, maintained that race relations in the United States were generally good and that real progress had been made in lessening racial discrimination, their perceptions of racial realities made it seem like whites and blacks were "living on different planets." While 51 percent of blacks believed that too little had been made of problems facing black people, 75 percent of whites thought there was too much or just the right amount of attention given to those issues. Although 58 percent of whites felt that blacks and whites had "about an equal chance of getting ahead," 57 percent of blacks maintained that whites had a better chance of succeeding. Blacks were four times more likely than whites to say that blacks were treated less fairly in the workplace, shops, restaurants, and places of entertainment. A substantial proportion of both races thought that many or most white people disliked blacks and many or almost all black people disliked whites. The poll also made it clear that, even in the modern world, most Americans do not live, work or worship with those of other races. Two-thirds of blacks said that improving race relations was one of the most important challenges facing the country, while only one-fourth of whites agreed.*

The failure of the Reconstruction experiment in equal rights was a tragedy for blacks and for the whole nation. The issue of race remained a sore on the nation's body for years to come. Nevertheless, the amendments and civil rights laws passed during Reconstruction became the basis of a renewed and more effective struggle for equal rights almost a hundred years later, a struggle that continues to this day.

In evaluating the impact of the war and its aftermath in Reconstruction, one might reluctantly agree with historian Bertram Wyatt-Brown. " The Civil War was indeed a tragic, moral failure in many respects," he conceded, "but beyond that it was the only way for blacks to make that enormous leap from slavery to a kind of free peasantry, meager though that step toward restricted liberty appears in retrospect." In human history, he explained, it has always been difficult and painful for "any subject class or race to travel toward equality with former masters. In this grim context, the Union dead did not die in vain, though they left the larger task of racial democracy to future, thankfully less harried generations."

BIBLIOGRAPHY

PART I—ANTEBELLUM AMERICA

Life in the North and West

Melvin Adelman, *A Sporting Time: New York City and the Rise of Modern Athletics, 1820-1870* (1986).

Janet Farrell Brodie, *Contraception and Abortion in Nineteenth Century America* (1994).

Victoria Bynum, *Unruly Women* (1992).

Hasia Diner, *Erin's Daughters in America: Irish Immigrant Women in the Nineteenth Century* (1983).

Timothy Gilfoyle, *City of Eros: New York City, Prostitution and the Commercialization of Sex, 1790-1920* (1992).

Joan Hoff, *Law, Gender, and Injustice: A Legal History of U.S, Women* (1991).

Julie Roy Jeffrey, *Frontier Women: The Trans-Mississippi West 1840-1880* (1979).

Alice Kessler-Harris, *Out to Work: A History of Wage-Earning Women in the United States* (1982).

Leon Litwack, *North of Slavery: The Negro in the Free States, 1790-1860* (1961).

Louise Mayo, *the Ambivalent Image: Nineteenth Century America's Perception of the Jew* (1987).

Lillian Schissel, *Women's Diaries of the Westward Journey* (1982).
Carol Smith-Rosenberg, *Disorderly Conduct: Visions of Gender in Victorian America* (1986).
Christine Stansell, *City of Women: Sex and Class in New York, 1789-1860* (1986).
Stephen Thernstrom, *Poverty and Progress: Social Mobility in a Nineteenth Century City* (1964).
John Unruh Jr., *The Overland Emigrants and the Trans-Mississippi West, 1840-1860* (1979).

Life in the South

Ira Berlin, *Slaves Without Masters: The Free Negro in the Antebellum South* (1974).
Catherine Clinton, *The Plantation Mistress* (1982).
Paul Escott, *Slavery Remembered: A Record of Twentieth Century Slave Narratives* (1979).
Jennifer Fleischner, *Mastering Slavery: Memory, Family and Identity in Women's Slave Narratives* (1996).
John Hope Franklin & Loren Schweninger, *Runaway Slaves: Rebels on the Plantation* (1999).
Herbert Gutman, *The Black Family in Slavery and Freedom, 1750-1925* (1976).
Jacqueline Jones, *Labor of Love, Labor of Service* (1985).
Lawrence Levine, *Black Culture and Black Consciousness* (1977).
Patricia Morton, ed., *Discovering the Women in Slavery* (1995).
Ann Firor Scott, *The Southern Lady* (1970).

Age of Reform

Robert Abzug, *Cosmos Crumbling: American Reform and the Religious Imagination* (1994).
Barbara Berg, *The Remembered Gate- The Woman and the City, 1800-1860* (1978).
Fawn Brodie, *No Man Knows My History: The Life of Joseph Smith, Mormon Prophet* (1945).
Thomas J. Brown, *Dorothea Dix: New England Reformer* (1998)
Catherine Clinton, *The Other Civil War: American Women in the Nineteenth Century* (1999, rev. ed.)
David Donald, *Charles Sumner and the Coming of the Civil War* (1981).
Frederick Douglass, *Life and Times of Frederick Douglass* (1881).
David Brion Davis, *The Problem of Slavery in the Age of Revolution, 1770-1823* (1975).
George Frederickson, *The Black Image in the White Mind, 1817-1914* (1971).

David Gollaher, *Voice for the Mad: The Life of Dorothea Dix* (1995).
Elizabeth Griffith, *In Her Own Right: The Life of Elizabeth Cady Stanton* (1984).
Paul Goodman, *Of One Blood: Abolitionism and the Origins of Racial Equality* (1998).
Carol Kolmerten, *Women in Utopia: The Ideology of Gender in American Owenite Communities* (1990).
Aileen Kraditor, *Means and Ends in American Abolitionism* (1967).
Gerda Lerner, *the Grimke Sisters of South Carolina: Rebels Against Slavery* (1967).
Henry Mayer, *All on Fire: William Lloyd Garrison and the Abolition of Slavery* (1998).
William McFeely, *Frederick Douglass* (1991).
Steven Mintz, *Moralists and Modernizers: America's Pre-Civil War Reformers* (1995)
Nell Irvin Painter, *Sojourner Truth: A Life, A Symbol* (1996).
Leonard Richards, *"Gentlemen of Property and Standing": Anti-Abolitionist Mobs in Jacksonian America* (1970).
David Rothman, *The Discovery of the Asylum: Social Order and Disorder in the New Republic* (1971).
Shirley Yee, *Black Women Abolitionists: A Study in Activism, 1828-1860* (1992).

PART II—THE ROAD TO WAR

David Donald, *Lincoln* (1995).
Don Fehrenbacher, *The Dred Scott Case* (1978).
Eric Foner, *Free Soil, Free Labor, Free Men* (1970, new ed. 1995).
Politics and Ideology in the Age of the Civil War (1980).
William Freehling, *The Road to Disunion: Secessionists at Bay, 1776-1854* (1990).
Thomas Gossett, *Uncle Tom's Cabin and American Culture* (1985).
Holman Hamilton, *Prologue to Conflict: The Crisis and Compromise of 1850* (1960).
Joan D. Hedrick, *Harriet Beecher Stowe: A Life* (1994).
James McPherson, *Ordeal by Fire: The Civil War and Reconstruction* (1982).
William Lee Miller, *Arguing About Slavery: The Great Battle in the United States Congress* (1995).
Michael A. Morrison, *Slavery and the American West: The Eclipse of Manifest Destiny and the Coming of The Civil War* (1997).
Mark Neely, *The Last Best Hope of Earth: Abraham Lincoln and the Promise of America* (1993).
Stephen Oates, *To Purge This Land with Blood: A Biography of John Brown* (1970).
The Approaching Fury: Voices of the Storm, 1820-1861 (1997).
David Potter, *The Impending Crisis, 1848-1861* (1976).
Robert Remini, *Henry Clay: Statesman for the Union* (1991).
Daniel Webster: The Man and His Time (1997).
Kenneth Stampp, *America in 1857: A Nation on the Brink* (1990).

Anders Stephanson, *Manifest Destiny: American Expansionism and the Empire of Right* (1995).
Albert J. Von Frank, *The Trials of Anthony Burns: Freedom and Slavery in Emerson's Boston* (1998).
Daniel Weber, *The Mexican Frontier, 1821-1846: The American Southwest Under Mexico* (1982).
Steven Weisenberger, *Modern Medea: A Family Story of Slavery and Child-Murder in the Old South* (1998).

PART III—THE CIVIL WAR

Iver Bernstein, *The New York City Draft Riots* (1990).
Gabor S. Boritt (ed.), *The Gettysburg Nobody Knows* (1997).
Bruce Catton, *The Civil War* (1985).
David Donald, *Lincoln* (1995).
James P. Duffy, *Lincoln's Admiral: The Civil War Campaigns of David Farragut* (1997).
Drew Gilpin Faust, *Mothers of Invention: Women of the Slaveholding South in the American Civil War* (1996).
Joseph Glatthaar, *Forged in Battle: The Civil War Alliance of Black Soldiers and White Officers* (1990).
Herman Hatttaway, *Shades of Blue and Gray* (1997).
Elizabeth Leonard, *Yankee Women: Gender Battles in the Civil War* (1994).
All the Daring of the Soldier: Women of the Civil War Armies (1999).
Glenn Lindend and Thomas Pressly, *Voices From the House Divided* (1995).
Thomas P. Lowry, *The Story the Soldiers Wouldn't Tell: Sex in the Civil War* (1994).
William McFeely, *Grant* (1981).
James McPherson, *Abraham Lincoln and the Second American Revolution* (1990).
Battle Cry of Freedom (1988).
Drawn With the Sword: Reflections on the American Civil War (1996).
For Cause and Comrades (1998).
The Negro's Civil War (1965).
Reid Mitchell, *The Vacant Chair: The Northern Soldier Leaves Home* (1993).
Mark Neely, *The Fate of Liberty: Abraham Lincoln and Civil Liberties* (1991).
The Last Best Hope of Earth: Abraham Lincoln and the Promise of America (1993).
Geoffrey Perret, *Ulysses S. Grant: Soldier and President* (1997).
Carol Reardon, *Pickett's Charge in History and Memory* (1997).
James I. Robertson Jr., *Stonewall Jackson: The Man, the Soldier, the Legend* (1997).
Stephen Sears, *George B. McClellan: The Young Napoleon* (1988).
Chancellorsville (1996).
Lonnie Speer, *Portals to Hell: Military Prisons of the Civil War* (1997).

Wendy Hamand Venet, *Neither Ballots Nor Bullets: Women Abolitionists and the Civil War* (1991).
Bell Wiley, *The Life of Billy Yank* (1952).
The Life of Johnny Reb (1943).
Garry Wills, *Lincoln at Gettysburg* (1992).
Terrence J. Winschel, *Triumph & Defeat: The Vicksburg Campaign* (1999).
C. Vann Woodward, ed., *Mary Chestnut's Civil War* (1982).
Steven E. Woodworth, *Six Armies in Tennessee: The Chickamauga and Chattanooga Campaigns* (1999).

PART IV —RECONSTRUCTION

Edward L. Ayers, *The Promise of the New South: Life After Reconstruction* (1992).
James E. Bond, *No Easy Walk to Freedom: Reconstruction and the Ratification of the Fourteenth Amendment* (1997).
LaWanda Cox, *Lincoln and Black Freedom* (1981).
W.E.B. Du Bois, *Black Reconstruction* (1935).
Eric Foner, *Reconstruction: America's Unfinished Revolution* (1988).
A Short History of Reconstruction (1990).
Eric Foner & Olivia Mahoney, *America's Reconstruction: People and Politics after the Civil War* (1995).
George Frederickson, *The Black Image in the White Mind* (1971).
Herbert Gutman, *The Black Family in Slavery and Freedom, 1750-1925* (1976).
William Hesseltine, *Lincoln's Plan of Reconstruction* (1960).
Tera Hunter, *To Joy My Freedom: Southern Black Women's Lives and Labors after the Civil War* (1997).
Leon Litwack, *Been in the Storm So Long: The Aftermath of Slavery* (1979)
Trouble in Mind: Black Southerners in the Age of Jim Crow (1998).
Eric McKitrick, *Andrew Johnson and Reconstruction* (1960).
Michael Perman, *Emancipation and Reconstruction, 1862-1879* (1987).
Willie Lee Rose, *Rehearsal for Reconstruction* (1964).
Theodore Rosengarten, *All God's Dangers: The Life of Nate Shaw* (1974).
Daniel Stowell, *Rebuilding Zion: the Religious Reconstruction of the South, 1863-1877* (1998).
Hans L.Trefousse, *Andrew Johnson* (1989).
Thaddeus Stevens: Nineteenth Century Crusader (1997).
Joel Williamson, *The Crucible of Race* (1984).
C. Vann Woodward, *Origins of the New South, 1877-1913* (1951).
The Strange Career of Jim Crow (1974).

CHRONOLOGY

1793	Eli Whitney invents the cotton gin, reviving slavery
1808	Congress bans importation of slaves to the United States
1820	Lowell mills opened
1822	Denmark Vesey's attempt at slave rebellion in Charleston is crushed
1825	Erie Canal is completed
1830	Baltimore & Ohio Railroad commences operation
	Joseph Smith founds the Mormon Church
	Charles Finney's religious revival meetings (through 1831)
1831	Nat Turner leads violent slave revolt in Virginia
	Garrison first publishes *The Liberator*
	Alexis de Tocqueville begins his travels through America, the basis for *Democracy in America*
1832	Virginia has last serious southern debate on slavery's future
	Restrictions on slaves increase in the South
1833	American Anti-Slavery Society founded
1834	New York Female Moral Reform Society founded
	Cyrus McCormick patents his mechanical reaper
	Women workers strike at Lowell mills
1836	Texas declares its independence from Mexico
1837	Mt. Holyoke college for women opens
	Oberlin college admits women and blacks
	Sarah Grimke writes *Letters on the Equality of the Sexes*
	Horace Mann appointed secretary of the Massachusetts Board of Education (until 1848)
	Ralph Waldo Emerson delivers his "American Scholar" address
	Mt. Holyoke opens – the first four-year women's college
	Oberlin becomes the first coeducational college
1840	Liberty Party founded
1840-1	Transcendentalists start utopian communities Hopedale and Brook Farm
1843	Dorothea Dix issues her report on the treatment of prisoners and the insane
1844	Joseph Smith murdered in Illinois
	Polk elected president
	Samuel F.B. Morse sends first telegraph message

1845	Irish potato famine starts, leading to massive immigration to America
	Invention of the rotary press makes rapid printing of newspapers possible
	Texas admitted as a state
1846	War with Mexico breaks out
	Wilmot Proviso introduced in Congress
1846-7	Mormon migration to the Great Salt Lake
1847	Frederick Douglass' *North Star* begins publication
	Popular sovereignty proposed for territories
	John Deere manufactures steel plows
1848	Failure of German revolutions increase immigration to America
	Treaty of Guadalupe Hidalgo ends Mexican War
	Zachary Taylor elected president
	Free Soil party founded
	First women's rights convention held in Seneca Falls, New York
1849	California Gold Rush stimulates growth of West Coast
1850	Compromise of 1850 passes; California admitted to union
1850s	Cotton boom sweeps the South
1852	Harriet Beecher Stowe's *Uncle Tom's Cabin* is enormous best seller
1854	Kansas-Nebraska Act passes, sparking controversy
	Know-Nothing Party is launched
	Republican Party is founded
	Thoreau's *Walden* appears
1855	Massachusetts becomes first state to end public school segregation
	Walt Whitman's *Leaves of Grass* is published
1855-6	"Bleeding Kansas" divides nation
1856	Brooks attacks Sumner on Senate floor
	James Buchanan elected president
1857	Supreme Court issues Dred Scott decision
	Buchanan supports Lecompton constitution in Kansas
1858	Kansas popular referendum defeats Lecompton constitution
	Lincoln-Douglas debates take place
1859	John Brown raids Harper's Ferry
1860	Democratic party splits
	Lincoln elected president in four-way race
	South Carolina secedes

1861	Six other Deep South states secede
	Confederate States of America founded
	Civil War begins with attack on Fort Sumter
	Lincoln calls up militia and suspends habeas corpus
	Union blockades the Confederacy
	Trent incident endangers U.S.-British relations
	First Battle of Bull Run
1862	The *Monitor* battles the *Merrimac*
	Battle of Shiloh
	Second Battle of Bull Run
	Battle of Antietam
	Battle of Fredericksburg
	Confederacy institutes military draft
	Homestead Act passed
	Morrill Land Grant College Act passed
	Union Pacific Railroad chartered
1863	Lincoln issues Emancipation Proclamation
	Congress enacts military draft
	Battle of Chancellorsville
	Battle of Gettysburg and surrender of Vicksburg
	New York City antidraft riots erupt
	Food riots break out in the South
1864	Battle of the Wilderness
	Siege of Petersburg
	Sherman's army marches through Georgia and "to the Sea"
	Congress passes Wade-Davis Bill
	Lincoln reelected
1865	Lee surrenders at Appomattox
	Lincoln Assassinated (April 14)
	Thirteenth Amendment abolishes slavery
	Freedman's Bureau Established
	Black Codes enacted by Southern Legislatures
1866	Congress approves 14th Amendment
	Congress passes Civil Rights Act and Freedmen's Bureau Act over Johnson's veto
	Ku Klux Klan founded in Tennessee
	Republicans triumph in congressional elections despite Johnson's efforts

1867	Congressional Reconstruction Act passed
	U. S. purchases Alaska
1868	President Johnson is impeached but acquitted
	Fourteenth Amendment ratified
	Ulysses S. Grant elected president
1869	Ratification of the Fifteenth Amendment
1870	Last four Southern states admitted to the union
1871	Ku Klux Klan Act passes to end terrorism in the South
1872	Grant re-elected president
1873	Financial panic leads to five-year depression
1875	Whiskey Ring scandal further discredits Grant administration
1876	Disputed presidential election of Hayes vs Tilden
1877	Electoral commission awards presidency to Rutherford B. Hayes
1890s	"Jim Crow" laws passed in the South
1896	*Plessy v. Ferguson* upholds segregation "separate but equal"

WEB SITES

GENERAL SITES:

Major sites that often link to other sites as well:

www.civilwarhome.com
http://americancivilwar.com
http://www.civilwaralbum.com

University of Michigan has hundreds of sources

www.umdl.umich.edu/moa

U.S. Civil War Center and Southern History

www.cwc.lsu.edu

The History Net

www.americanhistory.about.com/cs

AFRICAN AMERICAN HISTORY:

Library of Congress on African Americans
http://lcwb.loc.gov/exhibits/african/intro.html

Smithsonian's Anacostia Research Center for African American History and Culture
http://www.si.edu/anacostia

The Gilder Lerner Collection of first hand accounts of slavery
http://vi.uh.edu/pages/gilder.htm

Duke University's Collection on African American Women
http://scriptorium.lib.duke.edu/collections/african-american-women.html

SOME MORE SPECIFIC SITES:

Mexican War
www.dmvw.org/mexwar

Dred Scott Decision Documents and Other Specific Events and Issues
http://grid.let.rug.nl/~usa/E/dred_scott/scottxx.htm

National Park Service on the Underground Railroad
http://www.cr.nps.gov/ugrr/

Editorials of the Secession Era
http://history.furman.edu/benson/docs/

A Tour of the Lincoln White House
http://www.mrlincolnswhitehouse.org

Photo Tours of Lincoln Places and Discussions Among Lincoln Scholars
www.netins.net/showcase/creative/lincoln.html

BATTLEFIELD SITES (in addition to the general sites):

National Park Service on Military History
http://www.cr.nps.gov/military.htm

Wonderful panoramic views of major battlefields
http://www.jatruck.com/stonewall

Peninsula Campaign
www.peninsulacampaign.org

RECONSTRUCTION:

Harper's Weekly - America's Leading Magazine during Reconstruction
www.harpweek.com

Report of the Joint Committee on Reconstruction
http://odur.let.nl/~usa/D/1851-1875/reconstruction/repojc.htm

Index

A

B

T

U

V

W

Y